Gower Handbook of Call and Contact Centre Management

Gower Handbook of Call and Contact Centre Management

Edited by
NATALIE CALVERT

GOWER

Published by
Gower Publishing Limited
Gower House
Croft Road
Aldershot
Hants GU11 3HR
England

Gower Publishing Company
Suite 420
101 Cherry Street
Burlington,
VT 05401-4405
USA

Natalie Calvert has asserted her right under the Copyright, Designs and Patents Act 1988 to be identified as Editor of this work.

British Library Cataloguing in Publication Data
Gower handbook of call and contact centre management
   1. Call centers - Management
   I. Calvert, Natalie II. Handbook of call and contact centre
   management
   658.8'12

ISBN 0 566 08510 0

Library of Congress Cataloging-in-Publication Data
Gower handbook of call and contact centre management/edited by Natalie Calvert.
   p. cm
   ISBN 0-566-08510-0
   1. Call centers -- Management. I. Title: Handbook of call and contact centre management. II.
Calvert, Natalie.
   HE8788.G68 2004
   658.8'12--dc22

2004047538

Typeset by IML Typographers, Birkenhead, Merseyside
and printed in Great Britain by MPG Books Ltd, Bodmin, Cornwall.

Contents

List of Figures

List of Tables

Notes on Contributors

ANDY BARKER, HEAD OF MOBILITY, FUJITSU SIEMENS

Andy Barker's business experience includes Head of e-Business and TeleSales for Xerox Europe, where he helped run and set up Xerox TeleWeb Centres across Europe, together with Xerox's Europe-wide eBusiness strategies and initiatives. As Head of Channel Strategy for Compaq Computers EMEA, he oversaw Compaq's main strategic project reviewing their approach to Channels in the Internet Age. He started at Compaq in 1994 by helping to set up their Consumer PC business, and then moved on to become Head of European Distribution for Compaq in 1996. Former Marketing Director of Virgin Retail, he went on to found GAME Ltd, the specialist computer and game store.

CHERYL BLACK, CUSTOMER SERVICE DIRECTOR, SCOTTISH WATER

Cheryl Black is Director of Customer Service with Scottish Water. This role has responsibility for all customer-facing activities within SW, including Contact Centres, billing and collection, and Cheryl's main remit is to bring private-sector customer service standards, efficiency and focus to a publicly owned organization. Cheryl was formerly Customer Services Director for ntl, North East and Midland division, at a time when both ntl itself and its product range were facing dramatic change. Prior to this, Cheryl was responsible for Cable&Wireless/ntl's largest call centre in Swansea, which had 1200 seats covering high-volume telephone and email traffic. Previously, she was Head of Customer Services with London Electricity and Orange plc, as well as Head of Call Centre Services for Acxiom Ltd.

CAROL BORGHESI, DIRECTOR OF CUSTOMER CONTACT CENTRE, BRITISH TELECOM AND CHAIRPERSON – CCA

Following 17 successful years with BC Tel, Vancouver, Canada (now Telus), Carol Borghesi joined BT in August 1997. As General Manager of Outbound Call Centres (Telemarketing), she led the very successful implementation of a two-year strategic plan, focused on cost, revenue and quality objectives. Carol is currently Director, Next Generation Contact Centres for BT Retail and is leading the evolution of their call centres and the development of a common support management and shared infrastructure capability for all BT Retail's volume contact centres. She is also Director, London Region, responsible for advancing BT's agenda in the region and supporting the development and execution of the company's London strategy through key relationships and targeted programmes. She was appointed Chair of the CCA in 2003.

MICHAEL ESAU, ADVISOR, ORGANIZATIONAL EFFECTIVENESS, PREMIER FARNELL

Michael Esau was the Performance and Development Manager for Scottish Power plc, one of the leading utility suppliers in the UK. In what is now a very competitive market, he played a major role implementing a performance development programme across their four call centres. The key areas of the programme were the structured development of the entire team manager population in performance management skills and the implementation of a web browser performance management solution, which has provided a greater ownership of performance to the agents within the call centres. Michael's current focus includes developing group management and leadership development programmes and the redesign of a global performance review process, which is aligned with organizational values and competencies.

CAROLINE GRIFFITHS, MANAGING DIRECTOR, INTEXT MEDIA (UK) LTD

Caroline Griffiths is a consultant specializing in the new media and telecoms markets. In the 1980s she set up the UK's first premium-rate telephone business and went on to work for the BBC, running all their broadcast interactivity, as well as becoming the preferred consultant of Channel 4 and Channel 5. She advised the European Broadcast Union on running successful pan-national televotes and spent two years leading the BBC's involvement in video-on-demand trials and interactive TV around the world. After leaving the BBC, Caroline ran the UK's largest automated call-handling business. In March 2002 she set up her own business to provide specialist consultancy and whole-response management solutions to media businesses.

MIKE HAVARD, MANAGING DIRECTOR AND FOUNDER, CM INSIGHT

Mike Havard is Managing Director and Founder of CM Insight Limited, a customer management solutions consultancy with a heritage in contact centre outsourcing mediation and procurement. CM Insight has broad practical and strategic competence in helping organizations optimize value and reduce cost from their customer management activities. The organization is responsible for managing or procuring outsourced customer management operations for clients across all commercial and not-for-profit sectors. Prior to establishing CM Insight, Mike held senior positions in BT, and was a board director at Sitel, a global outsourced services provider.

DAVE HOWARD, EXECUTIVE DIRECTOR AND FOUNDER, CATALYST IT

Dave Howard is the founder of Catalyst IT Partners and has worked as both a business and technical architect for blue-chip finance organizations in the UK, Europe, South Africa, the US and Canada. During this period Dave has either designed, implemented or optimized contact centres for over 50 major blue-chip clients. Prior to founding Catalyst, Dave ran the IT department for Prudential in Reading and has held a number of posts with a variety of software development and engineering companies.

MELANIE HOWARD, CO-FOUNDER, THE FUTURE FOUNDATION

Formerly a marketer, Melanie Howard became head of IT and Media Consulting at the Henley Centre where she was responsible for Teleculture 2000, Dataculture and the Loyalty Paradox, before setting up The Future Foundation with Michael Willmott in 1996. As well as her continuing interest in the evolution of telemarketing and call centres, key research areas at The Future Foundation have included the impact of changing gender roles; the implications of growing mobility; changing time use in the 24-hour society; and the effects of new technology on networks and communication. She is an associate of Demos, Bristol Business School and the Helen Hamlyn Centre at the Royal College of Art.

ANGELA HUNTER, MANAGING CONSULTANT, CALCOM GROUP

Angela Hunter's career in contact centres began just under ten years ago with her role in the creation of the pioneering IBM pan-European Helpcentre in Greenock, Scotland, which became the blueprint for a family of customer contact operations across the globe. In 1998, Angela moved to her next pioneering project – the launch of the new Barclays b2 brand, which took Barclays into the direct market for wealth management products. As Head of the Customer Service Centre, Angela and her team won a number of industry awards – including Best UK Contact Centre, and in 2000 Angela was awarded the Kevin Hook Memorial Award for Innovation and Creativity at the annual European Call Centre Awards. Angela joined the Calcom team in June 2002, working with client partners to realize the potential of their contact centre organizations.

COSTAS JOHNSON, MANAGING DIRECTOR AND FOUNDER, QUALTRAK SOLUTIONS LTD

Costas Johnson is the founder and Managing Director of Qualtrak Solutions Ltd, a customer experience management company. Prior to starting Qualtrak in 1996, Costas held a number of HR Director positions with Avis Rent A Car, Otis Elevator and Thorn EMI. Qualtrak provides a range of products and services that enable contact centres to deliver a consistently positive customer experience. Qualtrak has recently launched its flagship product, QCoach, a unique integrated Behavioural eLearning, Online Coaching, Competency Management and Quality Monitoring system.

DONALD MacDONALD, TELECOM ORGANIZING OFFICER, COMMUNICATION WORKERS' UNION

Donald MacDonald is Telecom Organizing Officer for the Communication Workers' Union, and sat on the European Contact Centre Qualifications project's UK working party. He has a keen interest in the contact centre industry and has been highly supportive of cooperation between contact centre employees and employers.

COLIN MacKAY, DIRECTOR OF QUALITY AND STANDARDS, CCA

A Director and Company Secretary of CCA since 1997, where he was responsible for developing the CCA Standard: A Framework for Best Practice, Colin MacKay previously held a range of management roles within Financial Services throughout the UK. He is currently involved in developing the CCA Training Accreditation and Professional Qualification programme.

DAVID MACKENZIE, CONTACT CENTRE FUTUROLOGIST AND FOUNDER, CT CONSULTING

David Mackenzie, Principal Consultant and founder of CT Consulting, has been working on projects related to the convergence of voice and data technology in call centres and customer service for more than 14 years. He provides independent consultancy advice to companies that are implementing call centres and contact centres. His particular specialization covers the area of computer telephony, Web technology, IP-ACD and its use in integrated contact centres including inbound call routing, software predictive dialling, call scripting and the setup of web-enabled call centres and email contact centres.

CLIVE McAFEE, MANAGING DIRECTOR, INTERDEC

Clive McAfee has been Managing Director of interdec *working spaces*, the workplace and call centre design specialists, for five years. Clive, previously with BDG McColl, has developed interdec into one of the most respected organizations within its field. interdec *working spaces* specializes in the space planning, interior design and construction of offices and call centres. Its clients include Sky, Zurich Insurance, Thomas Cook Direct, NFU Mutual Direct and Norwich Union.

KAI McCABE, MANAGING DIRECTOR – NORTH, SEARCH CONSULTANCY

Kai McCabe joined Search Consultancy, the leading independent recruitment business, in 1995 as Director of their Edinburgh operation and within three years was appointed managing Director for the overall business in Scotland and the north of England. Since becoming part of the management buy-in/buy-out team in February 2000, Kai has played a key role in developing Search's successful business model within the Scottish market. While firmly establishing Search as the leading independent player in Scotland, Kai has also supported Search's substantial growth south of the border as the company has opened locations in Manchester, Crawley, Derby and Leicester, and increased staff numbers from 170 to over 300 within 14 months. As a result, Search is now recognized as one of the UK's 100 fastest growing private companies.

PETER McCARTHY, CHAIRMAN, iSKY EUROPE

After studying electronic engineering and business administration, Peter McCarthy worked in marketing and general management before starting his own business. Initially the company provided consultancy on call handling issues. Following client requests, it expanded into outsourced customer contact, becoming known for the quality of its technical solutions with many blue-chip clients. Peter is now Chairman of iSKY Europe plc, the UK arm of iSKY Inc., the US customer care group that purchased his company in 2000.

LAURIN McDONALD, MANAGING CONSULTANT, SITEL

Laurin McDonald is a managing consultant with vast experience in the contact centre industry. Formerly General Manager of SITEL's operations in the Midlands and as a senior member of SITEL's management team over many years, she has successfully contributed to the development of the industry in all its aspects from programme planning, design and implementation through IT and technology, operations and HR in all its applications and across a host of industries. SITEL is one of the leading providers of contact centre services. It designs, implements and operates multi-channel contact centres around the world offering services in 25 languages and dialects.

TONY McSWEENEY, MANAGEMENT CONSULTANT

Over the last ten years Tony McSweeney has provided operational consultancy in the IT, finance and utilities markets, primarily focusing on business performance, management reporting and business planning. By bringing together his experience of contact centre operations and his auditing background he is able to ensure that the qualitative aspects of call centre performance are driven by commercial objectives. Prior to this, Tony's background was in accounting and he held many financial positions including internal auditing and Finance Manager with a major contact centre outsourcing operator.

STEPHEN PARRY, HEAD OF STRATEGY AND CHANGE, FUJITSU SERVICES

Stephen Parry's career in contact centre operations spans over 15 years. During that time he has been responsible for building and operating large-scale international contact centres. He has extensive experience in the areas of operational management, strategy development, change and turnaround management, e-commerce and e-CRM. He has developed an innovative approach to rapidly transforming and managing call centre operations, called 'Sense-&-Respond' for which he was awarded the European Call Centre of the Year award for Innovation and Creativity 2001.

ROB PIKE, DIRECTOR, TELEPHONY OPERATIONS, ROYAL BANK OF SCOTLAND

Rob Pike was assigned Director of Telephony Operations for the Royal Bank of Scotland shortly after its takeover by NatWest. He has had a varied career, much of it spent in Central London. Following highly successful roles as Branch Manager and Senior Corporate Manager, Rob moved into operations, where he held three senior positions in the past ten years, during which time he also had a spell in the Group Strategic Planning Department. He joined the main board of the CCA in 2003.

STEVE PINK, MANAGING CONSULTANT, TELECOMMERCE CONSULTANCY

Steve Pink is Managing Consultant at Telecommerce Consultancy, a contact centre and customer service consultancy experienced in the provision and operation of customer interaction centres. Steve specializes in combining people, processes and technology to deliver profitable customer relationships. With over 17 years' experience managing call centres and contact centre projects, Steve has a significant record of success in managing telesales channels, direct marketing operations, e-commerce channels and customer-focused call centres.

SALLY POLLOCK, HEAD OF TRAINING, CALCOM GROUP

Sally Pollock is Head of Training for the Calcom Group, managing the design, delivery and innovation of training solutions for major blue-chip companies operating within the contact centre industry. Sally has over ten years' experience in contact centre operations and training, having set up and managed contact centres for a variety of financial services organizations in both inbound and outbound sales and service environments. Prior to joining Calcom, Sally expanded her skills, moving away from operations and taking on the role of Planning and Training Director for Charles Schwab Europe's multi-site contact centre.

SIMON PRIESTLEY, HEAD OF CAPACITY AND YIELD, THOMAS COOK DIRECT

Simon Priestley has over five years' experience in call centre management. He is currently responsible for contact support functions including resource management, planning and forecasting, telecoms, analysis and call quality at Thomas Cook. Prior to his position at Thomas Cook, Simon held similar roles with One 2 One and Air Miles; he also worked in change and project management for several years.

DAVID RANCE, CHAIRMAN, ROUND

David Rance is the driving force behind Round's holistic customer centricity proposition. Prior to the merger with Round, David was the Managing Director of Customer Centricity Ltd, a consultancy he established in 1988 to help organizations increase their business performance through improved customer management. David has over 30 years' experience in managing all major business functions including sales, marketing, customer care, product management, IT, software development, programme management and operations. He has held various posts including European Managing Director in Telecommunications and IT enterprises and Customer Care Director of BTCellnet.

DAVID SECCOMBE, CONTACT CENTRE MARKETING SPECIALIST

David Seccombe has worked in the contact centre consultancy business for 12 years. Between 1993–1997 he worked for OgilvyOne, consulting on UK and pan-European strategy, planning and implementation for, amongst others, American Express and Royal Mail. He started a tele-consultancy at Bates Dorland in 1997 and worked on both contact centre and general customer communications auditing, planning and implementation. David re-joined OgilvyOne in 1999 to head up the BBC TV licensing account and to develop the business.

ARCHIE SHEVLIN, CLUSTER TRAINING MANAGER, INLAND REVENUE

Archie Shevlin has been a learning specialist for five years. Prior to this he was in management. For the past three and a half years Archie has specialized in the delivery of telephone skills, customer service and coaching training. He is also responsible for Team Development and ICT. He is part of the team bringing contact centre practices to the Inland Revenue.

PAUL SMEDLEY, EXECUTIVE DIRECTOR, PROFESSIONAL PLANNING FORUM

The Professional Planning Forum is the independent industry body in Europe for call centre resource planning specialists. Paul Smedley established the Forum's training and benchmarking programmes and is rated highly for creating enjoyable, interactive sessions. Paul was previously operations manager for British Airways' call centres and his wide consultancy experience includes work with Halifax, HSBC, Egg, American Express and Vertex. Paul has tutored with Lancaster University Management School and is a member of the Institute of Directors, the Institute of Direct Marketing and the OR Society.

JIM SPOWART, FOUNDER, STANDARD LIFE AND INTELLIGENT FINANCE

Jim Spowart joined the Halifax in October 1999, where he launched and developed a twenty-first century consumer champion banking proposition. At launch, Intelligent Finance represented Europe's largest Internet-enabled call centre. In 2001, its first full year of business, it delivered a record performance for a new entrant bank in the mortgage market, winning 9.2 per cent of the UK net mortgage market. Intelligent Finance is now the fastest growing new-generation bank in terms of overall balances attracted. Before joining Intelligent Finance, Jim set up and launched Standard Life's telephone banking operation. Within 18 months he had built it into one of the fastest growing telephone banks in the UK. Between 1993 and 1997, Jim was MD of Direct Line Financial Services, and before that he worked at Royal Bank of Scotland establishing the blueprint for its telephone banking operation.

RICHARD STOLLERY, GLOBAL CONSUMER SERVICES DIRECTOR, LEGO DIRECT

Richard Stollery is responsible for LEGO consumer services in 18 countries and 13 languages. Before joining the LEGO Company, Richard was General Manager for Direct Operations for Xerox

Europe. There he was responsible for setting up eight contact centres across Europe, covering the disciplines of telesales, telemarketing and customer service.

JOHN TAYLOR, MANAGING CONSULTANT, MAPLE COMMUNICATIONS MANAGEMENT LTD

With more than 30 years' experience as an independent telecommunications consultant, John Taylor helps a wide range of public- and private-sector clients to select, manage and improve their communications systems and services. Complementary to his consultancy role he also provides training services to users and suppliers. He is the Leader of the Communications Management Association Consultancy Forum.

FABIENNE TYLER, HEAD OF MARKETING, THOMAS SANDERSON

Fabienne Tyler is Head of Marketing at Thomas Sanderson and also runs The Direct Marketing Consultancy, providing marketing and training services to a range of private clients. During her 20-plus years in the direct marketing industry, Fabienne has provided client support across all marketing disciplines, and has been actively involved in the industry through the DMA, where she chaired the DMA Royal Mail awards for over ten years, championing high standards and effective use of direct marketing.

GRAHAM WHITEHEAD, PRINCIPAL CONSULTANT, BTEXACT TECHNOLOGIES

Graham Whitehead has worked for BT, and previously the GPO, for 34 years and has been involved in most aspects of telecommunications from designing integrated chips and packaging lasers to manufacturing and laying of optical fibre submarine cable systems. After two years in the USA working for DuPont on the manufacture of Advanced Opto-electronic Research Devices, he returned to the UK in the early 1990s to lead an econometrics-modelling group looking at business issues that would be affected by the Information Revolution. Since 1996 he has specialized in presenting the future of communications and IT to customers around the world.

GREG WILKIE, HEAD OF CUSTOMER CONTACT, PHILATELIC BUREAU, ROYAL MAIL

Greg Wilkie has held a variety of positions at the Royal Mail over the past 16 years, and the majority of these roles have been directly related to customer services. Amongst his achievements in this area are the introduction of a single national telephone number to replace more than 70 previously in existence; the implementation of a networked complaints handling system for Royal Mail; and the migration of around 1600 staff and managers from ten separate business units into a single unit, reducing the senior and middle management tiers by over 50 per cent in the process. He has also been responsible for a range of customer satisfaction and mystery shopper measures covering the whole of Royal Mail's operations.

JOHN WILKINSON, VICE PRESIDENT, SALES AND ALLIANCES – EUROPE, WITNESS SYSTEMS

John Wilkinson joined Witness Systems in January 2002 and serves as Vice President of Sales and Alliances for the Europe, Middle East and Africa region. He is responsible for the strategic direction of sales, customer acquisition and partnerships, as well as continuing to build a strong market presence throughout EMEA for the company's industry-leading performance optimization software suite that helps global enterprises capture customer intelligence and optimize workforce performance. Prior to joining Witness Systems, Wilkinson worked for SeeBeyond, a California-based enterprise application integration software company, as managing director of the UK subsidiary – a role that expanded to include positions on the European leadership team that focused on field operations and strategic alliances.

Foreword

The Call Centre Association (CCA) was founded in 1996 and is recognized as the leading body representing the industry. As an independent, not-for-profit organization it has over 600 members from both private and public sectors. CCA is established as a conduit for building new relationships with other professional bodies, government departments, overseas agencies and bodies which have an interest in the successful development of contact centres.

CCA launched the Standard framework for Best Practice© in November 2000. The framework is a guide to support and develop internal processes which ensure improved performance and increased customer satisfaction. The principle of the Standard Framework is 'happy and fulfilled staff dealing with satisfied and content customers'. CCA's vigorous promotion of best practice in contact centres through the use of its Standard Framework has continued to bear fruit. The framework, which covers issues like training, communication, policies and legislation, is now used by well over 80 per cent of CCA members as a performance improvement tool and appreciation of its potential benefits has reached critical mass within the industry. Standards awareness workshops to enable delegates to undertake a gap analysis on current activity and devise a development action plan have proved highly popular.

The contact centre sector has grown and diversified and is recognized as a key provider of UK employment, accounting for 400 000 jobs. On a wider front, India, South East Asia and other areas have continued to attract contact centre operations relocating from elsewhere. Indeed, customer service is now a global proposition that can be delivered anywhere and many organizations require advice around realizing the investment in their contact centre in terms of enhanced customer service. CCA is in a unique position to assist today's contact centre market-place in their quest for improved delivery.

Call and contact centres are facing major challenges that are being driven partly by their own success and partly by the spectre of globalization. We should certainly be concerned about the prospect of jobs going overseas; however, the CCA is convinced that there is still room for sustainable growth providing we face up to the challenges of customer service, advancing technologies and building a profession for call and contact centre employees.

Most of the internal challenges facing us have been around for some time. Recruitment and retention issues, training provision, technology development and, perhaps most importantly, the public perception of the service provided by call and contact centres. This book will support and guide both new and experienced call and contact centre managers towards the focus needed to resolve these issues.

Anne Marie Forsyth
Executive Director
The Call Centre Association (CCA)

Introduction

Over the past 20 years the role of the call centre has dramatically changed from simply handling calls into a complex, sophisticated multi-channel environment, which now sits at the heart of many organizations. It's often far too easy to forget that call and contact centres are fundamentally all about customers – acquiring, retaining, servicing and valuing them – and ultimately, providing an excellent customer experience through winning hearts and minds every step of the way.

In the early years we have witnessed the 'cost call centre' with a strong 'command and control' ethos driven by productivity metrics that were all about achieving the fastest way to handle call volume. This has been followed by the 'profit contact centre' whose aims are to sell or add value on each and every contact, whether it is by phone, email, internet or mobile services. Now we are entering a new phase 'The customer experience centre': a centre that recognizes the power of behaviours, which has highly flexible, brand-driven communities and creates its value not only through profits or value, but also by eliminating the cost of failure across organizations. It is a model which is fully integrated within a company not sitting in isolation like its predecessors.

The customer experience centre not only deploys clever technologies and creates dynamic processes, it really understands the relationship between delivering a great customer experience and a great people experience. It understands that staff loyalty and customer loyalty go hand in hand. In a world where 'taking out the cost' is a business mantra, truly valuing people is often one of the greatest challenges. However, it is only through a highly motivated, well-skilled workforce that organizations can realize the potential of its customer base, deliver competitive advantage and really WOW the customer!

In compiling a handbook like this the challenge has been knowing where to start and where to stop. There are so many more topics I would love to have included, or existing topics that should have been covered in more detail, or even some that you the reader might feel should have been reduced! Overall, I have endeavoured to achieve the right mix for call and contact centre managers.

Whether your role is to manage 5 or 5000 staff you will find many pearls of wisdom and insight within these pages to help and support you develop your call and contact centre operations. This book is designed to be a handy, must-have guide which takes you through the journey of running your contact centre successfully, so that you, in turn, can WOW your teams, customers and organization – winning hearts and minds every step of the way.

Natalie Calvert
Managing Director
Calcom Group
nataliecalvert@calcomgroup.com
www.calcomgroup.com
August 2004

Acknowledgements

This book has over 35 contributors, and each one has worked hard to distil their wealth of knowledge and experience. While editing the contributions, I have often been in admiration of many of their writings. I only hope that my editing has ensured that not only the meaning but also the spirit of their words has been captured correctly. Please forgive me where I have failed. My heartfelt thanks go to each contributor for this incredible collection of expertise, and I am confident many contact centre managers will thank you for years to come. A special thank you goes to to Steve Pink for his collaboration on the technology section.

I am very grateful to Amanda Griffiths and Karen Levent, who have been an enormous help in compiling this book. I don't think that any of us knew or suspected just how challenging it would be to coordinate, craft and edit a handbook of this kind. Thank you both.

I would also like to acknowledge the wonderful team at Calcom, whose talent, expertise and commitment is an inspiration to the organizations and people we have the privilege to work with – as well as a daily inspiration to me. With special recognition to Matthew Taylor – thank you.

An indebted thank you to my mother Sylvia, my late father Malcolm, Michael, family and friends who have loved and supported me throughout the last 20 years of my career, I owe each of you an apology as often I have not been able to share enough time and laughter with you. Thank you to Eliyaho Yardeni for sharing your wisdom. Moshe Katz, I really love and appreciate you for being a terrific and very patient husband.

NC

EWAN GOWRIE, CHAIRMAN, CALLPOINT EUROPE

'If you were to pick the one invention which has most profoundly shaped the world over the last 100 years, then it would undoubtedly be the telephone.

Of course, there would be plenty of competition for this award – the internal combustion engine; the aeroplane; radio; television; the X-ray machine. The telephone is, however, by far the most important. It defines not only the way we do business, but more distinctively, the whole way in which global society is now constructed.'

PIERRE DANON, CHIEF EXECUTIVE, BT RETAIL

'Customer satisfaction is the cornerstone of BT Retail's strategy. As a part of our business that handles 2.3 million calls a day from customers, our call centre operation is at the heart of the drive to make our strategy a success.

These multi-functional contact centres will use leading-edge customer relationship management (CRM) technology and allow our customers to deal with us through the medium of their choice. The skills of our advisers are crucial to success.

This network of next-generation contact centres have the aim of delivering the best customer experience in the industry and increasing our efficiency.'

PETER SCOTT, CUSTOMER SERVICE DIRECTOR, T-MOBILE UK

'Contact centres are becoming the lifeblood of business, connecting with customers to create loyalty and stimulate growth.

In delivering great service, clever technology and processes help, but people make the difference.

The role of our people is to engage with our customers and to build loyalty through emotional experiences.'

JIM SPOWART, FOUNDER OF BOTH STANDARD LIFE AND INTELLIGENT FINANCE

'Call and contact centres have been a dynamic growth sector in the USA and UK for over 15 years, and are now being replicated in other territories on a worldwide basis. Call centre methodologies have been applied to a wide range of business processes, which are increasingly characterized by complex and sophisticated applications. Such operations require high-level management and knowledgeable agents, therefore continuous professional development of our people is the key to capitalizing on our leadership position.'

RICHARD STOLLERY, GLOBAL CONSUMER SERVICES DIRECTOR, LEGO DIRECT

'When you recruit the right people into the right environment, when your staff know what they are doing and why (and the Board does too), when they have the confidence and knowledge to add value to every contact, when you give them your trust, the support and the resources to add that value, you then have an operation that drives people and customer loyalty and meets its business objectives – this book will help you achieve those goals.'

GLENN HURLEY, DEPUTY CHAIRMAN, PNS GROUP

'With an almost unique insight into the development of our industry, this is a book that only Natalie Calvert could have written. The fact that she has managed to make it such an accessible read for her audience illustrates the understanding and empathy she has with the real people who make it great. With over twenty years' experience synthesized into one volume, it represents great value and will no doubt become a standard text for many training programmes.'

ANDREW TILLARD, CHAIRMAN, SITEL

'As I look forward to the future of the call centre industry I have the following thoughts ...

We all know that product differentiation for any significant period of time is difficult to maintain, so we have to make a big difference in the level of customer service so that we increase customer loyalty. But then there is the constant pressure to reduce costs ...

So how can we, as an industry, help?

We must have the proof that good customer service increases profit and have define what the "good" means for our industry and continually improve it to keep it top quality. We must use intelligent tools – be they well-trained people or clever ways of delivering useful, fast information to the customer – available to our trade to help generate profits and reduce costs. We must formulate the management information to help the decision-makers make the right decisions and make them aware of the cost of getting it wrong. Those of us who have been in the industry a long time need to reflect on how new products were developed that changed the way the industry operates – shopping direct, the 24-hour help lines, and the welcome call to mention a few. And we must look forward to generating more industry-changing models. But, to sound a note of caution, we must be careful that, in 20 years' time, we will not be reflecting on how our industry helped generate faceless banks, or helplines where we allowed management to over-focus on cost and forget what the customer wants ...

Finally, some words of advice to those of you entering the industry: enjoy it and every now and then sit back and reflect on just how you can help re-engineer the methodology of today's corporation ... a rare treat.'

MELANIE HOWARD, CO-FOUNDER, FUTURE FOUNDATION

'To meet the needs of customers in a more fluid, flexible society, organizations must use new, interactive technologies to create a transparent, porous skin through which the customer can navigate to get what they want from any interaction at any time. Real progress will be achieved by bringing together new thinking with new technology, not just replicating old bottlenecks in new ways. The biggest challenge for the industry is to give up trying to make the customer convenient to deal with, and instead, create real convenience for the customer.'

About the Editor

NATALIE CALVERT

Managing Director, Calcom Group

Natalie's wealth of call and contact centre experience has been developed over the past 20 years. An impressive range of international organizations have benefited from her business insights, passion and unrivalled expertise.

Undertaking global and local assignments, she is totally commited to raising professionalism, standards and skills for sales, marketing and customer services. Over the past decade she has undertaken pioneering work in this area, including:

* Ambassador for the European Contact Centre Qualifications
* Chair of London First Call Centre Task Force
* Founder and fellow of the Institute of Direct Marketing
* Chair of People Group for DMA Telecommerce Board
* Masters in Contact Centre Management Verifier
* Editorial Board for the *Journal of Database Marketing*
* CCA Standard Advisory Council member.

Natalie is frequently asked to chair and lecture at major events, regularly publishes articles and judges industry awards.

In 1992 Natalie founded Calcom Group, a highly respected and award-winning organization that significantly improves the performance of its clients. Calcom's clients include companies such as Royal Bank of Scotland, Royal Mail, Department of Work and Pensions and LEGO. The team at Calcom is renowned for really making a difference to bottom line business results and customer and employee satisfaction.

The Business Plan

This section of the handbook examines the fundamental components of developing a call or contact centre:

- Vision and Strategy
- Putting the Customer at the Heart
- Financial Planning and Budgeting
- The Contact Centre Environment
- Case Study: Intelligent Finance

1 Vision and Strategy

Rob Pike, Director of Telephony Operations, Royal Bank of Scotland

In this chapter we look at creating a vision and a strategy for your contact centre or a network of contact centres.

This chapter is not intended to be an in-depth guide to building a contact centre, but rather a checklist of the elements that should be considered, enriched with the benefit of hindsight and practical experience.

ENGAGING TEAMS AND SUPPORT

Whether developing a plan for a new contact centre or looking to revisit plans for an existing operation, there are three key teams whose needs should be considered. If these resources are used correctly and the needs of the stakeholders really understood then a framework can be created for the delivery of an effective operation. Figure 1.1 outlines the three key teams and stakeholders in question. If you do not have a 'large' internal team you will still need to replicate the methodologies in this chapter to build a successful vision and business strategy.

While the process of developing a strategy is largely sequential, it is also to a degree an iterative process. It is appropriate to note that, wherever possible, those who are to implement the

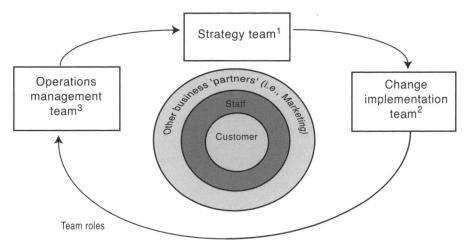

1. To define the longer-term structure and position of the operational centres within the wider organization and to articulate the changes that (2) will need to deliver next.
2. To develop and deliver the next set of tools to support the operational centres.
3. To support the operational centres – by developing and delivering the current tools set.

Figure 1.1   Key stakeholders, shareholders and internal players © Natwest

Three key internal players:	Three key stakeholders:

• The strategy team
• The change management team
• The operational management team.
	• Staff – the people within the contact centre(s)
	• Partners – within the business:
	  1. Marketing department (which might include customer segment owners)
	  2. Other channel owners (for example, in retail banking – the owner of the branch channel)
	• Customers – most importantly, the customers must be at the heart of everything your contact centre does.

strategy and those who will ultimately manage the operation should participate in the strategy development.

In order to create a vision and strategy that are robust, consider the following key steps:

1   The 'why' question
2   Decide the vision and create the values
3   Goals and objectives: creating the operational plan
4   Measures and targets.

To understand what to build and how the vision and strategy will be used for maximum benefit, the '4D' approach is often used:

1   Decide
2   Define

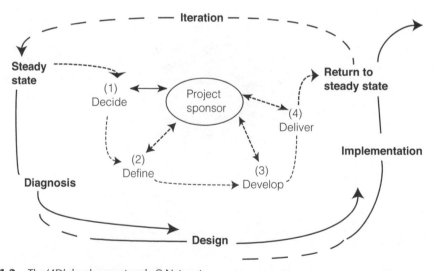

Figure 1.2   The '4D' development cycle © Natwest

3 Develop
4 Deliver.

The '4D' development cycle, depicted in Figure 1.2, illustrates this approach.

Having the wider team (strategy, change and operations) engaged at the Decide and Define stage is very important to the overall success of any project.

The vision and the strategy has to be owned. While it can and should be developed by the key players referred to above, as they should be close to the staff and customers' needs, it must be owned by the CEO and other key business executives.

Gaining the buy-in of senior management will serve two key purposes. First, it is inevitable that there will be challenges in implementing the finally agreed proposal, be they budgetary, resource or customer related. Management buy-in enables these challenges to be effectively actioned. Second, senior sponsorship will ensure that other areas within the business see the change as an essential element for your business's future, a point that will be useful during the implementation phase. Be prepared for critics who become much more vocal with the benefit of hindsight!

THE 'WHY' QUESTION

It is likely that not everyone who has built a call centre or contact centre will be able to clearly articulate why he or she did so, what its objectives were and how they evaluate its success.

To start the development of the contact centre strategy it is important to answer the question 'why are we doing this?' which will strongly determine people, process and technical requirements. Sometimes I wonder how many have started with the answer and then worked backwards to the question!

There are essentially four possible objectives:

- Improve customer service
- Deliver greater customer choice (that is, open a new channel)
- Reduce operational costs (centralize operations, reduce operational overheads)
- Increase sales income (sales/cross sales through lead identification).

It would be easy to say, all of the above. If that is the case, analysis should be undertaken to understand the order of priority.

Remember what Michael Porter says:

> The notion underlying the concept of genetic strategies is that Competitive Advantage is at the heart of any strategy and achieving competitive advantage requires a firm to make a choice – if a firm is to attain a competitive advantage, it must make a choice about the type of competitive advantage it seeks to attain and the scope within which it will attain it.
>
> Being 'all things to all people' is a recipe for strategic mediocrity and below average performance because it often means that a firm has no competitive advantage at all.
>
> Michael E. Porter, *Competitive Advantage*, 1985

A good and very simple way to check the underlying purpose and viability of a high-level proposal for change is to write the letter that would be sent to your customers explaining what you are doing, why you are doing it and what it means for them.

DECIDE THE VISION AND CREATE THE VALUES

Does the organization have a clear vision and set of values? Do staff understand these and buy into them?

On the assumption that it does, will contact centre plans fit with, and complement, what is already there? Develop the contact centre vision and values to give clarity of focus and to motivate and mobilize teams, but ensure they fit with other areas of the business.

If the objective is to reduce costs but one of the values is 'to put the customer at the centre of everything we do', then be clear how you communicate plans, not only to the customers but also to staff who may receive the message with a degree of cynicism.

When, in the case of large organizations, staff are spread far and wide, not just within contact centres but also in other channels, then having a clearly articulated vision and an understandable set of values will go a long way towards having all staff heading in the same direction.

If your business has not yet developed a vision or a set of values then the contact centre team you appointed to develop and build your contact centre strategy should have this high on their agenda. Ensure that they are aligned to the vision and values of the wider business, while personalizing goals for the centre.

It is important that the vision is short, simple and jargon free. An example might be:

> We will recruit, develop and retain the best people so that together we consistently exceed our customers' expectations.

Similarly, the values should be short, meaningful and easily identifiable by staff as supporting the overall strategy and objectives of your business.

Likewise, value statements should be jargon free and not include words that staff will find patronizing or embarrassing to use. The aim is to create identification with the vision and values within the team so that the statements gradually become a natural part of their vocabulary. They should be easy to remember. If your staff have to go to their desk to dig out a piece of paper then they will not work.

An example of a simple set of values might be:

We will achieve our vision by:

- being customer driven
- investing in our people so that they will look after our customers
- treating colleagues as we would wish to be treated ourselves.

Lower-level detail can then be developed to put actions beneath these values to bring them to life within the business and in so doing add real value.

GOALS AND OBJECTIVES: CREATING THE OPERATIONAL PLAN

Having agreed the vision and set of values to live by, together with why your organization needs to establish a contact centre and what products and services can be offered to your customers, it is now time to develop a more detailed operational plan.

The operational plan should be an organic document which sets out in some detail what you intend to do during the next period, usually 12 months. In other words, short to medium-term goals and objectives should be underpinned by a plan to show how you will achieve those objectives. An example of one entry might be:

We will reduce the number of complaints that reach the CEO by 50 per cent, to one complaint per one million customer calls by:

- increasing the number of agents qualified to level 3 from 60 per cent to 80 per cent
- increasing our mystery shopping scores for our core processes to 99 per cent
- creating a small pool of 'super agents' to whom all customer concerns/complaints are handed immediately for resolution
- ensuring the staff bonus scheme includes recognition for achieving this reduction.

To be effective, these goals need to be clear, logical and understandable but, above all, the staff need to know what they must do to achieve them and why that makes sense. To be really effective the goals need to be measurable and the targets which are set must be realistic but challenging.

The operational plan should take up several pages and detail a set of actions, the owners for those actions, and delivery milestones.

MEASURES AND TARGETS

For key goals and objectives to be meaningful, they must be measurable. It is advisable to ensure that measures are manageable in number, say between 10 and 15.

It is often easier and more logical to organize your goals and objectives into a cluster based on the quadrants of a balanced business scorecard. For example:

Customer	People
Internal effectiveness	Financial

If you find the right measures and targets in the first three quadrants, the fourth, the financial quadrant, will look after itself. That may be an oversimplification, but by investing in staff and process improvement, the financial benefits will flow naturally. Of course, all businesses have to operate within bugetary constraints; however, budgets should be driven by the plan and not the other way round. For further illustration see Figure 1.3.

COMMUNICATION

Plan to communicate at all stages. Whether during the strategy formulation stage (Decide/Define), the build phase (Develop/Deliver) or subsequent operational phase, ensure that there is communication, communication and communication!

When you develop your message, remember you have probably lived and breathed the proposition for months so don't assume your wider team will understand everything that you take for granted. However, it is even more inadvisable to patronize your team.

Keep your message clear, concise and consistent and don't be afraid to repeat certain parts of your message to reinforce its importance. Good leaders have a consistent storyboard and will align their messages to that storyboard, regularly reinforcing the same simple messages. They will talk in terms of this is where we have come from, this is where we are now and this is where we are headed, and why that makes sense.

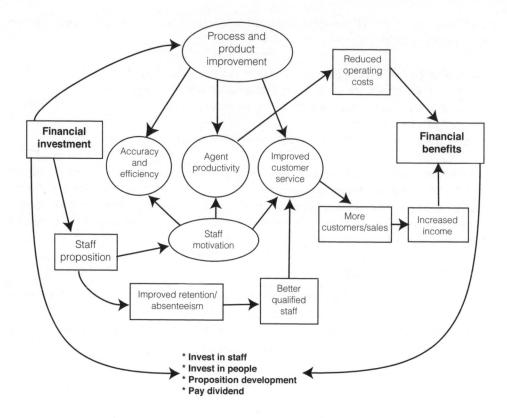

Figure 1.3   The virtuous circle of financial investment and benefit © NatWest

LEADERSHIP

Leadership is the key factor that makes everything else come to life. Like a great conductor and his orchestra, or Sir Alex Ferguson and Manchester United, the leader will often make the difference between success and mediocrity.

The leader will envision and communicate, energize and motivate, and quite simply provide leadership and direction. Leaders will help create the vision and will certainly own it, and 'sell' it to the wider team. They will develop the values and will always be seen to live them. They will drive a demanding set of objectives and will set challenging but achievable targets. They will ensure that plans are revisited and refreshed regularly in line with the vision and values.

Figure 1.4 serves to show each of the components discussed as a whole.

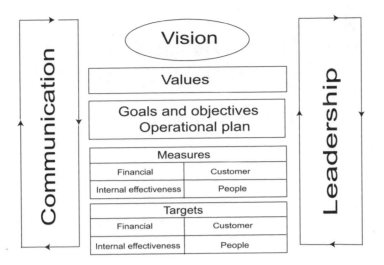

Figure 1.4   Bringing it all together © NatWest

RECOMMENDED READING

Porter, Michael E. (1985), *Competitive Advantage*, Free Press.

2 Putting the Customer at the Heart of your Contact Centre

David Rance, Chairman, Round

This chapter discusses ways to position the customer at the centre of contact centre operations, so that the customer drives and leads all aspects of operational delivery.

BACKGROUND

In an age of multinational power brands and mass marketing, customers are finally finding their power. So, how does a company become customer-centric and what role does the contact centre play in the future?

CRM (Customer Relationship Management) professionals from across the world were asked, 'How can we make CRM really work?' As with all powerful ideas, the answer is amazingly quite simple. Create five horizontal strands that 'join up the dots' across the business, as follows:

1 **Business journey**: Where is the business going? Create the plan to lead the organization from being product-centric to becoming customer-centric.
2 **Customer strategy**: Decide first what you want to do with each customer and then what each function needs to do to make it happen. End-to-end processes is the key here.
3 **Organization design**: Evolve the organization to be able to cohesively deliver the customer strategy, rather than a series of discrete functional strategies.
4 **Information architecture**: Continuously improve the customer experience by defining how all information (not just data) flows though the company.
5 **Performance measures**: Identify new performance measures that will really change the behaviour of your customer-facing personnel.

The business journey is the most important strand, as it describes how the company will change. There are four key milestones on this journey:

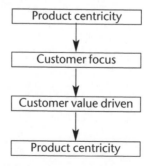

1st BASE

The role of the contact centre changes significantly as the company moves towards customer centricity. A 1st base company is completely focused on efficiency. For them, this is still the main reason why customer care or contact centres exist at all. These companies are aware of the levels of productivity and the cost of everything but often the value of nothing. The contact centre is a cost to the business and therefore the key performance measures are utilization, call-handling times and backlog.

2nd BASE

When the company moves to 2nd base, the focus shifts towards satisfying the customer. This usually means taking more time with customer contacts; making more outbound or proactive contact; or just waiting for high-value customers to call. As a result, utilization falls and costs rise. Most companies panic at this point and haul the centre back to 1st base to regain maximum utilization. This can then lead to the implementation of an *end-to-end customer process*, which will work to 'join up the dots' across the business to provide a consistent and high level of customer service.

This is when the contact centre comes into its own. Engaging the contact centre to identify improvements to both processes and business practices is important and this begins to drive changes across the company. The result is often very satisfied customers and highly motivated employees. And the added bonus is that costs fall as processes become streamlined and things happen more quickly.

3rd BASE

A 3rd base company builds on the foundation of consistent service to derive maximum customer value. They do this by helping the customer and often are assisted by good propensity analysis and other account information to help them decide what is best for a customer's particular needs at that time. And, of course, the more the agent 'helps' the customer, the more the customer trusts them and the more they buy. But it is impossible to build any kind of valuable relationship without first establishing trust. Trust is similar to rapport. It can be built, layer upon layer, by many different people. The key is first to be consistent, then to acquire the customer's permission to develop a relationship. Everyone can then use those permissions to enhance customer confidence and to strengthen those relationships. The 3rd base contact centre is there for the customer, to help them and guide them through the maze of confusing and often contradictory engagement channels. Once they have established trust agents can then use the relevant information to identify products or services which will appeal to the customer who, in turn, will buy more. There is no need for a hard sell.

4th BASE

4th base is nirvana. Here, the customer becomes so engaged that they become a stakeholder in the company's success. These customers aren't just loyal, they're genuine fans. The contact centre is their window into the company, their partner in the service creation, execution and constant improvement process. Customers then become part of the extended resource pool, with customer communities often helping other customers. Employee satisfaction becomes the key performance measure for a 4th base company because if the personnel are having a great time, then the customers will be too.

3 *Financial Planning and Budgeting*

Tony McSweeney, Management Consultant

This chapter provides the key tools for ensuring that the contact centre is robust in terms of its financial planning and financial performance, together with how to build a business case.

BACKGROUND

Budgeting is normally undertaken annually, three to six months before the commencement of the budget period. Typically, the budget process will start in June and end in September, with the new budget year starting in January.

For a contact centre manager the budget process generally focuses on costs, that is, identifying the centre's funding requirements for the budget period, which is usually a year's duration. Some centres may be allowed input into the income side of a budget but this is rare; normally, income budgets will be coordinated by marketing or sales, with budgets or targets passed down to the contact centre to be negotiated and agreed. For this reason, this chapter will focus primarily on the cost side of budgeting.

It is fair to say that most contact centre managers probably experience the budgeting process in terms of presenting a wish list to the finance department and then spending months negotiating to retain as much of this wish list as possible. To understand and benefit the most from the budgeting process, it is worth considering the process from the perspective of the senior managers making the final decision and the finance departments who will be coordinating funding requirements for the entire organization.

THE BUDGETING PROCESS

The finance department receives budget proposals or wish lists from all departments, which, if approved, will most likely eradicate all company profits for the period. For this reason, the first action is likely to be to send all budgets back with an instruction to reduce requirements by a significant amount. From this point the negotiating process begins, and the winners in the budgeting process will tend to be from those areas where the expenditure is seen to generate greatest return for the organization or where there is significant support from senior managers to deliver on a corporate initiative, for example improved customer service.

FINANCIAL PLANNING

The description of the budget process identified above is useful when considering the role and importance of financial planning for a contact centre. Financial planning creates a context for the budget process where it is agreed in what direction the contact centre wants to go over a longer period and identifying funding requirements over that period. By producing a medium-term financial plan based on clear business objectives and delivering the benefits outlined in the plan, a department is well placed to benefit most from the budgeting process, possibly at the expense of those who are seen to seek more and more funding with no clear benefit to the organization. Financial planning will be addressed in detail later in this chapter when we look at business models.

Management accounting principles and practices are far too numerous to address in any detail in this type of book. Therefore, we have attempted to isolate only those principles that may have a direct impact on budgeting and financial planning in a contact centre. Some of the principles below are very basic and you will probably be already aware of them; however, they are included for completeness.

PROFIT AND LOSS AND CASHFLOW

The definition of cashflow is simple: it is a measure of the cash coming in and going out of a business. As a very basic example, the business receives £4 million, it spends £3 million, net cash in hand is £1 million and this can be confirmed by checking the company's bank statement.

In very simple terms, profit is net cash adjusted to reflect timing differences. In this sense a company could spend £3 million and set that against income over five years although the cash is all paid upfront. In this case, over a five-year period, expenditure will be £3 million and cashflow will be £1 million. This example is shown in Table 3.1, which clearly highlights the difference between cash and profit calculation.

Table 3.1   Cashflow and profit and loss statement

Cashflow	Year 1 (£)	Year 2 (£)	Year 3 (£)	Year 4 (£)	Year 5 (£)
Cash receipts	4.0 m	0.0 m	0.0 m	0.0 m	0.0 m
Cash payments	3.0 m				
Net cash	1.0 m	0.0 m	0.0 m	0.0 m	0.0 m
Cumulative cash	1.0 m	1.0 m	1.0 m	1.0 m	1.0 m
Profit and Loss					
Income	4.0 m	0.0 m	0.0 m	0.0 m	0.0 m
Expenditure	0.6 m	0.6 m	0.6 m	0.6 m	0.6 m
Profit	3.4 m	−0.6 m	−0.6 m	0.6 m	−0.6 m
Cumulative profit	3.4 m	2.8 m	2.2 m	1.6 m	1.0 m

ACCRUALS AND PREPAYMENTS (CONSISTENCY)

A major concept in accounting is consistency. Consistency states that all costs and income needs to be matched across accounting periods. A good example is where a builder builds a home for £200 k in year 1 and sells it for £300 k in year 2. Reporting this on a strictly cashflow basis would show the builder making a loss of £200 k in year 1 and a profit of £300 k in year 2. In Table 3.1 the £3 k expenditure is written off over five years because the operational benefit is realized over a five-year period. In a contact centre this could represent the cost of refurbishment.

INCOME

In general, income or sales is relatively simple to understand and measure; however, there are times when it is not clear cut or where income may be the wrong thing to be measuring. An example of where income generation is complex is the finance sector. What is the sales value of a credit card sale or a savings account, or even a mortgage? In complex situations like these, performance is usually measured based on contribution, also known as marginal income.

> Contribution = income – variation cost of delivery
> Contribution ratio = contribution/income

In the finance sector, contribution rates for all products are calculated by underwriters, who take account of average product values, average duration of product holding and other measures. In all other organizations the finance department calculates a contribution figure or ratio.

Except where income calculation is more complex, one other example of when contribution is the appropriate measure of value is in the creation of business cases. This will be covered later in this chapter.

CAPITAL AND REVENUE EXPENDITURE

Revenue expenditure is expenditure that only benefits the current accounting period. This means that all revenue costs are debited from the current year's budget. Capital expenditure is the proportion of capital spent that is attributable to a specific accounting period.

The issue of timing has already been touched upon in the section on cashflow versus profit. In budgeting it is very important to understand these differences and how they affect your budget requirements. In this regard operations vary from organization to organization, so the only way to obtain a clear understanding is to ask a member of your finance team to take you through the specifics. Some of the issues that need to be clarified are:

- Are separate budgets prepared for capital and revenue spend?
- Does the write-off of past and current capital investment need to be covered in the revenue budget, that is, as depreciation? If it does, then the revenue budget will need to be large enough to cover the current year's write-off of past and proposed capital investment.
- What is regarded as capital investment? Many areas are clear cut, such as machinery and motor vehicles, but the treatment of others can vary. The major items to clarify are small equipment costs such as PCs, computer software and consultancy fees.
- Is the process for sign-off on capital and revenue spend different? If so, how?

Hopefully the issues raised above should highlight the need to acquire a clear understanding of the budget process. One tip: don't worry about looking a fool because you don't understand the terms or how the process worked. Having worked in accounting and with call centres for over 15 years, I have to study the idiots' guide to budgets and business cases every time I embark on a new operation.

DEPRECIATION

Depreciation is the way in which capital investment is written off over the useful life of the investment. Depreciation rates are set by company policy for each class of investment ranging from, say, 2 per cent per annum for property to 33 per cent per annum for motor vehicles. It is important that a manager knows how this impacts on budgeting and financial planning.

FIXED AND VARIABLE COSTS

Fixed costs are those costs that are incurred irrespective of the level of sales or production – examples are rent, bank interest and depreciation. Variable costs are those that vary with output or activity – examples are salaries, telephone costs and motor expenses. The difference between fixed and variable costs is important when it comes to effective budget management. Call centre managers can rarely directly affect the fixed-cost base, particularly within the current financial year, so their area of control is the variable element of the budget. Given managers' inability to affect fixed costs, many operations will manage fixed costs centrally so this never becomes an issue for functional managers.

It is worth highlighting the fact that costs are rarely totally fixed or totally variable. Salaries, though identified as variable above, will not exactly match production or output for example, as notice periods may need to be served in to reduce staff, and thus managers would need to be able to forecast requirements perfectly. Rent, though identified as fixed, can change if new space is acquired or if space is released.

BUILDING A BUDGET

A budget is an itemized listing of the amount of all estimated revenue and costs for a particular period, usually a year. Here, the focus is solely on the cost side of the equation and, more specifically, on the revenue costs, that is, excluding capital expenditure.

If a contact centre is a profit centre rather than a cost centre it probably will and definitely should build and report on both income and costs, as that is the basis on which it should be measured. If a contact centre operates as a cost centre but generates income it could also decide to report on both income and costs in order to emphasize the value that is generated by the operation.

HEADCOUNT

In some organizations there may be a headcount budget as well as the financial budget. There is obviously a direct link between these two budgets but it can make a big difference if a contact centre has a strict headcount budget as well as a financial budget. For example, if a contact centre has a headcount budget of 200 and this cannot be exceeded at any time throughout the year then the operation may have too many staff during quiet times and too few for seasonal peaks. Alternatively, if the budget is set as full time equivalents (FTEs) across the year then the operation could have perhaps 100 at quiet times and 300 at peaks. The latter option is obviously far better for the contact centre.

BUILDING A BUDGET

When constructing a budget, contact centres need to start with demand, that is, how many contacts do we expect to receive and how many do we expect to make. The first reference for building this forecast is what happened a year ago. Almost all contact centres will have this information in one form or another. If the contact centre uses a roster system the information will be there as will the tools for using the previous year's performance as the basis for the following year's. If no roster system exists, call statistics can be obtained from automatic call distribution (ACD) reports or whatever manual reporting is in place.

Although this starting point seems clear enough, it begs the question: should we use calls offered or calls answered? If a centre has a high abandon rate this can be a major problem. In reality, you must opt for the answered call rate, as many of the calls offered are likely to be repeat calls. Some allowance should be made for abandoned calls; assuming a service-type operation as a rule of thumb, only between 10 to 20 per cent of abandoned calls result in actual calls once a decent service level is achieved. This figure may be higher in a sales environment where the customer will have a variety of options on who they buy from. In addition, calculation and forecasting volumes for email, correspondence and administration should be incorporated into the budget.

FORECASTING GROWTH

Once the current activity volumes are known, estimates on the extent to which volumes will grow or reduce over the next period need to be developed. The forecast should be linked to the key drivers of call volume, for example:

- Historic growth
- Expected income growth
- Expected customer growth
- Marketing plans for the next period.

If an income budget is being developed it should also start from this point.

Once the forecast volumes are identified, the resource requirements need to be calculated. As mentioned previously, roster systems exist that can model various scenarios for future contact volumes and also calculate resource requirements down to a half-hour slot based on forecast and historic call patterns using Erlang C calculations.

> Erlang C is a mathematical calculation used to forecast the number of agents required to deliver a defined service level for inbound call handling given defined volumes and call 'Average Handling Time' (AHT). For details on Erlang C, contact your resource manager, read one of the many books on the subject or browse through www.erlang.com.

It is not necessary to have access to a roster system in order to make a reasonable forecast of resource requirements for budgetary purposes. This can be done using the basic information in the following table:

Resource requirements

Inbound call volumes	2 000 000
AHT in seconds	325
Inbound workload in hours	180 555.6
Inbound occupancy	70%
Inbound person-hours required	257 937
Outbound call volumes	500 000
Outbound call completed per hour	5
Outbound person-hours required	100 000
Total person-hours required	**357 937**

Days per working-year	260
Less:	
Annual leave	26
Public holidays	11
Sickness and absence	12
Training and briefing	24
Performance management	4
FTE days per annum	**183**
Call handling hours per working-day	6
FTE hours per annum	**1 098**
Total agent FTE requirement	**326**

The calculation of 326 full time equivalents (FTE) above can be broken down into the following equations:

FTE requirement = Inbound resource requirement (IRR) + Outbound resource requirement (ORR)
(326 = 235 + 91)

IRR = Inbound workload in hours (IW) / Inbound occupancy / FTE hours worked per annum
(235 = 180 556 / 0.7 / 1098)

IW = Forecast call volumes x Average handling time (AHT) / 60 / 60)
(180 556 = 2 000 000 x 325 / 60 / 60)

ORR = Outbound workload in hours (OW) / FTE hours worked per annum
(91 = 100 000 / 1098)

OW = Forecast outbound calls / Outbound calls completed per hour
(100 000 = 500 000 / 5)

Data/assumption	Value	Source
Annual inbound calls	2 000 000	Forecast based on historic data, expected growth and planned activity
Annual outbound calls	500 000	Forecast based on historic data, expected growth and planned activity
Inbound AHT	325	Estimate based on historic data and incorporated expected process changes
Outbound calls completed per hour	5	Estimate based on historic data and incorporated expected process changes
Inbound occupancy*	70%	Estimate based on historic data and Erlang C validation

FTE hours per annum	1098	Calculated based on agreed absence, operational requirements and historic unauthorized absence

* The one data item from the list above that may require further discussion is inbound occupancy. Within the calculation above occupancy has been used to short-circuit the need to run detailed Erlang C calculations for an entire year.

Occupancy = Agent time spent on call handling (including *wrap time*) or Calls answered
× AHT / Agents logged on time

OCCUPANCY LEVELS

The level of occupancy achieved is dictated by the volume of resources available to handle inbound call activity. All things being equal, the lower the resource, the busier the agents, the higher the occupancy and, therefore, the lower the grade of service achieved. Conversely, the higher the resource, the less busy the agents, the lower the occupancy and the higher the grade of service achieved.

Erlang C calculations fix the grade of service to calculate the agent numbers required. Once this calculation has been carried out, occupancy can be calculated as the number of agent hours required to deliver service level/inbound workload. If the working environment is changing significantly it is important to run an Erlang C validation to ensure the estimated occupancy figure is reasonable; usually, a test based on a typical week is sufficient.

The possible agent occupancy level based on Erlang C calculations is determined by the call distribution across the day, the level of service aspired to, the AHT and, most especially, the volume of calls. The ability to achieve a high occupancy level is mostly down to economies of scale.

Once the resource requirements are known, the rest of the budgeting process is usually relatively straightforward. In all areas of call centre resourcing, historic data is the ideal basis for forecasting. In simple terms, if a cost is variable it should grow in line with activity; if it is fixed it should remain unchanged unless known factors impact on it. Variable costs may be variable based on income (for example, commissions), activity (for example, phone bill) or other variables such as space (for example, utilities). These factors will dictate what item you index the cost against.

An issue worth raising here is inflation. Many operations will automatically increase all or selected costs to reflect inflation. For a contact centre, the most important issue in this regard is wage inflation as salary costs typically represent in excess of 60 per cent of a contact centre's costs. It is recommended that guidance be obtained from the finance department on how to address this issue.

MANAGING A BUDGET

Before we discuss the mechanics of managing a budget, here are a few questions that should be clarified regarding the operation of budgets in your particular organization:

- Can budgets be rolled over from year to year? There may be some flexibility here, but it is important to know; otherwise, budgets that are hard fought for could disappear.

- When is a budget considered spent? This sounds strange, but this issue could arise when a purchase order is raised, when an invoice is received or even in some cases where payment is made.
- Are cost categories interchangeable, that is, can I offset an over-spend in one area against an under-spend in another?
- What, if anything, can be done to change budgets during the course of the year due to unforeseen circumstances?

The main reporting tool associated with budget management is variance analysis. Variance analysis is usually carried out on a monthly basis, and reports what was spent against each budget area for that period and cumulatively each year to date. Many organizations will also include a forecast for the full year figure. A typical variance analysis report is shown below.

April budget report

| | April | | | | Year to date | | |
	Budget	Actual	Variance	Budget	Actual	Variance
Direct costs	£'000	£'000	£'000	£'000	£'000	£'00
Salaries	800	750	50	3200	3251	-51
Additional staff costs	20	32	–12	80	93	-13
Outsourcing costs	100	112	–12	400	168	232
Recruitment	20	15	5	80	52	28
Training	30	35	–5	120	87	33
Printing postage and stationery	10	12	–2	40	68	–28
Telephone costs	60	50	10	240	253	–13
Total	1040	1006	34	4160	3972	188
Indirect costs						
Rent	70	65	5	280	240	40
Council tax	20	25	–5	80	80	0
Services	10	5	5	40	20	20
Utilities	3	4	–1	12	18	–6
Business continuity	5	12	–7	20	45	–25
Security	5	4	1	20	18	2
Cleaning	3	3	0	12	12	0
Entertaining	4	5	–1	16	15	1
Travel	5	12	–7	20	35	–15
Professional fees	10	43	–33	40	43	–3
IT/Telecoms maintenance	20	20	0	80	80	0
IT/Telecoms support	20	20	0	80	80	0
Total	175	218	–43	700	686	14
Depreciation	62	54	8	248	186	62
Total running costs	1277	1278	–1	5108	4844	264

In this report a positive variance represents an under-spend of budget (good news), and a negative variance represents an overspend (bad news). If income were reported within the variance report, a positive variance would be overachievement of target and a negative underachievement.

The variance report will normally be produced by the finance department and, in many cases, will mean very little to the contact centre manager. This obviously creates problems in managing these budgets. As all reporting systems differ, it is not possible to outline a detailed approach on how to address this issue; however, in general terms, the contact centre manager or a nominee should review all cost items allocated against the contact centre budget and agree or query them with the accounts department. Where a strict adherence to a purchase ordering system exists and the contact centre signs off all orders, this may not be a major issue.

As salaries are such a major cost element for all contact centres and the volume of staff is often very high, it is important that the final payroll is always checked to ensure that everyone who should be on is, and those who shouldn't be aren't.

PRINCIPLES OR TIPS FOR WORKING WITH THE FINANCE TEAM

BUILD A RELATIONSHIP

Relationships between contact centre and finance are extremely varied which, in turn, means the relationship between contact centre managers and finance representatives vary also. Many large centres will either employ a finance manager as part of the management team or a nominated finance manager within the finance department. Having this sort of a relationship makes a contact centre manager's role much easier. It allows the manager to develop a working relationship with a finance expert who can represent the contact centre to the finance department and provide expert support in the development of both budgets and business plans. For this relationship to work well, the finance expert needs to develop an understanding of the dynamics of how the contact centre works, the issues that face it and the impact it has on the overall business.

UNDERSTAND KEY METRICS

A good financial representative should be involved in more than just the budget management for the contact centre. The effectiveness of a contact centre is driven by the contribution the centre generates and the efficiency of the operation in delivering the required service at an acceptable unit cost. An effective management accountant should be able to model activity and cost, 'Activity-Based Costing' (ABC), to develop 'Key Performance Indicators' (KPIs) that can be used to measure the performance of the operation and inform managers of significant issues.

MANAGE INFORMATION CLEARLY

In many large and almost all other contact centres, the relationship with finance is via the contact centre manager and a finance manager with some support from subordinates. Most of the data analysis is carried out using a 'Management Information System' (MIS) function within the contact centre. The biggest problem with this arrangement is that the finance team usually do not understand the value or benefits generated by the contact centre; it is seen as a cost centre and, as such, a drain on limited business resources.

Whatever the organizational structure, the objective of educating the finance department to understand how the contact centre works is still core to experiencing a productive relationship with the finance function. Other useful tips for managing the relationship with finance are as follows:

- Understand the role they play, what they need from you and what they will provide you with.
- Honour your side of the relationship by providing the information they require.
- Do not treat them as a bureaucratic irrelevancy; if you do, that is what they will become and they will make your life more difficult.
- Try to develop the relationship in order to maximize the data and expertise that they can provide to you. Finance is a hive of information that can be used by the contact centre for developing business plans and managing performance.
- If possible, try to get a dedicated member of the team who can take responsibility for this area on your behalf.

FINANCIAL PLANNING AND BUSINESS CASES

Financial planning is the process of translating business plans into income and cost projections over an extended period of, typically, three to five years. It may be little more than an extension of the budgeting process to provide a longer-term view of growth and resource requirements; however, it may identify significant change in the way the business operates in the future. A business case is similar in content to a business plan. The use of the word 'case' rather than 'plan' reflects the fact that the business case is presenting the case for change and, as such, the business case will need to show the value to the business of the proposed change. Value in this case may or may not be directly quantifiable in financial terms, for example improvement in customer service, but it will deliver benefit to the business and this benefit needs to be presented convincingly in the business case.

Business cases will normally be produced for any major investment initiative, and the financial element of the business case will be presented as a summary Return on Investment (ROI), probably with supporting documentation. It is important that a business case is not seen as a financial document. The case for change must be based on business logic and market awareness. Figure 3.1 outlines the key elements in a business case and it can be seen that the business model and the ROI are the outputs of the business case, not the business case itself.

It is important to note that business cases are usually presented as a cashflow not a profit and loss account, therefore capital expenditure is included at the time of purchase, as explained earlier in this chapter.

CONTENT OF A BUSINESS CASE

In order to direct the focus of the business case process on to contact centres, Table 3.2 shows some of the objectives, strategies and implementation plans that will have a direct impact on the cost and income generated by a contact centre. The implementation planning areas are not exhaustive and will be dictated by the strategies identified for the particular change programme.

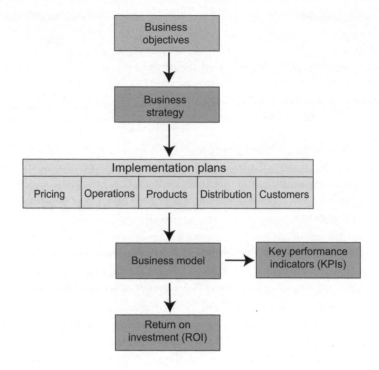

Figure 3.1   Business case flow diagram © Tony McSweeney

Table 3.2   Business case implementation plans

Elements of business case	Contact centre examples
Business objectives	• Improve customer service • Reduce costs • Increase revenue • Increase customer product holding
Business strategies	• Consolidate existing contact centres • Upgrade technology • Sell via service centres • Increase staff productivity
Pricing implementation plan	• Increase prices • Reduce prices
Operations implementation plan	• Redesign contact centre processes • Improve staff training • Implement performance management • Upgrade management information • Redesign call routing
Product implementation plan	• Introduce new products • Focus on core products • Improve customer proposition

Distribution implementation plan	• Use faster distribution channels
	• Use cheaper distribution channels
	• Distribute via the web
	• Use local intermediaries
Customer implementation plan	• Increase customer communication
	• Use customer targeting for proactive selling
	• Introduce customer satisfaction surveys

BUSINESS/FINANCIAL MODEL

Business model is a term that can be used to explain any business interaction, for example the business model might be used to sell directly to end-users, cutting out external distribution channels. In this case we are not talking about a model in that sense; we are talking about modelling the way the business operates and will operate in the future. The business model models the process of doing business, the right way.

There are many tools available to model the way a business works, from basic spreadsheets to highly advanced simulation systems costing £100 000 plus. The principles are the same and we will focus on modelling using spreadsheets. All business models should be designed so that any assumptions can be changed; the impact of that change will be carried through to the bottom line of the business model.

CALCULATING DEMAND

As with budgeting, covered earlier, the starting point for the business model will be demand. Depending on the strategy being modelled, historic data may or may not be of use in identifying demand. In many cases assumptions will be generated by the implementation plans, often developed by marketing, to reflect new customer products or customer contact strategies. These assumptions will need to be worked through to identify demand year on year.

The table below shows a simple example of demand and sales calculation for outbound telemarketing activity. Customer contacts are 700 000 per year for year 1 to 5 and sales generated are 245 000. Once these have been calculated, total sales value or contribution and staffing requirements can be derived. Apart from years 1 to 5 the table also shows year 0 or the base case. The base case shows the current level of performance and serves two purposes: (1) it provides a starting point on which to base or assess targeted performance improvements and (2) it is necessary for the ROI where you need to calculate the incremental benefit and incremental costs associated with the change. In the example below, the incremental benefit is £160 688 sales per annum (the difference between £245 000 and £84 312).

Telemarketing	Y0	Y1	Y2	Y3	Y4	Y5
Gross leads identified	3 372 460	5 000 000	5 000 000	5 000 000	5 000 000	5 000 000
Net leads provided	1 686 230	3 500 000	3 500 000	3 500 000	3 500 000	3 500 000
Total contacts	562 077	1 750 000	1 750 000	1 750 000	1 750 000	1 750 000
Total customers contacted	240 890	700 000	700 000	700 000	700 000	700 000
Sales closed	84 312	245 000	245 000	245 000	245 000	245 000

Data and assumptions
Telemarketing

Contacts made	33%	50%	50%	50%	50%	50%
Complete presentations	14%	20%	20%	20%	20%	20%
Conversion from total customers contacted to sale	35%	35%	35%	35%	35%	35%

Once demand is calculated it is necessary to calculate any one-off/capital costs of the change and also the operating costs going forward. As mentioned in the introduction to this business modelling section the business model needs to be driven by assumptions which are to transcend all the way through the model, for example, new PCs will be required at a cost assumption of £2000 each; the number required will be staff at end of current year minus staff at end of the previous year. By building models in this manner any change to staffing or unit cost of PCs will follow through to the cost of new PCs.

Return on Investment (ROI)

The return on investment is the benefit derived from an investment. It can be expressed as either a value or a percentage. To complicate the matter further, it may also be calculated on a discounted cashflow basis. A discounted cashflow basically allows for the fact that £1 million next year is not the same as £1 million today. The rate at which money is discounted is often referred to as the 'hurdle rate'. The table below shows the value of £1 million in current year, year 0, to year 5. The consequence of using a discounted cashflow approach is that significant benefits down the line may struggle to justify significant investment in the present day.

Year	Investment	Discounted cashflow
Year 0	£1 000 000	£1 000 000
Year 1	£1 000 000	£ 892 857
Year 2	£1 000 000	£ 797 194
Year 3	£1 000 000	£ 711 780
Year 4	£1 000 000	£ 635 518
Year 5	£1 000 000	£ 567 427
Discount/hurdle rate		12%

Return on investment = Incremental income − Incremental cost − Initial investment
(Incremental meaning additional income or cost)

The table below is a typical ROI for a business case. The hurdle rate in this case has been set at 20%. The Net Present Value (NPV) is £1.9 million. With a discounted cashflow, if the NPV is greater than 0 the investment achieves the target of 20%; if the NPV is less than 0 the investment would fail to achieve the desired return.

	Y0	Y1	Y2	Y3	Y4	Y5
Incremental sales	£0	£1 000 000	£2 000 000	£2 750 000	£3 500 000	£3 500 000
Cost summary						
Set-up costs	£520 466					
Running costs		£1 549 371	£1 503 310	£1 468 828	£1 440 273	£1 416 603
Total	£520 466	£1 549 371	£1 503 310	£1 468 828	£1 440 273	£1 416 603

Cumulative	£520 466	£2 069 836	£3 573 146	£5 041 974	£6 482 247	£7 898 851
Net benefit	−£520 466	−£549 371	£496 690	£1 281 172	£2 059 727	£2 083 397
Hurdle rate	20%					
NPV	£1 938 648					

KEY PERFORMANCE INDICATORS (KPIs)

Key performance indicators are measures that will indicate success for a business or business case. These KPIs will often be the assumptions contained in the business, such as contact rates or staff occupancy. When a business case is presented it is useful to present the KPIs in addition to the ROI. This will allow senior managers to understand what will drive performance in the future, assess the feasibility of the performance improvement, and track performance against these KPIs once the programme is implemented. The lists below highlight some contact centre KPIs that could drive a business case.

Appropriate KPIs for an <u>in</u>bound operation:

- Percentage of calls abandoned
- Logged on time
- Percentage of calls answered
- Schedule adherence
- Speed to answer calls
- Volume of calls handled
- Percentage of calls answered within ten seconds
- Occupancy

Appropriate KPIs for an <u>out</u>bound operation:

- Number of diallings made
- Number of Decision-Makers Contacted (DMCs)
- Conversion rate to sale
- Agent time spent on call activity

Appropriate KPIs for an <u>in</u>bound or <u>out</u>bound operation:

- Turn-round time on queries
- Sales generated (volume and value)
- Percentage of calls resolved first time
- Up-selling achieved (volume and value)
- Cross-selling (volume and value)
- Data accuracy and quality – S
- Call quality – S
- Staff absence
- Staff turnover (internal and external)
- Training days delivered (staff)

S = Soft measure (unquantifiable)

PRESENTING BUSINESS CASES

When obtaining the sign-off on business cases, you must 'always present it'; this is especially so if the business case is produced in a presentation format. Although the content of a presentation is normally very clear to those who produced it, bullet points in a presentation can be interpreted differently by an audience based on their knowledge or lack of knowledge of the subject matter. With this in mind, the decision on format needs to be made early on. Often a detailed written document will be produced and a presentation extracted from this document. If this approach is taken, the detailed document should attempt to educate the audience on the subject matter as well as include the core information of the business case. A common practice is to distribute this document in advance so that the attendees to the presentation are up to speed. Another option, if pre-meeting is a common practice, is to distribute a summary with key elements withheld for the presentation itself. A major concern with issuing the document in full as pre-meeting reading is that busy managers may then de-prioritize the presentation as they feel they have all the information they need and the presentation itself becomes a non-event.

Know your audience

Knowing your audience is very important when presenting contact centre business cases. Senior managers not operating in the field have a notoriously poor level of awareness of how contact centres operate. It is important that the people in the room perceive the role of the contact centre as important and not, as can be the case, as a necessary evil to keep customers happy. If the level of awareness is low, ensure that early on in the presentation the value of the operation to the business is presented and understood. Knowing your audience extends to individuals as well as the group as a whole, particularly those key to the decision-making process. No matter how big a group, rarely do more than one or two directly affect the ultimate decision.

In general, finance people will only be interested in the bottom line and whether the route to the bottom line is convincing; marketing people will be interested in the marketing approach and customer experience; human resources in the impact on staff; and IT in the complexity of the technology solution. Keeping them all happy may be impossible but each department needs to be considered.

In most situations, either you will be the project sponsor or there will be a project sponsor in the room. If this is not the case pre-presentation work is advisable to invite some advocates to the presentation. Also, it is important to consider who and how many from your team should attend. You don't want to outnumber the audience but it is helpful to choose people who can field specialist questions and contribute generally to the discussion. It is often helpful to share the presenting role in order to make your team members feel involved and also give you time to think. People who sit there and say nothing will not assist you and can have the effect of making the team look weak, so consider your team wisely.

Know the decision-making criteria

Most organizations will have set criteria that must be followed by all business cases before they can be signed off. This is normally a financial criterion, perhaps a particular hurdle rate that must be achieved. The business case may or may not meet this criteria but being aware of these is essential, as they will be raised during the presentation. Larger organizations will normally have a business case process, which possibly includes the following phases:

- Phase 1: Initial business case, top-line business case that will release funding for further investigation.

- Phase 2: Detailed business case, detailed to allow divisional managers to agree and sign off.
- Phase 3: Executive business case, much the same as phase 2 but less detailed and possibly taking a higher-level view.

If your organization does have a standard business case process, know what phase you are at, what, if any, templates are to be used, and ensure that the templates are included or attached to the presentation. Having said this, it is not advisable to slavishly follow the process. The presentation should say what it needs to say ensuring that all the basic requirements are covered.

Structure

Ensure that the presentation is punchy, to the point and can be delivered within the time allocated. Rarely will you get a second chance, so everything that needs to be covered must be done at the presentation. To this end try to minimize the number of slides; there probably should be no more than 30. There is no set structure for a presentation; however, it should allow the story to be told in an ordered fashion. A possible structure is set out below:

1 Objectives of the presentation, for example sign-off on business case.
2 Background to business, including current performance and the rationale for change.
3 Identify the scope of the business case, that is, what areas are included or not included, for example includes all telephone activity but excludes back-office functionality.
4 Business objectives and strategy for the business and contact centre. This is assuming that the business case is not proposing a new strategy for the business.
5 Review of what is happening in the market generally and what the competition is doing.
6 Educate audience with regards to 'best practice', and what you are aspiring to create.
7 What options have been identified? If they have been discarded, why? What option or options are you presenting today?
8 If more than one option is being presented, summarize pros and cons, cost and benefits and any non-financial benefits associated with each.
9 Overview of more detailed costs and implementation plans, if available.
10 Future actions.

Appendices may be supplied, which cover any additional data including more detailed costs and perhaps an overview of project timescales The appendices will not be covered in the presentation except to answer questions and for background information.

4 *The Contact Centre Environment*

Clive McAfee, Managing Director, interdec

Within this chapter the environmental factors associated with contact centres are discussed, including the benefits of a good working environment and some other vitally important details.

THE ENVIRONMENT REALLY DOES MATTER

Research has proven that underestimating the effects of working in poorly designed areas can be disastrous. At best, personnel under perform. At worst, personnel move on to somewhere more appealing, somewhere that makes them feel good even as they walk into the room.

A contact centre might hold statistical proof that it is doing well but, if a visitor's first impression is of a poorly lit, obviously cramped and poorly maintained environment, this impression will last.

The key benefits of a good environment are:

- Less churn
- Better productivity
- A happier working environment.

The environment is not only about choosing new paint, new desks or new lighting. It is about *fluidity*. It encompasses every aspect of a business. A well-designed contact centre says:

- we are a company that is concerned for the welfare of our staff
- we are forward thinkers
- we will not compromise by putting profits before people
- we are trustworthy
- we are successful
- we get results.

An environment with good design enabless the exploitation of space to maximum effect, so that more people might be placed within the space without sacrificing either their comfort or the overall look of the scheme.

> A company will spend thousands of pounds training and coaching an agent to their level of expectations, only to lose that person because another company is offering better working conditions.
>
> Anne Marie Forsyth, Executive Director of CCA

APPROACH

Any company when deciding on the design of its working environment must ask itself, what are its key operational needs?

Once these needs are established, the decisions regarding the look of the interior follow more easily. There are, of course, still key decisions to be made. Is the area to be themed – perhaps, a three-dimensional representation of a corporate identity?

From a recruitment and retention perspective, the contact centre working environment is vital to a company's return on investment in their staff. Here is an early opportunity for team building. Talk to the agents. What would make their working days better? Involve them in the design.

Allowing your agents to feel valued, that their day-to-day comfort matters, is the fastest and most direct way of ensuring staff loyalty. 'Ownership' and pride in workplace surroundings transcribe to balance sheets.

THE MINUTIAE

Key questions to consider:

1   Do teams who work closely together need to have easy access to one another?
2   How much will you need in the way of support facilities such as training rooms and meetings rooms?
3   Which teams need to have easiest access to these rooms?
4   To what degree do agents engage in team working? (This leads the decision on how much screening is required and whether there is a necessity for space in which ad hoc meetings can take place.)
5   How can you best balance operational requirements against building and technical constraints?

DUMMY WORKSTATION

Placing *in situ*, at the earliest possible juncture, a mock-up of a workstation that is being considered for installation will be of great value, in order to obtain agents' feedback. Considerations such as effective cable management and ergonomics are more often than not taken into account, but there can be aspects of an agent's working day, such as accessibility for technical support, that could be overlooked. If an operator's system should go down on the workstation being tested, will technical support be able to gain quick and easy access to everything they need?

Remember: A successful call centre is designed for people, people, people.

THE PRACTICALITIES

Here are some design rules that can be easily followed.

WORKSTATIONS

Asymmetric workstation clusters arranged on the call-centre floor will immediately break from the much-maligned traditional layout.

Workstation clusters not only improve the human image of a company but also, with their apparent randomness, introduce some rhythm and flow to the layout. If you have enough space for the number of people you intend to employ, then you also have enough space to break free from the dehumanizing environment of lines of desks.

The diagrams below represent possible contact centre desk layouts. Diagrams A and C have been voted the most popular with contact centre staff, while diagrams B and D are actually the most common.

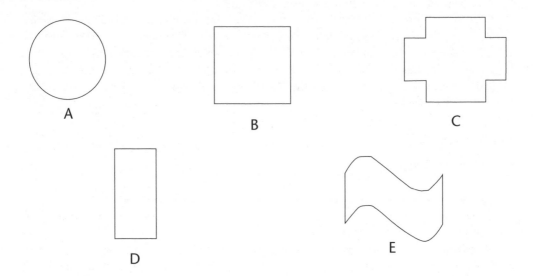

Ensure that the workstation reflects the business process and the functions performed by agents to ensure desks are sized appropriately.

DESKTOP

It is often financially worthwhile to invest in flatscreens and mini CPUs for agents. They take up far less room on the workstation top, which can pave the way for the installation of many more stations, thus increasing usage of expensive office space. Furthermore, flatscreens consume less power, resulting in an added saving in the long run.

HOT-DESKING

Given that workstation sharing is standard practice in contact centres, the provision of adequate storage facilities/personal storage is vital. Not just from the security point of view; they are also a huge help in keeping the contact centre tidy. Some companies have even gone so far as to put heaters to warm clothes in the storage area for that little added luxury – touches like this can sometimes be cheaper than you think and go a long way towards making agents feel valued and appreciated despite having no fixed workstation.

SEATING

What will your agents sit on? It is more difficult to specify seating for call centres than any other type of business environment due to the numbers of different people of completely different proportions who may well use the same seat. However, seating is becoming ever more user-friendly and quicker to adjust, and the investment is without doubt worthwhile. Back complaints, which lead to time off work, are an ever-increasing drain on productivity, and many cases can be directly attributed to inappropriate seating in the workplace. Ergonomic seating used to be a hugely expensive investment, but the technology involved is now becoming more commonly employed in less expensive chairs. The major factor here is to avoid workers being entirely sedentary; seats that allow for a certain amount of movement increase the flow of fluids in the spine, which prevent back complaints. Think of the spine as the engine of a car. Without oil running around the engine it quickly seizes up – surprisingly, the same is true of spines. As can be expected, cheaper chairs have a shorter life expectancy. However, keeping employees fit and healthy, quite apart from the humanitarian aspect, is certainly a worthwhile investment.

COLOUR

Colour is one of the most direct mood-altering devices and one of the most effective ways of introducing a desired mood into an environment. For example:

- very dark, unbroken colours on walls have been proven to lower spirits
- lighter, cheerier colours create a positive feeling.

LIGHTING

Lighting works in much the same way as colour on people's moods. Working under stark, bland strip lights is far from inspiring. But working in a dull, gloomy atmosphere is every bit as oppressive.

The installation of good diffused lighting is strongly advisable. Nothing can be gained from glare obscuring an operator's screen.

Coloured lighting effects on walls and ceilings are often extremely striking, acting as an attractive point of interest to liven up a space. It can also be an effective, and inexpensive, way in which to mark transitions between different areas of a facility. The fixtures themselves can be a visual livener. Many companies produce bespoke lighting fixtures that are so attractive that they become a talking point for visitors and agents alike.

BREAKOUT SPACE

It really is essential for contact centres to have areas where staff can take a break away from their desks – and, of course, to comply with regulatory needs for rest periods. These can take the form of breakout spaces, rest areas and/or canteens.

It is not difficult to create a high-street style café, where staff can enjoy their lunch and build up their reserves for the afternoon – it is just a matter of specifying more 'designer-look' furniture which doesn't by any means have to cost a fortune, but does make a huge difference to the look of any call centre.

The same goes for breakout spaces. They don't have to take up huge amounts of floor space and, in fact, can cost a great deal less to equip than many average workstation clusters. At a bare minimum, companies put in place soft furnishings (or even bean bags) in a partitioned-off section of the space to create an area which staff will appreciate and which suggests that the company is keen on alternative methods of motivation. At the opposite end of the spectrum, some companies invest in entertainment such as pool tables, table football tables and all manner of, what are in essence, stress-busting toys. Some provide televisions, or computers with Internet access so that staff can use email when on their breaks. Employers are coming around to the idea that these seemingly large outlays actually bring in better results for them in the long run thanks to their stress-busting qualities.

FLEXIBILITY

It is essential to consider how to build flexibility into your contact centre. For example, training and meeting areas that have fold-back partitioning and movable walls can be very useful. This flexibility is a simple practicality: to have a space which can be opened up into a large meeting area makes considerably more sense than to set aside a designated area for large meetings which might well be underused, or not used effectively, for example when there are far fewer people in a room than it can accommodate while others need the space.

In meeting rooms and training rooms it is possible to turn even whiteboards used for brainstorming and training sessions into part of the design. Some companies turn entire walls into whiteboards, which not only saves money on paper, but is also good usage of otherwise dead space. How many good ideas have been forgotten over the years for want of somewhere to jot them down?

It is the attention to this kind of detail that gives set-ups the edge. The subliminal impact of beautiful surroundings, on staff and visitors alike, pays dividends – often quite literally.

THE ESSENTIALS

- As much column-free space as possible
- Avoid splitting functions between floors
- Correctly sized workstations
- Space for personal storage – (lockable) lockers, for example
- Good quality seating, ergonomic considerations taken into account where possible
- Correctly sized and equipped training facilities
- Rest/break areas
- Appropriate levels of security
- Good air conditioning/air-flow
- Ceilings – go for as much height as is possible
- Lighting – don't allow glare to obscure the screens. Use diffused lighting.

EXTRAS

- Light, airy rooms, with, preferably, a view of daylight from each workstation are infinitely attractive, and always the best option. If that's not possible for some reason, installing lighting that lifts the spirits goes a long way towards creating the same effect. 'Full-spectrum' fluorescent tubes are phosphor-balanced units, the same technology used in the treatment of Seasonal Affective Disorder (SAD). Used in a working environment it keeps people bright, alert and motivated.
- Avoiding sharp edges sounds obvious but it's an often overlooked factor. In busy environments very large numbers of people hurt themselves on the corners of workstations, storage lockers and the like.
- Although this is often difficult, it is best to try and cut down on territorial demarcations. A room has to work as a whole and if it's possible to avoid a sense of segregation it encourages agents to feel more a part of a team.

FUTURE-PROOFING YOUR CONTACT CENTRE

It is true of all design, not just contact centres, that the more extravagantly *à la mode* a scheme is, the shorter-lived it will be. Of course, no company wants to find itself working within a scheme that was at the very cutting edge for six months, and is now embarrassingly dated, but equally no one in any way concerned with design would want a space that does not embrace any contemporary elements. Without a doubt, the trick to striking this balance is to build flexibility into the scheme so that as styles change so can elements of the design – with as little expense accrued along the way as possible. For example:

- Specify removable and reusable items
- A versatile and durable furniture system
- Partitioning rather than erecting walls
- Simple, classic colour schemes.

SUMMARY

- First, to gain the best results, understand the working practices and company philosophies as clearly as is possible – only then can the design be fully functional.
- Second, engage the staff. Staff knowledge of what would improve their output comes directly from their day-to-day usage of the facilities at hand and this knowledge is priceless.
- Finally, beware of the biggest mistake that can be made – to believe that there is a template around which all call centres are built. A design is organic, structured around specific needs, and the strengths – or even weaknesses – of your building.

5 Case Study: Intelligent Finance

Jim Spowart, Founder of Standard Life and Intelligent Finance

This case study summarizes the organizational impact of setting up a successful contact centre business. Intelligent Finance is a highly respected organization that has used direct contact to develop an innovative customer solution.

BACKGROUND

Call and contact centres account for the most widespread use of telephony within a customer-facing business framework. The only thing that is really surprising about them is the length of time that it took for them to become established. Conducting business on the phone, even in consumer terms, is hardly new: people have been doing it since well before the Second World War. So it is really quite astonishing that call centres did not appear on the business scene extensively until the mid-1980s.

I am not claiming to be a visionary, but I did recognize at an early stage in my career that the use of telephony in a highly structured way would represent a groundbreaking approach to dealing with customers and be a major aid to the process of transacting business.

The financial services sector is now one of the most dynamic, innovative, customer-focused and technologically driven of all industries. It has not, however, always been like that. When I first entered banking as a young man, it was still a profession – honest and credible, yes, but also profoundly staid, conservative and fusty. The closest most bank branches got to the use of technology was adding machines and double-entry bookkeeping.

As a young worker in the Cowdenbeath branch of the National Commercial Bank, time and again I noticed customers patiently queuing at the counter, awaiting a member of staff who was assisting a telephone enquiry. A ringing telephone is a highly intrusive and demanding thing: the one thing you cannot do is to ignore it. The customers who were calling by telephone received a priority service.

I was later involved with the establishment of Direct Line Financial Services, which was a pioneer in telephone banking and quickly became a market leader. Since then, my entire career has been built on the notion of delivering banking via call and contact centres.

I founded Standard Life Bank, which brought the freshness and innovation of the delivery of telephony-based financial services to one of Britain's oldest and most successful companies. My division managed to create more business for the company within a matter of months than other parts of the organization had managed during the better part of two centuries. It was a practical and eye-opening demonstration of the power of the call centre.

The next step in my career has been the establishment of Intelligent Finance. Once again, the willingness of the public to buy financial products and to transact via call and contact centres have been demonstrated. In our first full year in business, we captured no less than 9.2 per cent of the UK net mortgage market, having achieved £9.5 billion in new and pipeline business. The number of current accounts alone held by our customers is in excess of 70 000.

INTELLIGENT FINANCE

As our trading figures show, Intelligent Finance is among the most successful of the new generation of so-called direct banks. We now employ around 2500 people in our contact centre operations.

One of the most exciting aspects of using call and contact centres in the financial services industry is that it does not just give you the opportunity to provide a new way of transacting with the customer – it allows you to build completely new business models.

At Intelligent Finance, we knew from the start that we wanted to create a completely new form of banking, one that would genuinely break the mould in terms of delivery of financial products. We were determined that the technology we put in place would allow us to do this.

One of the things that had consistently annoyed me about traditional branch-based banking was that it was failing dismally to provide customers with the level of product and service they should reasonably expect. In fairness, I was not the only person to feel this way; others in the world of direct banking were of much the same opinion.

One of the main issues was the fact that the traditional high street banks were offering paltry interest rates – as low, in fact, as 0.1 per cent – on current accounts.

One of the reasons why this uncompetitive rate was being offered was that the banks were constrained by an old-fashioned and out-of-date mindset. They had failed to adapt to the direct banking revolution which call centres had forged and they still had a cost base driven by their traditional outlook.

TELENET: GOLDEN OPPORTUNITY

We recognized that this presented us with a golden opportunity. Our telenet-driven operation was not saddled with the high overheads associated with a high street branch network. We were lean, which meant we could afford not to be mean. The savings associated with our much lower costs could be passed back to our customers by offering them much better returns on their savings or uniquely competitive rates on their borrowings.

There is sometimes a perception among the general public that the somewhat anonymous nature of call centres means that customer service is compromised. In our experience, this is not the case. The key commercial driver of our contact centre is to improve service and retain customers. We certainly strive to fulfil both of these objectives.

Compared with the traditional method of banking – making a personal appearance at a branch and transacting either across the counter or in a face-to-face meeting with a member of staff – contact centres offer vastly improved customer service. There are no queues while customers wait to be seen. Staff are not harassed, so the conversation with the customer is neither rushed nor surly. Transactions take place quickly, easily and efficiently, either via the web or via our agents, who are trained to the very highest levels of service. It's a fact of life that no one ever gets over-excited at the prospect of organizing their banking, but our staff work extremely hard to ensure that the experience is as positive as possible.

THE VALUE OF CONVERSATION

The value of conversation, I believe, is one of the major benefits the contact centre sector can offer. Much of the interfacing between contact centre staff and their customers is of a routine nature. However, well-trained operators, whether dealing with inbound or outbound calls, can bring a feel-good factor to the converstion, which would be lacking in other forms of contact, such as mail. The attitude and positiviseness of staff can reflect well on the company concerned and lead to an enhanced experience which raises the likelihood of repeat business.

An example of this is in the handling of complaints. If there is some sort of a breakdown between company and customer – and this is something which can and does happen in any organization, large or small – then the contact centre business model allows it to be resolved quickly and courteously. Where this happens, the end result is that the customer will often go away completely satisfied with the outcome, meaning the relationship between company and client is actually improved. That in turn leads to increased goodwill and word-of-mouth promotion for the business involved.

EMPOWERING PEOPLE

Of course, empowering people can only be achieved successfully if you have quality staff. At Intelligent Finance we aim to be the kind of company people want to work for. The pay is good; the organization is people- rather than technology-centric; we have specific methods of ensuring that the work is varied and interesting; we encourage best practice and the active discussion of ways in which we can improve our service at every turn; we allow our agents to control the workflow, rather than having them feel that the workflow is controlling them; we do everything we can to reduce stress and to make working with us both fun and rewarding; we aim to hold the reputation of being a world-class company.

When we engaged in our recruitment process before the launch of our contact centre, we also set our parameters as wide as possible. We did not, for instance, look for previous call or contact centre experience. We were more interested in whether or not our potential employees had a background which meant that they were comfortable dealing with people.

We actually took the view that anyone who had worked in a customer-facing environment was every bit as suitable for call centres as seasoned agents. As long as they were friendly, warm, helpful and eager to please, that was fine by us. In our view, you can train people to the task in hand, but you cannot train them to have the right attitude with the customer. That is the most important attribute, and it has to be there from the beginning.

What, though, about the practicalities of the operation? Our centres are much bigger than the call centre industry average, although when compared with other household name financial services providers, they are not particularly large.

BUSINESS MODEL

The business model we have built could only work in a call or contact centre environment. This is not only because of the people, but the underlying technology. In order for a contact centre-driven direct-banking organization such as ours to succeed and beat off some highly capable competitors, three elements need to be in place:

1   First-class staff
2   Leading-edge technology

3   Innovative product and service ideas.

All of which can be delivered by the technology and the people.

INTEGRATED BANKING

We were aware from the start that we had to use our contact centre delivery mechanism to harness and use the power of phone and Internet banking in a way that had never been done before. The way in which we did this was to come up with the idea of *integrated banking*, a truly revolutionary concept linked directly to our contact centre technology.

We wanted to use our phone and Internet capability to create a product set so compelling that it could not fail to attract customers. By doing this, we realized, we could quickly build a high-volume business that did not compromise levels of customer service.

Our answer was to allow our customers to offset the money they had on deposit with us, either in their current account or savings, with the money they borrowed from us via a credit card, mortgage or personal loan. This revolutionary model, which we still use today, has been an enormous success.

We simply could not have done this using conventional banking techniques because of the high overheads involved. It had to be delivered in a contact centre environment. In this way, Intelligent Finance provides an excellent example of an organization that is not just using the contact centre to market its products: it has built its entire business model on the use of this type of delivery model.

We also took the view from the start that we had to offer genuine multi-channel delivery. This is critically important. We carried out extensive research before the launch, notably in the USA, and quickly discovered that the most successful contact centres were those that did not confine themselves to a single channel – principally, phone or Internet – but which allowed customers to pick their preferred method of contact.

We recognized that many people like the speed, flexibility and interactivity of online banking, but we were also aware that the web is by no means ubiquitous yet and that it is essential to provide phone-based contact. According to the *Journal of Database Marketing* ('Today's Changing Call Centre: An Overview' by Natalie Calvert, January 2001), penetration of the Internet continues to increase rapidly in the UK, but saturation point will not be reached until about 2015. It is certainly our experience that many people continue to want to use the phone.

We therefore have no plans at present to change the delivery mix. In fact, we have found that while customers may like initially to set up a product or plan by talking to an agent on the phone, the split between phone and web applications is roughly equal. But of those 50 per cent of people who open their plans on the phone, a subsequent 60 per cent of them will then go on to carry out their day-to-day transactions via the web.

FRIENDLY TECHNOLOGY

It need hardly be said that, in a mission-critical environment such as a transactional contact centre, the technology is as important as the people. When we launched our contact centre, we decided to use the full suite of customer management applications. One of its biggest advantages is that it can actually intelligently read the content of each email and route it to a representative depending on the words it contains. It can even deliver automatic responses based on the content of the original message.

Our software is also configured so that if our customers feel they have become stuck at a certain point during a web session, or if they feel they want more information before they proceed, they can contact us by telephone. Our representatives can then bring up the customer's web session on screen, replicating the information on our contact centre representative's own monitor. So both the customer and the member of staff are looking at the same thing on screen at the same time, which makes the process of resolving the issue at hand extremely straightforward.

This proves that technology has turned out to be a wonderful – indeed, essential – enabler. It provides us with the capability to work smarter, to understand our customers, to obtain a single view of their activities, and to give them what they want. We can create a memory snapshot of their behaviour which, of course, becomes further refined and more useful as time goes on.

When you are deploying technology in this way you are, of course, very much at the leading edge. Without discipline, it would be easy to lose sight of the fact that the contact centre operation must be run by its managers, and not by software applications, no matter how sophisticated they may be. Of course, you come to rely on the systems, but you have to be realistic enough to be aware of their potential failings too.

THE CUSTOMER IS KING

There is one rule about the contact centre business which is absolutely fundamental: never be so beguiled by the success of your business, the capabilities of the technology or the achievements of the staff that you forget that, as with any trading entity, the most important person is the customer. Everything any successful contact centre-based operation does must be aimed at improving and developing the relationship with those who buy your product and service.

Our phone lines, for instance, are manned 24 hours a day. They have to be, because there are some people who want to transact at 2 a.m. or to apply for a personal loan at daybreak. There are even people – quite a lot of them, actually – who will spend part of Christmas Day applying for a mortgage. It is not for us to question their reasons – although most are pretty innocuous, such as the demands of shift working – but simply to be there for them so that they can conduct their banking business at a time of their, and not our, choosing.

Of course, though, you don't just have to keep your customers – you have to train your staff too. Staff churn is one of the biggest issues facing the contact centre industry, and one of which we at Intelligent Finance have been acutely aware.

In fact, because of the way in which we work not just to recruit our operators but to keep them challenged and satisfied in the work they do, our churn rates are extremely low.

PEOPLE DEVELOPMENT

One of the most critical things we know we have to get right is the training. This is the key to staff satisfaction and retention. We have put huge effort and resources behind ensuring that we get our personal development processes absolutely right. Before our launch, we recruited no less than 65 trainers, which ensured that our staff felt confident and in control before the phones went live. In this way, we were ready to deliver first-class customer service right from the first hour of the first day.

We recognize, however, that training is very much an ongoing process, and that staff need to be encouraged to continually develop their skills. Keeping staff trained is essential, and you have to get the education process absolutely right. To this end, we have Learning Centres at our Edinburgh, Livingston and Rosyth sites.

It is imperative, then, to ensure that you get the best out of your staff. How? At Intelligent Finance, we deliberately give our representatives as wide a range of products to handle as possible. We don't corral them into the restrictive and ultimately unchallenging practice of dealing with single products. We don't have mortgage agents and personal loan agents and credit card agents and current account agents and savings agents. All our representatives are trained to deal with all our products. This keeps their interest alive by providing a wide variety of tasks during their working day.

It is also critically important that the overall burden of stress on staff is minimized. Any successful contact centre operates by necessity as a high-pressure environment, but there are ways of minimizing the effect of this pressure on staff. Indeed, it is essential that every company operating within the sector does so, or morale will slip very quickly indeed and churn rates will begin to reach unacceptable levels.

One way of reducing stress is to allow the agents to feel that they are controlling the workflow. As soon as they begin to feel that the workflow is controlling them, then they are on a slippery slope, which quickly leads to exasperation and eventually to resignation.

REMOVING STRESS

Another move we have made to keep morale high and improve corporate efficiency is to take the decision-making off the shoulders of our agents when it isn't appropriate or necessary for them to be burdened with any unnecessary stress.

One example of this lies in the regulations that govern advice within the financial services sector, which are necessarily extremely demanding and complex. There's a fine line between selling our products and giving advice on them. If a customer asks one of our representatives what action they would take, those representatives are trained to explain the options clearly and simply and to encourage customers to then choose for themselves because we do not offer financial advice.

Another potential source of stress is workflow. In most contact centres, calls are either made (outbound) or received (inbound) at high volume. If the call distribution is not managed effectively, then calls start to stack up on hold as the operators struggle to deal with them. If this happens, then customer service starts to be badly and unacceptably compromised. Operators feel stressed, and the person on the other end of the phone becomes an enemy rather than a friend. The representatives feel they have to deal with the enquiry as quickly as possible and then take the next call, which they also have to clear quickly. And so it goes on. Instead of helping customers, they feel they are simply shovelling enquiries, and both morale and service levels begin to suffer.

GIVE PEOPLE TIME

To combat this, we have a very straightforward but effective policy: we give our representatives the time they need to handle calls properly. We never make them feel we're rushing them on to the next call. The first priority is to give the customers the service they require, no matter how long it takes.

I cannot overestimate the importance of this kind of approach. Allowing our representatives to see their enquiries through to completion doesn't just reduce stress levels; it also gives them a sense of ownership of those enquiries. They build up a relationship with the customer, help steer the transaction or request through to a satisfactory conclusion, and can then take pride in a job well done.

There are also plenty of other steps we take to ensure that morale is upheld. For instance, I know that a lot of contact centres employ wallboards which give a live report of how many calls are waiting. We do not. In fact, we've quite deliberately excluded them from our operation because we don't think they add any value at all. How does it really benefit the representatives to know that seven or 73 calls are waiting? The truth is that it doesn't. If anything, it simply hikes up the pressure. I know that many people working in the industry call them stress boards. So you won't find them at Intelligent Finance.

We also work hard to ensure that our people feel valued – which, of course, they are. We encourage social interaction, insist that they take their breaks, and ensure that they recognize that they are at the centre of what the company does, not peripheral to it.

I also ensure that I visit both of our contact centres regularly. It's important that I meet the staff, and that they have the opportunity to know who I am and to talk directly to me. Vertical management structures are all very well, but this is a people business and I want to know what my staff are doing and thinking. By the same token, they have every right to know what I am doing and to ask questions of me.

The interaction between us is all very informal and friendly, which is the way it should be. But if the representatives know that the Chief Executive is available, on their side and listening to their concerns, then that can only help morale and, with it, productivity.

LISTEN, UNDERSTAND AND ACT

We do not just listen to what our staff say – we act on their opinions, ideas and concerns. We actively encourage them to think, to respond, to innovate and to challenge decisions. It doesn't matter who makes that decision – whether it's me, the Chief Executive of HBOS, our parent company, or anyone else. Challenging an idea or a concept puts it under the spotlight and forces its justification. It may lead to a new application of that idea, or allow it to be refined and improved.

It is a fundamental rule of business that people work better in teams. The more people you have in the team, feeding in their ideas and their reservations, then the better the business will be and the more the customers will benefit. And I really do personally appreciate what our people have done in making our company the force in consumer banking which it is today.

STANDARDS

I honestly believe that, at Intelligent Finance, we are working to the highest standards found in the contact centre business today. We have no choice: if we fail to interact properly with our customers, then our business is directly affected. There are no other outlets. We do not sell our products over the counter and, while they are available to customers through independent financial advisers, those advisers also deal with us through our contact centre delivery channels. So our staff and our systems do not just represent Intelligent Finance: they *are* Intelligent Finance.

Our standards are, I believe, the very highest that can be found in the marketplace – though I must stress that does not mean we do not still have things to learn. However, the contact centre sector is doing itself no favours if it fails to recognize that there are still some practitioners – a minority and becoming fewer all the time – who do not work to the standards of best practice that the leading companies have set for themselves.

There are still too many companies that regard their staff as an expendable resource or that adopt a sanguine attitude to a high attrition rate among customers who shy away from their aggressive inbound or outbound sales techniques. At least the customers are able to terminate the call – and their business with the company involved – by putting the phone down. For the staff involved, they only have the option of putting up with the working conditions or finding another job to go to.

The industry still has to fully recognize that companies with poor track records exist; it must do everything it can to encourage such companies to realize that the adoption of best practice is the only way forward. There is still an element of cynicism among the public at large about the way in which contact centres – particularly outbound ones – operate, and companies that fail to adhere to high standards simply damage the name of the business as a whole.

There can be no substitute for investment in technology and training, for exemplary customer service and for providing end-users with the service they want and expect. Good practice boosts the reputation of the industry as a whole. This, in turn, leads to more demand for contact centre services, leading to more jobs, more investment and a more positive experience for customers.

SO WHAT OF THE FUTURE?

I have no doubt that contact centres will become an ever more important part of the process of customer interaction. Customers receive good, efficient and flexible service; businesses benefit from the use of technology, new business processes, and reduced costs. In other words, everyone wins.

In my opinion, there is likely to be a move away from phone-based call centres towards broader-based contact centres, with the emphasis increasingly on the provision of web-based and online services. This, however, will take time, as public acceptance (in the UK, at least) of the use of the Internet for consumer-based transactional services is at present far from universal.

My view is that this will change, and that the Internet will eventually become the dominant force. However, there will continue to be a role for phone-based activity for many years to come, and quite possibly always.

The contact centre industry may be mature, but that does not mean that it cannot continue to develop and improve. We will continue to learn from both our successes and our mistakes, but, by sharing best practice, we will ensure that the former outweigh the latter.

BRINGING MAN AND MACHINE TOGETHER

We are all on a journey – a journey towards ever higher standards, ever more understanding of what our customers want, ever more determination to meet their needs, and ever more awareness of the importance of people as well as technology.

By bringing man and machine together, we are reaping the benefits of both and serving the customers in the best possible way. Which – just in case we ever forget it – is what this whole business must always be about.

RECOMMENDED READING

Calvert, Natalie (January 2001), 'Today's Changing Call Centre: An Overview', *The Journal of Database Marketing*, 8(2).

▌▌ *The People Factor*

This section of the handbook reveals some of the technologies employed to ensure that the right people are recruited, with the right skills and the right development process to ensure a well-balanced, motivated workforce is retained.

- The Contact Centre Manager
- The Role of the Team Leader
- Coaching
- Recruiting the Right Teams
- Building a Training and Development Strategy
- Performance Management
- Working Conditions
- Retaining Staff

6 *The Contact Centre Manager*

Cheryl Black, Customer Service Director, Scottish Water

This chapter examines the pivotal role of the contact centre manager, and provides a true understanding of the attributes needed for a successful contact centre manager.

BACKGROUND

The business role of the contact centre has evolved dramatically over the past 15 years from a basic call centre set up to reduce administration costs and deal with customer 'problems', to the sophisticated customer management tool of the present day. In short, it has advanced from a tactical to a more strategic role. Naturally, as the contact centre grows in importance within the wider business context, the importance of the contact centre manager also increases, as do the demands and scope of the role.

WHAT IS THE PURPOSE OF THE ROLE?

The role of the modern contact centre manager (CCM) has evolved from that of the traditional call centre manager. The range of skills and experience needed are no longer limited to people management and organizational skills, but encompass much wider attributes of leadership and commercial awareness. On the basis that there is a direct correlation between staff satisfaction and customer satisfaction, the CCM is both customer champion and staff champion within the organization and must have the range of competencies and knowledge to influence both groups. Ensuring that the contact centre 'machine' works effectively and efficiently is only one part of the new role. Equally important are the links the CCM must develop within the business to ensure that the contact centre is not only operating in line with the look and feel of the brand values, but is involved in developing products and services that will be delivered via the contact centre. It is not effective for the CCM simply to be told what the focus of the centre will be. The strength of the role is in using the intelligence which comes from your unique knowledge of your staff's skill sets and the customer base you are serving, along with real feedback from staff and customers, to help develop new opportunities for the centre. In this way, the CCM really adds value to the business by contributing to the development of new initiatives, rather than being the stumbling-block for product launches, for example, when products have been developed in isolation. With this input, the customer support strategy is developed alongside the product itself. Similarly, the CCM is in a perfect position to identify possible cross-marketing and customer retention opportunities operating in a constant loop of product development, feedback and continuous improvement.

HOW TO MAKE THE MOVE FROM REACTIVE TO PROACTIVE MODE

The traditional call centre manager operated in reactive mode, waiting to be told about issues to which the call centre had to respond, or often just reacting to customer activity stimulated elsewhere in the business. The challenge for the new-style CCM is to play a proactive, influencing role. In order to behave as a leader, contributing fully to the running of a business, as opposed to a manager managing an isolated part of the process, the CCM must build an extensive network of contacts throughout the company and externally. They must also be prepared to do their homework!

The CCM needs to influence the following key individuals/groups:

- Brand marketing
- Customer relationship marketing
- Sales/acquisition marketing
- Corporate communications
- Legal department
- Strategy and planning
- Finance/billing
- Operations
- HR.

In fact, almost every part of the organization! This takes considerable effort, but the benefits are very real. However, it is not enough just to decide to influence these groups. You must be able to articulate what the benefits of this approach are. In other words, what's in it for them?

BRAND MARKETING

The brand is the personality of the organization. You must understand what values and behaviours your staff and the service they provide should portray. This is shown at its simplest in the greeting a company uses on the telephone. A company that wants to portray a professional, established brand may choose to answer 'Good Morning, Smith and Son, how can I help you?'. Alternatively, a company with a brand that portrays a more informal, contemporary approach may choose 'Hi! You're through to Smith's'. Rather than wait to be told which greeting to use, work with the marketing department to understand all the nuances of the brand and weave this into the behaviours and processes in the centre. Applying a consistent look and feel in all parts of the operation is a tremendous opportunity to reinforce the brand and is likely to endear you to this group.

There are some simple things you should check to ensure brand consistency:

1   Is your IVR (Interactive Voice Response) consistent with the one used on calls?
2   Is the tone and style of letters, emails, and so on, also consistent?
3   Are the customer processes consistent? Customers buying into a modern brand don't expect to find bureaucracy when dealing with its customer service.
4   Is the language used in advertising, literature, and so on, carried through into the contact centre?
5   Is this backed up by insistence on the use of the same language, terms, and so on, internally as well?
6   Is marketing collateral highly visible within the centre?

CUSTOMER RELATIONSHIP MARKETING

The customer relationship marketing (CRM) department will usually have a programme of initiatives designed to impact on customer behaviour either for retention or revenue generation. Working with this group to develop the programme will influence the nature and timing of the plan. Without input, the centre will be trying to respond to increased call traffic or customer enquiries for which it is either unprepared, or more usually, could have been far more simply absorbed into the operation. For example, could the timing of a customer mailing be moved by a few days to avoid clashing with a bill run? Small changes could make the difference between an effective CRM campaign and a public relations disaster for the centre. This is also an opportunity to provide feedback to the team designing the CRM initiatives from direct experience of customer behaviour and views. Is the script suitable for staff and compatible with the call-handling process? Input at this stage can very often improve the effectiveness of the whole campaign.

SALES/ACQUISITION MARKETING

As with CRM, involvement in the planning stages of any sales campaign will confer an advantage to the centre when preparing for response, and also to the design of the campaign. For example, previous campaigns may have been successful in terms of absolute numbers of sales, but perhaps calls were received by customer service rather than telesales, due to the design of the sales media, thus adding cost and customer dissatisfaction. Contribution at this stage can make the next campaign more efficient.

CORPORATE COMMUNICATIONS

Even the most innocuous press statement can generate calls into a contact centre and, unless the centre is aware of the content, staff will again be in reactive mode. The challenge here is to convince the corporate communications team that all and any press material is of interest to the contact centre. Most corporate communications departments also run a press-cutting file that can be easily accessed. Often in large organizations, staff are unaware of charity or community initiatives that the company is involved in. This news can have a positive effect on the morale of your team by generating pride in their employer. The benefit for corporate communications is the assurance of a consistent message leaving the centre.

LEGAL DEPARTMENT

A contact in the legal department is a must for all CCMs. Even in the best-managed companies, complaints from customers and staff can reach legal proceedings. Having a contact in the legal department will mean that issues can, hopefully, be minimized by taking informal advice before action is taken or put into writing. Merely discussing things can often help to avoid major errors. Because of the increasing need to be aware of the Data Protection Act and other corporate legislation, this relationship is likely to become even more important. In my experience, legal people are usually delighted to be asked their opinion on anything, so there is not much influencing to be done here!

STRATEGY AND PLANNING

Even if your organization does not have a separate strategy and planning department, there will be someone responsible for this role, often within the finance team. In terms of moving from reactive to proactive mode, this is the group who possess the information required. Knowing the plans for other parts of the business can prevent you spending time and money on projects that may not be meaningful in the long term. The benefits here are, in effect, business benefits, which is what this team is all about.

FINANCE AND BILLING

If the operation involves handling billing enquiries from customers, then this is likely to be one of the CCM's key relationships. The timing and accuracy of bills, and reminders, will have a huge influence on the performance of the contact centre. As well as being aware of the detail of billing cycle dates and volumes, it is well worthwhile developing a dialogue with the Billing Manager at a higher level. Issues such as the layout of the bill, the information contained on the reverse, or use of important sections on the bill can all be influenced by the CCM to the benefit of both the customer and the efficiency of the centre. It is also worth checking that the terminology used on the bill is consistent with that used by contact centre teams and with the brand, as discussed above. Knowledge of customer behaviour from calls and letters will influence decisions on payment methods, direct debit penetration, frequency of billing, and so on. Anything that improves cash collection is likely to find favour with this group.

The management accounting team will help the CCM to understand the costs within the operation, both from an expenditure and efficiency point of view. A CCM should, of course, understand the salary costs and other expenditure associated with running the centre. However, to operate as a commercially focused business manager, you should also understand the cost of transactions with the centre. For example, how much does it cost to handle a call compared with an email or letter? How much does it cost to acquire a new customer compared with retaining an existing one? What is the average value of goodwill credits given to customers compared with the average margin? These are all pieces of information which you need in order to be able to make genuinely commercial decisions about the running of the centre.

The management accounting team will also be your allies during the budgeting and forecasting cycle.

OPERATIONS

Operations, in this context, means any group that deliver part of a service or product to the customer and are outside of the contact centre itself. For example, in the mail order industry, this would be the group that selects and delivers the products. In the cable telephone/TV industry, this would be the group that installs the cables, deals with faults and maintains the network. Once again, relationships are key to ensure that information affecting the centre's performance flows effectively. If Operations are in contact with customers, it is also important that a consistent message is given. Commitments made in the contact centre, but delivered by another group, are open to misunderstanding and failure. If a customer service representative (CSR) says that someone will be with a customer within the next four hours, they need to know that that is the case. Service level agreements are a good place to start, but act only as a framework. The real effectiveness of the agreement is in the close working relationship that develops between the two groups.

HUMAN RESOURCES

The Human Resources (HR) department is one where strong operational links will almost certainly already exist with the contact centre team. However, it is also necessary to develop a link at the strategic level. From your knowledge of your own centre's staffing needs and performance, you will wish to influence the HR strategy in almost all areas. The HR department may have very firm views on recruitment and selection, for example, and you must be able to influence this department if you are to be responsible for the performance of your team. What kind of people do you wish to recruit, and what kind of skills will you need them to develop? Do you have access to best practice in the contact centre industry that HR may not be aware of? As with all your other departmental relationships, you respect the specialist knowledge that the function has, but wish to influence it from hands-on experience, direct feedback and hard evidence. This is an area where it is important not to be defensive. For example, if staff turnover or absence levels are increasing in your centre, do not see this as only your problem, to be dealt with 'in house'. Work with HR to review the selection process or absence management policy to identify flaws or areas for improvement. However, the bottom line is that you are responsible for performance, so you must have the final say in the people you employ. Selection decisions should never be made without input from your team, at the most senior level possible. This takes a lot of time, but then so does dealing with the effects of recruiting the wrong people.

Having a member of HR situated in the centre, on an open-surgery basis, is an excellent way of demonstrating this relationship. The HR team are usually delighted to be able to work closely with operational areas as it helps them be more effective too.

OTHER DEPARTMENTS

Clearly, the range of people you wish to influence will depend on the nature and scale of your organization. This is not an exhaustive list, but merely an indication of the groups likely to confer the biggest rewards. Departments such as IT and training are also important but are perhaps more obvious. In small companies there may be just a few key individuals with whom you need to develop links. Regardless of scale, the objective is to put yourself in the position of influencing any activity that will affect the operation of your centre, either by submitting ideas or proposals or by receiving information to help you prepare. Figure 6.1 shows the spread of influence a contact centre manager should aim for.

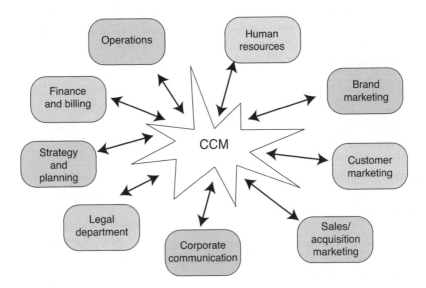

Figure 6.1 CCM departmental influences

COMMERCIAL MANAGEMENT

One critical success factor is your own credibility as a business manager. This is where the homework comes in. To improve perception of your role as a commercially focused manager, always seek the best business solution to any problem, rather than just the one that suits your area. However, in order to do this, you must have information on which to base your decision. This means staying abreast of what is happening in your company. Make sure you read the Annual Report, for example. Read the Strategic Business Plan, or at least the parts that can be made publicly available. Ask to receive copies of the monthly reports of departments that support yours. Offer copies of your own to them. Obtain copies of all advertising schedules and marketing activity plans. If you work in a regulated industry, make it your business to be aware of changes in relevant regulations and legislation. Keep up to date with changes in employment law and other corporate legislation. Read the financial press to understand activity in your industry sector, even if it has no direct relevance at the moment. Mergers and acquisitions happen so frequently today that it is important to be aware of key players in your market. Be aware of competitor activities. Read all the market research on your company, including customer satisfaction surveys. Find out if the marketing team is running focus groups and procure an invite.

In short, enhance your contact centre skills with as much business information as possible in order to build a credible and valued role for yourself within your organization. Remember, however, that this is not purely for self-aggrandisement. These are the skills and tools you will need to make your contact centre truly effective.

LEADER OR MANAGER?

So far we have looked at the role of the CCM outside the centre, but the role inside the centre itself has also changed dramatically. In the past, the CCM was often seen as the guardian of the contact centre's staff, defending them from all the terrible things that other departments wished to do to them. There was very often a 'them and us' culture between the centre and the rest of the company. The changes in the role of the CCM, described above, are the key to changing the internal aspects as well. Supplied with information and support from the rest of the business, the focus of the role widens to include more than the traditional hands-on people management aspects. As a result, the range of skills and competencies required in the role has broadened considerably. The key aspects of the traditional role would have been:

- People motivation
- Performance management
- Organizational skills
- Communication skills.

The new role also requires the following:

- Change champion
- Culture shaper
- Figurehead/mouthpiece both internally and externally
- Management of conflicting priorities between departments, for example, cost of customer retention vs. control of spend on goodwill credits
- Planning and forecasting
- Business/commercial awareness

- Influencing and negotiating skills
- Coach/mentor to your team
- Technical awareness
- Communication and presentation skills
- Financial skills
- Leadership skills.

The old role was a specialist, functional role. The new role is a general manager in a leadership position. The leadership aspect is highlighted by the change in culture of the contact centre. Gone is the victim culture of a centre at the mercy of sales and marketing activity. In its place is a vibrant culture where people feel valued for the role they play within the business. The role of the CCM is the link between the centre and the rest of the company; the credibility of the CCM, and by extension, that of the centre's, is what provides the improvement in self-esteem and job satisfaction for everyone who works there. The contact centre is no longer an afterthought. Its role is designed into all new products and services.

HOW DO YOU BALANCE INTERNAL AND EXTERNAL ASPECTS OF THE ROLE?

As a result of the need to spend time nurturing relationships outside the centre, the CCM is likely to be less hands-on than his or her former counterpart. It is therefore vital to ensure that a strong leadership team exists to manage the day-to-day running of the centre. The CCM must ensure that he or she devotes sufficient time to supporting and coaching the team. Regular team meetings and one-to-ones with team members are essential to ensure that the CCM does not become remote from the operation, but remains the solid bridge between the two. Part of the duties of the CCM as coach to the team must be to motivate the team to develop relationships within the wider business and to develop their own business skills. If all the contacts and business skills reside only with the CCM this will not only act as a bottleneck for information flow, but will also serve to alienate the CCM from the team. The CCM must create opportunities for members of the team to attend meetings or presentations where they feel secure and can develop their own network of contacts and business information. Remember also to keep your team updated on what you are doing. Circulate your diary so they know where you are and always be contactable by phone. At your own team meeting, update them on meetings you have attended. Otherwise, you run the risk of being seen as distant and accused of spending all your time at meetings while they do all the work!

UNDERSTANDING THE CONTACT CENTRE

In the same way that it is important to understand what is happening in the wider business, the CCM must remain aware of what is happening within the centre itself. One very effective way to do this is to set aside time each week to spend in various parts of the centre, for example, listening to calls or sitting with administrators. There is no quicker way to get a feel for both morale in the centre and customer issues. Small, informal staff sessions such as coffee mornings are also good ways to acquire feedback, but are dependent on the dynamics of the group itself. It is important not to rely only on these but to spend time within the centre talking to people in their own workplace.

For the CCM to be effective at influencing groups outside the centre, they must be confident that their own patch is running smoothly, both from a people and efficiency point of view. The CCM must not lose sight of the basic disciplines of centre management, ensuring that both performance and customer management processes are adhered to.

From a leadership point of view in the centre itself, this means being aware that the manager is a barometer for the concerns of the staff. Remember that you are their representative in the wider world and that you are on stage every time you walk through the centre or talk to someone. If you leave a meeting looking concerned or angry, within minutes a rumour will have spread across the floor that the centre is to be closed down or you are going to resign. Whatever is happening personally or on a wider business scale, keep a calm look on your face when you are in front of your 'audience'. The contact centre staff take their lead from you and it is surprising how much impact a word or gesture can have. So smile!

WHAT ABOUT EXTERNAL CUSTOMERS?

Along with their many internal responsibilities, the CCM must not lose sight of their role as customer champion too. One of the many benefits of having a more influential role within the company is that the CCM can ensure that the customer's voice is heard. If a policy decision is being taken that will reduce the service to or otherwise adversely impact on the customer, the CCM is the person best suited to make the case against it. For example, if Operations currently give two-hour appointment windows to customers and they inform you that this is to move to four hours, your knowledge of the customer base will let you judge the impact of this on attrition or revenue.

It is in preparation for such debates that understanding your customer base is vital. It is not sufficient to know how many calls or contacts the centre receives each day or month. Detailed analysis of the reasons for contact, frequency, response rates and resolution and so on are also required. In addition to this transactional information, you should understand the makeup of the customer base. How many? What products do they use? How long do they stay? What stimulates a contact with your company? All this information may well exist already. But if not, make it your job to accumulate as much of it as you can. This is the knowledge that gives you the edge when debating customer-affecting issues. If you can state with confidence, based on fact and experience, that customers will react badly to something, and you can make this argument from the standpoint of a manager respected within the business for their commercial view, then you will have a great advantage. And what's more, the right decision will be made first time. How many times have you heard customer service representatives (CSRs) saying, 'If only they had asked us before they did that, we could have told them what would happen'? It is your role to prevent that happening in your centre.

Keeping in touch with customers is also a large part of the role. The CCM should provide the example to all of the team in being genuinely happy to talk to customers. Not only will customers be satisfied that they can reach a manager if they want to, but you will also learn a lot about your organization and your own centre. Try to talk to at least one customer every day. It is not always comfortable, but it is rewarding.

WHAT SUPPORT DOES THE CCM NEED?

ORGANIZATIONAL STRUCTURE

The organizational structure chart of a contact centre will be affected by a number of variables, which will undoubtedly change and develop over time.

When deciding on structure, take the following into account:

- **Volumetrics**: Audit of the nature of customer contact, that is, calls, emails, texts. web and staff skills have to be analysed.

- **Management ratios:** This is dependent on the complexity and key components of each role – a ratio of between 8 to 15 often works best.
- **Technology:** Availability, utilization and expertise of systems and technology especially for management information.

  For example: Databases are an invaluable business asset, which, when integrated into a marketing and operational system, will reduce the number of support staff required, as management information becomes automated, rather than a manually intensive process. Conversely, a high degree of manual processes and procedures will mean more team leaders and associated support staff.
- **Business support:** Teams need to be supported by a layer of management to provide consistency and direction. In addition, it is recommended that further dedicated support is provided by a Business/Operations support section. This dedicated team consists of:

  Training: to ensure high skill levels

  Capacity planning: to maximize resource utilization

  Technical support: to manage local system and telephony needs

  Quality control to monitor customer satisfaction staff consistency and to achieve quality standards.

  The ratio of support staff to advisors is dependent upon the degree of workflow and process automation.
- **Additional support:** There is a constant need for ongoing support and dedicated resources from Human Resources, Training, and Technology departments. It is strongly recommended that any specialist skill resources are dedicated to contact centre activities and sit comfortably with the contact centre environment.

Figure 6.2 depicts a typical contact centre structure.

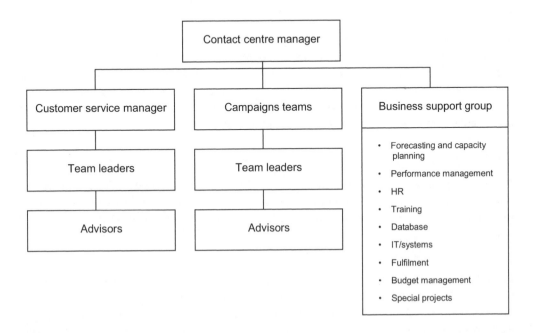

Figure 6.2   A typical contact centre organizational structure

The customer service function may be allocated by:

- Skills (sales, service, credit control)
- Functionality (phone, email, admin, correspondence)
- Rotas, shifts, and so on
- Product groups (mortgages, banking, and so on).

Whatever organizational structure you decide on, you will need to take into account all of the functionalities and roles discussed.

The key to a successful contact centre is the role of the manager who, like the conductor of an orchestra, has the role of bringing all components together and ensuring delivery of business objectives.

As well as a network of contacts in the business as explained in the previous section, and the operational team running the contact centre, there are a number of other support roles that are required to enable the CCM to do their job well.

MANAGING YOUR MANAGER

The most important support that a CCM needs is from their own line manager. It is essential to develop a strong relationship and communication links with this person. Depending on their style this may be close or remote, but the important thing is that it is positive. Without your line manager's support you cannot build the network you need to develop your own role. The critical factor is to understand their vision for the department and to agree with them your game plan for achieving your part of it. It is vital to develop two-way communication rules as well. You need to be well informed if you are to be effective, and team working with your colleagues is essential.

PLANNING AHEAD

It is important to have a strong planning/forecasting team managing the traffic volumes, resourcing and activity plans for the centre. This group provides the platform for all other activity in the centre and even in a small centre I would recommend that this is a dedicated group. The skill sets are very different from the team leaders (TLs) or people managers and both sets are rarely found in one person. Maintaining control over headcount numbers and scheduling is an arduous task in larger centres and this group can make a huge difference.

THE NUMBERS!

Support for finance and budget-related issues is also required to produce regular and ad hoc reports on aspects of running the centre. With strong support in this area, you will have access to the types of report needed to make your case with other parts of the business.

MANAGING CHANGE

In most businesses there is a long list of projects, both big and small, which are ongoing at any time. A team responsible for centre development can bring all those together and apply some kind of priority to each one. In larger centres, it is not unusual to find two teams unknowingly working on the same project. This role can act as a mini Programme Office to control and coordinate change. Depending on the size of centre, this person may lead a small team of project managers who actually carry out some of the work. However, it is useful if some projects are carried out by CSRs and TLs themselves, as these provide excellent development opportunities. This group may also look after technical developments and liaise with the IT department on system changes, new technology, and so on.

COMMUNICATION

The final support role concerns communication. This is often the most difficult area to handle well in a contact centre, or any other operation that is run in real time, and transcends core business hours. The wider aspects of communication are discussed below, but suffice to say that a dedicated person or group is required to ensure a smooth flow of information into, out of and around the centre.

Information or communication

In almost any contact centre, a staff survey will tell you that people think communication is poor and managers will almost tear their hair out in frustration and point to a plethora of newsletters, bulletin boards, briefing sessions, and so on. It is therefore important to understand what people mean by communication. There is often confusion between communication and information. There may be lots of communication going on, but if it doesn't give the right information, it is deemed to be ineffective. Similarly, if the right information is available but it is difficult to access, communication will be blamed. It may also be the case that the flow of information is only one-way. If staff do not perceive they have the opportunity for consultation and discussion, they are likely to blame the problem on poor communication.

Providing information within the contact centre

There is a wide range of information that contact centre staff need to have access to and it normally falls into the following categories:

- Corporate information: what is going on in the company I work for?
- Business information: what do I need to know to do my job?
- Local information: what is happening in the centre I work in?
- Job-specific: what is changing that will affect my role?
- Social: what interesting things are my colleagues or the company doing?

However, to provide this we must first of all find a way to transfer the information to the centre. The quality and timing of information is crucial and the key to obtaining it again lies in the internal network of business relationships. For example, if the IT department needs to carry out some planned system maintenance, there would normally be an arrangement where this was done between set hours and the contact centre was always informed in advance. However, if a system crisis occurs and the system has to be taken down, can you be sure that you will receive a call either in advance or telling you when it will be available again? In the meantime, what do you tell your customers? If you have forged your network carefully, then your IT contact will automatically call you as soon as they can. And you are prepared. So make sure you have an information map for your centre with agreed timescales and contacts for formal communication, and others for when you have to fall back on the informal route.

Traffic light system

Once the information is available, it must be communicated to the team. Each item is important in its own way, but the amount of time available in a day to absorb new information is limited. A way must be found to help prioritize the time they have. One way to do this is through a traffic light system (see Figure 6.3).

Red	* Something you need to know to do your job today * Something that will affect you personally or your role	Time is made available to read this information
Amber	* Something you need to know to do your job in the future * Something you need to know about the context you work in	Information to be read at your own discretion
Green	* Something of general interest or amusement related to your work	Information to the read at your own discretion

Figure 6.3   Communication traffic light system © Scottish Water

This system can be used in all communication media and allows individuals to prioritize their own time. It is, however, recommended that time is made available to everyone at the beginning of a shift to absorb the Red information. The Amber and Green can be read at the member of staff's own discretion. Creating a daily newsheet in this format, as electronic or printed copy, can be very effective. It creates a 'bible' for your centre – a place that people can be sure of finding accurate information.

Providing the right information

Before producing any documentation, however, you must first be sure of the accuracy of the information. It is very common in contact centres for staff to build up their own reference documentation and to rely on word of mouth from colleagues when checking policy details, numbers, and so on. Obviously this poses a risk. Misinformation cannot be corrected as the source cannot be defined. As I know to my cost, an incorrect telephone number once in circulation within a centre can take months to eliminate. While working for a mobile phone company, a CSR in my centre had transposed a digit when taking down a telephone number, and the Managing Director's (MD) number was being given out instead of the number of the Change of Ownership department. It took nine months and many embarrassing conversations with my MD to resolve. I finally resorted to a desk-by-desk search of individual notes and reference books and finally found the number in question in a list belonging to an experienced CSR whom people regarded as a font of knowledge for the centre. For this reason, I would recommend that within the communication team, you create an information section. This person and their team, depending on the scale of your centre, would have responsibility for the accuracy and timeliness of all information. As other departments pass information into the centre, for example network downtime, product availability, policy changes, this section would be responsible for validating the information and approving it for circulation. In this way, you can prevent incorrect information being published inadvertently. This is particularly common with Intranet use where something is published incorrectly and not spotted until it is too late. To be effective, the members of the information section must have a wide knowledge of the business so that they can understand the implications of changes and make judgements about how best to validate data provided to them. This role may sit comfortably with the quality management role within the centre where document control may already reside.

How to dispatch information to the people who need it

Once the information is available, it is necessary to make it available in the most appropriate way. It is important to make the distinction between information that can be presented and absorbed by an individual and information which should be communicated in a forum where it can be discussed.

One-way communication includes media such as the Intranet, newsletters, news boards, screensavers, onscreen messages, bulletins and wallboards.

Two-way communications can include team meetings, coffee mornings, presentations, and so on. It is important in these sessions to distinguish between a meeting of which the purpose is for one person to deliver information to the others, with time for questions built in, and an open-forum discussion. Remember to ensure that the person taking the session possesses the appropriate skills for this type of session as they can be difficult to keep on course.

Remember also that in any communication that contains an instruction, the use of a positive phrase will have a greater effect. For example, a sign that says 'Please use black ink only' will have a much more positive effect than one which says 'Do NOT write in red pen'. Treating our teams as colleagues whom we respect and not as schoolchildren is one of the most important examples that a leader should set.

External communication

Communication upwards and out of the centre is another area that is often overlooked. Ensure that your boss and your colleagues are well briefed on the centre's performance, plans and initiatives so that they can make informed decisions and comment. Producing a monthly pack of statistics and narrative, which can be circulated widely, not only allows you to publicize the centre's successes but also provides a single point of reference for data relating to the centre. This ensures that everyone is looking at the same numbers no matter what their interest in the contact centre.

It is often the small things that are overlooked in the field of communications. Remember to keep staff informed about anyone who is visiting the centre. A group of people in suits walking round the centre, listening earnestly to your Managing Director and taking notes can start the rumour machine going in no time. For want of communication, an innocent Chamber of Commerce visit has been turned into rumours of mass redundancy and a day's productivity has gone through the floor.

Celebrating success

Finding new and inexpensive ways to celebrate and communicate success in the centre is also a worthwhile exercise. Invest in a digital camera and have the Communications team take photographs at opportune events. Post them on the Intranet and on the walls. Find reasons to recognize people who wouldn't normally stand out. I believe that the most important factor for anyone who works in a contact centre is self-esteem and recognition is a sure-fire way to improve this. The leadership role for the CCM is to be available as often as possible to make that recognition. Present prizes, draw raffle tickets, and pose for a hundred photographs shaking hands with somebody. This may be the hundredth time for you, but it is the first time for them. Make them feel special and you will reap the rewards.

SUMMARY

The challenge for today's contact centre manager is to build their own credibility within their organization to allow them to shape the current and future role of the centre. A contact centre can be a business tool or a business overhead, and a determined, commercially focused CCM can help to determine that role, and in so doing, determine their own future too.

7 *The Role of the Team Leader*

Angela Hunter, Managing Consultant, Calcom Group

Supporting the contact centre manager is the team leader, a role generally with a significant span of control. This chapter reviews the role, skills and behaviours required by team leaders.

THE TEAM LEADER WORLD

The team leader role is arguably the most critical within any contact centre environment. Realizing cultural visions and delivering operational standards, team leaders are the local leaders who execute plans and initiatives.

Team leaders do not have an easy job. Every day, they are obliged to distil immense quantities of information and demands from a whole range of sources – marketing, sales, fulfilment, 'back office', and of course ourselves – and must somehow translate all of this information into one single menu of practical objectives for their team. The pace is fast, change is frequent and no two days are ever the same.

Team leaders are generally a mix of skills and behaviours, knowledge and experience, dreams and aspirations. In a typical team of ten, there is a whole range of personality and capability. A typical day for the team leader involves many tasks from motivating the team, to making decisions about shift rotas, to solving customer issues. In a fast-moving, ever-changing environment that involves a large number of people – both staff and customers – therefore, consistency in the team's approach to managing the operation is absolutely critical.

STANDARDS

To achieve consistency, objectives should be translated into 'method and behaviours' covering:

- Routine
- Discipline
- Controls.

Routine enables:

- Spending time together as a management team, leading to consistency in approach, clear messages and good decision-making.
- Understanding customer wants more and delivering them (that is, callbacks when promised, authorization of the database that releases customer payments for processing, and so on).
- Minimizing risk (that is, regular live testing).

Discipline enables:

- Prioritization of time for performance reviews, coaching, training, team meetings, call monitoring and feedback.
- Reward and recognition becoming the norm.
- Standardization and common ways of managing.

Controls enable:

- Consistency, especially in performance management.
- Understanding today to plan for tomorrow.
- Proactive management efforts.
- Achievement of service level agreements with other parts of the business.

Table 7.1 gives some examples of the most basic routines, disciplines and controls that help to manage the team effectively.

Table 7.1   Team leader routines, disciplines and controls

Routines	Disciplines	Controls
• Line test at 8 a.m. each day	• Agent performance reviews are documented each month and delivered within five working days of the new month	• Agents reporting in sick by 8.45 every morning – record on central spreadsheet
• IVR (Interactive Voice Response) scripting reviewed each month to ensure customer communication is cohesive	• Listen to three calls per agent per week, document feedback and allow 30 mins per agent per week to coach observations. The agent must be allowed time to listen to their own calls in advance of the feedback session	• Return-to-work interviews must be completed by 11 a.m. on the day of return, documented and filed in personnel folders
• Management information reports are available by 8.15 a.m. every morning and distributed by email to person x, y and z		• Lateness of 15 mins or more must be recorded on the central spreadsheet
• Sunrise Group at 8.30 a.m. each day to review previous day's performance and agree today's operational plan	• Assess individual training needs each quarter and review collective observations with the training department	• Three instances or more of lateness in any given month to be discussed, documented in personnel folder and reflected in performance review
• Regroup at 2 p.m. to share operational issues and agree actions, for example overtime requirements to clear down callbacks	• Motivation programme looks like this and works like so. We reward people every month for demonstrating behaviours x, y and z and delivering outputs 1, 2 and 3	• No more than five agents on holiday on any given day
• Fortnightly team meetings with agents		• We review our manual processes and procedures every six months
• Four weeks' notice when making changes to our shift rota		

SETTING EXPECTATIONS

We can communicate and reinforce our expectations at a practical level in several ways:

- Build an organizational mission statement that captures key themes
- Facilitate a session with the team leaders to examine:
  - what behaviours they expect from their own teams
  - what behaviours they believe are expected from them
  - what behaviours they expect to be demonstrated
- Translate expectations into the performance contract, ensuring that the behaviours can be measured or at least evidenced
- Regularly and publicly recognize and reward the behaviours, not just the output.

In our expectations of team leaders, perhaps the greatest expectation is that they coach and develop their team. Coaching and development should be an important part of contact centre culture: the capability and motivation of people to deliver objectives and output is an item for daily discussion, and responsibility for the results is firmly in the team's hands.

SUMMARY

The role of the team leader is the most crucial in making the contact centre machine work. Many organizations have to remove this role at various times; however, they often end up replacing the role with a new or shared job function as, fundamentally, in such a demanding and dynamic environment the role of the team leader has significant impact. The importance of team leaders is further highlighted through their role as coach, which is examined in the next chapter.

8 *Coaching*

Archie Shevlin, Cluster Training Manager, Inland Revenue

Within contact centres, coaching plays a vital role in improving performance. The impact of coaching can be extremely significant. This chapter considers how coaching can be effectively implemented.

THE ROLE OF THE COACH

Coaching is more than simply providing feedback on performance. Effective coaching is where the individual understands what the skill or technique being coached is, why it is appropriate and how to apply it in a way that works for them. A big part of coaching is also taking the opportunity to offer praise and encouragement for good performance. Coaching activity over a period of time enables individuals to perform to the best of their ability.

The aim of coaching is simply to improve individual performance, continuously. It's a skill and it's about development and performance enhancement, not assessment.

MANAGER AS COACH

When a manager steps into the role of coach, they leave behind the role of overseer and manager. The coaching relationship is different and requires mutual trust and respect. The coach needs to know how to motivate and get the best out of individuals.

A coach must be prepared to put their reputation on the line by demonstrating to their staff exactly how to do the job. For example, 'Do as I say' is not enough. Say 'Do as I do'.

Coaches develop and maximize the talents of their staff. The coach may routinely perform some of the duties of their staff but should recognize that their true role is to enable other staff to perform.

A coach is:

- a counsellor
- a supporter
- an adviser
- an ally
- a guide
- a mentor
- a sounding board
- a sage
- a role model
- a cheerleader

- a teacher
- a confidant.

COACHING BENEFITS

Staff may feel uncomfortable if a team leader is sitting with them, analysing their performance and behaviour. You will need to put them at ease. Their worries are likely to disappear if you explain why you are coaching and what you hope to achieve.

Coaching has many benefits:

- A regular opportunity to talk about performance
- An opportunity to share best practice
- It builds rapport between staff and manager
- It's flexible and can be organized around business needs and the needs of the individual
- It can be designed to meet individual learning requirements
- It creates effective communication
- It's an opportunity to set goals and targets together
- It's a bridge between formal training and putting training into practice
- It improves individual performance.

Coaching places the focus of attention on individual performance, which creates regular dialogue about performance between manager and individual. This, in turn, becomes the norm.

COACHING FOR CONTINUOUS IMPROVEMENT

Coaching should be used to encourage and support staff, but is separate from performance assessment. It is an opportunity to build upon existing strengths and to develop and improve. It is not an empirical measure of achievement; it reflects current performance and provides the opportunity to plan for improvement. This continuous cycle of improvement is illustrated in Figure 8.1.

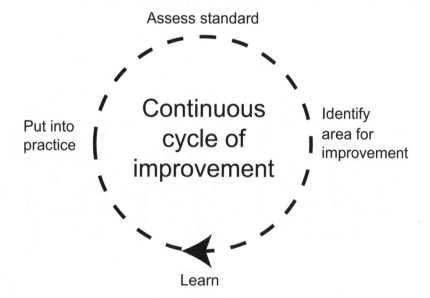

Figure 8.1   Continuous cycle of improvement © Inland Revenue

A coaching session does not stand alone, as each session builds upon the previous one. In this way the coach and 'coachee' can gauge whether areas for development have been improved. This locks the learner into a continuous cycle of improvement.

Coaching is on-the-job training which is designed to take place in the workplace rather than in the classroom. It may occur on an ad hoc basis, by the manager picking up on performance development needs via random listening of calls. This would occur in addition to structured and planned coaching sessions.

COACHING AND RESULTS

When coaching is first introduced, performance gains can be significant.

Don't stop coaching when an agent reaches peak performance and no further performance gains in terms of output and results are anticipated. Congratulate the individual on this achievement but keep coaching to maintain performance. It is often harder to maintain this peak performance than to reach it in the first place. To keep coaching requires nerve and commitment from management.

When 'good performance' becomes the norm it is easy to become blasé. The natural assumption may be that results arise from self-motivation in staff and that having trained them to peak performance the importance of coaching can be discarded. Coaching, previously dynamic and motivational, can become perfunctory. To stop coaching too early, or simply pay lip service to it can only lead to a decline in performance.

The following chart demonstrates the concept that performance is not constant. Individuals can be trained to peak performance. When this peak is reached, performance naturally declines. Coaching intervention prevents this decline from being terminal. The trick is to ensure that troughs in performance do not fall below what is considered to be acceptable.

In our example (see Figure 8.2), acceptable performance is 90 per cent while ideal performance is 100 per cent. With regular coaching the individual operates within those parameters. Each time performance dips, this is dealt with in the following coaching session. Leave it too long, though, and the climb back to the top is more difficult.

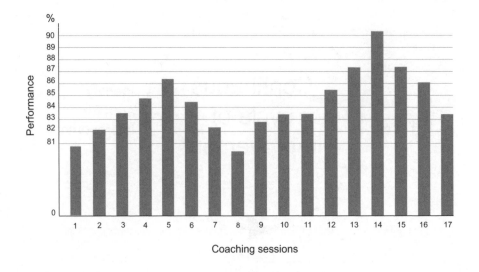

Figure 8.2   The effects of coaching on performance © Inland Revenue

FIVE TIPS FOR SUCCESSFUL COACHING

1 Take care of the practical stuff

- Put a system in place for recording calls. For example: this can be downoaded from the telephone system to the PC desktop, or recording equipment plugged into the agent's telephone set.
- Make playback equipment such as PC desktop, mini disc player or tape recorder/player available for coaches and staff.
- Set aside a suitable area for coaching, that is, with suitable equipment installed and furnished informally. If a room is unavailable then find a quiet place away from the workstation.

2 Consistency

- Allow individuals to hear and assess their own calls before the coaching session
- Managers should assess calls before the session
- Coach at regular intervals
- Set clear guidelines for performance standards
- Meet regularly with your peers to discuss and agree these standards.

3 Have constructive dialogue

- Start the session with an informal chat to loosen the throat and break the ice
- Ask staff for their thoughts first
- Seek agreement on strengths and areas for development
- Listen
- Ask questions
- Don't judge
- Praise good performance
- Encourage
- Demonstrate
- Never miss a good opportunity to let the coachee to do the talking.

4 Goals are important

- Recognize strengths and build on these
- Highlight a key area for development and agree on how to improve this
- Set this as a goal to be achieved for the next coaching session
- Provide support in achieving this goal
- Consolidate the learning point back in the workplace.

5 Coach the coach

- Ensure your coaches are capable of delivering the business improvements required.

9 *Recruiting the Right Teams*

Kai McCabe, Managing Director – North, Search Consultancy

Finding the right people is not easy. Here in this chapter we share tried and proven methods for recruiting staff.

BACKGROUND

Recruitment and selection is such an integral part of the entire process of contact centre establishment and maintenance that the programme must be coordinated, planned and measured throughout to ensure success.

Recruitment is also becoming increasingly challenging. In today's contact centres, we are now looking for professionals who can handle a wide variety of complex transactions, make sales and provide unparalleled service.

Therefore, to combat costly attrition rates and to make sure you are recruiting the correct employees for the job, the entire recruitment process has to be carefully constructed to include a blend of:

- psychological analysis
- educational skills
- presentation and social skills
- interactive skills.

The following eight stages will take you through the recruitment process:

1 Identify your needs
2 Plan the framework
3 Source the candidates
4 Meet the response
5 Face-to-face with candidates
6 Interviews
7 Letters and documentation
8 Following up.

STAGE ONE: IDENTIFY YOUR NEEDS

Ensure that you have measured your key criteria before the project begins.

Taking into account the business model (see Chapter 3), determine how many calls you are going to take and therefore how many front-line staff will you need. Build a matrix according to your criteria.

Ensure that you have taken into account the number of calls that an agent could take allowing for official breaks, follow-up paperwork, natural breaks, sickness allowance and holiday time.

In addition, focus on your service levels: how many staff do you need to ensure that your abandonment rate is constant, and what allowance do you have to make for ongoing staff training and development?

It is essential also to work continually with your marketing and sales departments to forecast demand in terms of customer calls.

Decide whether all new staff should begin in the department on the same date or if it is more appropriate to stagger their employment. Liaise with the marketing department to ascertain their expectations, and the training department to assess their capabilities.

STAGE TWO: PLAN THE FRAMEWORK

Provide the framework for the recruitment programme.

Identify the date on which you need to 'go live' and create a workflow project plan working backwards. Allow sufficient time for:

- designing and placing advertisements
- creating job descriptions
- briefing your response team
- adequate response to your advertisements
- designing assessment centres
- running assessment centres
- interviewing candidates
- assessing performance at assessment centres and selecting candidates
- distributing job offers, contracts and letters of employment
- candidates to give notice to their current employers and reply to your job offer
- training: product training, skills training, corporate induction, systems training, telephone techniques training.

Create job descriptions so that there is a clear understanding of each role including salaries, earnings, additional benefits and any other elements of the full package.

Agree key competencies for each role so that you are sure you are testing for key, defined skills for each role. This is a different process from the job descriptions and will establish the criteria that you will use to identify appropriate candidates and their key skills for the role at both assessment centres and interview.

STAGE THREE: SOURCE THE CANDIDATES

How you source your employees will be dependent on the size of the call centre and budget available; however, Figure 9.1 and the next section detail some of the more commonly used techniques:

- Referral and word of mouth
- Internal advertising
- External advertising
- Internet advertising
- Private agencies / Selection consultants
- What to consider when selecting your recruitment supplier.

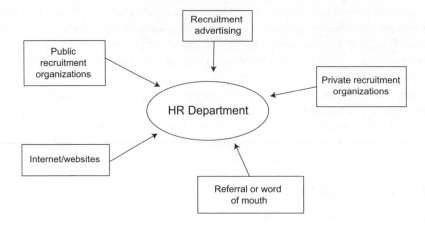

Figure 9.1   Sourcing model © Search Consultancy Ltd

REFERRAL AND WORD OF MOUTH

This can be the least expensive source of recruitment for some organizations. On that account, do not neglect your own employees as a method of sourcing applicants. A satisfied employee can be the best salesperson for vacancies within your organization. While some employees will inform their friends and acquaintances about vacancies without being encouraged, many organizations will incentivize their employees to attract potential employees. For example:

> Refer-a-friend initiatives:
> £000s bonus if friend hits first set of targets.
> £000s bonus when friend completes three or six months' service.
> £000s bonus when friend completes/passes the initial training period.

For those organizations with limited budgets, an alternative could be retail vouchers.

INTERNAL ADVERTISING

Opportunities for advancement or to broaden experience should always be advertised internally before external sources are used. Managed appropriately, organizations can create a highly motivated workforce.

In today's competitive market, perception is everything; hence, be forewarned that this method should always be completed prior to sourcing applicants externally. Organizations that offer posts internally at the last minute may leave external applicants with the feeling that their time has been wasted. Conversely, promoting internally can be a positive message to the market.

EXTERNAL ADVERTISING

Advertising is a costly business, therefore it is important that the recruitment advert is targeted at the right audience and gives them the information they need to encourage a positive response.

Writing an effective recruitment advert is often more difficult than it seems. Descriptions of both the organization and the position(s) on offer should be clear and attractive, but sufficiently tight to discourage unsuitable applications. Display adverts are the most expensive but can be effective in reflecting the calibre of the organization. The format of the advert needs to be eye-catching but the style should be appropriate to the organization and the people it wants to attract.

Checklist for placing an external advertisement

1   **Targeting:** When you place an advertisement, think carefully about the medium and title you choose. Consider what will offer the best/most effective coverage of your target audience. (Find out what newspapers/journals your best employees read or which radio station they listen to. Be aware that although you may be offered what initially seems like a cheap deal, if no one relevant is going to respond to the advert then it is not worth doing.)

2   **Renumeration**: Where possible, include salary and benefits information. It is a fact that a significant proportion of applicants won't even bother taking the first step if a salary is not included. It is assumed, whether correctly or incorrectly, that the salary is too low.

3   **Get the basics right**: Make sure that the job title, salary/benefits, and job location are prominent within the advertisement, rather than hidden somewhere within the body of the text. Likewise, ensure that the contact details are obvious and give the candidate clear instructions as to the next step in the recruitment process.

4   **One to one**: Speak to an audience of one. Always assume you are talking directly to the ideal person for the job. Use phrases like 'You'll be a team player with…' rather than 'The ideal candidate will be…'. Use language that your target audience will be comfortable with; relate to them, ask them to qualify themselves in or out of the role, stimulate a desire and call to action.

5   **Benefits lead**: Always remember that you are trying to encourage someone to contact you regarding the vacancy. Rather than focusing on a list of demands that you require from the applicant, think about the benefits the job will bring to them – free parking if the job is based in the city centre, non-contributory pension schemes, flexible working hours – anything that will set you apart from your competitors.

6   **Size matters**: A large advertisement can dominate a page, will catch the eye first and can convey credibility and quality of an organization.

7   **Create interest**: Where possible, use colour. Colour, design, use of shapes, as well as white space, draws the eye to an advertisement.

8   **Use of space**: Do not try and pack too much information into a small space thinking that this will get you more for your money – it has the opposite effect. Your advertisement will look crammed and applicants may decide not to read it. Book a bigger space or reduce the amount of information until it fits the space appropriately. The look of the advertisement may be the first impression a potential employee has of your organization.

INTERNET ADVERTISING

Internet advertising is significantly less expensive than press advertising hence the rapid growth in its usage. Whilst the above list may be relevant to Internet advertising there are some other key points to highlight:

1   **Clever use of space**: You are always restricted in terms of space. Accordingly, job title, location and salary are a must and should be obvious. Remember, unlike press advertisements there are likely to be at least 20 similar opportunities competing for attention.

2   **Key words**: Focus your content on key words (keeping in mind the applicants' point of view) and include as many 'searchable' words in your description as you can.

3 **Bullet points**: Although bullet points are not always encouraged in press advertising, they can work well in Internet adverts where space is limited.
4 **Response mechanism**: Make sure potential applicants can contact you via an email address.

PRIVATE AGENCIES/SELECTION CONSULTANTS

Agencies typically operate by building up a database of suitable candidates who are either qualified or interested in certain types of work. They should have pre-screened these individuals prior to introducing them to organizations. The agency will be paid by employers who recruit candidates introduced by the agency, mainly on the basis of a percentage of starting salary.

Selection consultants work primarily by accepting a brief to fill a specific vacancy (or vacancies) for an employer. They will carry out the initial stages of the selection process on behalf of the employer, that is: preparing and placing the advertising; response management; conducting initial interviews and/or assessments; providing a shortlist of suitable applicants.

The consultant will normally be paid on a percentage-of-salary basis; however, in volume recruitment the supplier may charge a fixed management fee that is agreed at the start of the process and is dependent on volumes and resources needed to manage the project.

Checklist for selecting your recruitment supplier

- How extensive is their experience of recruiting within call and contact centres?
- Is contact centre work an area in which they specialize?
- Capability – for example, case studies and client references
- Financial stability – percentage of turnover attributable to contact centre recruitment
- Scope and range of products, for example, temporary, permanent, contract, consultancy, and so on
- Processes, for example, response handling capability (volume), recruitment and selection processes, account management techniques, referencing procedures
- Quality accreditation
- Synergy of cultures
- Creativity
- How important your business is to them
- Market perception – ask other contact centres
- What relationships they have with external partners, for example, the Employment Service
- Value added services offered, for example, salary surveys, labour market analysis
- Ability to produce management information
- How they could work with you to become a true partner
- How much will it cost
- Trust
- Would you be comfortable with them representing your company.

For high-volume projects, you should also take the following into account:

- Company size and level of resources available
- Experience of the account management team.

Other methods of recruitment to consider:

- Recruitment fairs
- Direct marketing campaigns (for multilingual candidates try special interest groups)
- Colleges and universities (students tend to be good for late and weekend shifts, although bear in mind exam time and holiday periods)
- Radio advertising
- Billboard advertising (target travel-to-work routes)
- Residential leaflet drops
- School leaver initiatives.

STAGE FOUR: MEET THE RESPONSE

Identify the most appropriate interviewing and assessment techniques for each role.
   Successful techniques include:

- Initial screening telephone interviews
- Follow-up, in-depth telephone interviews
- Face-to-face interviews
- Assessment centres to measure suitability
- Open days
- CVs.

An initial screening interview enables candidates to be assessed, establishing the appropriateness for progression to the next stage. This, followed by an in-depth telephone interview for each role lasting on average 45 minutes, allows a cost-effective, quick and manageable method of assessing each individual's skills and experience without having to schedule one-to-one interviews.
   As these interviews can take a considerable amount of time, many candidates will have to be contacted at home in the evenings, so you might need to plan for some shift work among your interviewing staff.
   Plan the initial call-handling capabilities:

- Allow sufficient telephone lines so that candidates will be able to get through at any time.
- Train the recruitment staff to be able to manage the calls.
- Create call scripts and training for the recruitment staff who will take the calls to ensure consistency and accuracy. The call scripts are a crucial part of the process and each job role should have a tailored call script designed specifically to determine the candidates' suitability for that particular role.
- Ensure that all details will be captured, including the source code (where the candidate heard about the position).
- Ensure the database will allow you to recall all the information you will require during and after the campaign.
- Anticipate every question that an applicant will ask and build this into the training. In case an applicant asks a question that cannot be answered by the recruitment team, ensure that you have an escalation process in place so that all questions can be answered. Applicants will ask about the company, the role, the working environment, salaries and on target earning (OTE), holidays and every aspect of the position.
- Remember to include your brand values in the scripts and the training so that every agent and communication is reflecting the brand.

- Test your recruitment agents by making some calls to ensure that the whole process is running smoothly.

STAGE FIVE: FACE-TO-FACE WITH CANDIDATES

Organize assessment centres or open days. The major benefit of running assessment centres is that you can give each candidate a series of tests that will determine, in an objective and impartial way, their suitability for the role. They allow you to assess each individual in a way that will test the actual skills that they will use in their role.

The major benefit of running an open day is that you are able to attract a large number of candidates on the same day. These are often recommended if you are looking to recruit large numbers of staff in a short space of time.

ASSESSMENT CENTRES

Assessment centres are more commonly used for both high-volume recruitment and management development assessment. They can last from a few hours or up to two to three days dependent on the type and level of skills and competencies being assessed.

Tips for successful assessments:

- Photograph each candidate as they come to the assessment centre as it makes everyone easier to recall later.
- Plan your resources not only in terms of staffing, but also computer availability, separate testing rooms, amenities and logistics.
- Remember also to reflect the brand at all times in the design and layout of the assessment Ccentre.

Contact centre assessments typically invite eight to twelve applicants to attend; however, for more senior roles there could be only four to six. More significant is the number of assessors available to observe the participants and score the exercises they are involved in.

A typical assessment may include some or all of the following:

- Presentation
- Group exercise
- Aptitude testing
- Personality profiling
- Teamwork exercise
- Key skills testing.

The content will be derived from the competencies required for the role.

A competency-based interview is used in assessment centres, which is a structured interview where questions are related to specific competencies and interviewees give examples of situations where they have demonstrated the required behaviours. In addition, this technique enables the interviewer to build up a picture of the interviewees' strengths and weaknesses on each competency and can be applied subsequently in their development programme.

Different tools can be used to 'measure' different competencies, See Figure 9.2 for the competencies required from a contact centre agent.

Key result area	Competence	Definition level	Telephone interview	Method	Quiz/skill assessment	Teamwork exercise	Face-to-face interview
Customer service	Customer focus	Creates and re-inforces a culture of customer service for all types of customers	X		X		X
Planning and reviewing	Results focus	Ensures that their own performance and activities achieve objectives	X	X	X	X	X
Business solutions	Information gathering	Requests and compiles information from established sources			X	X	X
Business solutions	Problem solving	Solves problems requiring simple solutions within well-defined procedures		X	X	X	X
Team effectiveness	Team working	Co-operates with other individuals from own and other teams	X			X	X
Personal drive	Adapting to change	Shows high levels of adaptability and ability to respond to change	X				X
Personal drive	Handling pressure	Remains calm and effective when under pressure	X		X	X	X

Figure 9.2   Contact centre agent competency-based matrix © Search Consultancy Ltd

PERFORMANCE AND PERSONALITY TESTS

Some recruitment tests have a long and respectable history; others, however, have been devised with insufficient development or defective thinking. Whatever the pedigree of the test, it is unlikely to aid selection unless you know how the test performance relates to performance in the positions to be filled.

OPEN DAYS

Tips for a successful Open Day:

- Establish exactly what you would like the candidates to do, for example, if they are to go through an interview, do you have the resources required, and if they are to be assessed, do you have enough space, resources, computer availability?
- Ensure that you have enough space within your own building to manage the Open Day.
- Which areas of your business would you like the candidates to see and what security risks does this involve?
- Manage existing staff perceptions of the day well in advance.
- Ensure that all data on each candidate are captured and stored.

STAGE SIX: INTERVIEWS

Ensure that you have planned all your interviews and have sufficient personnel to manage the process. Following the interview, candidates will expect to hear very shortly whether they are to be offered a position, so you should prepare beforehand to let all the applicants know the result of the selection process, whether successful or not, as soon as possible.

Ensure that your interviews follow a set format to retain impartiality and consistency, particularly if you are using more than one interviewer for a range of candidates.

The interview is commonly defined as a 'conversation with a purpose'. A good interviewer will control and manage the progress of the conversation using effective questioning. The main benefits of effective questioning are:

- Common understanding
- Effective two-way communication
- Relevant information obtained quickly
- Interviewer controls the flow of the information
- Interview objectives are achieved
- Professional impression created

Types of question:

Open questions cannot be answered with Yes/No or one-word answers. These questions encourage applicants to 'open up' and talk freely. Open questions begin with: Who/where/what/when/how/which/explain or tell me. 'Why?' can be viewed as aggressive or confrontational. Examples of open questions:

How did you achieve your target?
What were your duties and responsibilities?

Closed questions require only a Yes/No answer or a short factual answer. Examples of closed questions:

> Do you use a PC?
> Have you used Microsoft Word previously?
> What is your current salary?

Probing questions investigate further and uncover information which might otherwise have remained undiscovered. Probing questions usually follow an open question and allow you to focus in more detail on a specific issue. Examples of probing questions:

> What exactly do you mean by...?
> And then what happened?
> What exactly did that involve?

Recap questions demonstrate that you have established a full understanding of what has been said, by repeating the sense of the question briefly in your own words. Examples of recap questions:

> Just to recap on that, what you have just said to me is...?
> So as I understand it then, what you have just told me is...?

Leading questions should be avoided as they imply the desired answer by the question asked, for example, 'So you are good at dealing with people?' Multiple questions, a series of questions in one sentence, should also be avoided as they will confuse applicants.

Two of the most important questions often not asked are: 'What is the main reason for leaving your present job?' and 'What are your salary expectations?' Consequently, potential employers will not match job offers with expectations, which, in turn, is given as some of the main reasons why applicants turn down job offers.

COMPETENCY-BASED INTERVIEWS

There are many definitions of 'competency', one of the most simplistic being:

> Competencies are the set of behaviour patterns that the incumbent needs to bring
> to a position in order to perform its tasks and functions with competence.
> Woodruffe 1999

The goals of the competency-based interview are:

1   To be able to predict or estimate what individuals will do in a given set of circumstances.
2   To ascertain what skills and attributes they will be able to bring to bear to complete the job or assignment effectively or how well they will fit into the organization.
3   To collect enough information to be able to predict how the applicant would fare in that environment and whether or not they could apply those skills effectively in the assignment under consideration.

STAGE SEVEN: LETTERS AND DOCUMENTATION

Ensure that the database is set up and the text of your letters is organized well in advance so that you can notify candidates as soon as possible of their success or failure.

Test your database and system. On no account can the wrong letter go out to applicants at any stage.

Ensure that you have letter text for:

- rejection at first stage
- an invitation to attend an assessment centre
- an invitation to attend an interview
- rejection at a later stage
- offering a position.

Ensure you have contracts of employment and are able to take up individuals' references if required.

STAGE EIGHT: FOLLOWING UP

FEEDBACK

Allowing each individual to receive personalized feedback on their performance can be a positive experience for candidates. The provision of a dedicated telephone number supported by trained staff equipped to deliver feedback is essential. Make sure the applicants are aware of this feedback mechanism at the beginning of the process.

REPORTING

Prepare full reporting on the entire process, including candidates' scores from the assessment centres or Open Days so that the company has full accountability for the project.

ANALYSIS

As a basic minimum, you should include the following:

- how many candidates replied to each medium
- how many from each medium 'passed' each stage
- what was the cost of employment from each medium
- what percentage qualified for each stage of the process

EVALUATION

Evaluate the cost, effectiveness and quality of each aspect of the programme:

- what was the cost of each reply from each medium
- what was the cost of handling each telephone call
- what was the cost of each individual attending an assessment centre or Open Day
- what was the overall cost of employing each individual?

SUMMARY

In summary, whether call and contact centre organizations employ specialist recruitment organizations or have the resources to do it themselves, selection processes must be designed with the job role in mind, and be compatible with organizational culture. As consumers become more sophisticated and the call and contact centre market matures expectations will increase and applicants will initially rank organizations based on the perceived benefits of your recruitment process.

RECOMMENDED READING

Iles, P. and G. Salaman (1993), 'Recruitment, Selection and Assessment'. In John Storey (ed.), *Human Resource Management: A Critical Text*. Routledge.

Mitial Research (2001), *UK 2001 Call & Contact Centre Study*.

Taylor, P. and P. Bain (1998), 'An Assembly Line in the Head: The Call Centre Labour Process', *Industrial Relations Journal*, 30(2): 101–17.

Woodruffe, Charles (1999), *Winning the Talent War: A Strategic Approach to Attracting, Developing and Retaining the Best People*. John Wiley and Sons Ltd.

10 Building a Training and Development Strategy

Sally Pollock, Head of Training, Calcom Group

With contributions from:
Sonia Keheyan Dodd, Training Consultant, Calcom Group
James Cowlin, Business Development Manager, London Qualifications

This chapter examines how to create a training and development strategy for contact centre teams, through the life cycle of an employee from induction onwards. Career development and qualifications are discussed towards the end of the chapter.

RAISING THE SKILL BAR

The skill bar is rapidly being raised for people within the contact centre industry, thus driving the need for effective training and development frameworks that enable people to be successful, keep them motivated and, above all, maximize their talents.

This chapter takes you through the main components of training and development within the contact centre and aims to provide you with a valuable framework, whether you are new to the training arena or just looking to enhance your existing environment.

As with customer life cycles, there are four key stages within the life cycle of a member of the contact centre team:

1 Recruit
2 Induct
3 Develop
4 Progress and retain

Training and development is a key contributor to finding, nurturing and keeping staff. Best practice in this arena can influence an organization's ability to acquire and retain the most talented people. There are a number of components that make up the framework for creating a training and development plan that supports and enables people as they move through each stage of the life cycle. This chapter will take you through each component of the framework and provide you with practical suggestions and examples to help you create an effective training and development plan in the contact centre environment.

We'll begin by looking at developing a competency framework (see Figure 10.1).

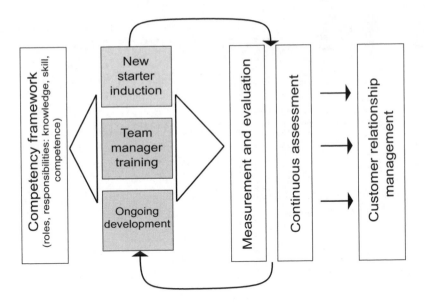

Figure 10.1   Framework for creating a training development plan © Calcom Group Ltd

CREATING THE SKILLS AND COMPETENCY FRAMEWORK

The first stage in any training plan is to gain a full understanding of the knowledge and skills required for each role in the contact centre. In well-structured environments, this should simply be a case of reviewing existing role profiles for each level or it may be that a competency framework is already in place. In the absence of either, sufficient information can usually be obtained from interviews with managers, side-by-side observation and reviewing procedural documents.

Contact centres come in many shapes and sizes, and providing a 'one-size-fits-all' framework is impossible. Job knowledge, process and systems will always be unique; however, there are many skills and competency requirements that are standard regardless of the nature of the centre. The important output is a clear framework from which to draw for recruitment, initial induction training and future development planning.

The framework in Figure 10.2 shows some examples of contact centre roles and the knowledge, skills and competencies that may apply. The job knowledge section can be broken down in more detail and will always be unique to each centre. It's also worth pointing out that I have yet to find two organizations that have the same definitions of what classifies as a skill, a competency or behaviour. What is important is that your framework captures the things you need people to be able to do and the way in which you want them to do it.

The next level of detail behind the framework is the definitions that support the headings. You may also consider building different levels of competency within a specific skill to differentiate between job role requirements. Table 10.1 shows how skills can be defined and divided into levels. You may then wish to assign different levels to different roles in your competency framework, depending on the requirement to deliver against that skill. Having worked with many frameworks, the advice would be to keep it as simple as possible. Too many roles with differing levels of skill and competence make for a major challenge when attempting to continuously assess, monitor and develop people within the performance management system.

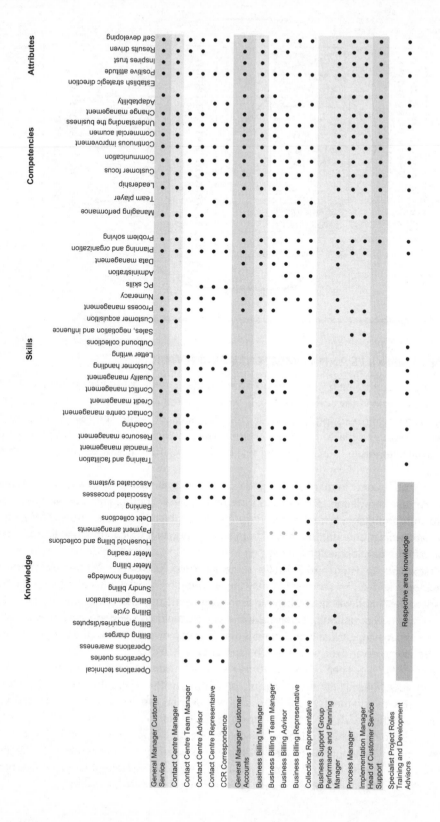

Figure 10.2   Competency framework © Calcom Group Ltd

Table 10.1   Customer focus framework

Customer focus		
Level 1	*Level 2*	*Level 3*
• Appreciates importance of customer service • Takes ownership of the customer query • Takes action to meet expectations • Is receptive to change	• Works to meet the needs of both internal and external customers • Anticipates and addresses customer service issues beyond scope of own role • Tailors service to suit customer needs • Identifies and recommends improvements to working practice	• Takes proactive action to deliver customer service • Goes the extra mile • Works to eliminate organizational barriers to customer service • Fosters an environment in which customers are seen as a priority

The framework can be used to build effective recruitment scenarios for stage one of the life cycle and provides the foundation from which to design your training programmes as people move to stage two. We'll begin by looking at the induction process for new agents joining the contact centre.

BUILDING A NEW STARTER INDUCTION PROGRAMME

In many contact centres, resourcing is a challenge, recruitment is a regular occurrence and high on the management agenda is the question 'how quickly can we get new recruits on the phone?' The answer is, of course, 'as quickly as you like'; however, the trade-off is clearly what you can expect from your time invested in training and the impact this has on both customer and employee satisfaction!

Induction training is not only the means to teach new people the skills to 'do the job', but also the opportunity to provide the context for their role, communicate the brand and inspire them to embrace the values of the organization in delivering service to the customers. A tall order for those in the training arena!

Induction is the opportunity to take your newest recruits on a journey from knowing nothing about your organization to becoming able and confident in their role. A good induction follows a logical structure built around a funnelling technique to ensure induction is a journey and not a quick trip through a few processes and systems before being hurled in front of customers.

THE FUNNELLING TECHNIQUE

The funnelling technique, as depicted in Figure 10.3, ensures that new employees joining the organization first learn about the organization through corporate induction, followed by an overview of the contact centre and where it fits within the 'bigger picture'. They can then start to learn about the products, processes and systems they need to eventually be able to do 'their job', not forgetting, of course, to wrap all of the learning with how to practically apply the new skills

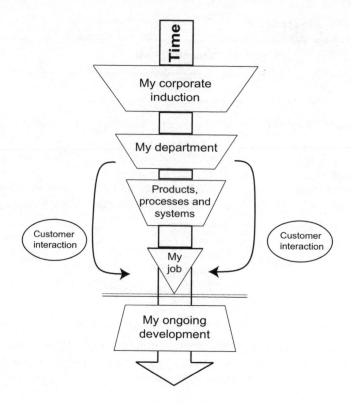

Figure 10.3   The funnelling technique © Calcom Group Ltd

within the context of the branded customer experience to every customer interaction.

Corporate induction will usually fall outside of the responsibility of the contact centre, however, it is critical that messages from the corporate induction are aligned with any materials in the new starter induction programme. New starter induction usually begins at the 'my department' stage and should immediately follow corporate induction where possible.

SO WHAT GOES IN THE INDUCTION?

What goes in the induction depends largely on what you have identified in the knowledge and skills section of the framework. It is highly likely that there will be an incredible amount of information to take in and therefore any opportunity to keep induction at a basic skill level should be taken. This is clearly dependent on the means to separate out simple transactions from the more complex in the live environment. This then provides a route for ongoing development and progressive up-skilling over a longer period of time, which will be discussed later in this chapter.

Following the funnelling technique, here are some examples of core modules to consider in the new starter induction:

New Starter Induction Modules

Contact centre overview

- Department structure
- Who does what – introductions
- Customer life cycle – interaction points

Customer interaction skills	• Product and services overview
	• Call handling and call control
	• Email and letter writing
	• Internal and external service orientation
	• Embracing the company brand
	• Complaints handling
Products and services	• Detailed products and services
Process and procedures	• What to do with every interaction
	• Integrated within interaction skills
Systems and technology	• Using the automatic call distribution (ACD) correctly
	• Knowledge management tools
Regulation and legislation	• Detailed compliance module
Sales skills	• Product promotion
	• Customer lifetime value/segments
	• Outbound/inbound sales
Other departments and teams	• End-to-end customer processes
	• Key hand-offs
	• Service level agreements
Performance management	• Targets
	• System and culture
	• Reward and recognition
	• Ongoing development
	• Career paths

It's not just what goes in the training that's important, but also how the training is structured.

Training on customer interaction skills prior to anything else creates the opportunity to *reinforce the learning* through every process and procedure section in the induction.

In general, people tend to recount information in the way they have learned it, so structuring your material around customer interactions, what to do, what to say and how to say it, rather than individual modules on product, process and systems, will make the transition from the training room to the live environment much easier. People are also better at retaining what they learn first, so putting the customer interaction skills up front is a good way to embed customer culture prior to any system and process work.

HOW LONG SHOULD THE INDUCTION BE?

How long is a piece of string? The induction should be as long as it takes to equip people with the knowledge, skills and competencies to deliver a branded customer experience that reflects the brand and values of the organization. In reality, the length of time will vary depending on the needs of the centre. The most common length of time is three to four weeks. Credibility lies in the ability to define in measurable terms the value added by each module of the induction and the impact on the business of reducing the length of time through elimination of specific areas.

Table 10.2 shows some example timescales for each module – it's easy to see how the days add up!

Table 10.2   Example timescales for each module

Module	Example number of days depending on complexity of environment and commitment to depth and practical application of learning		
	Complexity and commitment level 1	Complexity and commitment level 2	Complexity and commitment level 3
Contact centre overview	1	2	3
Customer interaction skills	1	2	5
Products and services	1	3	5
Process and procedures			
Systems and technology			
Regulation and legislation	0.5	1	2
Sales skills	1	2	3
Other departments and teams	0.5	1	2
Performance management	0.5	1	1.5
Practical application and assessment of skills	1	5	10
Total number of days	6.5	17	31.5

Producing a table like the example here is useful for planning and justifying the length of time required within your own centre. The training methods used will also have a major impact on the length of time it takes to induct a new starter.

DELIVERY METHODS

Methods will vary depending on the nature of the training. Classroom training is still by far the most popular form of delivery within contact centres, but it is not always suitable. For example, in smaller centres where recruitment may take place in very small numbers, having a one trainer to one new starter ratio is not cost-effective. In this scenario, side-by-side learning may be preferable and can be effective as long as specific learning objectives are identified and methods of evaluation are in place prior to direct customer contact. The variety of training methods used and their current and future usage is displayed in Figure 10.4.

Technology such as multimedia software and web-based training tools are readily available. However, their use is not yet widespread as many products have either limited flexibility, or require a high degree of maintenance to keep the information up to date, thus eating up valuable training resource time.

Training modules that are most suited to online learning are those where the content is fairly static and the learning is on hard skills, rather than softer behavioural competencies.

A list of the most common delivery methods used for contact centre training includes:

- Classroom sessions with trainer facilitation
- Side by side with structured learning objectives
- External suppliers
- Multimedia/Software/CD-ROM-based training
- Ad hoc coaching and training 1:1 with trainer or coach
- Open/distance learning
- Web-based learning.

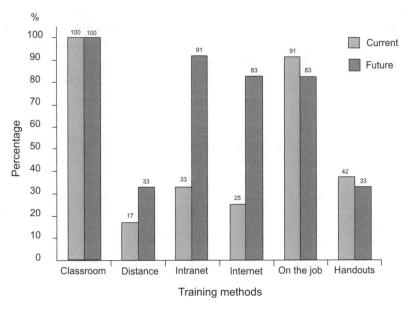

Figure 10.4   Delivery methods © Calcom Group Ltd

If we refer back to the components of the training and development plan, the next stage once the induction is built is to ensure measures are in place to both evaluate and continually assess employees as we move on to the develop stage of the life cycle.

MEASUREMENT AND EVALUATION

Measuring the success of any training intervention can often be difficult, but following the theory that everything comes back to a number, it's critical to identify the numbers that will demonstrate that the training has added value. For example, you wouldn't deliver sales training unless you believed it would impact sales ratios. What's the point in customer service training, unless it has a measurable impact on customer satisfaction? You'd expect multi-skilling to impact on first-time contact resolution and so it goes on.

The following table provides examples of where training can add measurable value across a balanced scorecard.

Financial

Call-to-order value
Customer order ratios
Customer lifetime value

Operations

Grade of service
Data quality
First time call resolution
Repeat calls
Productivity

Consumer

Customer satisfaction
Retention

Individual

Employee satisfaction
Sickness/absenteeism
Attrition

Measuring the success of your new starter induction programme is about more than just evaluating whether an agent is ready to 'go live' with customers. In many contact centres, the induction programme extends to a product knowledge quiz where the inductee is scored out of 20 and then handed a headset and left to get on with it!

The induction programme is the first opportunity to assess competence and provide the individual with a meaningful development plan for their transition into the live environment.

Aligning the training evaluation with the performance criteria provides:

- the team leader/manager with the immediate development needs of the individual
- the individual with an indication of how they measure up to the requirements in the live environment
- a set of criteria against which to target the training team and measure success.

Assessment of call quality can be gained through setting up role-play scenarios, which are then scored against the contact centre quality monitoring templates. The outcome of this assessment gives the green light for the agent to 'go live'. However, assessment of productivity needs to take place in a 'safe' environment where full support is provided.

TIME ON THE NURSERY SLOPES

The nursery slope can be considered the period of time following training where agents are practically applying their skills in a 'live' environment; however, full training support is provided and revision sessions are carried out in areas where individuals feel under-confident. This period usually lasts one to two weeks and can be used as a period of intense coaching to build confidence and improve performance against the agreed criteria.

At the end of this period, the official evaluation is complete and a formal handover to the line manager should take place where strengths and development opportunities are discussed and a development plan put in place for the first month.

Of course, evaluation is never a one-way street and the second area to evaluate is the overall effectiveness of the training from the perspective of the delegate. This can be carried out using an evaluation form and needs to be constructed in a way that gives you ample information from which to make improvements to the programme ready for your next influx of new starters!

Areas to consider when evaluating are as follows:

- Content
- Pace
- Training methods
- Trainer style
- Practical application
- Evaluation and assessment methods.

So, now you've built the new starter induction; however, there is another group of people that often gets left off the induction agenda: team leaders and managers.

BUILDING THE TEAM LEADER INDUCTION PROGRAMME

Team leader and manager induction training is an under-developed area, where much of the initial learning takes place 'on the job', followed up by scheduled events often provided by the corporate training function. While it can be argued that the responsibility for management training falls under corporate training to a greater degree than for agents, there is still a responsibility within the contact centre to ensure that new managers are equipped with the knowledge and skills to hit the ground running. This is particularly true of team managers, where the performance of their team has a direct and immediate impact on customer satisfaction. If you wouldn't put an agent on the phones without training them first, why wouldn't the same apply to your managers? For this reason I will focus on induction at team manager level; however, the same process can be applied for any new manager joining the contact centre.

SO WHAT GOES IN TEAM MANAGER INDUCTION?

As with new starter induction for agents, the team manager induction programme largely depends on what you have identified in the skills and competency framework. From a practical perspective, it makes sense to draw out from the framework any knowledge and skills that are absolutely essential for a team leader to function as a supervisor to the team from day one. Everything else can be tackled as ongoing development to be discussed later in this chapter.

Team Manager Induction Modules

Contact centre overview	• Department structure
	• Who does what – introductions
	• Customer life cycle – interaction points
	• Product and services overview
	• Role of the team manager
HR policies and procedures	• Appraisals
	• Absence/sickness
	• Disciplinary procedures
Customer interaction skills	• Call handling and call control
	• Email and letter writing
	• Internal and external service orientation
	• Embracing the company brand
	• Complaint handling
Products and services	• Overview of products and services
Process and procedures	• Quality monitoring
Systems and technology	• ACD/workforce management software
Regulation and legislation	• Monitoring for compliance
Sales skills	• Product promotion
	• Customer lifetime value/segments
	• Outbound/Inbound sales
Other departments and teams	• End to end customer processes
	• Key hand offs
	• Service level agreements
Performance management	• Targets

- System and culture
- Reward and recognition
- Ongoing development
- Career paths
- Managing performance
- MI tools and reports

Coaching
- Coaching for performance
- Skills and systems

Whilst the list looks almost identical to the new starter induction, you'll notice that the content emphasis is on developing the sufficient knowledge and skills to be able to coach their teams in delivering the required branded customer experience. The key to driving up the quality of interaction with customers lies in the ability of this group of people to reinforce the learning from the agent training programmes. The only way to do this is to train them too! I have been in many centres where customer service training is rolled out to all agents, but the team leaders and coaches are not provided with the skills and tools to bed-in the new learning and reinforce the skills. The impact is, of course, skills are not put in to practice, behaviours don't change and the training is soon forgotten all at great cost and no value to the business.

Time and investment in developing the team leader group pays off from both a performance and a cultural perspective.

DELIVERY METHODS

There is clearly a difference in the level of detail required in the product and process areas and it is therefore unnecessary to duplicate all elements of the new starter induction programme. What has worked well in some organizations is the development of a 'fast track' programme for team leaders and managers where the product knowledge, processes and systems elements of the programme can be completed as distance learning, with assessments at the end of each section. Again, there is opportunity to develop online tools for some of the more difficult skills development.

With your induction modules in place, the next step is to create the tools and structure to support and develop people as they move through to stage three of the employee life cycle.

ONGOING DEVELOPMENT

This section will focus on the ongoing development of contact centre agents and look at performance management development.

BUILDING THE ONGOING TRAINING PLAN

Ongoing development is a critical component within the employee life cycle and can mean the difference between people viewing the role of the contact centre agent role as a stepping-stone to a 'better job' or a structured career with opportunities to grow and learn over a long period of time.

Ongoing training and development can be structured in a variety of ways and is influenced by skill levels and agent group structures depending on the make-up of your centre. Figure 10.5 gives an example of how different types of skills development paths can be created.

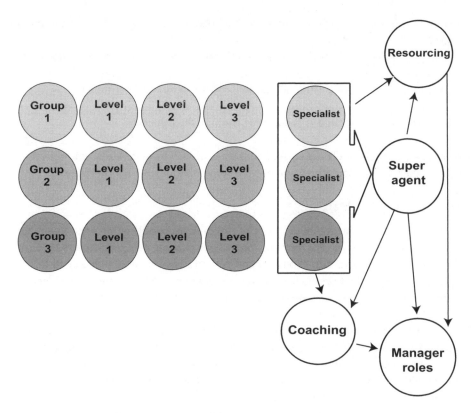

Figure 10.5   Example career paths © Calcom Group Ltd

Whether agents are grouped by interaction channel (calls, emails, letters), product (investment or personal banking products) or role type (payments team and sales team), a clear development path can be mapped over a defined period of time, creating pools of highly skilled agents and helping to keep people motivated. As shown in Figure 10.5, skills development can be used to up-skill agents within their current group, multi-skill agents in across several roles or begin the process of succession planning for future managers.

The rules of progression are entirely down to the individual contact centre: for example, it may not be necessary to be a super agent before one can become a coach, or to become a specialist before one can transfer to a role in resourcing. What is important is that the route maps to personal development, learning and salary progression are clearly defined.

As shown in Figure 10.5, an agent can become a specialist in their own group, a super agent by multi-skilling, and then develop into coaching or a role in resourcing before moving on to manager positions.

SUCCESS FACTORS FOR PROGRESSION

A successful ongoing development programme is dependent on the following:

- Structured modules that can be delivered through a means appropriate for the contact centre without a negative impact on valuable resources

- Structured measurement and evaluation to ensure people are accredited with the appropriate skill level
- Ongoing practical application of the new skills learned (new skills are quickly forgotten if they are not practically applied)
- A means to track skill levels within all roles across the centre so that training needs can be prioritized
- Reward and recognition linked to progression through the career paths.

In many centres, a visible display of accreditations has proven to be an excellent motivator and great if you need help with something and need to know who knows what pretty quickly!

CONTINUOUS ASSESSMENT

It can be said of contact centres that the most knowledgeable people in the department are the new recruits and it's probably true. Over time, procedures change, new products are brought out and people develop their own 'bad habits' for completing transactions. The degree to which this happens is highly dependent on the knowledge management and communication methods of the centre; however, continuous assessment is a great method of keeping knowledge up to date.

This can be something as simple as a series of questions on products and procedures completed on a quarterly basis to highlight knowledge gaps and requisite training needs. Web-based tools are ideal for continuous assessment as this is not an area that requires a human interface. In highly regulated areas, continuous assessment provides an excellent means of ensuring regulatory requirements are being met.

Continuous assessment of the quality of interaction with customers should be conducted through an ongoing quality monitoring and coaching regime.

The information provided from continuous assessment can be fed into the performance management system and used to evidence competencies under the job knowledge section.

LINK TO PERFORMANCE MANAGEMENT

It would be very difficult to talk about training and development without mentioning performance management, but at what point does performance management become the responsibility of the line manager and not the training team? The simple answer is, it's an ongoing partnership. A good performance management system facilitates the assessment of competencies in the areas identified in the competency framework and allows managers to identify gaps and build meaningful personal development plans for individuals.

To this end, assessment of performance should not just be against achievement of objectives, but also against criteria under the headings of job knowledge, skills and behavioural competencies. Through this thorough appraisal system, development needs can easily be identified and individuals provided with the appropriate training and coaching to support them towards excelling in their roles.

Some development needs can be satisfied by the use of coaching, observation and self-development tools, which is often the case for management development. Other development needs warrant structured training, thus the baton is passed back to the training team. The extent to which development needs are passed back as a training issue for resolution depends largely on the level of skills of the operational managers in managing learning and, in particular, their knowledge of different learning tools and methods.

With the training and development framework in place, we can now turn our attention to the group of people that the framework serves to support.

KEEPING YOUR CUSTOMERS SATISFIED

The success of any training and development plan can be measured entirely by the satisfaction of your customers. In this case, the 'customer' is the operational management team and the relationship between this group and the training team is crucial.

Feedback and measuring customer satisfaction is key. This can be done through a regular customer satisfaction survey that checks to what extent the training team has:

- delivered value to the operation
- been flexible and responsive in meeting operational needs
- embraced the brand
- inspired performance through innovative methods
- worked in partnership with the operational leaders.

Of course, the result of the satisfaction survey is as much about how well the trainer has managed perception as it is about delivering a fantastic service to the operation. In my experience, providing a monthly training report that details achievements and next month's activities is a great method of managing this perception. Detailing activities taking place in periods of non-delivery is a particularly good idea as there can often be a question mark over what trainers actually do if they're not delivering!

The following table provides some examples of information to capture within the training report.

Monthly delivery summary	Monthly activities summary	Next month planned delivery	Next month key activities	Summary trainer time
<ul><li>No. of courses</li><li>No. of delegates</li><li>Evaluation scores</li><li>Measurements of success actual</li></ul>	<ul><li>Research and design</li><li>Training needs analysis (TNA)</li><li>Other training activities</li></ul>	<ul><li>No. of courses</li><li>No. of delegates</li><li>Measures of success planned</li></ul>	<ul><li>Summary of planned activities</li></ul>	% time spent in:<ul><li>TNA</li><li>Research and design</li><li>Evaluation</li><li>Updating modules</li><li>Administration</li><li>Delivery</li><li>Coaching</li><li>Supporting the operation</li></ul>

It can be easy to forget that training is a service provider to the contact centre operation. This means creating a continual communication channel to ensure that operational plans are reflected in future training plans.

CAREER DEVELOPMENT THROUGH QUALIFICATIONS

CAREER DEVELOPMENT

> There is something rarer than ability. It is the ability to recognize ability.
>
> Elbert Hubbard

In an industry where people costs are high and we see that on average, a churn rate of over 20 per cent is acceptable, a structured career development path becomes critical.

Career development will offer the individual:

- a planned and structured future
- increased skills
- enhanced job satisfaction.

Benefits to the organization include:

- reduces attrition
- increases morale and motivation
- serves as an effective recruitment tool
- consistently increases performance and productivity.

Career development for individuals through qualifications further demonstrates not only recognition of their achievement but is also confirmation of their employer's commitment to them. The results can be seen by increased loyalty to the organization through to reduced levels of attrition and enhanced job satisfaction.

Qualification types within the contact centre industry are broad and range from knowledge-based tests through to competency-based qualifications, which require assessment of individuals while they are carrying out their normal work. Training provision is also very broad in nature, from specialist organizations offering single-topic training, for example customer service and sales, to more generalist training for a particular work role. Training delivery methods are also numerous and include classroom-based, distance and e-learning.

NATIONAL VOCATIONAL QUALIFICATIONS

National Vocational Qualifications (NVQs) are recognized as the benchmark for vocational competence. They are certificated by organizations called Awarding Bodies who have to consistently meet criteria defined by the Accrediting Body, who are responsible to the Government.

NVQs are formed by grouping units of competency together so that they reflect actual job roles. As units exist on their own it is possible that the same unit may be used in several qualifications. For example, the unit 'Contribute to developing and maintaining positive caller relationships' is not only applicable in the agent qualification but also in the team leader and supervisor qualifications as well.

Job roles at the same level across the call and contact centre sector are not only labelled differently by organizations, for example advisor, representative, agent and so on, but can also vary in the tasks to be undertaken. The development of the sector's occupational standards has therefore had to be broad enough to accommodate the majority of tasks undertaken across the sector, as well as reflecting the responsibilities of different job roles, for example advisor, team leader and manager. In recognition of the autonomy, leadership and management responsibilities within job roles, each qualification is graded between one and five. A level one qualification is applicable to a repetitive job, for example working on a production line, while level five is considered a professional qualification, for example chartered status. Figure 10.6 shows the National Qualifications framework, which outlines how NVQs relate to equivalent qualifications.

NVQ Level 5		Professional Development Diploma BTEC Advanced Professional Award/Certificate/Diploma	Postgraduate and Professional
NVQ Level 4	Higher National Certificate Diploma Professional Development Certificate BTEC Professional Award/Certificate/Diploma	First Degrees	Higher National Certificate Diploma Professional Development Certificate BTEC Professional Award/Certificate/Diploma
NVQ Level 3	Advanced GNVQ	National Certificate/Diploma Professional Development Award BTEC Advanced Award/Certificate/Diploma	GCE A Level
NVQ Level 2	Intermediate GNVQ	First Certificate/Diploma BTEC Intermediate Award/Certificate/Diploma	GCSE
NVQ Level 1	Foundation GNVQ	BTEC Foundation Award/Certificate/Diploma	National Curriculum
Entry Level	BTEC Introductory Award/Certificate/Diploma		

Figure 10.6   National Qualifications framework

Four nationally recognized vocational qualifications focusing on advisor (level 2); senior advisor and supervisor (level 3) and manager (level 4) form the suite of qualifications for people within the call and contact centre sector. Consisting of mandatory and optional units, each qualification addresses the competency of a range of similar job roles by the selection of those optional units that best reflect the job role. Thus an advisor who deals with inbound calls within a mail-order contact centre might choose units which address 'the needs of callers', 'authorize transactions' and 'use a computer system', while an agent in outbound sales might select 'address the needs of callers'; 'offer products over the phone' and 'use a computer system'.

There are 47 units of competence, which make up the suite of contact centre vocational qualifications from levels two to four. To be awarded a full qualification the candidate is required to achieve specific mandatory units and a defined number of option units, which best reflect their job role.

Table 10.3 identifies which units of competency are mandatory and which are an option within each qualification, as well as providing a comparison of unit content across qualifications.

Table 10.3   The relationship between the units of competence and the call handling qualification frameworks © London Qualifications

CH02 – Call Handling Operations at level 2
CH03 – Call Handling Operations at level 3
SCH3 – Supervising Call Handling at level 3
MCH4 – Managing Call Handling at level 4

M – Mandatory, O – Option, * either one is required

No.	Unit title	CHO2	CHO3	SCH3	MCH4
1	Contribute to developing and maintaining positive caller relationships	M	M	O	
2	Address the needs of callers	O			
3	Develop and maintain supportive relationships with telephone callers		O		
4	Solve problems for telephone callers		M	O	
5	Provide specialist assistance using telecommunications		O		
6	Make arrangements on behalf of callers	O			
7	Authorize transactions using telecommunications	O			
8	Generate sales leads for follow-up calls	O			
9	Offer products/services over the telephone	O	O		
10	Undertake telephone research	O			
11	Enter and retrieve information using a computer system	O			
12	Communicate information using email facilities	O			
13	Design and produce documents using word-processing software		O	O	
14	Design and produce spreadsheets		O	O	
15	Manage the operation of telecommunications facilities for call handling activities				O
16	Enhance telecommunications facilities				O
17	Process telephone calls	O			
18	Provide information and documentation to meet requirements	O			
19	Research and supply information		O		
20	Maintain performance and an effective working environment			M	
21	Contribute to the handling of incidents and resources	O	O		
22	Manage call handling activities to meet organizational requirements				M
23	Ensure the quality of call handling services				M
24	Develop and maintain team activity schedules			O	
25	Contribute to an effective and safe working environment	M			
26	Contribute to improving the quality of service provision	M			
27	Develop and maintain an effective and safe working environment		M		
28	Create effective working relationships			M	
29	Develop productive working relationships				O
30	Contribute to improvements to call handling activities		O	O	
31	Contribute to influencing change within the organization				O

32	Manage information for action			O	
33	Provide information to support decision-making				M
34	Facilitate meetings				O
35	Manage yourself		M	M	
36	Develop your own resources				M
37	Facilitate learning through demonstration and instruction		O		
38	Lead call handling team and individuals to meet their objectives			M	
39	Support the efficient use of resources			O	
40	Contribute to the selection of call handling personnel			O	
41	Manage the use of physical resources				O*
42	Manage the use of financial resources				O*
43	Select personnel for call handling activities				O
44	Manage the performance of teams and individuals in the call handling facility to promote good practice				M
45	Respond to poor performance in your team				O
46	Develop teams and individuals to enhance performance				O
47	Remotely provide, modify or cease telecommunications service	O			

Confirming ability

The method of confirming an individual's competence is through assessment, which is undertaken by an assessor. An assessor is an individual who has achieved not only their own qualification in assessing vocational competence but is also competent in the area they are assessing. While they may not be able to undertake the task they are assessing they must have sufficient experience to relate that task to the occupational standards. Assessment is a partnership between the assessor and the individual being assessed (the candidate) and if correctly planned should be a stress-free and non-bureaucratic process. Assessment takes into account:

- task or technical ability to carry out the task
- task management ability to manage all the other tasks
- contingency management ability to cope with non-routine situations
- environment management ability to perform the function within particular environments.

As nationally recognized vocational qualifications are independent of the learning route taken, an individual who has been in a job role for a number of years may already be performing to the national standard. Thus assessment will be supported by the gathering of existing evidence (Accreditation of Prior Achievement) providing that it is current, applicable, reliable and sufficient. An individual new to a job will need longer to prove competency.

Fundamentally, NVQs cannot replace skills or knowledge-based training but can act as a vehicle to support training and development within an organization while also recognizing the competencies of individuals.

FURTHER QUALIFICATIONS

Employment in contact centres is increasingly being seen as a career rather than a stop-gap to other employment. Further and Higher Education are increasing their subject base to enable individuals to develop through to degree level. Organizations that recognize the pivotal role of contact centre personnel in winning and retaining customers are investing in their greatest asset – staff development.

Apprenticeship

Apprenticeship frameworks that incorporate the development and recognition of life skills as well as the technical skills to undertake work have been developed and adopted by the sector. With Government funding available for individuals under the age of 25, these frameworks have defined outcomes so that both employers and trainees will know what their capabilities are at the end of the apprenticeship period.

Composite qualifications

Composite qualifications incorporating NVQ content, together with related modules, for example in team leadership, delivered either in a college environment or distance learning, provide individuals and employers with more focused development opportunities.

Foundation degrees

Foundation degrees provide a development path for individuals into Higher Education as they bridge NVQ level four competencies with the strategic aspects demanded by the sector.

General management

When choosing a Management Development programme there are a number of options available, ranging from generic management courses delivered through Business Schools and Management Development Centres through to more specific courses designed specifically for contact centres.

CCA professional

The Contact Centre Association is increasing the professionalism of the industry by providing a framework for training and development, which leads to individuals becoming recognized CCA Professionals. This programme ranges from approved, endorsed and accredited training programmes provided by in-house training departments or approved providers.

e-skills

The e-skills Career and Skills Framework identifies a comprehensive set of contact centre competencies linked to the role and career routes of the contact centre professional. It highlights the competencies required to deliver exceptional customer service, acquire and retain customers, and manage effective contact centre operations.

The framework offers practical support to contact centre employers in developing the multi-skilled, technology-literate contact centre professional of the future. The intention is to help employers build a talented and professional contact centre workforce able to add value to each customer interaction across multiple channels and products.

THE COST OF TRAINING

Costs will always vary considerably. In a recent Calcom Group 'Training Methodologies' study, a number of Training Directors were asked how much they would consider spending on training for advisors and managers. The results showed a trend towards higher spend for management than advisors, with totals in excess of £1000 per head in 80 per cent of answers regarding management, while advisor spending ranged from £100 to £2500 per head.

SUMMARY

The training and development framework is in place and the key to success now lies in your ability to keep focused in all areas. Just as there is an employee life cycle, so too is there a continuous training cycle of identify, design, deliver and evaluate. To summarize, here are some attributes of great contact centre training and development frameworks:

- Clear understanding of role requirements
- Induction that is a journey not a trip
- Measurement that ties back to organizational goals
- Team leader development that reinforces agent learning
- Ongoing development for motivation and progression
- A cycle of continuous assessment that links to the performance management system
- A partnership with the operational management team
- Trainers that inspire, motivate, encourage and support
- Above all, an environment that allows people to have fun and be themselves.

The contact centre industry has recently seen an increase in the number of specific qualifications available. When choosing a qualification, whether for advisors or management, think about what you are looking to achieve – is it recognition of something they already do or will it be based on assessing competency?

Many of the industry bodies are proactively working towards recognizing the industry as a profession. Qualifications will not only help to recruit high-calibre people into the industry, but as we have seen, can help retain our stars and increase morale and motivation.

11 *Performance Management*

Michael Esau, Organizational Effectiveness, Premier Farnell

Performance management is a key component of increasing results, motivating teams and building talented individuals. In the right hands it is a powerful management tool – in the wrong hands it becomes a 'command and control' monitoring system. This chapter discusses how to develop performance management as a highly motivational and powerful tool.

PEOPLE, PEOPLE, PEOPLE

Working with teams, whether as leader of a single team or manager of several, is an essential part of a manager's remit. Team working is rapidly becoming the preferred practice in many organizations, as traditional corporate hierarchies give way to flat, multi-skilled working methods. Teamwork is the foundation of all successful management. Managing teams well is a major and stimulating challenge to any manager, from novice to experienced hand.

All successful teams demonstrate the same fundamental features:

- Strong and effective leadership
- Shared vision and objectives
- Informed decisions
- Communicating freely
- Providing clear targets
- Right balance of people prepared to work together for the common good of the team.

THE MANAGER'S ROLE

These days, a team manager in a contact centre should no longer be the team's system expert or policy expert. To create a people-centred environment within the contact centre today, it is imperative that we have people managers who understand how to work with and develop the skills and capabilities of a wide range of individuals. Team working has become a preferred practice and this is largely due to the strong performance that can be delivered by a multifaceted team. The dynamics of a team are forever changing and the role of a manager is to facilitate this change. All leaders need strong personality traits to assert influence and function. Some of these are internal, such as vision and belief, but they must be complemented by the visibility required to produce the utmost from team members. A manager needs to be both facilitator and inspirer to provide their team with the support to grow. A true manager will facilitate, inspire and implement rather than control.

THE EMPLOYMENT RELATIONSHIP

The relationship between a manager and a member of staff can be described in many ways. Any relationship is formed within a context of rights, expectations and obligations on the part of each individual. There is now a more individual relationship between managers and their staff over such things as the nature of trust, openness, willingness to cooperate, and acceptance of different points of view. This has best been summed up by the phrase 'psychological contract'. It includes factors that affect feelings, motivation and loyalty, and is itself affected by the climate of the organization and the nature of the management style.

AGENTS' RIGHTS, EXPECTATIONS AND OBLIGATIONS

Contact centre agents should have certain basic rights. They have the right to know exactly what is expected of them; therefore the workplace should have clear goals and standards of performance. Agents have the right to know how they are performing, not just annually, but continuously. If each and every agent was provided with unbiased, objective feedback on a regular basis, the expectation of enhanced performance from both parties is more likely to be achieved.

The performance variations between experienced contact centre agents are usually huge and the cause is not simply a lack of motivation. Low productivity does not happen because some agents have bad attitudes but is strongly influenced by the agent's relative isolation in their day-to-day activities. Because an individual agent often doesn't have the opportunity to observe other agents doing the job, they are unable to learn better behaviours in that way and frequently acquire habits and work patterns that limit their own and the organization's performance.

Agents have the right to be helped to improve their ability to do their jobs. If a business presumes to measure them in terms of performance, it seems appropriate to suppose that the business also knows the skills and knowledge that are necessary to master the job. Once the business judges a particular individual to be deficient in one or more areas, it seems fair for the agents to turn to the business and ask for help in improving their abilities.

In the contact centre industry, employee costs account for 60 to 70 per cent of operational expenses. Leveraging this resource has the potential to yield substantial returns for organizations and therefore agent performance is mission-critical to the business goals of the contact centres.

PERFORMANCE MANAGEMENT ETHOS

The increased interest in systematic management in the last ten years has led to the development of performance management. There are a variety of reasons for this, such as the need for organizations to be more efficient in their performance in what is now a very competitive world. Another possible reason is that industries decided to put people at the heart of their business strategy and performance management was the vehicle to exploit this. Whatever the reasons, the change in approach has taken a long time to be accepted and understood, not only by organizations themselves, but also the managers that operate within these organizations. This is why, in my opinion, the change of focus for managers is still taking place and has not been a seamless transition. Some managers will tell you that being a system expert is easier than being a people manager. They are probably right, but who or what delivers the best results in the long term?

Plachy, *Performance Management: Getting Results from Your Performance Planning and Appraisal System* (1987) has one of the best explanations of the term, 'performance management'. This was the first book to be exclusively devoted to performance management. He described what had become the accepted approach to performance management as follows:

> Performance Management is communication: a manager and an employee arrive together at an understanding of what work is to be accomplished, how it will be accomplished, how work is progressing toward desired results, and finally, after effort is expended to accomplish the work, whether the performance has achieved the agreed upon plan. The process recycles when the manager and employee begin planning what work is to be accomplished for the next performance period. Performance management is an umbrella term that includes performance planning, performance review and performance appraisal.

Plachy encapsulated in one paragraph what managing people is all about, creating an understanding of what is to be achieved, how it will be achieved and then, upon completion, recycling for the next period. Within the contact centre industry, the timescales required for this cycle to work can vary dramatically, depending largely on the manager and members of staff concerned. We have all seen individuals achieve extraordinary results in a very short time period, and this is largely down to the vision, belief, know-how and focus that have been instilled in them through discussions with their manager. The challenge for managers is to provide that focus to all of their team members all year round. It requires a tremendous amount of energy and verve, but these qualities are essential in such a result and performance-driven environment.

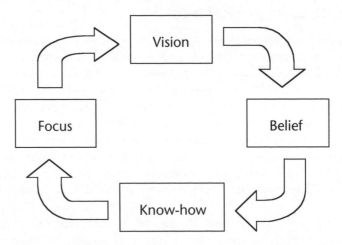

The contact centre has always been, and always will be, the high-performance and high-pressure environment where you have to continually meet both the customer and business demands. To deliver sustainable performance, there needs to be a strong focus on the employee and the development of a better balance between business pressure and performance.

DATA INTO POWER

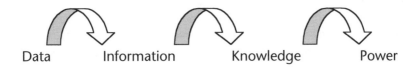

Data   Information   Knowledge   Power

The two key challenges for performance measurement and its management are that it should be a managed process and the output should be intuitive. In terms of a managed process, the data that is being produced must be measured. It is fundamental that you implement specific objective measures, which ensures that a fair approach is adopted and removes subjectivity. These measures should be timely, as there is no point in looking at last week's or last month's data if the opportunity to put things right has passed. Managers need to be managing the outputs and not the inputs.

Performance outputs should be intuitive and should be to remove information overload. The information needs to identify the root cause of performance issues to facilitate proactive decision-making and development actions.

A successful performance management programme is one where the goals are aligned at all levels of an organization. The critical element is to analyse and align the business-based performance measurements with the employee-based performance objectives. When you get it right, the performance of the individual will drive the performance of the team.

By breaking down the goals into key performance indicators (KPIs) and aligning them with individual objectives, you can then identify your high and low performers, but also the root causes behind the lows. To do this, you must understand the performance components at the ground level and measure them.

ENCOURAGING INDIVIDUALS TO IMPROVE THEIR OWN PERFORMANCE

The primary objective is to improve and maximize individual performance. It is important to support and empower individuals to be more responsible for improving their own performance. Most agents within the contact centre will be at the 'average performance' mark. By giving agents the responsibility of achieving their own specific objectives and empowering them for their own development, the average performance mark will move closer towards the high performance end of the scale.

By implementing a performance management culture, which is understandable, measurable and visible, agents and management will strive to improve on their results. This will apply to the vast majority of employees and it is those you must focus on.

Determining performance expectations is that stage at which employees are made aware of their individual objectives and the performance standards that are expected of them. This is a critical time in which to establish understanding about and commitment to wider business or departmental goals.

Supporting performance refers to the day-to-day informal interaction between managers and their team members. This support can come in the form of coaching or mentoring or merely an informal conversation to ensure that everything is going okay. It is vitally important that this stage of the process is continuous and ongoing in order for it to be effective. It is often this kind of interaction that is overlooked by managers, as they juggle the demands of the business with the development of their teams.

The third stage in the process is *review and appraisal*, which not only allows managers and staff time to review performance, but allows time to further build and develop their working relationship. The contact centre industry is so dynamic and performance-driven that it is crucial that managers carry out their reviews on a regular basis. The danger with any review process is that managers view it as purely a monthly or yearly exercise, where an individual's objectives should be reviewed against target.

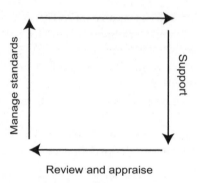

Figure 11.1   Torrington and Hall performance management cycle

The final stage in the process is the *management of standards*. This is when actions are taken to deal with issues that have been highlighted during performance reviews. The focus could be on how performance could be improved and sustained or possibly some training and development activity that the individual might have attended. It is very important that all parties are in agreement over any courses of action and that these are then supported through the cycle process again. Too often, we see managers agreeing actions with their team members and neither supporting or reviewing how they are progressing with their actions. They then ask themselves the question, 'Why hasn't the performance improved?' The focus should not be on 'what is to be done' but 'how will it be done'.

The Torrington and Hall model (see Figure 11.1) is a very simple process for managers to follow, whether you are a new or experienced manager. A model or process such as this can provide managers with the basis or framework to clarify performance and behaviour. The process can be tailored to all individuals, whether they are a top performer or an under performer, and is considered to be an excellent guide for managers. In my opinion, the model also lends itself to the concept of continuous improvement. The process is built around the ideals of constant reviewing and resetting of performance expectations. This shift in approach and almost change of mindset is still alien to a lot of managers and has involved a big shift in their way of working. Moving the focus from the normal 'what is to be done' to the 'how will it be done' is a very qualitative way of thinking. It is extremely motivational for all concerned and, once begun, builds up a momentum that very rarely slows down.

The contact centre is a very skilled environment, so the desire to improve the performance of people should always be evident. From experience, this is not always the case, so the challenge is to create a want in managers to continuously develop their people.

CONTINUOUS IMPROVEMENT

What is the difference between performance management and continuous improvement? The answer is, not a lot really. In principle they are the same thing, both striving to improve the performance of the organization and the people within it. The fundamental difference is the process-driven approach of performance management, as compared to the philosophical or mindset approach of continuous improvement.

The philosophy of continuous improvement is that contact centre managers and agents must constantly seek new ways of improving the quality of their process, performance and service to customers. Performance management is concerned with creating a culture in which organizational and individual learning and development are a continuous process. It provides means for the integration of learning and work so that everyone learns from the successes and challenges in their day-to-day activities. A display of the components concerned with performance management are shown in Figure 11.2.

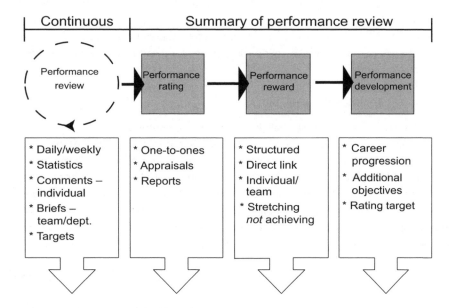

Figure 11.2   The components of performance management © Premier Farnell

The significance of continuous improvement is that it is a daily process in which everyone is involved. Continuous improvement changes the way people think about their work and it is the process of change that is important, as well as the results achieved. Its significance also rests on the fact that continuous improvement uses the contribution of all employees.

The introduction of continuous improvement is by means of communications, involvement, process development and training. The processes used in continuous improvement can include activities such as focus groups, problem-solving groups or suggestion schemes. Managers play a key role in all these activities. Managers have an important leadership role in gaining participation and commitment from their teams. This should result in support rather than issuing directives. Contact centre managers should look to act as enablers, consultants, facilitators and coaches to individual employees. It is important to note that these activities *must* be encouraged and facilitated by managers; they will not happen by themselves and perhaps there lies one of the reasons why this ethos does not exist in every contact centre today.

The conditions under which continuous improvement is most likely to work well exist when:

- Top management provides the leadership and direction and ensures that the values underpinning continuous improvement are made clear to all concerned and are acted upon.
- Middle management supports the philosophy of continuous improvement and is ready to support its introduction and to ensure that effort is sustained.
- There is trust between management and employees and vice versa.
- There is a high-involvement, high-commitment culture in the organization.

FEEDBACK

Providing feedback to agents based on fact, not subjective judgement, is a crucial part of any performance discussion and, in general, the management of a group of individuals. Constructive and positive feedback can go a long way towards cementing an employer–employee relationship. It is important that the information presented to people on their performance helps them to understand how well they have been doing and how effective their behaviour has been. Feedback acts as reinforcement, and positive feedback can be a powerful motivator because it is a recognition of achievement.

OPPORTUNITIES TO PROVIDE FEEDBACK

Technology has moved on so much that the methods of communicating with each other have increased dramatically. In contact centres today, applications such as email, company intranets, electronic bulletin boards and text messaging are all available for people to communicate with each other. Would it be fair to say, though, that these applications have made us rather lazy when it comes to communicating and in some ways has stifled the growth of personal relationships as the face-to-face interaction between people has declined? Prior to email, we were all accustomed to leaving our desks and walking to see someone at the other end of the building. Maybe we are more efficient with our time now, but when it comes to personal relationships, how effective are we?

The following are some of the common methods that are still used today to provide feedback:

1 **Annual performance appraisal**: This is a well-established way of providing feedback and guidance to staff. The appraisal, which is an activity central to the good management of staff, plays an important role in any performance management programme. It celebrates the culmination of an individual's performance for a whole year and is a great opportunity for both parties to evaluate events that have taken place. The appraisal process in some organizations is linked to pay, which can sometimes distract from some of the softer benefits of the process. The appraisal should also be used to display and support the culture of the organization.

2 **Monthly one-to-ones**: Someone once said to me that a lot can happen within one month in a contact centre. Contextually, I wasn't sure what the statement meant. Over time and through personal experience I have found that comment to be very true indeed. The contact centre

environment is quite unique. The dynamics are very different to anywhere else. The most common method of communication with the outside world is via the telephone and an interaction with a customer via this medium is very challenging and requires a great deal of skill and (often) patience. Depending on the type of contact centre you work in, a typical call centre agent could realistically receive in any one month up to and above one thousand phone calls. To ensure that an agent is performing against agreed expectations and they themselves are comfortable with their output, the one-to-one is a great opportunity to exchange views and ideas and identify any potential training needs. It ensures that nothing remains outstanding and all parties are comfortable with where they are. It is good practice to document and record the outcome of any one-to-ones as they can feed into the appraisal at the end of the year.

CONTACT COACHING

The outcomes of any call coaching session can be fed into the monthly one-to-one meeting. In most contact centres, the objectives set for an individual can be both qualitative and quantitative. This is more commonly known as the balance scorecard. It is considered good practice for agents to have a sample of their calls recorded each week or month. The objective would be to review the quality of each type of contact (telephone, email, text, web and so on) against the contact standards for the contact centre and identify any potential development areas. Contact coaching is a very important avenue of feedback, as contact is one of the key outputs of any agent. It is vitally important that managers are trained not only on 'how to coach', but also on the sills required – so that they reinforce best practice, not poor practice.

There are various methods of coaching and feedback; this area is discussed in Chapter 8. Some contact centres will expect the analysis and coaching of the call to be carried out by the team manager, whereas other contact centres will have a centralized quality team to analyse the calls and distribute the feedback to the respective manager, who can then coach the individuals concerned. There are arguments that can be raised for the merits of both methods in terms of their success, but the adoption of one of these methods depends largely on how the contact centre is structured.

Some contact centres provide feedback in two ways. Some follow a scoring system, whereby the agent will receive a score for how they dealt with the call. Other methods prefer to concentrate purely on constructive comments and tips. There has been much discussion about scoring and its lack of objectiveness. Anecdotal feedback from agents suggests that they don't always understand why they are an eight out of ten one week and a five the next. Some find the process very disheartening as the subjectivity and lack of consistency is prominent. Recent visits to other contact centres suggest that the majority seem to be shifting their focus away from scoring and concentrating purely on coaching tips.

OBJECTIVE SETTING

A primary function of managers within any performance management process is to define the challenge facing the organization. This means setting objectives. As Drucker (1994) wrote:

> Objectives are needed in every area where performance and results directly and vitally affect the management of the business. Objectives enable management to explain, predict, direct and control activities in ways in which a single idea like profit maximisation does not.

WHAT IS THE VALUE OF OBJECTIVES?

The ultimate value of objectives is that they focus individual performance on the areas that are critical to departmental and organizational success; in so doing, generating a clear understanding between the line manager and staff member as to what is expected to fulfil a role effectively. If objectives are set at an appropriate level, they should be motivational. A lack of clear work objectives is de-motivational.

The best means of clarity is through discussion and mutual checking of understanding. This needs to be accomplished through the one-to-one process. A performance record completed by a team manager and an agent can be used to capture the essence of what has been discussed and agreed. Objectives should as specific as possible. An individual should be left with no uncertainty as to what are the expected achievement of those objectives.

Objectives need to be agreed through a process of dialogue between the team manager and agent – not imposed without discussion. They should be realistic – given the nature of the job, the individual's experience and the business climate.

KEEP IT SIMPLE

Employees need simple and tangible information to increase motivation and satisfaction, highlighted by clear and purposeful activities linked to reward and recognition. To show agents the value of their efforts relative to the overall performance of the organization in order to generate motivation, organizations need to provide agents with a steady flow of information about their performance.

Contact centres need to employ a system that offers clear, constant, business-driven performance information, which aligns their activities and measurement to the organization's primary business objectives. It is important to remember, though, that the effective use of any process, no matter how sophisticated, requires a high degree of skill as well as a positive attitude and an emotional involvement. In contact centres it is imperative that a people-centred environment is established.

You will know you have succeeded when:

- Contact centre objectives are cascaded to all employees.
- Everyone has individual objectives, which are business focused and result in improved performance.
- Managers have the skills and knowledge needed for all elements of performance management and personal development.
- You have achieved increased employee involvement, satisfaction and the desire to be successful.
- Individuals take even more responsibility for their own performance and development.

CASE STUDY

At the beginning of 2001, Scottish Power conducted an employee opinion survey entitled 'The way you see it'. The primary objective was to understand how staff felt they were being managed and rewarded for their individual contributions. For the contact centre, two clear areas were highlighted. The survey showed that the staff wanted clearer objectives and regular feedback on their performance.

The response by Scottish Power was to set up a designated Performance and Development team, whose role was to introduce a consistent performance management framework across all of the call centres. This framework contained individual objectives for all, including intensive training and development for the managers so they would be able to carry out their role within the programme.

The approach that was taken was to get back to basics. The programme, entitled 'Keep It Simple', has adopted the simplest principles of effective performance management and applies the process laid out in the Torrington and Hall performance management cycle. The essence of 'Keep It Simple' very much lies in the name. The objectives and measures used within Scottish Power's four contact centres are both clear and easy to understand and are reviewed continuously. Each individual also has access to a web browser Performance Management solution, which provides them with the results of their performance from the previous day. They also receive continuous call coaching, which constitutes part of the monthly one-to-one process.

Keep It Simple objectives:

- Creating a shared understanding about what is to be achieved, how it is to be achieved and managing people so it will be achieved
- Focusing people on personal development to improve individual and team performance
- Improve the organization's performance by optimizing the contribution of individuals.

Keep It Simple process:

- **Planning** – agreeing team and individual objectives and performance measures which will enhance individual development
- **Managing** – monitoring progress, coaching and providing feedback
- **Reviewing** – reviewing performance and individual development against expectations in terms of end results and measures of success.

Keep It Simple is:

- a day-to-day process based on two-way communication
- an opportunity to develop people and therefore improve overall quality and performance.

THE OUTCOMES AND BENEFITS OF 'KEEP IT SIMPLE'

'Keep It Simple' outcomes and benefits for team members:

- Ensures team members know what is expected of them and ensures participation in setting objectives and responsibility for achieving results
- Provides regular and consistent feedback about how they are doing
- Provides an open forum for discussing performance, recognizing strengths and identifying development needs
- Provides the opportunity to build on strengths and address development needs
- Promotes effective performance in the current job and supports further career development
- Provides an opportunity to identify opportunities for progression and potential career paths.

'Keep It Simple' outcomes and benefits for team managers:

- Translates company objectives into meaningful objectives for individuals who will in turn contribute to the achievement of customer service goals

- Provides a framework for initiating discussion on performance and helps keep performance 'on track'.
- Promotes open and honest discussion of personal development needs and future opportunities
- Promotes a motivational climate leading to superior performance
- Develops better relationships with individuals and allows the leader to deal with performance issues in an open and constructive way.

'Keep It Simple' outcomes and benefits for the call centre:

- Supports an improved organizational climate, encouraging strong performance
- Increases customer satisfaction
- Increases success in achieving business objectives
- Direct impact on the bottom line.

The overall philosophy of Keep It Simple is to improve business performance through people.

RECOMMENDED READING

Armstrong, Michael (1999), *Managing Activities*, CIPD.
Armstrong, Michael and Angela Baron (2000), *Performance Management: The New Realities*, CIPD.
Drucker, Peter (1994), *Managing for Results*, Butterworth Heinemann.
Heller, Robert and Tim Hindle (1998), *Essential Manager's Manual*, Dorling Kindersley.
Placy, R.J. and S.J. Placy (1987), *Performance Management: Getting Results from Your Performance Planning and Appraisal System*, AMACOM.

12 *Working Conditions*

Donald MacDonald, Telecom Organizing Officer, Communication Workers Union (CWU)

This chapter examines the unions' perspective on providing good working conditions, including the relationships between unions and organizations.

> We must indeed all hang together, or, most assuredly, we will all hang separately.
> Benjamin Franklin

BACKGROUND

For many people, call and customer contact centres are distinctly unglamorous places. Much of the work is routine, repetitive, and closely monitored. It has prompted trades unions and the media to characterize them as 'dark satanic mills of the 21st century'. While this view does not properly reflect the wide range of experience within the sector, it does raise issues that need to be addressed.

This chapter considers some of the issues for staff and looks at ways of improving conditions. In particular, the related issues of stress, management style and people issues will be examined with observations made from a trades union perspective that reflects the many comments made on a daily basis by union members in call centre environments. Finally, there will be some suggestions as to how best practice in career development may contribute to a dynamic approach to technological change in the UK.

RELATIONSHIPS BETWEEN UNIONS AND COMPANIES HAVE OFTEN BEEN UNEASY

The development of inclusive and supportive management practice is critical for commercial success and the maintenance of employment in the sector. This has not always been evident, and industry bodies and leading employers are quite correctly taking on the setting of standards and benchmarks that will freeze out the rogue companies.

While there are many extremely well-managed call centres where management have positive staff relationships and welcome trade union involvement, the relationships between trades unions and companies operating customer contact and call centres have often been uneasy.

In truth, most trades unions are not unfairly highlighting bad conditions, but rather are trying to tackle the worst workplace abuses as they arise, and, more strategically, to work with employers and industry associations to raise standards and to expose the second-rate and the downright appalling employers.

The Royal National Institute for the Deaf (RNID) estimates that 8.7 million people, one in seven of the UK population, suffer a range of difficulties from hearing loss to deafness. In an increasingly noisy world, the RNID is very conscious of the changing nature of work and believe people working in call centres are in a high-risk category. Today, acoustic shock is very much a 'white collar' issue, and temporary hearing loss or tinnitus is not an unusual problem in call centre environments. There are widespread concerns that there will be far greater numbers of people with work-related hearing problems in the future.

Hearing problems, eye strain, repetitive strain injury (RSI), sore throats, stiff necks, backache, and exacerbated sinusitis conditions are common enough in any call centre, but should not be regarded as an inevitable by-product of working in that environment. All are preventable provided that the will of management is there – and staff have a voice in the workplace that articulates their problems and perceptions, and ensures that action is taken.

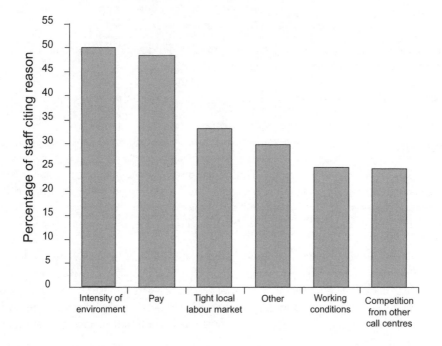

Figure 12.1 Reasons cited for staff leaving employment © CWU

Figure 12.1 shows the key reasons why people leave call-centre employment. While it is relatively straightforward to remedy some problems with improved workstations, seating, lighting and ventilation, other issues are not so easily addressed. For employees, particularly those performing basic job functions, the problems are numerous and varied, but can be summarized as:

- work intensity and management style
- stress
- training and career development
- pay and conditions.

The final point above is an extensive subject that is beyond the scope of this book.

WORK INTENSITY AND MANAGEMENT STYLE

The traumatic process of de-industrialization in the 1980s was described as 'post-Fordism', but the call-centre phenomenon has been dubbed the 'new Taylorism', where factory-style methods of manufacture and staff management were being applied to information handling. Despite the technology's capability to disperse work, call-centre staff are often concentrated into very large units with unprecedented levels of individual monitoring.

Traditional office-based work functions in areas such as sales, order handling, billing and customer service have been irrevocably changed by the impact of automatic call distribution technology. Associated with the technology was the introduction of standard salutations and scripts. The intensification of labour made for great efficiencies, but at a price – employees felt that their role had been de-personalized ('de-humanized' is a word often heard in this context) and that they had become ciphers, mere extensions to the technology.

One of the challenges of realistic job design is to ensure that people know what is expected of them. The CCA (Contact Centre Association) Standard (A Framework for Best Practice), as described in Chapter 24, stresses this:

- Employees at all levels are given mandatory training and development to support them in their role so as to enable achievement of their own and the organization's objectives.
- Individual employees are aware of their personal and/or team objectives and organizational goals, together with the means by which they are monitored.

MANAGEMENT ROLE

However, the CCA Standard must be backed up by clear management structures as well as professional training for supervisors in management and 'people' skills. Without these, poor job design and crude call-handling monitoring can create additional tensions in the work environment leading to the development of a ruthlessly competitive culture where unprofessional supervisors increase the pressure on the agents. This raises the staff's stress levels and contributes to a downward cycle of low performance, poor customer satisfaction, and increased agent attrition rates. Call centre and team targets therefore need to be openly shared with agents in a supportive and sympathetic management environment. Conversely, staff need to have the facility to input their experiences and views.

MANAGEMENT BEHAVIOUR

Management behaviour and style must also be addressed. One of the startling effects of call-centre work intensification (and poor training) has been the use of harassment and bullying as a managerial or supervisory tool. This unwelcome development is not confined to the call-centre sector, but many of the sector's characteristics may lend themselves to such abuses in the absence of conscious management adherence to best practice. As with company policies on equality and diversity, there have to be clear processes in place that are understood and followed by management and staff. Trades unions can make a valuable contribution in assisting employers by involving staff in developing policies and processes that can identify and deal with problems.

TACKLING STRESS: LISTENING TO STAFF

One of the many frustrations experienced by contact centre staff is the failure of supervisors and management to act upon simple suggestions that could easily reduce stress levels. For example, staff regularly complain about losing pay because of log-on difficulties (many staff spend up to ten minutes going through slow log-on processes), and being expected to attend team briefings and to deal with 'pick-ups' (such as reading company notices and familiarizing themselves with new scripts) in their own time. These are not seen as problems for managers or senior staff on unconditioned hours. But it is grossly insensitive to expect lower-waged staff, who may have family responsibilities and tight life-balance commitments, to work unpaid.

In the competitive environment there has also been a tendency to ignore staff requests for redesigning jobs. This is particularly the case in non-union work environments, where requests are usually made on an individual basis (rather than a collective one) and can be interpreted by managers, and sometimes colleagues, as a sign of personal weakness. For a largely female employment sector, there has been too much of the macho 'it was good enough for me' attitude from supervisors, many of whom had previously worked on the same duties with the same problems. For example, headset sharing at hot-desks may seem an efficient way to run a centre, but can create new problems and increase long-term costs because of the health risks involved. To expect agents to share headsets is not only demeaning to their self-esteem, but potentially exacerbates sick absence rates through ill-health, caused by the transmission of diseases, or acoustic shock from unreported or unchanged faulty headsets.

Although day-to-day problems are frustrating, the greatest challenges to reducing stress involve getting to grips with the real nature of contact centre work and the fundamentals of job design.

WORK-RELATED STRESS

Much remains to be done in the field of work-related stress, particularly in developing understandings that are gender-sensitive and are more related to *new economy* activities.

This is possibly the greatest challenge to the call centre sector. Despite the good work already undertaken by the CCA, HSE (Health and Safety Executive) and other industry and government bodies, it remains to be seen whether the competitive pressures (particularly acute in outsourced activities) can leave sufficient room for the creation of a fully humane and supportive environment that is conducive to positive workplace relationships.

Unions can assist firms in making this possible by providing professional support to staff and their workplace representatives in building clear representative and communication channels within call centres. Without those channels, companies will never fully understand the collective issues and the perceptions of their staff.

Good managers will listen to each individual, but will also encourage a collective approach as that is often the only way in which staff can articulate shared views and experiences. Unfortunately, neither is universal practice and, in the worst cases, people who speak up are classed as troublemakers. Contact centre managers that operate an authoritarian command structure will probably find themselves in some difficulty, as staff become aware of the European directive on information and consultation rights.

While some managers may feel challenged by the collective views of staff, it is still better that they are articulated and addressed. After all, for contact centre staff, the perception *is* the reality. The ability to respond positively is the mark of good management.

PREPARING FOR THE FUTURE

Despite the rapid expansion of contact centre activity, there is also vulnerability that has to be faced by government, employers, staff and trade unions:

- staff 'burnout' issues (addressed, in part, above)
- sensitivity to shifts in global economic activity
- greater capability of other transaction technologies, for example voice recognition software for simple transactions, Internet, e-enablement, third generation mobile technology
- low telecommunications costs that allow the transfer of work functions to lower wage economies.

Preparing for the future is a responsibility that needs to be shared by employers, employees, government and unions – all have a stake in ensuring the long-term viability of the sector, and the employment and employability of the people who work within it. Central to that is a coherent training and career development plan that has a broader horizon than simply developing personal development plans, welcome as they are.

What is needed is a sectoral approach that can not only accommodate personal career enhancement, but one where individuals and firms are future-proofed as far as possible.

ROLE OF TRAINING

Many of the sector's early (and present-day) problems arose through lack of training. Contact centre training was wildly inconsistent, and supervisory training in management skills was unknown in many companies. Firms with high attrition rates were therefore spending almost their entire training budgets on the most basic skills, very often training staff who would promptly job-hop to a contact centre with better pay rates. Even in the better centres, it has been the norm only to train up to the minimum level required by the job functions.

Now, faced with competing customer service and order-processing technologies, and the growing reality of contact centre work being diverted to lower-paid parts of the world, the sector and the government really need to take a fresh look at the whole approach to training. If the objective is future-proofing and maintaining a competitive edge, it is questionable whether the UK sector will be able to prosper from existing technologies and basic job skills.

While up-skilled staff may later choose to take advantage of enhanced career prospects in other companies, they will retain affection, and be an ambassador, for the firm that made it possible. And who knows? They may return with a much more responsible role in the future.

GETTING IT RIGHT

Getting it right therefore requires a shared understanding of the management objectives and the needs of staff. Positive approaches to training, qualifications, career development, employee relations, health and safety, information sharing and respect for the needs of staff tend to be the hallmarks of the organizations that will weather the challenges of technological change and global competitiveness. Conversely, contact centres that have a sloppy approach in one discipline have a good chance of failing other tests of best practice.

For key call centre unions, it is critically important to play a *strategic* role with government, employers and industry associations, rather than simply being reactive to either management initiatives or failures. There has to be a buy-in and a trades union recognition of the key role that call centre activity plays in the new economy, where transactions and customer decision-making takes place in 'real time'.

For all the inherent remote and impersonal qualities, customer contact handling is likely to become an even greater driver in the world's economy and commerce. Change is the only constant factor in the customer contact equation.

13 *Retaining Staff*

Greg Wilkie, Head of Customer Contact, Philatelic Bureau, Royal Mail

Staff churn rates have long been the topic of debate for many contact centre organizations. Fundamentally, there needs to be a complete shift in management approach towards staff in order to retain people in the longer term. This chapter provides excellent insights into how to achieve lower staff churn rates and increased loyalty.

BACKGROUND

Despite the many significant advances in contact centre technology, for most companies and applications, the work remains as labour-intensive as ever. The consequence is that contact centre service providers' biggest area of investment is its people. Why, then, is it that many of these companies do not have a clear and focused approach to recruiting the right people in the first place, or subsequently protect that investment by ensuring that their people stay with the organization long enough to make a positive contribution to the company's success? Customer loyalty measurement and schemes are widespread and companies think little of investing large sums in such areas. Staff loyalty, however, has not generally attracted the same level of attention.

> **Staff loyalty = Customer loyalty**

Staff turnover in the service sector is generally recognized to be increasing, leading to an increasing importance placed upon staff retention. This is certainly the case in the contact centre industry where annual turnover rates as high as 20 to 30 per cent are not uncommon. Additionally, the relatively high use of agency, seasonal or temporary workers in contact centres could be masking turnover rates of even higher levels. Replacing experienced contact centre workers at a time when the industry is experiencing relatively high growth and customer service is perhaps becoming the key driver of customer loyalty is also getting harder. In areas with a high concentration of contact centres, employers experience a form of musical chairs as staff hop from one centre to another, looking for better salaries, conditions and career opportunities and often returning to the original employer after a time.

You might assume, then, that with that sort of cyclical movement of staff, surely no employer is losing out, as each will benefit by the training investments of its competitors? Not so. Apart from fairly clear differences in the quality and amount of training offered by each employer, the cost and the effect on the customer experience are two key reasons why this phenomenon needs to be addressed.

STAFF ATTRITION

The estimates of industry analysts vary widely but it is probably safe to say that the cost of staff turnover in the contact centre industry is in excess of £1 billion per year in the UK. That is without attempting to quantify lost business from customers whose poor experience at the hands of an inexperienced customer service advisor causes them either not to purchase or to move their account. It could be argued, of course, that it is simply inadequate training that results in poor customer experience. While that is certainly one factor, when employers are effectively replenishing upwards of 20 per cent of their workforce each year, it is inevitable that there will be some impact of advisor experience on customer experience.

The learning curve for an advisor to reach the required standard of contact handling and product knowledge can stretch to several months. This varies according to the complexity of the product offering. The challenge is measuring this learning curve and the effectiveness of individual advisors. In some types of work it is easy to produce some measurement, for example, sales achieved. In others, however, there is often little available to managers other than productivity measures. Qualitative measures, such as customer satisfaction, are often difficult to track in a meaningful way at advisor level. Mystery-caller approaches can help but become expensive if results at advisor level are required. Of course, the role of team leader as coach will be a valuable source of measurement; however, unless there are clear standards of expected performance, which have been communicated and understood by both the team leader and the advisor, even coaching has its limitations in this respect.

HIGH STAFF TURNOVER IS A DRAIN

If it is accepted that the provision of high-quality customer service is a key driver for success in the contact centre industry, then it is difficult to argue against investing in learning and development of front-line staff in order to deliver that. Recruitment, training and development of a company's workforce represents a significant cost to the organization. As technology and knowledge management are increasingly able to provide the product-specific knowledge for any given application in the contact centre industry, so the skills of an advisor become more and more sophisticated. Investing in acquiring new people and providing skills training, only to see a competitor benefit as people leave after gaining these skills and a basic level of experience, is galling for any director. With recruitment and initial training costs representing approximately the equivalent of the annual salary of the person recruited, it is easy to see the drain on both management and financial resources that high staff turnover represents.

APPROACH TO STAFF RETENTION

Faced with this drain on investment and on customer loyalty, what should an employer do about it? The first thing is to recognize that this area of management is worthy of a focused strategy in exactly the same way as customer relationship management (CRM) strategies are becoming ubiquitous in business. There will be benefits for the staff as well as the company, but many of the elements of a retention strategy will mean that advisors will become more accountable for their own performance and there may also be a degree of self-management required. This can be seen as putting additional pressure on individuals, asking them to do more and to work harder. Careful positioning may be needed to persuade the workforce that the benefits outweigh the perceived impositions.

STAFF RETENTION MANAGEMENT

It is only through having good people that good customer service can be provided. The fact that staff retention management (SRM) is only now beginning to be addressed by many employers in this industry is probably a reflection of the roots of the industry. Once seen as a low-cost marketing channel, contact centres have grown to be an integral part of the marketing and customer service strategy of most businesses. Just as marketers have long talked about making their product, service or company the first choice of customers, likewise contact centre operators and HR managers need to make the contact centre a place where people choose to work and want to stay. The trick is how to make it happen.

ELEMENTS IN A STAFF RETENTION MANAGEMENT STRATEGY

There are a wide range of potential elements in a SRM strategy, and deciding which ones are appropriate will depend on the industry segment in which the employer is working, the maturity of their workforce, the prevailing culture within their company and the competitiveness of the local employment market. The elements described here are those that are most likely to have benefit regardless of the factors listed above. The key elements of a generic SRM strategy, therefore, are:

- Pay progression through achievement
- Professional qualification
- Planning a career
- Adopt a coaching approach
- Encourage self-development
- Communication
- Management style.

Pay progression through achievement

Pay is a tricky area when discussing staff retention. If an employer is paying a competitive salary and one which is attracting the required quality of candidates when recruiting, then pay is not likely to be a major factor in staff retention (except, that is, in areas where competition for contact centre advisors is high and people are leaving for small salary increases). In general, people do not leave the contact centre industry, just a particular employer, and the jobs they are leaving to go to are not offering significantly different salaries.

While not advocating that employers inflate salaries in order to retain staff, there are some things that can be done to manage staff retention using pay. One is to use regional pay rates where a company has multiple locations. This ensures that salaries are competitive for the local employment market but also give the employer some degree of flexibility when managing attrition across the company. Another is around pay progression. Traditional progression by means of annual increments rewards loyalty but doesn't necessarily reflect the effectiveness of the individual advisor. An alternative approach is to link progression to the achievement of certain standards or qualifications. This can help to tie staff to the employer for at least the duration of the qualifying period but often staff stay much longer.

Professional qualification

Career development strategies are one very successful way of reducing turnover, giving people the skills and marketability that make them feel valued. It is an irony that developing your people to make them more marketable to your competitors is actually likely to help keep them within your company.

Using professional qualifications, as already discussed in this book (Chapter 10), as a route to staff retention can be very effective, as mentioned earlier in this chapter. A professional qualification in customer service has the benefit of giving the individual advisor a greater sense of achievement and pride in what they do, improving customer service and staff retention for the employer, at the same time as driving up the professionalism of the industry as a whole.

Royal Mail experience
In my own experience, a generic qualification such as a National Vocational Qualification (NVQ) in Customer Service can be a fruitful route to reducing staff turnover. When Royal Mail (Customer Management) Limited introduced a scheme to encourage the uptake of NVQs and Institute of Customer Service (ICS) awards, one of the primary aims was to lock our advisors into a longer-term skills development programme and demonstrate our commitment to them as individuals. We also took the decision to link NVQ achievement to progression through the salary range. This meant that the company's commitment had to be as firm as that of the advisors, as their pay progression depended on our ability to register them for the awards as fast as they were demanding them.

The NVQ programme was not only introduced as a mechanism for pay progression. It also provided a platform for training and development activities, career paths and the competency framework against which job roles and development plans are assessed. The objective was to create a flexible and responsive climate that was ready to absorb the introduction and utilization of new technologies, new processes and, most importantly, stable enough for employees to feel that they have a clearly defined role to play and a clear career path to follow. Such up-front commitment to personal development via NVQs was also expected to have a positive impact on the key business measures of staff retention, churn rates and employee satisfaction. The expected reduction in annual turnover was in the region of 10 per cent, enough to offset the cost of establishment and maintenance of the programme.

The actual results from the first ten months of the programme can be seen in Figure 13.1. Clearly, not only is the turnover rate for staff pursuing qualifications very low, but the overall turnover rate has dropped by more than 10 per cent.

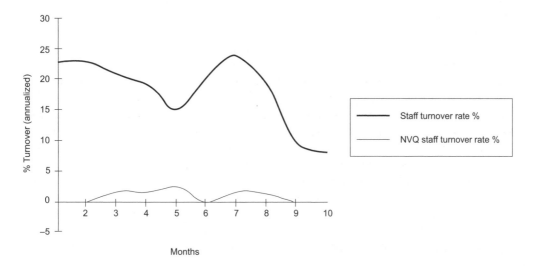

Figure 13.1   Comparison of annualized turnover rates © Royal Mail

In summary, this strategy gave the following benefits:

- provided a clearly defined route for people to achieve a recognized qualification in customer service
- offered advisors the opportunity to work their way up the pay scale, based on their level of NVQ achievement
- gave a clear signal to employees as to the company's commitment to learning and development, particularly for those staff who were, by their age, excluded from the government-funded NVQ programme for 16–24 year olds
- locked advisors into a progressive longer-term development programme designed to have a significant impact upon retention and churn rates, and therefore on overall recruitment, selection and development costs
- freed up budget from recruitment and induction training for re-investment in other areas
- raised, in the longer term, the quality of our customer service advisors
- directly addressed the issues around boredom and lack of challenge that featured heavily in our exit interviews
- a potential spin-off benefit of being seen as a more attractive employer to future recruits.

Planning a career

A related approach to both pay progression and professional qualifications, although one which can stand alone, is that of career paths for customer service advisors. One potential driver of the rapid movement of staff from one employer to another is that working in contact centres is seen as more of a job than a career. If an employer can describe to its workforce how their career might develop, what alternative paths are available to them and what exactly they need to do to have a better chance of succeeding in their chosen path, the result is likely to be a workforce that has better focused individuals, feels more valued and is potentially more willing to embrace changing demands in the organization.

Be realistic in career opportunities

Individual career paths which enable staff to plot their short, medium and longer-term prospects can be relatively easily introduced as part of the normal coaching and development or performance review activities that take place in most companies. Illustrative paths can be developed to show the typical routes, and the individual advisor in conjunction with their team leader or other support can determine where their interests and abilities lie, as well as making a judgement on the likelihood of succeeding in a particular path. Indicative or minimum expected timescales can also be applied to these illustrative paths to help manage expectations. A word of caution on timescales. It is possible to draw a path that indicates that it is possible to go from being a newly recruited advisor to running a major contact centre in just a few years. While that may be true, the likelihood of a large number of advisors being able to follow that path to its conclusion within the stated timescale is clearly non-existent.

The main risk of describing career paths is that they are either badly communicated and seen as 'promises', which are then not fulfilled, or they are not backed up with a commitment to help people develop into new roles. If either of these things happen, introducing a career development strategy will have, at best, short-term improvements, which are then undermined by a disaffected workforce who believes that management have misled them on what they might expect.

Adopting a coaching approach

While pay, qualifications and career mapping all provide benefits in terms of reducing attrition, they are at the periphery of what occupies an advisor's day. In management terms, they are all medium to long term in their payback and of little use to the team leader in the day-to-day task of managing performance. Only by keeping the interest levels and motivation of advisors high on an ongoing basis, will an employer be able to create a workplace where people enjoy working and want to be there.

That is where the role of the team leader is crucial in keeping staff turnover at an acceptable level. In the most successful contact centres, much of the administrative burden has been stripped from team leaders. Nor are they expected to spend significant amounts of time acting as 'super advisors' dealing with escalated calls and contacts. Instead they are required to manage as coaches, spending 70 per cent or more of their time with individual advisors or their entire team, guiding them towards better performance levels.

Of course, it is not enough just to remove the administration from team leaders and tell them to go and coach their teams. The team leaders will need to have the skills and knowledge to successfully coach performance in a way that encourages advisors to develop within the organization. Otherwise, it is likely to have the opposite effect and to drive up turnover by being seen as a company that always 'wants more from its employees'.

Coaching is the culture, not just part of it. To be wholly successful, coaching must be embedded as a mechanism to manage business results, including staff retention, and not just used for isolated incidents to help staff with their communication skills. A coaching approach can make advisors feel more satisfied with their work and more valued, leading to lower attrition, in the following ways:

- Employees' suggestions for process improvements are more likely to be listened to and implemented.
- Consistent deployment of process changes are easier to achieve as employees have more opportunity to raise questions and team leaders have more opportunities to observe actual behaviours.
- Better identification of the caller demand type will lead to high levels of first-time resolution and increased customer and employee satisfaction.
- Fewer complaints from customers will reduce the stress levels associated with the job.
- Employees will feel more in control of calls, again leading to increased employee satisfaction.
- Improved relationships between team leaders and advisors.
- Increased team working and cross-team cooperation.
- Better motivation from advisors and team leaders.

Encourage self-development

A coaching approach will certainly go a long way towards making advisors feel that they are working in an organization that values its employees and wants to keep them and develop them; however, this may not be enough on its own. If an employer can supplement its approach by encouraging self-development through a range of means then staff attrition is likely to be lower still. Investors in People feedback indicates that easily accessed and suitably equipped learning centres are a positive factor in retention/development initiatives.

Potential ways of adding to traditional training and a coaching approach include:

- **Learning knowledge centres**: Provision of learning knowledge centres (LKCs) in contact centres means making both facilities and support available for employees to develop skills and knowledge at their own pace in their own time. Some work time can also be used, if required, but generally the provision of the opportunity is the employer's part of the bargain.

- **Work-time learning packages**: This takes the learning knowledge centre concept one step further and it may be that many of these packages are available through the LKCs. This approach would allow advisors to use allocated development time, which is not to be used for mandatory training sessions such as product updates, to develop skills and knowledge in a wide range of areas. Most of these learning packages will be directly related to the advisor's current or potential next role, but they can also be aimed at developing skills that may potentially benefit both employer and employee in the future, for example, languages.
- **Community projects and programmes**: Although these are likely only to impact directly on a few advisors, the visibility of the employer's support for them and for those advisors interested will send the message to the workforce as a whole that this company is serious about valuing its employees. Potential projects and programmes include the Prince's Trust, Operation Raleigh, school governor schemes and local community projects.

Communication

A common thread that runs through all of the approaches and initiatives described in this chapter is the need for communication. Feedback from employee surveys, exit interviews, informal listening sessions and formal reviews are frequent sources of expressions of employee dissatisfaction, which highlights that employees often do not know what is going on or what is expected of them. Workplace communication is the subject of many management handbooks. This section is limited to how communications can affect staff retention.

Without frequent and open communication, creating an environment in the workplace that encourages people to stay, while still delivering required levels of performance would be virtually impossible. Individual advisors and teams must know what is expected of them and what they can expect from their leaders. Likewise, they must know how they are doing in accordance with expectations and feel that their contribution is valued. Finally, they must have a route to express their ideas and suggestions where the feedback is transparent.

The key elements of communication for staff retention, therefore, are:

- Performance standards and performance management
- Recognition
- Employee input.

Performance standards

In the case of performance standards, these may be expressed in terms of productivity, behaviours or quality statements. For example, productivity standards may be expected number of contacts per hour, hours logged on, average handle times, and so on. For newly trained advisors these can be graduated to show expected standards increasing as they progress through the learning curve. Behaviours may be such things as dress code, call-handling techniques, business policies and company values. Quality statements are likely to be based on mystery caller or silent monitoring results, first-time resolution rate, and so on.

Without performance standards, which are communicated and understood, advisors will not necessarily understand exactly what is expected of them. In that situation, frustration and resentment can grow, either against the team leaders, who will be making demands for improved performance without being able to say what is expected, or against their peers as they witness people 'not working as hard' as themselves or 'playing the system', with team leaders doing nothing about it. Standards will also help in the coaching approach. With standards in place, team leaders are able to coach advisors towards a target level of performance. Without standards, the areas which the advisor needs coaching become more subjective.

Recognize results and individuals

Recognition is an obvious way of making advisors feel valued for their efforts in the workplace. The methods of recognition, however, can be many and varied. These range from a simple 'thank you' to a formal recognition award scheme. Schemes may or may not carry a tangible reward and can be limited to a certain number of specific awards, for example, Customer Service Advisor of the Month, or be more open-ended. Prominent display of awards and celebration of winners can also help to keep everyone involved. Whichever methods are used, recognition is a very cost-effective way of maintaining a sense of worth and belonging which, in turn, helps to reduce attrition. None of these methods replaces the need for regular one-to-one sessions between team leaders and advisors.

Employee input

Employee input is the third strand of communication that impacts on turnover. If advisors feel they have a voice then they are less likely to vote with their feet when frustration sets in. Again, there are a number of routes open to employers. A formal suggestion scheme can work but these have proved counter-productive in many companies as they became administratively unwieldy; feedback, if any, was not instant; and the scheme frequently abused with frivolous suggestions. An alternative is to hold regular listening sessions with groups of advisors. These generally work best if hosted by a senior manager who is able to answer questions about the company, give instant feedback or decisions on some issues and to progress more complex suggestions as required.

There is, of course, much more to communication than the above. These elements, however, are inexpensive and will directly affect both business performance and staff retention.

Management style

Few people arrive at their place of employment with the intention of doing a bad day's work, and few go home and complain about a new process they've learnt, a new client or even a difficult customer contact they've dealt with. It is more likely that a person complains about their boss. The behaviour of managers and leadership style in an organization can make a difference between a good and bad day for an advisor and, ultimately, may drive their decision to stay or to go to another employer.

The impact of leadership and management style on business results, including staff retention, is demonstrated by the European Foundation for Quality Management (EFQM) business model (see Figure 13.2). The EFQM sees leadership as the starting point of the business model, determining the management style through policy and strategy, allocation of resources and, most importantly for staff retention, people management approaches.

So what is the most appropriate management style for an organization? Naturally, this will vary from company to company but there are some common themes that will allow for reduced turnover as well as other key business results.

Make the management style a friendly one. Identify first with the company goals and values and then with the team. The aim is for all members of the team, advisors and managers to realize that they share a common goal. Management style drives the overall feel of the contact centre and the company – its cultural climate.

The first step is to develop the management team as leaders not managers. Leaders visibly demonstrate commitment to business values and goals. Leaders support improvement and involvement by providing resources and assistance and they recognize and appreciate people's efforts and achievements.

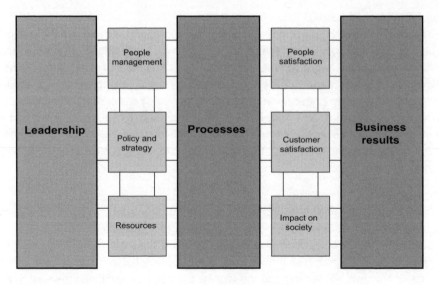

Figure 13.2   European Foundation for Quality Management model © Royal Mail

Visibility is one of the key elements of a good management style. Whether by structured 'coal-face' visits by senior managers and directors, or by regular open forums or breakfast meetings, the leaders of a business can do much to engender a feeling of being valued just by taking the time to listen to the people in the front line.

VALUE PEOPLE, VALUE CUSTOMERS

If the senior people in the company demonstrate a high level of interest and commitment to their people, it is more likely that all managers will be committed to creating a better working environment and recognizing the contribution of their people to business results. If advisors are rewarded for their attitude, skills and knowledge and helped to develop these in a positive atmosphere, it is much more likely that they will choose to stay. If managers value their people, they will see the contribution they are making to business results and feel proud to work for that organization and customers will notice the difference in the service they receive.

There is an inextricable link between happy employees and loyal customers. Recognize that link, value your staff and they will repay you not just with their own loyalty but with a more successful and profitable business.

> ... a business stands little chance of winning the loyalty of its customers if it does not take the trouble of winning the loyalty of its staff. Committed employees are far more powerful than any plastic card.
>
> Stuart Hamson
> *Chairman of John Lewis*

III Contact Centre Technology

Technology is the engine room of the contact centre. This section of the handbook explains what technologies are available, what they do, and demonstrates the benefits through case studies.

- Contact Centre Technology in Context
- The History of Call Distribution
- Convergence of Voice and Data
- From Call to Contact Centre
- Predictive Dialling Summary
- Automated Call Handling
- Integrated Messaging into the Customer Contact Centre
- Customer Management in Practice
- Self-service
- Quality Management Technology Perspective

14 Contact Centre Technology in Context

Steve Pink, Managing Consultant, Telecommerce Consultancy

This chapter and section is designed to put into perspective the role of technology and the variety of tools and systems available. Whatever the size of the contact centre operations, the same principles can be applied.

BACKGROUND

The beinning of the twenty-first century has seen the emergence of the contact centre. The marriage of the telephone with email and the Internet, has enabled centres to deal with various customer communications in one place.

The huge growth in contact centres has been one of the drivers behind the advancement and cost reduction of technology. As a result of the emergence of the Internet and web presence, customers demand choice. They are no longer content to 'phone'; they want to 'contact' via email, fax, web chat, text messaging and whatever else they choose.

CONTACT CENTRE TECHNOLOGY: AN OVERVIEW

Starting up a new contact centre or developing an existing call centre requires the organization to take a strategic overview of current customer contact media, the way in which relationships with customers are managed and the approach to quality management. This chapter of the handbook helps you develop a 'state-of-the-art' customer interaction centre in terms of defining the business requirements and identifying the technologies available to support them. However, you do not need to have or to be building a significant state-of-the-art centre – this section acts as a valuable reference to understand the current technologies available.

There are three levels of technologies:

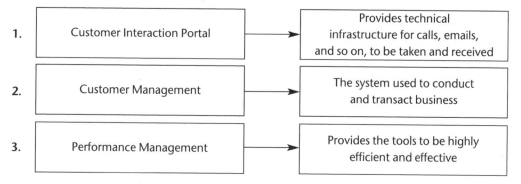

1.	Customer Interaction Portal	Provides technical infrastructure for calls, emails, and so on, to be taken and received
2.	Customer Management	The system used to conduct and transact business
3.	Performance Management	Provides the tools to be highly efficient and effective

Generally, you will find that the *Customer Interaction Portal* is the responsibility of the Telecoms/Facilities/IT/Support functions and it includes areas such as the network, the website architecture, and so on.

The *Customer Management system* is normally known as the front end (or back end system) that agents use every day.

The *Performance Management* tools such as customer analysis, quality, reporting, forecasting, and so on, are normally accessed by supervisory levels of staff and business support.

MANAGING COMMUNICATIONS

In today's business climate, customers can view our products and services on our website, place their order by email, call to amend the order and expect to be updated as to the progress of their order by SMS text messaging via their mobile phone. These days we need to create an integrated multimedia queue of customer interactions managed and routed by common business rules and accessible to all staff in the organization who might ordinarily be expected to interact with customers or provide direct support to those colleagues who do. We only have to look at the proliferation of mobile phone text messaging to also realize that the frequency of communications is increasing as well as the variety and complexity of the media. Interactive digital TV and third generation mobiles have also started to make an impact – all this, plus a substantial section of our customer base that still write in and expect confirmation in writing! In organizations where volume of communications and commonality of transactions is an issue, there will be pressure to manage emails, IVR (Interactive Voice Response) and web contacts with automation to keep control of costs. In this situation, organizations must think long and hard about the Customer Interaction Portal (CIP) that meets all of their current and near future business requirements.

MANAGING CUSTOMER CONTACT

There is a need to record and track a full contact history for every customer. That history has to include media/channel used, the time of the interaction, who initiated it, the issue under discussion, the outcome, and any follow-up action required. Having a clear vision as to whom the organization wants as its customers, when, how and why it wants to communicate with them and what choices will be made available to the customer (who probably does not want to feel 'managed'), is paramount for effective customer relationships.

If, additionally, the organization has well-mapped business processes, has defined business requirements for its supporting systems and is operating with a single customer and transaction database structure that has the flexibility to accommodate all departmental functions – then there is an infrastructure on which to develop this potential. If, on top of all this, the organization's staff and customers are given convenient, user-friendly access to make the transactions that achieve the organization's goals – then a true Customer Relationship Management 'system' is in place.

MANAGING CONTACT CENTRE PERFORMANCE

We've made contact with our customers and we have followed the processes designed to achieve our corporate objectives ... so, is that it? A two-dimensional model is unlikely to sustain an organization for very long: it possesses no capacity to evaluate its quality, identify opportunities for improvement and implement positive change and have the ability to:

- monitor contacts
- record communications with customers
- evaluate the quality of customer interactions
- undertake customer satisfaction surveying
- identify areas requiring improvement
- implement training/coaching solutions and provide feedback to staff on performance against agreed objectives.

The organization needs robust systems for capturing, publishing and learning from customer and staff feedback to move forward confidently and achieve its business objectives in an environment that focuses on customer interaction.

The basic principle of training, coaching, monitoring and evaluating staff against a common set of criteria is well understood. What is less well understood and poorly implemented in many call centres are the recording systems, access to records, the physical quality of records, the discipline of regular monitoring, the differences in monitoring methods and evaluation standards. This results in negligible feedback to staff on how well they are performing, or varying standards in different teams undertaking the same role. When such differences are reported upwards, contact centre directors often get an unrealistic picture of performance.

These inconsistencies are carried across into customer satisfaction tracking. If the sample is unrepresentative or not statistically significant; if the survey is not undertaken regularly; if the sample contains only customers who have contacted the centre and not 'silent' customers, the organization can be given a misleading impression of customer satisfaction indices. Additionally, consider the layers of complexity as we try to obtain a true picture of staff satisfaction or obtain feedback from emails and web contacts.

Now we have an appreciation of the need for effective quality management in our contact centre. Here, our attention should concentrate on the key 'levers' that drive contact centre performance including volumes, traffic patterns, resources (staff and telecoms technology), service standards, operational costs and productivity. In other words, we want to obtain maximum effective business benefit from the available customer interactions at the most efficient cost.

We need open channels of communication with the marketing, sales and service teams in our organization to develop accurate business models and demand forecasts for our contact centre. We need to integrate campaign-based traffic forecasts with historical and seasonal trends to provide reliable forecasts of workload for the contact centre. We need to provide long-term forecasts of required staffing and technology levels, plus short-term staffing rosters. Then we need to see if our forecasts were accurate and if our staff were deployed in the right place at the right time. That is a more balanced approach to performance management.

Today's integrated suites of applications have intelligent contact management capabilities that enable a company to interact with its customers via phone, web, fax and email across an enterprise of multiple switches, automatic call distribution (ACD), IVR, database and desktop applications. These suites provide centralized management control over customer contact, allowing organizations to implement a single set of business rules that uniformly address customer needs independent of contact channel or resource location and enabling consolidated reporting across dispersed resources. Regardless of how a customer interacts with the company, multimedia routing supports a company's ability to seamlessly integrate voice, email and web channels, including web chat, VoIP (Voice over Internet Protocol), web call-back and web collaboration, to create a central, Internet-ready contact centre. All interactions are handled in a consistent manner as equal 'events', funnelled to a universal queue and intelligently routed, according to a company's defined routing strategy.

15 *The History of Call Distribution*

John Taylor, Managing Consultant, Maple Communications

THE UNFORTUNATE CALL

Back in the days of the manual telephone exchange there was the 'Unfortunate Call'. This was the incoming call that lit a lamp in several places on the switchboard but never got answered. The operators were all busy answering calls, but the switchboard was lit like a Christmas tree and the Unfortunate Call was overlooked – just bad luck.

Much later on, it was the Key System that became favoured in small businesses that could not afford dedicated telephone operators. The Key System enables the incoming call to light lamps in several different places (again, on telephones), but with the bell ringing or lamp flashing it is not so easy to overlook. Indeed, many forerunners of the call centre employed a Key System to aid the functionality of the telephone handsets and multiple calling of individual lines. The parts department in your local motor dealership might still be using this system.

While small businesses used a Key System, big businesses used automatic call distribution (ACD). This was the first serious attempt to design a system specifically to deal with the caller in a single transaction. The systems were large and expensive and only the biggest and best-suited businesses could justify the expense. Airlines and mail order were typical of the vanguard in ACD, which was completely separate from the office telephone system. The ACD has queues. Death for the 'Unfortunate Call'?

In the 1980s the office telephone system evolved into that rare device – the dedicated computer. It ran only one programme – connecting telephone calls. That could not last for long, and soon the digital PABX (Private Automatic Branch Exchange) was sending out management information about the calls it was handling, as well as continuing to offer a range of standard features which had always been useful for answering calls in a group, such as hunting (automatic search for a free extension in the group).

TODAY'S SYSTEM

Today the modern telephone system is capable of providing ACD facilities as an integral part of its feature set, albeit often at an extra charge from the supplier. Even large call centres now operate on the ACD portion of a PABX, which also serves the back office with regular telephone service simultaneously. Like the PABX this functionality is scaleable, and so fully featured call centres can also be created for small specialist groups of just a few agents such as, for example, technical helplines.

What are the extra features that make a PABX into an ACD?

- Smart telephones – usually 'top of the range' digital handsets.
- Queues – the facility provided through software to create queues of incoming calls and decide, on the basis of rules, how the calls will be routed to the queues.
- Management information – specialist reporting on the activity of agents, volumes of traffic and overall service performance.

Despite the hype, most operators of UK call centres today are still in the position of having all this telephony quite separate from the IT network on which the customer transaction depends. This is the next big step: the convergence of voice and data in a single switching system. The relentless pursuit of the 'Unfortunate Call'…

16 *Convergence of Voice and Data*

David Mackenzie, Contact Centre Futurologist and Founder, CT Consulting

The most recent development to affect call centres is the use of Internet Protocol (IP) as the sole transport medium within the contact centre. Historically, in order to support voice, and email, web chat and web collaboration, contact centres have used a mixture of conventional telephony, and conventional Internet technology. This has meant that there needed to be two networks in the contact centre, and an integration process to allow the delivery of voice or data to an agent to be coordinated across the two systems. Often this required a complex integration allowing the Internet components to use the CTI (Computer Telephony Integration) interface of the ACD (automatic call distributor) to control the allocation of agents. It also meant that essentially a number of stand-alone technologies, ACD, email, web chat/collaboration were being bolted together. This led to a solution that worked but was a nightmare to manage.

In order to get over this problem, and to simplify the architecture, products have been developed which allow IP to be the sole transport mechanism.

It is essential to support customers using conventional telephony, so there is a gateway that converts the voice delivered from the traditional public network into IP and is delivered over the local area network.

Within the contact centre there are all the usual components required to manage calls, contacts and queues, but each is based on IP rather than voice. So there is the 'IP ACD' that is key to managing the activities of the agents, routing whichever activity the agent needs to handle next, according to the appropriate business rules. Similarly there are 'IP IVR', email, web chat and collaboration servers. The agent positions are connected using IP, with IP phones converting VoIP back into voice.

This simplified architecture makes the solution easier to maintain, simplifies staffing requirements, as you don't need staff with expertise in disparate networks, and also greatly simplifies moves and changes. In a conventional contact centre the phone is physically connected all the way back to the ACD. In the IP contact centre, the phone simply needs to be identified by its IP address, so that it might be moved to another room, another building, or another country and instantly be available for use by the IP ACD. This means that expansion into separate buildings, and using agents working from home or abroad, is as simple as dialling the Internet.

SOFT SWITCHING THE IP-CENTREX

Within the contact centre environment, a service has been available for businesses that don't want to buy a telephone switchboard. Called Centrex, and offered by major telecom providers, the telephones and agent turrets are rented, and these are connected to a remote telephone switch within the telephone company's telephone network. This eliminates all the work associated with choosing a switch, installing it, connections, and the ongoing management of the system. It also eliminates initial capital costs; instead there is an ongoing rental cost.

It is possible to offer the same service using IP-ACD technology. However, instead of needing a complex set of telephone cables, you simply need an IP connection, of suitable bandwidth, to the IP-ACD in the network.

It will be immensely flexible, easily supporting concepts such as home-working, tele-cottaging and so on. All that is needed is an IP connection to an agent's desk, so it doesn't really matter where they are. Configuration is simple too. Plug in a PC, log on to a network, and you are up and running. It will be possible to imagine a business with no fixed premises, allowing agents to work wherever they most feel comfortable.

WHEN TO CONSIDER CHANGING TO IP

Although these solutions offer many benefits in a contact centre, they don't fundamentally change the core functionality of being able to talk with customers. Therefore it requires a significant change in the contact centre before it is worth considering this technology. For example: moving to multi-channel interaction; opening a new call centre; integrating a satellite office. If any of these is happening then it makes sense to consider this technology.

AREAS TO CONSIDER

What do you need to look for in a solution? There are two key areas of functionality that need to be examined closely.

1 **Functionality**. If you are replacing an ACD, you need to be sure it gives you all the functions you would expect. The management tools available will also be critical, as the majority of the work in contact centres is in managing the staff and reviewing the performance of the centre.
2 **Resilience**. Voice systems are historically very reliable. Once you have moved over to the IP environment running on a LAN, any failure in the LAN will take everything down. Not just the PCs, but the telephones as well. Protection against viruses is also imperative.

17 *From Call to Contact Centre*

Markus Recker, Manager, DeTeWe Enterprise Solutions

GROWTH OF THE INTERNET

The explosive growth of 'non-traditional' Internet media is driving change. According to analysts The Gartner Group, over 35 per cent of call centre access will come from emails or web contact by the end of 2003. As more companies use websites to help drive consumer and business sales, there's a growing need for new applications that supplement traditional voice-centric technology. A contact centre solution now needs to provide queuing, routing and reporting solutions not only for voice calls but also for Voice over Internet Protocol (VoIP), email, video, chat, NetMeeting and web call-back functions.

Yet, rather than relieving inbound call traffic, this explosion in Internet media is presenting new challenges. While online customer service will grow, the uptake in usage of web applications – and the growth of new communication channels such as wireless application protocol (WAP) and digital TV – will fuel a further explosion of calls.

As customers choose to contact companies via email or the Internet, the contact centres need to have strategies to convert these contacts into sales or service. For example, real contact centres support virtual bookseller Amazon.com's online presence. The company's CEO, Jeff Bezos, has publicly stated that these centres are the most important part of Amazon's business. And with the current consumer trepidation over spending online, the contact centre winners, especially in the e-business, will be those who most successfully turn browsers into buyers, by whatever means.

So contact centres not only need to be able to handle and respond to mixed media requests, but also need to sharpen their phone call-routing capabilities too, to respond to ever-increasing traffic levels. So how do they do this?

NEW POINTS OF ACCESS

As the web offers an extremely cost-effective way of both providing information and requesting information, companies need to exploit it. This means integrating the company website and email server with the contact centre, to give customers the widest range of contact options without eliminating the opportunity of speaking to a real person. The web has simply become another access point for the call centre, alongside the telephone, fax and email. Figure 17.1 shows the required levels of integration of the operating system.

Web integration, in its basic form, provides an option on a company's website for customers to email the call centre. Alternatively, the website might provide a call-me button, which guides the customer through a simple menu from which the customer can request a call-back from a call centre agent at a convenient time. More complex applications of web integration can allow customers to access an agent directly, using synchronized browsing features such as

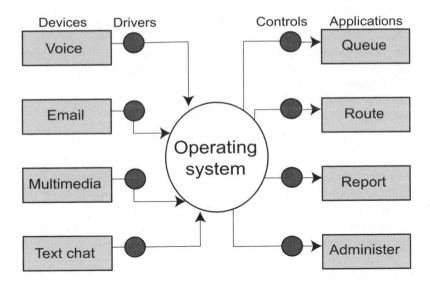

Figure 17.1   Devices, drivers, controls and applications of the contact centre operating system © DeTeWe
Enterprise solutions

'whiteboarding' while talking on a single telephone line. Integration tools from Microsoft,
Netscape and other leading vendors make services like these relatively simple to operate with
existing applications.

WORKFLOW MANAGEMENT

These new methods of contact fit well with the increasingly workflow-oriented approach that call
centres are taking to customer communications. Incoming contacts to call centres – whether
phone, fax or email – and their corresponding records, documentation, accounts and so on are no
longer just calls, but workflow jobs to be handled by agents of the appropriate capability.
However, to ensure effective workflow, the information relating to the communication – that is,
the entire 'job' – must also be routed, blending the queuing, routing and reporting of email, VoIP,
chat, NetMeeting and web call-back with traditional voice contact.

ROUTING MATTERS

Of course, it's no good giving customers the widest range of contact options without prioritizing
and managing incoming contact effectively. The trick is to blend these multiple contact points
smoothly into the centre itself, and present them to agents with the right skill levels to deal with
that contact.

Using management software solutions, a contact centre supervisor can establish the routing
criteria that suits the centre's exact business needs, bearing in mind the skills of available agents or
groups. The first step in doing this is to grade agents according to their competencies in
categories such as knowledge in a specific area, and language skills.

ROUTE AND MAP

To show how this works, imagine a contact centre within a financial organization. Customers may
ring or email with enquiries ranging from requests for product brochures, to a payment made to

or from their account, or someone needing to speak to an operator for advice on a complicated transaction. Rules-based weightings are applied to map the needs of the incoming communication to the available agents' abilities. For example, a supervisor can configure the system to consider a foreign language as a desirable skill, ideal in today's merging financial markets. The key points here are that a comprehensive set of routing rules allows any communication to be prioritized and weighted. This not only benefits designated customers, but improves service to all.

NETWORKS

Let's look at some further examples of how web calls and requests can be blended into a contact centre's communications, and the benefits that can be accrued by web-enabling the contact centre. For example, the call centre of a mail order company utilizes a typical computer telephony integration (CTI)-enabled automatic call distribution (ACD) switch with an integrated interactive voice-response system, linked to the company's databases. The company's web server is also linked to the ACD software of the contact centre.

In our example, the company is running a sales campaign, and has designed its web pages to reflect the promotion. One customer wants to place a substantial order online, but requires an increase in her credit limit to do so. In this case, a credit authorization form can be displayed on the customer's browser for completion and mailing back to the company. The information can be captured and blended into the company's workflow application, and using skills-based routing is passed to agents authorized to deal with it before the transaction proceeds.

In another example, a customer browsing a company's website may want to check availability of certain sizes and prices for a number of given items. The customer can request a call-back using the site's facilities, so that an agent can confirm the required details in a phone call at a more convenient time. In this simple case, the request is captured by the workflow application and logged, ready for presentation to a suitable agent at the right time. Companies can further exploit the potential of their websites by deploying push technology to deliver related content to the caller's Internet browser, helping to make the Internet 'call' more interactive and fulfilling for the customer. The enhanced efficiencies and overhead cuts enabled by use of such systems are clear.

PROTECTING INVESTMENTS

Of course, no one will want to undertake a wholesale replacement of their existing contact centre systems – the expense and downtime would be prohibitively expensive. The key to gaining maximum benefit from using web technology is to preserve existing investments, and extend them into new areas. This means that the routing and workflow applications that web-enable the contact centre must work with the 'legacy' call centre systems – switch, databases, document management and so on – to allow an evolutionary, rather than revolutionary, roll-out. Those companies that migrate their contact centres to an infrastructure that supports multimedia will be positioning their business to provide the widest range of customer service options.

18 *Predictive Dialling Summary*

Colin Chave, Managing Director, Melita

The Direct Marketing Association (DMA) defines predictive dialling as

> A process designed to maximize the time agents spend talking to contacts by automating the non-productive aspects of outbound calling, for example, deciding who to call, dialling numbers, waiting for an answer and filtering out telephone messages. Predictive diallers connect only answered calls to the agent and contact details appear on agents' screens as each call is connected. The dialling rate is adjusted automatically to provide a constant flow of answered calls to keep agents busy.

The first predictive dialler was developed in the 1970s after a utilities company developed an emergency need to locate people through the use of multiple telephone lines. It was discovered then that automatic diallers could do the work of many people, in less time for lower costs. They could complete the people-intensive task of calling thousands of people, utilizing an agent's time only when a party answered the phone.

KEY DRIVERS

The driver towards the predictive dialling technology that is used today is the result of the following call centre needs:

- Automation of call processing
- Calling list preparation and management
- Management of multiple telephone lines
- Predictability and information access.

ADVANTAGES

By applying the manual dialling process to business applications where thousands of outbound calls are made every day, one can easily see the enormity of time spent on non-productive call processing. The predictive dialler offers three powerful advantages over manual dialling:

1 It can manage all tasks associated with a call.
2 It can queue calls by using statistical averages to predict when an agent will complete the current call.

3   It increases productivity by simultaneously delivering the voice call to a telephone and the customer's records to a PC.

This increases the average productive 'talk time' per agent per hour to well over 50 minutes compared to an average 10 to 15 minutes in a manual environment.

MANAGEMENT OF INFORMATION

Automating the calling process requires the dialler to recognize and detect phone rings such as busy, ringing with no answer, a human voice, and answerphones. An important part of calling list management is the ability to work with a multitude of databases and host applications. Information on prospects and customers is often stored in multiple external systems; Calling List management must access all of these sources, combining them effectively to build the final lists. In financial and customer service applications, experience shows that once lists are transferred to the dialler, they often require additional selection and sorting for more focused campaigns.

AUTOMATION

In order for multiple telephone lines and agents to be managed, the dialler requires a switching platform to ensure virtually instant connections are created. By automating the process that connects the agent to a targeted party, predictive diallers can greatly increase agent efficiency and productivity. However, the real challenge for predictive dialling is taking the process one step further, to ensure that the moment an agent completes a call they are connected to a new party, keeping each agent as close as possible to 100 per cent productivity. In order to accomplish this, the diallers must predict the exact moment when an agent will complete a conversation. Since agents type at their own pace and differ in the way they handle inbound/outbound calls, the system must predict individual agent availability to take such calls. Predictive diallers must track and apply this information to individual agent characteristics.

BUSINESS BENEFITS

In general terms, a predictive dialler in business-to-consumer (B2C) contact increases agent productivity by 150 to 400 per cent, depending on the application of the call. The first difference between B2C and B2B is agent productivity, with general increases between 30 to 60 per cent for B2B. The difference in productivity is determined by the consumer being more likely not to be at home than the business customer not being at work.

MANAGEMENT CONTROL

A subtle, often unnoticed, major benefit of a predictive dialler is the management control, or operational streamlining, it provides over inbound/outbound calling campaigns. The dialler provides management tools to ensure rules and policies are followed by both agents and supervisors when they make their calling decisions.

The real dialling benefits to management are:

- It ensures that agents follow the call centre rules and policies.
- It obeys company rules that all first-attempt no-answers are called back throughout the day.
- It records every call attempt made and updates the relevant database.
- Workflow control assures accurate adherence to policy, regardless of which agent is on the phone.

- Supervisors are free to train and coach as there is no need to monitor agents' processing their work.
- As diallers know the exact length of each call, and who processed it, management therefore receives, as standard, comprehensive reports on system information.

In summary, we have seen that predictive dialling technology can provide significant results to applications such as collections, telemarketing and customer service in the right environment, with relatively quick return on investments. It is clear that the best investment is a dialler that provides individual agent pacing, lowest nuisance dropped call rates, the most talk time per agent hour and the greatest increases in productivity. The predictive dialler is a core technology in contact centres today and therefore the future of the dialler involves integration with emerging technologies such as the Internet. In the instance of a web call-back, the details of the customer will be fed into the dialler and the customer will be called back at the requested time. The predictive dialler is now one channel of the multi-channel contact centre, which offers true customer interaction management through telephony, email, web chat, instant messaging, VoIP, mobile-commerce and fax.

19 *Automated Call Handling*

Caroline Griffiths, Managing Director, Intext Media

AUTOMATED CALL HANDLING: WHEN AND WHY?

We are all familiar with the nightmare of some automated call systems. Indeed, which one of us has not felt like screaming with frustration when we have been sucked into the whirlpool of a poorly designed automated system? However, there is a time and a place for automation – it is just a matter of getting the right application, for the right service, and managing consumer expectations.

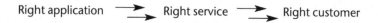

Right application → Right service → Right customer

No one can refute that well-run live operator call centres generally provide excellent solutions but there are circumstances when automated call handling provides equally excellent complementary support. There is also the issue of whether to use other forms of interaction and, if so, how they should be integrated. Other interactive media normally includes text messaging, web interfaces and digital interactive TV (DiTV), but increasingly one also has to consider rich media delivery by mobile phone using enhanced messaging services (EMS) and multimedia services (MMS).

However, the focus here is on IVR (Interactive Voice Recognition) and the pros and cons of implementing such automation. The commonest issues, which lead to IVR being of real value for an inbound campaign, include:

- cost
- speed of set-up
- the need for anti-social hour cover, for example 24/7
- the need to handle call surges prompted by TV or radio advertising
- caller confidentiality
- if the promotion or service needs to be self-funding or profitable.

COST

IVR systems are cheaper than live operators. The costs involved in setting up a service may include an up-front fee for the programming of the IVR equipment but this may be waived if the service is a standard application such as name and address and postcode capture. There will be a call-handling fee of typically 10 to 12 pence per minute payable for actual calls taken. This has the benefit that if the campaign disappoints the fees are proportionately less. There are no extra fees for out-of-hours working and if the campaign exceeds all expectations most systems have extra capacity which effortlessly kicks in at no incremental cost to the client other than the call-handling charge described above. All other costs, such as transcription, database management, fulfilment and mailing, will not be significantly different from those offered by a live operator call centre.

SPEED OF SET-UP

Provided that the service is either very simple or has been anticipated in advance so that the background preparatory work has been done, it is possible to launch automated services in a matter of hours. This is not possible with live call centres where the capacity and training issues require a longer lead-time.

OUT OF HOURS COVER

Working outside normal office hours is cheaper with IVR systems, as the equipment runs on a 24/7 basis anyway. Not only does it avoid high anti-social hour payments it obviates the challenge to find the right number of quality staff who can work overnight or at weekends, even if the client's budget can support the theoretical cost.

CALL TRAFFIC PEAKS

Nothing frustrates a client more than investing in an expensive promotional campaign and for the campaign to be so successful that many of the respondents hear the busy tone. IVR systems can support many thousands of simultaneous calls if necessary, and avoid the frustration of potential customers being aggravated by the engaged signal. Case studies show that once a caller hears the busy tone, only a few will try ringing again and virtually none will try ringing more than three times if they have still not got through.

CALLER CONFIDENTIALITY

While there are sometimes protests about the anonymous nature of 'speaking to a machine', on occasions this comes into its own. Two of the case studies illustrated below involve subject matter that was potentially personally embarrassing and respondents were more than happy to speak to an automated system rather than a real person.

Self-funding services

If the service needs to break-even or make a profit, it can be run on a premium-rate number, for which a share of the revenue generated from the phone calls is paid out to the service owner. If this is done in conjunction with an automated call-handling system, the service can be designed to make money. If a live operator solution is deployed it is extremely unlikely that the service will break-even or be profitable, though the premium rate revenues can make a useful contribution to overheads, as the many 'free' Internet Service Providers can attest. Premium-rate charging is also useful for deterring nuisance calls.

These issues are best illustrated by the three case studies that follow.

IVR CASE STUDIES

THE DISASTER EMERGENCY COMMITTEE GOMA APPEAL

The Disaster Emergency Committee (DEC) acts on behalf of 15 charities to coordinate massive fund-raising appeals in times of extreme emergency. When a major incident occurs, the UK's broadcasters give the DEC free airtime to announce the appeal, requesting donations from members of the public. The appeal comprises a call to action, which is to ring a national rate tariff number (charged at the cost of making an inland call of over 50 kilometres) to make a donation. During the hours of the live appeal, typically 6 p.m. to 12 p.m. on the launch night, calls are routed as a first option to a call centre manned by about 80 volunteers. Because the broadcasts prompt massive call surges, an automated overflow system is also put in place. This automated system works round the clock, even after the live operators have shut down for the night. The combination of live and automated systems addresses several issues. Being a charitable venture, cost is a major issue and the automated systems are low cost. Automation allows for major capacity to be put in place at short notice. It provides 24/7 coverage, and handles the massive call surges prompted by the powerfully persuasive appeals.

Audiocall, part of BBC Worldwide Ltd, managed this particular service. As well as the mass-access call-handling system, Audiocall provided speedy transcriptions of donation information and supported the process for the duration of the appeal. Typically such appeals generate over 300 000 records in a few days.

Table 19.1 is a summary of the key rationales for implementing an IVR-driven solution for the Goma appeal.

Table 19.1   Summary of the key rationales for implementing an IVR-drive solution for the Goma appeal

Reasons for using IVR – DEC	Issue for this service?
Cost	Yes
Speed of set-up	Yes
Round-the-clock-cover	Yes
Call surges prompted by TV or radio	Yes
Caller confidentiality	n/a
Need for self-funding or a profitable solution	n/a

'LOVE FOR LIFE'

'Love For Life' was an initiative organized by the BBC Social Action Unit. This unit has the role of tackling issues with a strong public service remit. The aim of 'Love For Life' was to de-stigmatize sexual issues and to promote sexual well-being. In support of the broadcast, it offered a booklet to members of the public. To receive the booklet the audience had to ring a premium-rate telephone number and the call was handled by automated systems. For this service, automation was chosen on the criteria of cost, 24/7 cover, management of potential call surges and the need to make the service break-even. Furthermore, this is an example of a service where callers enjoyed the confidentiality of 'talking to a machine' rather than speaking to real people. The service was self-funding with the cost of the booklet and despatch covered by the £2 call charge.

This was another Audiocall project. Audiocall provided call handling and fulfilment of the booklet and audiocassette.

Table 19.2 is a summary of the key rationales for implementing an IVR-driven solution for 'Love For Life'.

Table 19.2   Summary of the key rationales for implementing an IVR-drive solution for the 'Love For Life'

Reasons for using IVR – 'Love For Life'	Issue for this service?
Cost	Yes
Speed of set-up	n/a
Round-the-clock-cover	Yes
Call surges prompted by TV or radio	Yes
Caller confidentiality	Yes
Need for self-funding or a profitable solution	Yes

TANGO TALK TIME

The client, Britvic, ran an 'on pack' promotion offering free mobile phone airtime to customers who bought a 500ml bottle of Tango. The service involved a combination of Internet, SMS (text messaging) and IVR technology, supported by a live consumer helpline, available daytime seven days a week. This was the first time that Britvic used a multi-channel new media approach.

Each Tango bottle had a unique PIN number inside and instructions directed consumers to a microsite of www.Tango.com. Consumers could register for free calls using the PIN and leaving their details. Once registered, a text (SMS) message was sent within five minutes explaining how the free calls could be used. To redeem their free calls, customers had to make a call to an automated system. The live helpline was used to handle any queries relating to the promotion and the agents could register on behalf of any customers without Internet access.

After seven weeks the promotion had attracted 76 000 visitors to the website and 40 000 consumers had registered for free calls. Tango sales had increased significantly.

This service was managed by Telescope, which provided all forms of interaction for this Tango service.

Table 19.3 is a summary of the key rationales for implementing an IVR-driven solution for Tango.

Table 19.3   Summary of the key rationales for implementing an IVR-driven solution for Tango

Reasons for using IVR – Tango	Issue for this service?
Cost	Yes
Speed of set-up	n/a
Round-the-clock-cover	Yes
Call surges prompted by TV or radio	No
Caller confidentiality	n/a
Need for self-funding or a profitable solution	n/a

20 Integrating Messaging into the Customer Contact Centre

Andy Barker, Head of Mobility, Fujitsu Siemens

This chapter explains how email can be used for optimum customer communications; the impacts within the contact centre environment are discussed.

WHY DO WE NEED EMAIL TECHNOLOGY?

We are witnessing an explosion of email and web-based communication coming into organizations; yet their ability to handle this growth is woefully poor.

A Datamonitor study (*Serving the Customer in a Multi-Channel World: CRM Strategies for Success* – Kathleen Klasnic) indicated that on average only 29 per cent of emails are responded to in one business day. For those that were responded to, only 65 per cent of the responses were accurate – so in actuality only 19 per cent of emails were responded to accurately within one day. This causes huge customer dissatisfaction issues which Datamonitor describes as an 'email crisis'. As new messaging technologies such as instant messaging, web chat and SMS/MMS mobile messaging gain widespread usage within organizations this crisis is set to worsen.

Companies often give out email addresses and set-up web forms on their Internet sites and media with little thought that the end-user might actually use them! Typically, as the number of responses skyrocket, a response backlog builds up. It is at this point they seek 'emergency' solutions to solve the problem – often implementing email management systems and web-based self-service. But, by rushing in the technology, little consideration is given to what is really required and the technology is often not 'bound' by proper business rules.

Understanding email management is less to do with the technology itself and much more to do with how one implements and integrates it into a customer contact centre.

WHAT EMAIL TECHNOLOGIES ARE THERE?

A variety of email technologies are used in business systems; many of them are involved with the organization's network infrastructure and security. It is assumed that for contact centre management the responsibilities for basic technologies such as email servers, anti-virus/anti-SPAM systems, routers and so on, fall outside the CCM's remit. But those technologies that help the contact centre's agents to better perform their jobs are discussed below.

There are two types of technology that are being applied to email:

Email management systems: these are software-based solutions that generally route, track and respond (or suggest a response) to customer email and web form enquiries. Most packages have the following basic functionalities, including:

- Distributing and tracking incoming mails
- Multi-level email queues with workload management
- Central repository for automated responses (and part responses)
- Web form support
- Monitoring response time and individual customer service representatives' performance
- Tracking the history of a customer interaction.

Specialist packages have more advanced features such as:

- Categories email (automatic recognition of content and category of mail)
- Automated suggestions to assist agents' personalized responses
- Automatic responses (some with artificial intelligence that seek out specific answers from other IT systems, for example order status)
- Multi-site systems
- Multi-language systems
- Automatic email notifications (instant responses to customers)
- Secure delivery of emails
- Link to CRM systems (central store for emails)
- Link to telephone systems (blended queue)
- Integrated outbound mailings
- Terminology assistants (to ensure consistent corporate terms/responses).

Outbound email marketing and notification: these are email systems that act as an e-marketing tool for an organization performing such actions as:

- Newsletters and announcements
- Event promotion and registration
- Lead generation follow-up
- Customer surveys
- Product updates and recall.

The software packages often consist of such functions as:

- High-volume email delivery
- Targeting and segmentation tools
- Administration tools for managing email flow
- Scheduled mailings
- Sophisticated 'bounce-back' handling.

While the technology to manage email effectively is abundant, the skills and ability to implement it effectively are not. Therefore let's focus on what contact centre management can do to harness this technology better.

WHAT IS BEST PRACTICE IN EMAIL MANAGEMENT?

Plan before you start! Most practitioners make the point that, in order to take control of email, you must understand what it is you are trying to achieve. Find the answers to the following sorts of question (and more) before you start:

- How many consumers want to deal with you via email?
- Do you know who they are and why they are contacting you?
- How would they prefer to receive the support they require?
- What are their legitimate expectations (for example, response times, level of personalization)?
- What can you afford to do and what can you afford not to do?
- Is service going to be a key proposition for your organization?
- Do some types of service have the potential to become a revenue stream?
- Do you want to operate an online-only or a multi-contact service including personal contact?
- What is your coverage of regions/languages?
- Is there any integration with other parts of your organization?
- What parts of the process do you want to own in-house and what parts might you consider outsourcing?

UNDERSTAND EMAIL PERFORMANCE BENCHMARKS

Experience has shown that end-users expect a reply to all email within 24 hours. Faster responses may enhance the customer experience; but longer than 24 hours is invariably perceived negatively. You should also prioritize responses internally and give priority to such things as credit card authorizations, password changes and website help.

LEARN FROM OTHERS

Amazon.com found that by implementing the following procedures you enhance customer satisfaction is enhanced:

- Proactively send email confirmations, warnings, advice, answers and recommendations before the customer asks for them.
- Give quick, precise answers to their questions.
- Preferably provide web-based answers (self-service) where possible; but ensure human assistance is available if necessary
- Let one person handle all of a customer's query needs from beginning to end
- Customers place a huge premium on first-contact resolution:
  - Solve the problem
  - Explain why it happened
  - Offer advice to help them avoid recurrence in the future.

While customers do show a preference for personalized responses, they are quite happy with automated responses that follow the format above. What they hate is wrong and incomplete answers that are totally impersonal.

Even automated emails should contain a minimum of:

- Title
- Name

- Order detail (where applicable)
- Agent's name.

Change and adapt the tone of responses to fit with the different situations.

3Com are another company that has used email and electronic communication for many years. The key lessons they have learnt are:

- You cannot make users do what they don't want to do just because it is convenient to your business. You have to let them do what they want to do; then align your business in such a way that it benefits your business too.
- Content ownership must be in-house. Poor email content generates additional phone calls, therefore owning and improving the content saves costs.
- Provide appropriate levels of service delivery. One size of service does not fit all and you can save large amounts of money by directing customers to existing online knowledge – 80 per cent of customers ask the same 20 questions.
- There will always be a need to offer manual responses.
- For international operations, act globally; but be local in your responses.

Both 3Com and Amazon stress the importance of pre-sales *and* post-sales relationships. By capturing what product is bought, where they bought it and why they need support you can complete the manufacturing and product development cycle. Both also state that the critical aspect of introducing email technology is properly handling the people aspect within a contact centre.

TACKLE THE PEOPLE AND ORGANIZATION ISSUES

There can be no question that handling email within a contact centre provides many economies, if introduced carefully. By managing peaks and troughs effectively you can get clear economies of scale, as the example from an insurance company shows (see Figure 20.1).

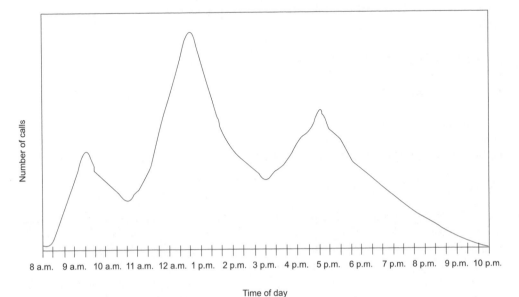

Time of day

Figure 20.1   Mid-week call traffic scenario – insurance (non-DRTV) © Andy Barker

However, you are asking your agents to multi-skill and add new and different skills to their repertoire. One must understand that the job changes substantially with the introduction of email-related tasks in a customer contact centre, as the table below shows.

	Telephone	Email
1. Skills required	Listening and talking	Reading and writing
2. Work activity	Verbal	Written
3. Response required	Often reactive	Often proactive
4. Primary tool used	Telephone	Computer
5. Interaction	Personal	Impersonal
6. Senses used	Hearing	Touch

Experience shows that contact centre management has to completely review the people aspects prior to the introduction of email handling by agents. These include:

- Recruitment and skills assessment
- Training
- Support tools
- New processes and methods
- Holistic view/knowledge management
- Sharing of learning
- Need for consistency
- Escalation support options
- New staff incentives
- Self-management and trust.

When looking to introduce relevant skills to existing agents, some of them will be completely new, such as:

- Understanding new systems and tools
- Written skills
- Keyboard operations
- Email control
- New language for replying to emails.

INTEGRATING INSTANT MESSAGING INTO THE CUSTOMER CONTACT CENTRE

WHAT IS INSTANT MESSAGING?

It can be said that the instant messaging (IM) market is in its infancy; but the speed of growth is staggering and it is the fastest-growing communications medium in history. The market for corporate IM is estimated to grow from 5.5 million users worldwide in 2000 to 181 million in 2004, according to a report from market analyst IDC.

Instant messaging enables users to share a window on their desktops with other users on a network; they can simply exchange short messages with one another in real time. This makes the text interaction and experience unique:

- **Similar to natural verbal communication**: the conversations can be threaded with one user or a group of users (often called group chat).
- **Presence**: you can make it known to other users on a network defined by yourself that you are present for communication.
- **Control over your information**: you can control who can and cannot send messages to you and how you appear to the outside world.

WHAT INSTANT MESSAGING TECHNOLOGIES ARE THERE?

IM products fall into three broad categories:

- **Public system products**: where anyone can download a client and establish an account with a central, Internet-based service. These products include Yahoo Messenger, Microsoft Messenger, ICQ and AOL's two technologies, AOL Instant Messenger and AIM Express.
- **Tied system products**: sometimes provided within the operating system or by a specific enterprise application vendor to which the organization subscribes. The software vendor provides the client in these instances.
- **Private system products**: where you purchase an instant messaging solution and set it up on your internal corporate network and, potentially, website. The client is then provided by a third party hosted service or by the solution vendor.

The choice of solution is not as complex as it seems, as there are key drawbacks to using public system product and some tied system products that make them unusable in a customer contact centre:

- **Security**: there have been numerous instances of hackers being able to use public IM as a means to enter a corporate's networks.
- **Control**: unrestricted usage of IM makes it very difficult to monitor usage and leaves organizations vulnerable to potential litigation.
- **Inter-operability**: many of the public and tied systems do not enable a user to communicate with someone who might be a member of one of the other systems (that is, they are 'closed' from one another).

Therefore for business-to-business and business-to-consumer communication, private systems have become the most common form of IM employed within organizations.

Most packages have the following basic functionalities, including:

- Public and private chat
- Presence (automatically detect who is online and in which status)
- File transfer quickly (using drag and drop)
- Web-based messaging
- Threaded discussions
- Secure interchange of IM across internal and external networks
- Group conference facility – ability to immediately switch to self-created or pre-created rooms
- Multiple levels of online status
- Send a contacts name(s) to other contacts

- Control of IM experience: see who is online, set online status, block, ignore or send away unwanted messages, save or forward IM chats and hold messages while offline. Control which contact list you are with.

Some packages have more sophisticated functions:

- Recording chat
- Generating message logs
- Multi-lingual functions
- Forwarding messages to wireless device or email address
- Conducting polls with charting
- Videoing
- Whiteboarding
- Application sharing
- Customization of messages (for example, fonts, graphics)
- Camp-on features
- Smart notifications (for example with end-users).

Web chat

Web chat is a derivative of instant messaging, in that it is a desktop area where you can interact with another person using IM. This technique is used in such areas as:

- Collaborative browsing: where an end-user and an advisor can interact using instant messaging techniques as they collaboratively view a specific web page together.
- Meet Me/Push Me: where a page is sent to an end-user's desktop and an advisor meets them on the page and interacts with them using instant messaging techniques. Page markup can be used to highlight crucial information that is then mirrored on the customer's browser.

These sorts of technologies are ideal for conducting demonstrations online and for more complex sales situations that need explanation.

WHAT ARE THE CORE BUSINESS BENEFITS OF USING INSTANT MESSAGING?

There are many benefits of using instant messaging within an organization and specifically its call centre. There are also great benefits when using it to engage with customers and prospects. IM saves companies money: by using instant messaging within large and widespread call centres and establishments it acts as a cheap information and community tool.

The key areas of cost saving are:

- Eases the burden on email servers
- Does not need online storage of data
- It is bandwidth efficient and produces minimal network traffic
- Reduces both telephone and travel expenses associated with remote communication
- Acts as central plank of a telecommuter strategy, thus reducing staff and office costs.

IM makes working more efficient. In fast-moving environments, using IM to broadcast and obtain information speedily and securely to topic-related interest groups is of major benefit – for example, the ability to impart prices and information between call centre staff or the sending of instructions in real time and escalating issues to gain advice while customers are on the phone.

Instant messaging creates a team environment for distributed work groups. You can detect team members' presence, exchange information in real time, involve different members in discussion, and gain input/debate – all done when staff may be physically remote or spread across different call centres and organizations.

More general benefits of IM are that it:

- allows users to get right to the business in hand and ask more in-depth questions
- eliminates time spent tracking someone down to answer a question
- improves synergy between different business communications
- fosters a collaborative approach
- creates a central meeting place
- enables a user to handle multi conversations
- enables real-time distance learning, mentoring and training.

IM also helps to increase revenue: it makes for a low-cost customer engagement route with customers in real time to receive their instructions and requests over the Internet, for instance, obtaining requests and delivery instructions (take-away food companies).

IMPROVING THE CUSTOMER JOURNEY

IM can create a customer community and improve customer experience: by implanting IM into a website, it acts as a community builder between like-minded people and interest groups. In effect, it acts as an interaction facilitator within a community, including the company (first used by portals, dot.com services and information companies; but now being incorporated in many companies' sites). An often-quoted adage is that for successful eBusiness you must first build a community before you can harvest revenue.

IM is a core CRM (Customer Relationship Management) tool for customer support and technical assistance: providing a customer route through your site using instant messaging directly into your contact centre provides enormous benefits for the company and the end-user, not the least being reduced costs (see below) because a customer service representative (CSR) can handle several enquiries at once and some amount of automated responses can be integrated in a similar manner to automated email.

However, while IM is not the cheapest support medium, it does provide one of the most satisfactory experiences for a customer:

- Instant speedy personal support when the customer wants and needs it
- Interacting and leaving personalized reference information and advice
- Increased resolved issues because the CSR is able to escalate an issue and involve better skilled people in the conversation as required.

Figure 20.2 shows how cost percentages vary between web-based support and telephone support.

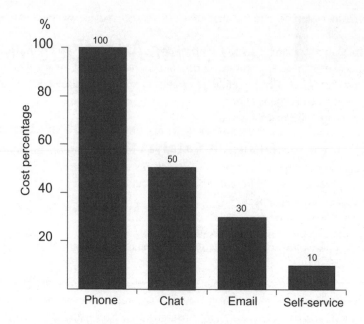

Figure 20.2   Web-based support costs compared to phone © Giga

COMBINING VIDEO WITH THE CONTACT CENTRE

An excellent example of using video to enhance the customer experience is the service provided by East Riding of Yorkshire Council, UK. As the largest unitary council in England and with a widely distributed population, the council decided to open 11 customer services centres providing a 'one-stop shop' for all council services. IT Development Manager, Jenny Sergeant said, 'this still was not enough for our chief executive or the council members. Our driver is to provide high-quality services accessible to all our citizens.'

The customer service centres provide a face-to-face service to personal callers and two integrated call centre sites provide a telephone service – with additional back-up as required from the customer service centres which are also integrated into the virtual contact centre infrastructure. With the council's catchment area at over 300 000, this still left many communities of around 10 000 people with no physical council presence. Thus the CitizenLink was 'born'.

Situated in local amenities (such as a Safeway's store) or built as a stand-alone unit, the CitizenLink provides a secure, welcoming environment equipped with video link, voice link and document scanner to interact with the council's contact centre team. As Jenny Sergeant reported 'One customer said it was just like talking to a real person – well, it is!'

This development is now an integral part of East Riding's CRM strategy and e-government strategy to deliver a holistic approach to the council's citizens utilizing information and communication technology. The council's aim is to enable public services that are accessible, responsive, innovating, high quality and efficient. The CitizenLink with its video, voice and image capability is an excellent example of customer-focused contact centre technology in action.

21 *Customer Management in Practice*

Dave Howard, Executive Direcctor and Founder, Catalyst IT

This chapter examines customer management and the role that technology plays in delivering a great customer journey.

BACKGROUND

Customer management is a comprehensive approach that provides seamless integration of every area of business that touches the customer – namely marketing, sales, customer service and field support – through the integration of people, process and technology, taking advantage of the revolutionary impact of the Internet. A typical organization will seek to create an integrated commercial environment by means of an enabling programme that will bring together information, technology, skills and processes so that useable, timely information can support effective customer relationship management. While definitions vary wildly, it is suggested that there are a number of key Customer Relationship Management (CRM) components.

ESTABLISHING CUSTOMER MANAGEMENT BUSINESS REQUIREMENTS

- **Marketing, sales and service functionality** needs to provide campaign management, lead generation, lead qualification and lead tracking capabilities with underlying support for market segmentation, opportunity management, brochure handling and product/pricing configuration to manage marketing and campaigns. Separate (but closely integrated applications) may be targeted by marketing to address the details of campaign management and customer database analysis tools. Specific sales needs include account management, contact management, order entry and proposal generators.
- **Customer service and support functionality** should include incident assignment/escalation/ tracking, problem management/resolution, order management and warranty/contract management in addition to business-specific transactions and workflow. CRM functionality may be required as part of a sector-specific application or may run in tandem with specialist sector-specific systems as a 'front end' customer contact system.
- **Contact centre and e-commerce functionality** should include call list assembly, telephony integration, scripting and call tracking to support the marketing, sales and service requirements of the call centre and e-commerce. Systems should provide web-based, front-end interfaces into the Customer Interaction Portal (CIP) and commercially available, third party e-commerce engines. The systems selected should be capable of supporting business-to-business as well as business-to-consumer e-commerce applications. This increasingly includes

customer self-service using a web-browser and web-based marketing/product encyclopedias. As well as a CIP to interface with customers, contact management systems require enterprise portals to provide distribution channels and end-users with direct access to real-time and historical information coming from internal applications, legacy databases, the Internet, and third-party sources, all via a web browser. As well as thinking about how to provide information to users, there need to be facilities to import and utilize data from external sources during online transactions.

THE GENERAL BUSINESS NEEDS OF THE ORGANIZATION

There are a number of general business requirements that may not come readily to mind when addressing contact centre needs – time management functionality (calendar/scheduling) and email being at the top of the list. Extensive and easy-to-use reporting capabilities are important, as is the integration with all other parts of the organization.

Enterprise Resource Planning integration functionality provides the tools to integrate CRM systems (front-office systems) with legacy systems (back-office systems), the web, and third-party external information sources. Providing the links is one thing – if the two sides of the link refer to different data we have a problem and so excellent data synchronization functionality becomes very important. This covers multiple field devices (wired or wireless), as well as business synchronization with multiple databases/application servers. A relationship with a customer cannot be managed effectively if systems show two current addresses in different areas of infrastructure.

While our focus is on customer interaction via call centres and e-commerce, the research and selection of CRM systems must take account of the organization's requirements for field service support functionality. This would include providing work orders, dispatching and real-time information transfer to field personnel using mobile technologies. Similarly, unless the organization has a strong focus on sales management, it is easy to overlook functionality to track future orders, sales analysis, forecasting, sales metrics and territory assignment.

While this section contains an extensive range of functionality, it is appreciated that an organization will probably opt to concentrate on delivering a few core modules in key business functional areas as an initial phase. However, to compete for first-class customer relationships the systems selected must be capable of being developed to meet the full scope of CRM requirements. During a recent project to evaluate potential CRM systems, a UK organization started with 132 potential suppliers on its 'long list' prior to the work aimed at producing a short list. Clearly, systems mentioned in this section can only be examples of what is available in the open market.

WHAT CRM CAN DO FOR OUR CONTACT CENTRE

The impact of CRM should be considered in terms of:

- The market proposition and the brand
- The products and services
- The competencies, cultures and behaviours
- The organization and partnerships
- The business processes
- The IT systems.

To check that the value exchange is preserved and the desired behaviour and performance from a customer's perspective is achieved, a performance improvement and benefit realization framework is used along with the customer experience model. Figure 21.1 shows how the approach fits together.

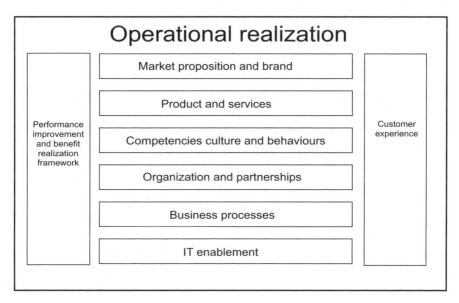

Figure 21.1   Operation realization of CRM © Catalyst IT

So how do you use this approach? This can be best illustrated by the case of a financial services company that recently launched a new investment management proposition targeted solely at the IFA (independent financial advisor) distribution channel. It was designed to give advisors access to modern portfolio construction techniques previously only available to large institutions such as pensions funds and insurance companies, and offers a sophisticated range of web-based investment tools supported by a true multimedia contact centre. However, the company's whole ethos was based around making the IFA's life easier, so if they didn't want to use the modern portfolio construction techniques, they didn't have to. Or if the IFA didn't want to use the web-based tools, business could be submitted on paper or over the phone.

This was a new business venture and, while there were no legacy constraints, the downside was that there was no fully formed management team to share in the shaping of the key decisions. The project was constrained by budget and the need to launch the business in a robust way.

The initial phase of the project involved making the following key decisions:

1   The long-term market proposition plus brand values and phasing of the product launch.
2   The key business processes that would be required, especially those required for launch.
3   The customer experience – what would it be like to deal with us across all our nominated channels?

Having made these decisions, the key enablers were then examined.

IT SYSTEM

IT decisions both in terms of functionality and suppliers needed to be taken early on which was not straightforward, as the management team had not yet been fully formed. The general philosophy was that if it was going to be complicated to build, or complicated to understand, then it would probably be complicated to use. As a result, it was kept simple for the launch and any additional complexity would be added later.

ORGANIZATION

This new venture describes itself as a 'clicks and people' business. The technology used would be for the sake of the business and not just technology for its own sake. An overriding principle was that anything on the web had to be intuitive and easy to use. Should anyone have any difficulty, they could call their named contact in the service centre for help.

The IT company's whole function is to make the IFA's life easier: by reducing paperwork, speeding up processes, helping with the complexities of regulation or easing the portfolio construction process, only then will the IFA become a repeat customer.

PERFORMANCE MANAGEMENT

The performance management framework assist in managing teams and key individuals to ensure that their performance is aligned to the key business principles. In this case study, both sales and back-office staff were offered bonuses based on sales generated over the web. This meant that if non-web business came in, staff would have an opportunity to talk to the customer (for example, thanks for the business) and at the same time try to understand why the customer didn't use the web. In all cases, the customer is happy because they've had someone do something that makes their job easier, and the business is happy because transactions are now coming in over the more economic web channel.

CUSTOMER EXPERIENCE

In reality there was considerable overlap between these enablers, but the one constant that was used to inform all the critical decisions was quality and consistency of the customer experience. To achieve a customer-centric solution, 'friendly' IFAs were consulted throughout to help drive and prioritize the system requirements and review the functionality throughout the development phase. This was a great idea, but the trouble with customers is that they all do things differently. So, while one IFA might want automatic portfolio construction, another would feel that it took away his or her control of the situation. If one thought submitting business over the web would solve all of the paperwork problems, another would point out how unreliable websites could be. But the key point is that this new business asked its customers what they wanted. The end result was a complete business proposition that was integrated and totally aligned to the IFA distribution channel.

SUMMARY

The idea that you can manage customer relationships is both arrogant and flawed as most customers don't want a relationship – they just want their business taken care of as promised. Managing customer interactions in a consistent way to an agreed service level is the real source of competitive advantage. However, the underlying concepts of CRM remain valid and the difference between success and failure is in the execution.

Using a proven approach and a framework for execution and using simulation to preview the future can significantly de-risk major change programmes and take the guesswork out of major decisions. This provides an accurate and detailed baseline of the current state and identifies the key levers that will result in the most significant payback. Finally, the adoption of programme and transition management that integrates tactical and strategic change will ensure that the desired changes actually happen and the benefits are realized.

22 *Self-Service*

Peter McCarthy, Chairman, iSKY Europe

SELF-SERVICE, BUT NOT AS WE KNOW IT

The concepts of customer relationship management (CRM), customer-managed relationships and 24/7 'any media' service (phone, web, mobile and so on) is compelling. The natural home for their delivery is the contact centre – which presents its managers with a broader and deeper challenge than ever before.

New and innovative ways of delivering service and information have, thankfully, developed. Having started life as a 'hole in the wall' to get cash, order bank statements and make balance enquiries, self-service has grown up into a sophisticated customer service tool ideal for routine transactions. Examples include booking cinema tickets through an automated IVR (Interactive Voice Recognition) system, or giving meter readings to a utility company.

The financial services sector still leads the way – for example, customers of at least one bank can register to receive SMS (short message service) texts on their mobile phone, giving a statement and balance – perfect when you are on the move. A leading building society is also working on enabling access via hand-held personal digital assistants (PDAs) to provide a wealth of data and information. Other sectors have adopted online self-service: it is used extensively by the travel industry, particularly airlines and ferries. However it is recommended that the appropriateness of an online approach is fully tested and sampled within individual markets and sectors.

Cheaper, wider access to phone, web and mobile means the boundaries of self-service are changing rapidly. The customer in each of us demands convenience and accessibility. We want to access the services we need, when we want to, using the channel we choose. As soon as we key in our account number or password, we expect that system – whether it belongs to a bank, airline or utility – to know who we are. Fast.

AUTOMATE FOR ACCESS

Self-service is driven by the need to optimize the relationship with the customer, but at the same time not let the cost of service spiral out of control. If you are an organization with a million customers, ten products and five different channels to market including web, phone and email, you have 50 million different permutations.

Automation facilitates self-service, while data capture, storage and analysis capabilities and data mining enhance its value. Successful self-service needs smart integrated systems that bring the data to the point of the customer's touch. Whether via a kiosk in a department store, an IVR application, mobile, SMS, email or website access, the data has to be delivered to that touch-point so that it is available to the customer when he or she needs it.

UNDERSTANDING CUSTOMER VALUE

Traditionally customer value has been considered the key to how we should respond, electing that high-value customers should talk to a live operator while low-value customers could use a cheaper form of communication, that is, self-service. This no longer holds true. High-value customers may prefer the convenience of access to self-service-type operations most of the time, while low-value customers will sometimes need help from a live operator.

Self-service is signalling a change in thinking behind CRM: it is about each customer managing their own relationships with an ever-widening range of organizations. We now know the approach preferred depends more on the type of transaction or information required, rather than the value of the customer. Offer your customers the right channel for the right occasion.

When fighting for funding, capital expenditure arguments will often quote the cost of service and ROI (return on investment). Offering attractive self-service options can cut the cost of a transaction to a fraction of its 'live assistance' counterpart – and today you can also legitimately argue that many of your customers prefer it.

Most importantly, however, self-service should be used to reduce the need for personal interactions, rather than an attempt to eliminate them from any particular application. This is as true for the Internet as it is for the phone.

HYPE OR HAPPENING?

Technology provides new ways of recognizing speech, so we rely less on having to key in numbers on a keypad. As IVR (interactive voice response) becomes more sophisticated, companies are developing ways of using it more creatively. Using words rather than keys to communicate is more natural for us, more accessible, and will bring into the equation new tranches of customers choosing self-service.

Historically, the web involved simply moving data across a network. Now, with collaborative browsing and the advent of VoIP (Voice over Internet Protocol), applications can more closely mimic a human interaction.

A great deal of hype has grown up around different technologies and mobile is no exception. Third generation mobile technology (3G) enables us to have not just text but data, video and more, pumped down the airwaves and into a mobile phone, making it more of a communications than a telephony device.

LOOKING AHEAD

More sophisticated SIR (speaker-independent recognition) technology will have a major impact on self-service. Before long, instead of giving instructions by keying in numbers or letters, customers will talk to a SIR system to place orders. Sitting alongside this will be software to analyse natural language more efficiently. As well as understanding what people say, the technology will seek and recognize commonality, thus speeding up the communications process. Orders will then be automatically transcribed and loaded into a business's database.

Another breakthrough for self-service technology will happen through the personal card. All our personal data will be held on one chip – protected by a security procedure, of course – and used as the 'key' to a number of different channels of communication. Swiped through the reader in your mobile phone, it will give instant verification of name and account details and validate transactions and credit.

When choosing technology for self-service, take care. Understand your customers and the contact processes, how they buy now and how this might change if a better approach was offered. Look at the technologies available to improve both the processes and level of service that can be delivered, and only then think about the kind of engine required to use that technology and serve your customers. After all, your aim is to make it as easy as possible for customers to use their preferred channel to communicate with you.

23 *Quality Management: Technology Perspective*

Paul Smedley, Execcutive Director, Professional Planning Forum and John Wilkinson, Vice President, Sales and Alliances – Europe, Witness Systems

We are no longer constrained by the idea of producing a staff roster to match call volumes and recording calls to provide 'evidence' proving we were right when the customer has the audacity to complain. This chapter looks at a landscape that includes sophisticated workforce management systems, which support forecasting of contact centre traffic and the scheduling of staff and automated resources to meet demand. This same landscape includes systems to record, track and analyse performance and customer experiences within the customer interaction centre. Additional functionality aims at improvement, by targeting specific performance measures.

WORKFORCE MANAGEMENT: PREDICTING QUALITY SERVICE

Despite all the technology, the Customer Interaction Portal can only route calls to an agent to deal with the customer enquiry – provided there is an agent available to take the call! Workforce management software ensures the right people are in the right place at the right time. A workforce management system should be capable of imitating exactly your current ways of operation in the contact centre. This will soon show you where improvements can be made and these can then be implemented at your own pace. So ensure, for example, that the software can manage rotating shifts if you use them.

Workforce management enables the efficient use of manpower to meet customer demand while managing overtime, breaks and other off-phone activities more proactively. Contact centre managers can manage their operation in a more dynamic fashion and provide all areas of the centre with coordinated support. This allows the business to be run more effectively and service levels can be maintained without overruns on budget and costs. Customers benefit from fast response times and having staff with the right training and knowledge available to deal with their enquiry.

Contact centre staff benefit from more sociable work patterns to meet their specific needs, with scheduled breaks, training and management time. Managers can assess the impact of giving breaks instead of relying on 'gut-feel' and staff are advised automatically of any roster changes.

If the forecasts of calls, emails and Web contacts are accurate, the staff scheduling functionality of a workforce management system will make best available use of staff, placing even more emphasis upon the quality of forecasting. In addition to past experience – historical traffic volumes and arrival patterns – we need to take account of seasonal trends and external influences (for example, a heat wave will impact on an air-conditioning hire company!). We also need to take account of internal influences controlled by the wider organization. In this way, the contact centre needs to be part of the decision-making process for marketing and sales campaigns that will drive either direct response or customer service feedback.

EVALUATING PERFORMANCE

Systems are available to record, track and analyse performance and customer experiences within the customer interaction centre and aims at improvement, by targeting specific performance measures. These systems can capture voice, screen activity and other data – the days of the tape recorder and even the voice recorder have passed by.

INTEGRATED SOLUTIONS

With the benefit of Computer Telephony Integration (CTI) capabilities we can support both fixed and hot-seating environments. By adapting to multimedia environments, including Voice over Internet Protocol (VoIP), email and Web interactions, the full range of customer contact can be recorded, monitored, played back and analysed. Play-back interactions are available via phone extension, dedicated speaker or through the local area network (LAN) using PC sound cards. This provides all the 'traditional' call logging-type capabilities used in the financial services arena and other sectors to record interactions as 'evidence' as to whether transactions have been carried out correctly. It also opens the door to much wider quality management applications.

There are really exciting solutions which provide all the tools needed to implement a world-class quality monitoring programme, including scheduled voice and screen recording, online call evaluation forms, and reporting calibration tools that ensure consistency between evaluators. By creating personalized, focused, online surveys, organizations can gather feedback on the customer experience – from the customer's viewpoint. This begins to provide organizations with a 360° view of the customer experience. Customers are invited to participate in web surveys whilst interacting online or via personalised emails. Organizations can then receive real-time customer feedback in the form of reports, tables, graphs, verbatim responses, mean scores and alert systems. This provides a side-by-side comparison from both the contact centre adviser and the customer aspects of the communications experience.

COMPLETING THE QUALITY CIRCLE

Once we have captured interactions and analysed the quality by evaluating voice, screen, email, chat, web co-browsing, and other contacts the obvious next step is to identify areas for improvement and take action. Collaboration between contact evaluation vendors and online knowledge-based training providers has resulted in solutions that can deliver smart multimedia training sessions directly to agent desktops. By using recorded content for training needs analysis, real-time reports automatically trigger the delivery of specific training modules to agents, based on quality evaluation results and on agent profile information. Online reports enable agents to view their own quality management and training scores as well as a summary of available training modules.

WORKFORCE MANAGEMENT CASE STUDY – STREAM INTERNATIONAL

EFFECTIVE RESOURCE PLANNING … AND HOW TO MAKE IT HAPPEN …

The need to understand your call workload and get the right people in the right place at the right time can often be seen most clearly in the stories of those who have grappled with the problems of improving service within a limited budget.

Take, for example, global outsourcers Stream International. In one contract, traditional staffing plans did not always match volume changes, so that service levels could be lower than expected despite being at budgeted staffing levels. As an outsourcer, Stream were accountable for improving service level within the agreed staffing budget. This meant they had to find ways of using existing agent-hours differently, to provide more consistent service at key times. The planning team did this in two phases.

Phase 1

First, the team went back to basics and identified specific patterns as identified in Figure 23.1 or factors behind the resource shortfalls:

- Agents were working the same shift patterns every week with no consideration given to changing requirements or the impact of holidays/sickness.
- The service level dropped throughout the afternoon but was high at the start of the day.
- The 'standard shift' of a nine-hour day with one hour lunch was causing huge problems in service levels between 12 p.m.–2 p.m.
- Mondays and Tuesdays were busy. Friday afternoons were quiet.

A key issue for this centre involved the scheduling of lunches and breaks. First steps for the planning team included:

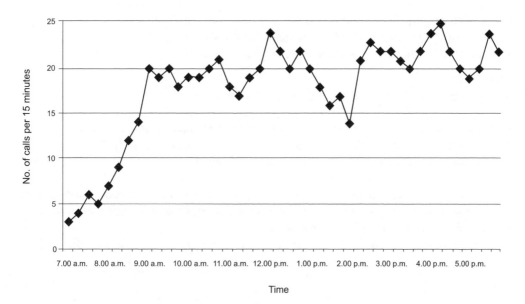

Figure 23.1   Call arrival pattern © Professional Planning Forum

- Asking for volunteers for a 30-minute lunch period and in exchange start at 8.30 a.m. instead of 8.00 a.m.
- Focusing on the afternoon – to make sure they had adequate numbers of staff across the afternoon.
- Implementing some longer shifts on Monday/Tuesday and giving the agents Friday afternoon off in lieu.

Phase 2

This phase included the implementation of a workforce management system and allowed the team to look at more detailed solutions such as:

- **Cross-skilling**: This was popular since it allowed agents variety in their work, and efficient because paying five agents £1000 extra per year is cheaper than hiring an extra agent and the effect on service levels is greater.
- **Flexing/moving shifts**: Agreement to move agents' start/finish times by 30 minutes meant that Stream could cover holiday/training/sickness with less impact on service levels.
- **Holiday allocations**: Restricting single days off on a Monday, because it was the busiest day and encouraging people to take long weekends by being off on Fridays, which were quieter.
- **Short-notice changes**: Stream created a 'fire brigade' team who would change their working hours at very short notice, to accommodate unpredictable volumes of calls and limit the impact on others.

Immediate results

Stream experienced service level increases of up to 15 per cent when compared to past performance. Overall, excellent service levels were achieved consistently with no increase in staffing costs. Key to the success was agreement on the scheduling or work rules for agents, such as:

- agreeing flexibility in breaks as well as avoiding fixed start/end times
- using template rotas to enable fairness and to make change easier
- regularly using the flexibility that has been agreed – or lose it!

Lessons to learn

So how do you get the best results? There are some basics:

- Track the right data by half hour or quarter hour in order to forecast your call workload.
- Identify and agree the working rules and practices that your centre requires.
- Have well-oiled processes for communicating resourcing needs.

In the past many call centre managers were required to forecast and schedule in their spare time with little training or no help. Even specialist planners in the larger call centres could be isolated, without formal training or accreditation.

Now, even the basics require a highly skilled specialist and it is a sign of the times that new call centres now look for this experience from the very beginning.

IV *Standards, Processes and Outsourcing*

Developing the processes, standards and governance within the contact centre operation ensures that synergy exists between people and technologies. Procedures, designed in a customer-centric manner, enable organizations to really add value on each and every contact in a planned, controlled and measurable way.

- The CCA Standard Framework
- Developing Customer-Centric Processes
- Workforce Management Process
- Resource Management
- Quality Monitoring and Service Improvement
- Outsourcing

24 *The CCA Standard Framework*

Colin Mackay, Director and Company Secretary, Call Centre Association

Can there be an organization anywhere that does not claim to work to a standard? There can be no doubt that standards are a good thing. Understanding how they impact on your business is critical to its success. How they should be set, including a proper focus on the standard and not on any targets by which it is measured, can be the difference between business success and failure. Measuring standards, and understanding and resolving the issues that are thrown up by that measurement process, can be one route to continuous improvement. This chapter examines the standard developed by the CCA.

BACKGROUND

The Call Centre Association (CCA), with Department of Trade and Industry (DTI) Support, has developed the CCA standard framework for best practice. This is a unique, commercially neutral and annually reviewed process that establishes guidelines around company policies in areas including staff training, review of customer complaints and career progression. All CCA members are now required to commit to the principles of the Standard and, optionally, to be independently assessed through the British Standards Institution to ensure they are meeting CCA framework criteria. The framework is monitored and kept relevant by a board of industry experts who have full control of its development. This is one of a number of standards available in the UK, including those of the British Quality Foundation, ISO 9000 and Investors in People. It is the one that is most relevant to contact centres, having been designed specifically as an operational standard for that medium.

WHY DOES THE CONTACT CENTRE INDUSTRY NEED A RECOGNIZED OPERATIONAL STANDARD?

The contact centre environment is constantly changing and will continue to develop as technology provides ever greater opportunities. The primary objective of a recognized standard is to support organizations with a framework in which clear decisions can be taken on the delivery of good performance and fulfilment of expectation for staff and customers.

Its people are a key element in any successful contact centre. A standard is an enabler to providing high levels of service and differentiation within the marketplace. Applying a recognized set of standards within a centre will facilitate moves towards the multi-channel, multi-skill environment of today's contact centre.

CONFIDENCE

Improving technology requires significant investment, and financial decisions must be backed by confidence in contact centre performance. Being aware that their centre adheres to a standard, particularly one that is specific while remaining commercially neutral, and is focused on staff and customers, will facilitate that confidence in senior managers. Promoting efficiency and growth through people helps to ensure that expected returns on investment will be achieved.

VALUING PEOPLE

Staff, aware of the detail of a recognized standard, will see it being applied. They will feel valued, which will positively impact on stress and attrition levels. If the standard has a training element that it is both measured and effective this will improve customer service and ensure efficient targeted spend.

CUSTOMER EXPECTATIONS

It is essential also that a recognized standard focuses on customers and is designed to improve public perception of individual organizations and the industry as a whole. It should be in the public domain, and customers should be able to identify what to expect from a well-run centre.

QUALITY

Overall, a standard can provide a comprehensive guide to the activities that *should* be taking place in a well-run call centre. It should reflect the views on contact centre management of successful companies, experienced individuals and serious players within the industry.

THE CCA OPERATIONAL STANDARD

The CCA standard framework provides a template for the development of a comprehensive, tailored organizational standard. It is complete in itself as an operational standard and comprises five sections, which can be seen in detail on the CCA website (www.cca.org.uk).

In summary, the framework covers the specific areas of:

- **People**, dealing with such issues as training and development, including the acquisition of recognized industry qualifications
- **Communication**, addressing the need to gather employees' views and to have formal dispute resolution processes in place
- **Culture**, covering the overarching issues of compliance, development planning processes and attrition rates
- **Policies and legislation**, addressing the need for managers and staff to be fully up to date with legislation, including data protection
- **Performance**, both in terms of service performance and organizational efficiency, encouraging organizations to have prescribed standards for all key activities in the call centre including the gathering of customer feedback information.

THE STANDARD IS NOT PRESCRIPTIVE

Critically, there is no sense in which the standard is prescriptive. Processes and the means by which the standard principle is achieved is at the discretion of the organization. The CCA standard simply creates a *framework* within which contact centres of all kinds can set measurable standards. As the framework enters more into the public awareness, the CCA intends that it will be a differentiator allowing the public to identify contact centres that subscribe to a clearly recognized standard.

CCA STANDARD: A FRAMEWORK FOR BEST PRACTICE©

The statements contained in the CCA framework are intended to identify key focus areas. The CCA acknowledges that there is no single route to standards achievement. Methods supporting the framework and inputs are entirely at the discretion of participating organizations although, eventually, each has to be approved by the Standards Board as being effective before accreditation can be granted.

1   Your People
   1.1   Employees at all levels are given mandatory training and development to support them in their role so as to enable achievement of their own and the organization's objectives.
   1.2   Training effectiveness is measured and the outputs acted upon.
   1.3   A Performance Development process is in place and employees' personal development plans are the norm.
   1.4   Individual employees are aware of their personal and/or team objectives and organizational goals together with the means by which they are monitored.
   1.5   Employees at all levels are encouraged and supported in achieving recognized Industry Qualifications and in ongoing learning.

2   Communication within the Call Centre
   2.1   Processes are in place to gather employees' views, disseminate information and take appropriate action.
   2.2   A documented process is available to resolve inter-employees and employee(s)/management disputes.

3   Culture
   3.1   A legally compliant recruitment Policy exists.
   3.2   There is a commitment to provide an honest forecast of potential for progression or development.
   3.3   A Development Planning process is in place covering all employees.
   3.4   Measures are set for attrition and attendance. Plans are in place to achieve or maintain these.
   3.5   Employees' benefit and welfare processes are in place and are communicated to all employees.
   3.6   Where rotas exist, the need for them and the process for their establishment is communicated to all employees.

4   Policies and Legislation Affecting Your Operation
   4.1   A process is in place to ensure that developing legislative requirements are brought to the attention of management.
   4.2   Managers and Supervisors are trained in the application of current legislation and are mandated to apply it.

    4.3   All employees are aware of the organizational commitment to the regulations imposed as a result of memberships of industry associations.

    4.4   All employees are aware of the requirements of the Data Protection Act.

5   Service Performance and Organizational Efficiency

    5.1   Standards have been set for key activities related to the call centre and are measured.

    5.2   Standards are understood by employees and plans are in place to achieve/maintain the standards agreed.

    5.3   Customer Complaints are logged and reviewed. Action is taken to eliminate recurring complaints.

    5.4   A complaints handling process is in place with target response times. Plans are in place to achieve/maintain targets.

    5.5   A process is in place to gather customer feedback. Measures are set for satisfaction and plans are in place to achieve/maintain targets.

    5.6   Arrangements are in place to manage call centre internal relationships with other business areas and to identify, review and resolve issues as they arise.

    5.7   Contingency and resiliency plans are in place, are kept up to date and are practised.

    5.8   Forecasting and business planning are in place to manage the impact of activity on the operations.

The CCA will maintain and develop the standard framework through the CCA Advisory Board. The CCA affirms its copyright of the standard and alterations or amendments not approved by the CCA Advisory Board are invalid. Formal accreditation of performance against the standard is only possible using options approved by the CCA Advisory Board.

25 Developing Customer-Centric Processes

Stephen Parry, Head of Strategy and Change, Fujitsu Services

In contact centres, as with any other organization, processes work at many levels. This chapter will deal primarily with the processes for products or services as these have the highest impact on the customer experience and work design.

WHAT IS A PROCESS?

A process may be defined as: 'An organized group of related activities that together create a result of value to customers' (M. Hammer, *The Agenda*, Random House, 2001). A company needs good processes to satisfy its customers and deliver excellent business results.

All work is a process and must be subject to constant improvement. In today's rapidly changing world, the nature of demand from customers is also changing. It is only through constantly improving processes that organizations can put their customers first. Where processes are unsuited to the needs of the customer, the service experience always worsens and costs rise. Customers can sense when a call centre advisor is sticking to ill-fitting processes or scripts, rather than solving their problems.

Once a contact centre organization has developed a method for identifying the nature of customer demand and has the ability to measure its response, it is far easier to recognize new demands, then react accordingly. It follows that any organization with effective process management is better positioned to deal with rapid change and maximize the potential return from its customers.

TIME-SHARING CUSTOMERS

Products and services are delivered via processes that often cut across functions. Most companies break work into functional specialities and pass the customer between departments where staff are usually focused on their local goals, budgets and targets. In effect, organizations time-share their customers. However, as far as the customer is concerned, functional boundaries and departments are of little interest. What matters to the customer is whether value is created and delivered to them.

All processes should be a natural reflection of customer needs. In spite of this, companies often design processes without considering the impact on their customers. The end-to-end process, from call arrival through to final delivery of products or services, creates customer value. Therefore, understanding how the combined efforts of teams and departments effectively deliver against customer demand-types and expectations becomes fundamental to the success of any organization.

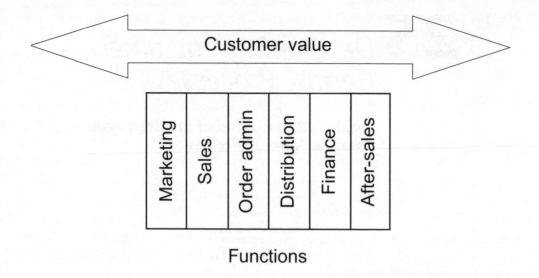

Figure 25.1   Customer values across the business functions © Fujitsu Services

Cross-functional, as shown in Figure 25.1, or end-to-end measures provide call centres with a solid foundation for establishing effective processes. This, combined with process management, will enable the organization to serve customers cost-effectively.

PROCESS MANAGEMENT

It is recommended that process measurement is in place before any attempts are made to improve customer service. Otherwise, the problem may worsen for both customers and call centre advisors. The priority is to define a 'measure' that records the end-to-end workflow, even when the service or product delivery is external to the call centre. The measure should also provide a means of investigation into operational performance, identifying and prioritizing areas for redesign and improvement.

The objective of process management is to:

- increase customer satisfaction
- increase revenue
- reduce operating costs.

These are achieved by identifying the work value, tracking its flow from start to finish, measuring how well the organization responds, and eliminating the causes of 'failure'.

VALUE DEMAND AND FAILURE DEMAND

In order to improve and redesign processes, organizations need to know what type of demand the call centre is attracting. In all contact centres, indeed any type of business, there are two types of demand: the type the business wants and the type it does not. Another way to describe this would be to class the demand the organization desires as 'value' and the other as 'failure'.

John Seddon, an occupational psychologist and author, describes value and failure demand in the following way:

Failure demand is demand caused by a failure of the system, for example 'it did not arrive on time', 'it's not what I ordered', 'my bill is wrong', 'you didn't get back to me' and so on.

Value demand is what companies should be designed to respond to, for example 'give me service', 'can I buy?', 'which is better?' and so on.

Seddon, Transforming call centre operations, *Journal of Call Centre Management*, 1999

SIX-STEP PROCESS

To understand how processes create value for customers, a 'six-step' process should be followed:

1 Understand the nature of demand, as expressed by the customer.
2 Create end-to-end measures, related to 'what matters to customers'.
3 Understand the cause(s) of performance variation.
4 Understand what creates value for customers.
5 Define the purpose.
6 Separate 'value' and 'failure' demand.

Most organizations begin by attempting to identify the purpose; however, this should be step five, not step one. For an informed definition of purpose, the company must first understand the needs of its customers and how well they are being served. Therefore, steps one to four examine what matters to customers, the nature of their demands, and how well the company responds. Steps five to six examine the actions required to improve the contact centre operation.

UNDERSTAND THE NATURE OF DEMAND

Listening in to customer calls and noting their first question or statement is a simple and effective way to gain insight into the nature of demand. After that, pose the following questions to advisors:

- How predictable are these types of demand in terms of frequency and volume?
- What value is created at the first point of contact and can it be increased?
- Is the call centre handling what it is designed to handle, or is other 'unwanted' demand appearing?

A common method for collating customer statements and questions is affinity mapping:

- Having listened to calls and recorded the customer's first statement, write all the comments onto separate Post-it® stickers.
- Group together the statements that have features in common. For example, 'it did not arrive on time', 'it's not what I ordered', 'my bill is wrong', 'you didn't get back to me', 'give me service', 'can I buy?', 'which is better?' and so on.

In general, a maximum of six to eight group headings will cover 90 per cent of the total customer demand. Experiment with different group headings until the results are satisfactory. Having identified the demand types, investigates how well the company currently performs in response.

CREATE END-TO-END MEASURES

There are two dimensions to processes: effectiveness and efficiency. To illustrate, a person may have a highly efficient car providing 60 miles per gallon; however, if the driver is in Cardiff and needs to be in London, heading towards Manchester is hardly effective. Understanding how processes perform in both dimensions is fundamental to the avoidance of costly mistakes. Processes need to be effective in delivering what matters to the customers (purpose) while being efficient for the organization.

In the early days, the call centre industry, in order to reduce operating costs, put measures in place to drive greater efficiencies, usually at the expense of the customer and the call centre employees. Many overlooked the effectiveness dimension. Using efficiency measures alone will always worsen customer service and increase stress in the workplace.

Effectiveness measures are not the same as efficiency-related output measures. Output measures, such as 'the number of calls answered' or 'total sales', may indicate that a problem exists but does not specify what to do about it.

End-to-end effectiveness measures indicate how well any process responds to demand. For example, whenever type 'A' demand arrives, the end-to-end measure indicates it always takes approximately one hour, give or take 15 minutes, to respond. In a telesales environment, a typical end-to-end measure could be 'the elapsed time from order taken to final delivery'.

End-to-end effectiveness measures predict how well organizations will respond, provided there is no change to the process or any unusual occurrences. Once the elapsed time for delivery is known, a company can make an informed decision as to whether or not it wants to improve matters. If changes to the process are made, the same end-to-end measure can be used to gauge the effectiveness of that change.

When focus is on the end-to-end effectiveness measure, people in the process begin to learn and understand what factors influence service. Once an effective process is in place, then the organization can set about making the process efficient.

UNDERSTAND THE CAUSES OF PERFORMANCE VARIATION

A plethora of sophisticated tools and software packages is available to contact centres for predicting volumes, resource planning and the like. While many of these tools are useful, the information they collect is only partial. The tools and software packages lack the ability to identify the end-to-end processes and practices that inhibit good service. However, the information is, and always has been, available if an organization knows where to look.

By tracking, over time, the end-to-end workflow, it is possible to identify the typical processes, procedures, practices, dependencies and bottlenecks that cause continuously deterioration to service. Collectively, these types of failure are referred to as the 'common causes of variation'. They are common to the way processes have been designed, implemented and operated.

If something out of the ordinary occurs, it is usually due to a special cause. The ability to separate special causes from common causes of variation in performance is fundamental to process management. Unless a company is planning for contingencies, it makes little sense to implement procedures or processes for events that are neither controllable nor predictable.

Use the skills and knowledge of front-line staff to establish what factors contribute to poor service. Some of these causes may be, for example, out-of-stock items, poor product or service information, and slow IT systems that inhibit performance. In such an environment, when advisors strive to meet their quota of calls, they are tempted to make the numbers and put the needs of the customer last.

Collecting this data is key to improving both customer and employee satisfaction. Once it is obtained, it is imperative that the company use it to make the necessary changes and use the end-to-end effectiveness measures to check if service has improved.

UNDERSTAND WHAT CREATES VALUE FOR CUSTOMERS

When ringing a call centre, customers want the person who takes the call to help them, or they want to be transferred quickly to someone who can. If advisors are only logging calls and then passing them to other departments, they are not adding value to the customer. In many ways, work is fragmented, increasing costs and customer dissatisfaction.

Processes should be designed that enable front-line advisors to give customers what they want or need in a single call. It may not be possible every time; however, the 'one-touch principle' should be a design rule for processes. When the work that actually creates value for the customer is moved closer to the first point of contact, customer satisfaction will increase and the end-to-end delivery costs will decrease, since the need for rework, call-backs, handovers and call stacking will have been removed from the design.

Providing advisors with access to information that will allow them to make decisions will improve overall quality. When demand has to be routed elsewhere, ensure that it is passed on without the need for rework or follow-up phone calls. In order to create value for customers, advisors need to have the correct level of product training, tools and systems, allowing them to make decisions based on what matters to the customer.

DEFINE THE PURPOSE

It is easy to become confused about what matters to customers and to lose sight of the real purpose. Unless the real purpose is known and articulated, it cannot be measured. Therefore, no improvements can be made. By contrast, once the real purpose is understood and measured from a customer perspective, it becomes obvious what needs to be changed.

If call centres were to look at the nature of demand they currently receive, they might identify a new purpose or re-appraise the delivery processes. When these centres re-evaluate the purpose, they may reclassify today's value demand as failure demand.

Organizations must have clarity of purpose from the point of view of customers; all activities must contribute to customer service. As self-evident as this may seem, many companies do not take time to establish their true purpose. They usually decide on purpose without understanding what matters to customers. Remember, a common purpose leads to common understanding, cooperation, and a common desire to see the whole organization succeed.

SEPARATE 'VALUE' AND 'FAILURE' DEMAND

Whatever the organizational purpose, some failure demand will always be present. The company itself will be responsible for most of it, in which case it should not be improving but removing those processes that deal with failure. By removing the root cause, failure demand will decrease. When call centres analyse the fundamental cause for incoming calls, many are surprised to find that typically 50 per cent to 70 per cent of the demand is in fact 'failure' demand. The golden rule is to automate the 'value' demand and remove the 'failure' demand. Once you have separated the demand you want from the demand you don't, simple action plans need to be constructed and executed, for example:

- List the demand types
- Evaluate demand against purpose and sort into value and failure types
- List actions needed to improve the processes for the value demand
- List actions required for removing failure demand.

CASE STUDIES

Case study one looks at the problems that occurred when a company was focused on functional goals and budgets, and how it took action to solve them. Case study two illustrates the six-step process in action. Case study three deals with Thomas Cook Direct and their adoption of a customer-centric model.

CASE STUDY ONE: BREAK-FIX ORGANIZATION

Figure 25.2 displays the process by which the customer travels from diagnosis to conclusion, described in detail below.

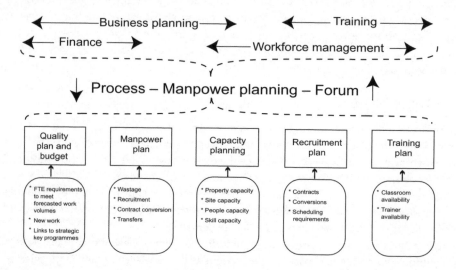

Figure 25.2   Resource management process © Fujitsu Services

This case study relates to a 'break-fix' organization, where customers' first point of contact is with a technician in the diagnostic call centre. The technician must identify the nature of the problem, propose a solution, and order parts.

The logistics group sends out parts, and an engineer arrives on the customer site to apply the 'fix'.

The diagnosis call centre manager has calculated that, based on the number of calls taken each day, the average call-handle time for printer problems is eight minutes. If it takes longer, the manager must hire additional staff, ultimately increasing cost.

The diagnosis technicians then learn how to complete their diagnosis within the allocated time.

The logistics team focuses on reducing the cost of inventory by making sure stock levels are minimized; therefore, infrequently-used parts are returned to the suppliers.

The manager of the field engineers concentrates on 'Customer fault calls per person per day' and first-time fix rate.

All three departments use measures (shown in Figure 25.3) designed to decrease local costs.

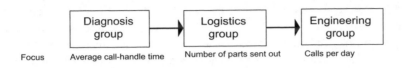

Figure 25.3   Resource management focus © Fujitsu Services

To meet the average call-handle time target, the diagnosis technicians begin to take short cuts. In many cases, they cannot decide whether they need part A or part B. Making this decision will increase the diagnostic time, so they order both.

The logistics team then ship both parts to the engineer, who uses one and returns the other.

The logistics manager notices that the engineers are returning a large number of unused parts. These parts are then returned for testing and re-packaging. The manager asks the question, 'If parts are being returned unused, then why do we stock them?'

The manager, therefore, establishes a rule: the logistics team must send one part only. 'If the members of the diagnostic team are doing their job properly', the manager reasons, 'they will order the correct part.'

However, the problem remains: the diagnostic team still cannot identify whether part A or B is required to repair the problem. The managers fail to realize that in order to get around this issue, the technicians now order part C, an assembly kit containing both parts A and B.

The logistics team, however, does not have the assembly kit in stock, because the planning profile shows that there is no need for part C. As a result, the logistics team places a rush order to get part C from the supplier. These 'priority-one orders' are more costly than regular ones. Finally, the logistics team, once it receives part C, sometimes several days later, sends it to the engineer.

The logistics team then notices that parts A and B remain on the shelves, so it sends the stock of parts A and B back to the suppliers in order to reduce the cost of 'unnecessary' inventory.

In this case study, the responsibility for customer satisfaction lies with the manager of the engineering team, because of the face-to-face interaction that the engineers have with the customers.

Case study one: summary

For some time, the company situation had been deteriorating. The rule that the diagnostic team could order only one part at a time led to the final collapse of the whole process. The team began to order expensive combination kits not normally kept in stock. There were lengthy delays in the delivery of parts. The engineers faced angry customers who had been waiting longer than usual to receive their engineering visit. Customer satisfaction results deteriorated which, ultimately, resulted in the dismissal of the engineering manager.

It seems logical that if the teams worked together, they would work towards a common purpose: to 'fix' the call as rapidly as possible in the most cost-effective manner. However, in this instance, the engineering manager was dismissed because each department focused on its purpose alone, rather than having a common vision of how the service should best be delivered. By using measures relating to their local costs, rather than having a common purpose, the managers acted at the expense of each other and the customer in order to develop short-term gains within their own teams. Over the longer term, with more priority-one part requests and expensive combination kits being issued, costs increased rather than decreased.

A side-effect of using measures that are related to local costs instead of having a common purpose is that people often mistake their measures with their purpose. For example, if the measures were based on local costs, it would be easy for the diagnostic team to begin to think along the following lines: 'What's my job? To pick up the phone within 20 seconds and pass this call on as quickly as possible.' Although this may create short-term gains in productivity and cost-savings within the local department, it create problems in the service system that inevitably will cause problems elsewhere. Each department and individual had a narrow goal with little or nothing to do with the common purpose. In fact, no one focused on the purpose or the end-to-end effectiveness.

Later the company introduced end-to-end measurements, resulting in a significant change of behaviour across the organization. Simply introducing end-to-end measures (total elapsed time to fix) and removing the average call-handle time targets from diagnostic technicians, call demand decreased by 25 per cent and first-time fix increased from 48 per cent to 70 per cent. Most significantly, technicians were able to service broken printers in seven hours, where previously it had taken eight days.

Therefore, for an organization to succeed, it is essential that every team member involved in the delivery of products or services have a common purpose and use end-to-end process measures to improve the service and reduce costs.

CASE STUDY TWO: TELESALES ORGANIZATION

This case study examines an office products direct marketing company. In this company, different departments had little or no communication with each other. The telesales staff members were responsible for taking orders; whereas, customer service teams dealt with after-sales enquiries and complaints. Furthermore, warehouse employees picked and packed the sales orders, and an external distribution company picked up the goods, took them to the distribution centre, and sorted them for next-day delivery.

The company had experienced numerous difficulties: sales targets were not being met, customer complaints and product returns were at an all-time high. Attempting to improve the situation, the distribution company was replaced, but customers still experienced delivery delays. As a result, goodwill compensation payments to disgruntled customers had risen, costing the company even more.

Customers, tracking their orders and complaining about products and services, inundated the call centre with calls. These calls outnumbered sales calls 2:1. As a result, over 18 per cent of customers hung up before speaking to a staff member, as waiting times were long. The overall working conditions worsened and staff turnover became high. Increasing costs even more, the new delivery company was having to re-deliver large quantities of goods, and merchandise returns were high because customers had been sent the wrong item(s) or because the merchandise was faulty.

The company realized it had to radically improve, so a cross-functional assessment team was set up to look at all the main processes throughout the company.

Step one: understand the nature of demand

The group began its task to improve conditions in the office products company by analysing the nature of demand placed on the call centre. In order to do this, over a two-week period, the team listened to calls received by the telesales and customer service departments. Rather than asking a standard set of questions, the staff members were instructed to ask customers open-ended questions to better assess what their expectations were.

The survey indicated that customers wanted the organization to:

- meet the next-day delivery promise
- deliver the correct product(s)
- provide good-quality products
- ensure advertised items were in stock.

Step two: create end-to-end measures

The assessment team used customer feedback to establish four end-to-end measures: (1) committed delivery time, (2) order accuracy, (3) quality of goods, and (4) in-stock items. They then investigated how well current processes performed against them and found the following results:

Measurement	% Achieved
Committed delivery time	68
Order accuracy	60
Quality of goods	63
In-stock items	67

Step three: understand the causes of performance variation

Process performance, by nature, is prone to variation; therefore, understanding the causes of variation and being able to predict its effects is the key to improvement. The statistical process control chart below illustrates this premise (see also Recommended Reading at the end of this chapter). In March, for example, 'Committed delivery time' has a mean figure of 68 per cent, with a possible variation of between 57 per cent and 80 per cent. Unless the process changes in some way, the high range of variation will remain the same. As a result, the assessment group at the office products company followed the processes throughout the organization, identifying the elements that predictably caused variation.

	March	April	June	July	Sept
Upper control limit %	80	88	100	96	100
Mean %	68	84	95	90	95
Lower control limit %	57	80	90	86	87

Figure 25.4 shows an example of the causes of variation in the percentage of orders arriving on time for office products direct.

While visiting the distribution centre, the group noticed a number of damaged products and asked the distribution supervisor if this was normal. According to the supervisor, products were frequently damaged because of inadequate packaging. Although the supervisor had informed the manager at the distribution centre, the manager had not communicated this to the warehouse where the goods were packed. Therefore, the team then went to the warehouse and spoke to the manager about the poor packaging. In order to reduce cost, the manager explained, the warehouse had begun to use cheaper materials.

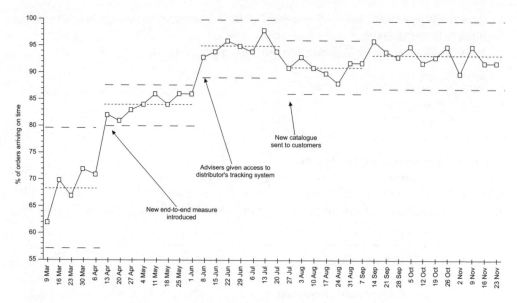

Figure 25.4   Committed delivery time: Office Products Direct © Fujitsu Services

During the visit, the staff made another discovery. While the label with the customers' name and mailing address was placed conspicuously on the outside of the package, any special delivery instructions were being packed inside along with the merchandise. Without these instructions, the distribution company could not, for example, deliver the goods at a certain time period specified, or leave them with a next-door neighbour. This resulted in a large number of customer complaints.

In addition, the group found the:

- product substitution lists were inaccurate
- post-code finder was five years out of date
- call centre staff were not informed of catalogue distribution dates
- order-entry system was slow
- customer invoices had errors
- warehouse computers were unable to reprint orders after printer jams, and these particular orders were lost.

By identifying these issues, the group began to understand the reasons for delivery problems and customer complaints.

Step four: understand what creates value for customers

Customers value quality products that are appropriate for their needs and, if delivery is involved, they value receiving them on time. This is what the telesales company learned once it began to ask those employees who knew most: the front-line staff.

Until this point, members of the telesales team were viewed as order-entry staff. Training was limited to simple sales techniques and to the order-entry system itself. However, they needed access to much more information and training. For example, the staff (and ultimately the customers) would benefit from faster order-entry computers, product demonstrations, and access to:

- detailed product information
- the order delivery status
- invoices and customer purchase history.

Step five: define the purpose

Having completed the analysis, the group and senior management team determined the organizational purpose as:

1 Selling and distributing stationary products on time.
2 Delivering accurate orders.
3 Selling quality products.

All activity must be related to this purpose, and progress would be measured using the new end-to-end measures. The previous purpose for the call centre was to meet sales targets. It viewed the distribution and quality of its products as someone else's problem. The call centre had failed to realize that it, too, was responsible for ensuring ordered items were fit for purpose and goods were delivered on time. To achieve this, the company had to redesign the role of its telesales staff and re-train them as necessary. Furthermore, it had to change its procedures and upgrade its systems.

Step six: separate value and failure demand

Once the team had identified the issues that reduced performance, the members set about classifying the demands. 'Value demands' are those that a company wants, and 'failure demands' are those that it does not want.

Value demand processes needed to be improved and then optimized, and the company did this by:

- automating the catalogue-ordering process using an interactive voice response (IVR) system
- decreasing the registration time for new customers from four days to three hours
- improving IT system performance by increasing the power of the computers
- giving telesales access to distribution tracking information
- updating the post-code finder
- increasing available stock
- product training and demonstrations
- upgrading the role of the telesales staff.

Conversely, failure demand needed to be removed at the source. This was achieved by:

- displaying special delivery instructions on the outside of the package
- improving the quality of packaging
- discontinuing poor-quality items
- checking order accuracy in the warehouse before package was sealed
- upgrading the computer system in the warehouse so that it would allow reprinting of orders
- providing telesales staff with access to information that was previously only available to customer service teams.

CASE STUDY TWO: SUMMARY

The team clarified the purpose by implementing measures that tracked performance against end-to-end measures. They were free to experiment with new methods. It became normal procedure for front-line staff to identify what processes were sub-optimized and where blockages and bad practices resulted in serious customer dissatisfaction. As illustrated below, service efficiency and effectiveness saw dramatic improvements.

Measurement	% Achieved before	% Achieved after
Committed delivery time	68	95
Order accuracy	60	96
Quality of goods	63	85
In-stock items	67	79

There were many other significant improvements. For example, the call centre saw a 26 per cent reduction in the number of incoming calls; customer complaints were reduced by 82 per cent, removing the need for a dedicated complaints department; the order-entry time decreased by 35 per cent; and, finally, customer compensation payments dropped by 75 per cent.

This case study exemplifies the need for call centres to:

- have advisors who understand true customer focus
- have advisors who understand the nature of demand
- respond appropriately to demand
- investigate and remove causes of variation in processes
- understand the needs of the customer, then quickly adapt the processes to keep servicing those needs.

This is about more than managing the call end-to-end; it is also about changing processes and procedures throughout the service-delivery chain.

CASE STUDY THREE: THOMAS COOK DIRECT

Thomas Cook UK is one of the UK's leading travel companies and one of the best-known names in travel, employing 11 800 staff across the UK.

Thomas Cook Direct offers customers the facility to book their holidays by phone. Over 1000 agents are employed at its five contact centres in the UK, which operates seven days a week, from 8 a.m. to midnight and handles up to 80 000 contacts each week. Workforce management at these levels has the potential to be extremely complicated, and Thomas Cook Direct sought a technology solution that could support and simplify the process.

Thomas Cook Direct wanted to shift the focus of its contact centre agents to a more customer-centric model – from simply taking bookings over the phone to building long-term relationships, identifying and influencing buying behaviour and cross-selling other travel arrangements. To do this it was necessary to develop multi-skilling in the contact centres, and to have the infrastructure to manage this. Historically, contact centre agents had mostly handled one type of contact, either as a product or a business stream specialization. Thomas Cook Direct wanted to change this by enabling the vast majority of agents to become multi-skilled in two or three product or contact types.

A technology solution was sought to provide the foundation for the development of a more customer-centric model for Thomas Cook Direct at a number of levels, which involved:

- Managing the scheduling and allocation of staff by skill against the level of contacts.
- Accommodation of seasonal variation (peak selling periods for travel bookings are during January and July/August).
- Integrating a customer database that could be used to route contacts according to past behaviour and give agents information during the contact to facilitate and improve customer service.
- Improve contact abandon rates and average hold times.
- Reduce agent turnover.

With people accounting for over 70 per cent of recurring contact centre costs it was essential that Thomas Cook Direct's workforce strategies were optimized in order for the overall customer relationship management (CRM) strategy to succeed.

Case study three: the results

As a result of developing a more customer-centric contact centre model and implementing a workforce optimization solution as its foundation, the results have proved impressive at many different levels. Since the project was first initiated, the following results have been achieved:

- Contact abandon rates have been reduced by up to 50 per cent.
- Average hold times have decreased from 40 to 15 seconds.
- Service levels have increased from 50 per cent to 80 per cent.
- 70 per cent of contact centre agents are skilled in handling contacts for two or more different travel product areas. Thomas Cook Direct has become more customer-focused and agents are better able to identify sales opportunities.

The financial return was evaluated by comparing staff availability to contacts handled. A higher percentage of contacts can now be handled with a given level of staffing. The financial benefits of this improvement per annum is several times the original investment in the system.

RECOMMENDED READING

Hammer, M. (2001), *The Agenda,* London: Random House.
Seddon, J. (1999), 'Transforming call centre operations', *Journal of Call Centre Management,* September/October: 31–39.
Wheeler, Donald J. (1993), *Understanding Variation: The Key to Managing Chaos,* Knoxville, TN: SPC Press, Inc.

26 *Workforce Management Process*

Simon Priestley, Head of Capacity and Yield, Thomas Cook Direct

This chapter considers the processes and working practices needed to effectively utilize resources, from planning and scheduling through to shift patterns and creating a plan for workforce management.

WHAT IS WORKFORCE MANAGEMENT?

I have never found an official definition of workforce management, but in practice it is a term usually used to differentiate between the basic practice of scheduling staff, and using an integrated set of tools and processes to cover all aspects of managing staff. In many contact centres, particularly those that have grown from a small operation over a period of time, each element of the staff management is often formalized at different times using systems that are not linked. Often the systems are designed in-house by expert users in spreadsheets or Microsoft Access, or relatively simple software solutions have been purchased at different times. It is still possible to bring these together into a coherent process, although as shall be discussed later, using workforce management software can make this much easier and more effective.

Throughout this chapter reference is made to the resource teams. This is taken to mean the group who forecast call traffic, and plan and create staff schedules. The actual responsibilities of this team will vary from organization to organization. If your contact centre does not have a specialist resource team, consider the merits of having one.

WORKFORCE PLANNING

Workforce planning is a key process in the operation of a successful, cost-effective contact centre. It is also one of the more complex processes in a contact centre, relying upon the application of planning principles to the particular environment in question. There are software solutions available to help parts of the planning process, some of which are very effective, but this is very much a situation where the software is only a small part. The key to workforce planning is to define the planning process for the organization in question and include the contact centres in this. Augmenting this with software then becomes a logical progression.

CREATING THE MODEL

In principle, the process is always the same. First, there needs to be a successful model for forecasting the contacts into the centre. This model is the same for call centres as for multimedia contact centres; each media is just another skill to accommodate. This is often the area that provides the greatest challenge for a centre. Unfortunately, if this model is significantly wrong the best scheduling in the world will not give the right result. The forecast then needs to be broken down into day of week and time of day.

FORECASTING

High-level forecasts can be used to determine quite closely the number of staff required to handle the contacts. Breaking the forecasts down within the week provides the framework for deciding what shifts the agents are required to work. Staff can then be assigned to shifts to create the schedule. In the case of a centre that handles multiple-media types or multiple-call types, the planning process needs to plan every call or contact type. Creating the schedules then relies upon working with the operation to develop a plan for staff by shift and by skill, to ensure that coverage for each type of contact is correct across the week.

MULTIPLE SITES

In the case of a centre with multiple sites, the process is mostly the same – the key to complexity is skills, not sites. However, multiple sites are harder to schedule from a functional point of view. The resource planning team needs to understand how the contacts are distributed between the sites. Does a network-level contact management product exist so that from a workflow point of view the centres can be treated as one unit, or are the skills and contacts allocated to centres unevenly, meaning that a combination of schedules has to be used to achieve the end result?

Each of these steps will now be discussed.

CONTACT FORECASTING

CREATING A FORECASTING PROCESS

In many cases, unfortunately, the contact centre management receives little communication from the rest of the business about the activities that are affecting contact volumes. Creating a framework where the contact centre is an integral part of the corporate planning process is vital. This has to be driven at a fairly high level. Ultimately, poor communication within the contact centre will lead to staff being in the wrong place at the wrong time. While the internal departments bemoan the failings this creates, the person who suffers most is the customer. Suffering customers generally migrate to a company that meets their expectations. Despite the obvious logic in this, many contact centres still struggle to stay in the planning loop within their organization.

Remember that to make a significant change to contact centre staff levels, you need to allow at least three months' notice. This is approximately the length of time it takes to advertise, screen, interview, appoint and train intakes of staff. If the planning shows that the capacity of the centres will be exceeded, then increasing physical capacity – another centre or outsourcing – could take significantly longer. In order to be truly effective, advance planning is the key.

There needs to be a process whereby each month all those who influence contact centre volumes sit down, ideally all together, and provide an up-to-date plan for their area of influence at least a few months in advance. Even if activity is still undefined ('our new catalogue will come out in six months – we don't know what it will look like but we know we will be doing it') it still gives the centre planners a chance to prepare. This planning forum could even include areas of the business such as website development – a glitzy new section to the website could affect the centre's performance more than a direct mailing.

A perfectly accurate forecast is obviously impossible. The key is to make as accurate a forecast as possible while understanding the uncertainties. In this way a 'most likely' plan can be created, but contingency measures for variations to plan can also be discussed and agreed. For example, if overall forecasts exceed expectations it helps to have business agreement as to which calls have the higher priority. If forecasts can be accurate to within 10 per cent overall, most operations can usually be flexible enough over the short term to accommodate this kind of variation. Over a long period of time, however, the ups and downs of the forecast need to average out fairly close to 100 per cent accurate, because long-term understaffing is bad for business and morale, and overstaffing costs money. With a regular review process for forecasts in place, this should be achievable.

COMPILING THE DATA NEEDED TO CREATE A FORECAST AND RESOURCING MODEL

The main information needed for a forecast model is the volume of contacts offered. If the operation in question exists already, then for the long-term capacity planning these statistics need to be compiled weekly, going back over at least a year. For new ventures then marketing forecasts will need to be used, but in such cases building-in flexibility due to the uncertainty in the forecasts will be essential. If the information has not been compiled accurately in the past and reports need to be compiled again, then 12 months will probably be the limit as many ACD (automatic call distribution) systems only hold 12 months' data.

UNDERSTANDING SKILL LEVELS

The contacts offered need to be measured at least to the skill level. In other words, if there are two skills in use, for example sales and service calls, then the past weekly calls offered will need to be compiled for both. If sales is broken down by products and each product area is a skill, for example sales of copiers and sales of printers, then the calls need to be measured at the same level of detail. Most existing operations will have this in place.

CALL PATTERNS

Having done this, for producing schedules the call data is needed by day of week, by skill, for the previous few weeks. Three weeks is usually adequate for this task. At the same time, compile the calls by day of week for any bank holiday weeks that are on file. The call patterns for these weeks differ and they need special treatment when the schedules are produced.

COMBINING CALL PATTERNS AND SKILLS

Finally, for each day of the three weeks being compiled, the calls offered by interval need to be compiled as well, for each skill. This level of detail is often not part of the regular reporting and may need to be done from scratch. The size of the reporting interval is usually limited by the ACD, as some will only report on 30-minute intervals while some have the option of 15 minutes. If scheduling software is being used then the smaller the interval the better to get an accurate intra-day call pattern. However, if schedules will be produced manually using spreadsheets then intervals smaller than 30 minutes will probably create an overwhelming degree of complexity.

ANALYSING HISTORY TO CREATE A CONTACT FORECASTING MODEL

Having compiled weekly contact volumes for each skill, it is now necessary to try to use this as a basis for predicting the future. There is usually one dominant factor that drives contact volumes:

- **The customer base model**. Contacts are a result of the size of the customer base or of general market awareness of the organization. In other words, each week the centres received on average one call per customer, for example. Centres where most contacts come from existing customers tend to fit this model, such as some areas of financial services and utilities.
- **The seasonal activity model**. This is an extension of the customer base model, but the calls vary noticeably according to time of year. Holidays, travel and consumer goods with heavy emphasis on Christmas sales tend to follow this model.
- **The growth model**. In this version the calls into the centre grow at a rate in line with awareness in the market or growth of customer base, usually in response to marketing initiatives. These growths can be short term, so that most of the forecasting is based on one of the first two models with extra contacts added in at certain times to match marketing activity.

GROWTH FACTOR

Growth in a centre is usually the hardest factor to deal with. Long-term growth trends can be hard to measure accurately – year-on-year comparisons are the best method, but these rely on consistent information going back well over a year, which may not exist. The rate of growth may be changing – speeding up or slowing down – which requires even more careful analysis. Finally, the growth may be erratic, depending on when marketing activity is taking place, or has taken place in the past. Adding 20 per cent on to the previous year's calls will not be an adequate way of allowing for growth if the timing of marketing activity is totally different.

MARKETING CAMPAIGNS

Allowing for the contact-volume variations of shorter-term marketing activity requires a different level of analysis, but the good news for most centres is that this is unlikely to be needed. By examining past campaigns and testing models you can arrive at accurate predictions for the number of contacts generated depending on the medium used, the size of audience and the duration of the activity. However, in most cases, 95 per cent of contact activity is core and follows the customer base or the seasonal model, with a simple treatment of growth where applicable. Sophisticated breakdown of marketing activity is only needed where direct response to marketing activity represents 10 to 20 per cent or more of the total contacts.

MULTIPLE SKILLS

Forecasting in environments where there are multiple skills – be those skills different call types or different media – is just an extension of the basic forecast principle. Forecasts will be created usually by some organizational classification, such as marketing channel, product type or media. To use these to forecast agent requirements just requires an intervening step to translate the forecasts created with the business into the skills used within the contact centres. One piece of marketing activity may generate calls for more than one skill area, and vice versa.

Turning contact volumes into staff requirements

At this point, hopefully, you will have a weekly contact forecast for each skill, be those skills call-taking or multimedia ones. From here, you then need to generate staffing requirements. While there exist software models for this, some of these have a 'black box' approach – you provide certain inputs and a result is provided, which many managers find uncomfortable to use. Most also rely upon the use of Ehrlang formulae (see Chapter 3), which are fine for simple scenarios but in multi-skill scenarios will not manage the sharing of activity. However, this area can be managed by reasonably competent spreadsheet users, using either Ehrlang formulae (most spreadsheets support this) or using a derived model along the lines of the suggestion below.

New formulae for multi-skilling

First, the contact volume forecast for each skill can be translated into a number of hours' work, by taking the handling time for that contact type and multiplying it. Then allow for the percentage of time that the agents spend performing that activity, as a percentage of the total time logged on. This gives a requirement for total logged hours. Then add on a provision for training, meetings, and other off-phone activities. It is often useful to formalize this area anyway for budgetary purposes. The amount of this provision will depend on the culture and demands of the centre. Those centres with complex products require more training and coaching. Those which have formal weekly team meetings will need more meeting time than those which have monthly meetings, and so on. This will provide a requirement for 'attendance hours': the number of agent hours that are actually needed on site. Finally, add on an allowance for the things that stop staff attending work, such as sickness and annual leave. Remember that using overtime increases your productivity.

Contacts offered (week)	10 000
Avg. contact duration (secs)	360
In contact/logged per cent	50%
Effective logged hours required	2000
Training, meetings, and so on	12%
Attendance hours required	2272
Sickness provision	6.8%
Planned attendance hours	2437
(equivalent planned agent days)	348
Holiday provision	5%
PLUS overtime	3%
Required trained FTE	71

A simple but quite accurate method for calculating FTEs (full-time equivalents) required. With experience, holiday, sickness and training provisions can be varied seasonally to match the forecast fluctuation in calls.

Advantages

The advantage of this kind of model is that for multiple skills or for changes in numbers of agents the operation can use its own parameters. Ehrlang formulae make assumptions of efficiency improvement against the size of agent pool using a standard model. In a multi-skill environment, efficiency improvements are far more complex; they rely upon levels of multi-skill and the extent of call and contact overflows, which are individual to each operation. These efficiency factors need to be measured and modelled for each contact centre operation. The operation can then use its own efficiency values in the models, and make its own assumptions about how this will improve over time or with changes in the operational size or structure.

ACHIEVING COST-EFFECTIVE GRADE OF SERVICE

A strategic decision that needs to be taken early in the staff planning process is the service standard(s) the company wishes to adopt. The natural answer is a good level of service, but for some companies this can have significant cost implications. Cost-effective service depends upon good 'end-to-end' workforce management, consistent or predictable call volumes, or having good response processes for unpredicted demands. The more uncertain forecasts are, the more staff will need to be hired to be sure of giving good service. The danger then becomes that, if call volumes are towards the lower end of the forecast, the overall cost per call can become too high. The organization really needs to decide how much it can afford to spend per call, and then, based on that, decide if it can afford to overstaff to guarantee service, or if it will have to be cautious.

Other factors affecting the ease of achieving good service are the size and complexity of the operation. Large operations with few agent skills are easier to forecast than smaller complex ones. If a range of different skills are needed, the more calls that can overflow into the different areas, the more the economies of scale can be achieved. 'Ring-fenced' teams for certain types of call may make skills training easier but can impact on the economic factors, and for many operations it is a matter of finding the right balance between the two.

The easiest way to plan for a given level of service is to look for periods of time when this has been achieved, and then look at staff efficiency during those periods, that is, the percentage of time taken to handle contacts versus being unavailable. Use this level of efficiency in your future planning (although as your workforce management improves, so will your efficiency!). If the target level of service has never been achieved then plot efficiency against service standards achieved so far, and extrapolate the curve to the point where the desired standard can be forecast. If you are numerically confident or your call centre is a simple one to model, there are functions and formulae in most spreadsheet packages to assist this.

LONG-TERM PLANNING: HIRING, TRAINING AND PHYSICAL CAPACITY

These models can be set up for an unlimited distance into the future. All they need is assumptions about contact volumes and contact-handling performance. Given a resource requirement picture into the future, other plans can be derived. Existing staff numbers can be compared with the requirements to understand basic ability to handle contacts. Remember that actual ability to handle contacts will depend upon the quality of the scheduling and the matching of staff to contacts. The number of existing staff will decrease over time as staff leave or are promoted. If this is added to the model then it can be predicted where and when hiring needs to take place to maintain staff numbers, or where up-skilling and cross-skilling need to take place to meet changes in the business.

SPACE PLANNING

It is also possible to assess the physical capacity requirements, which is important in any growing organization. While this can be modelled in detail, in my experience, given the uncertainties that can exist in long-term forecasting, a simple rule of thumb is quite adequate to give a guide to when space issues may arise. Given the FTE requirement, the minimum number of desks that is required will be approximately the FTE divided by 1.8. This works quite well for 24-hour centres with normal contact distributions. For contact centres that are open less than 24 hours a day, with contacts thus spread over fewer hours of the week, this ratio may prove a challenge and 1.6 may be more appropriate. For those with a reasonable amount of night-time traffic, it may be possible to improve on the 1.8. As well as this requirement for number of agent desks, the provision for team leader desks and other management positions need to be added, according to the management ratios used in the operation.

SCHEDULING

Forecasting leads to the ability to predict contact volumes according to interval through the week, by skill, and overall. From these predictions, it is possible to produce schedules for staff, which match these as closely as possible. For new, changing or growing organizations it is first necessary to decide what shifts need to be used, and how many people need to work each shift. Staff can then be moved or recruited to the correct shift mix.

How to design shifts to meet contact patterns
There is no right answer here: a mix of shifts is needed to cover the opening hours of a centre, and as long as a combination of the available shifts enables this to happen then the goal has been achieved. However, a number of shifts are fairly common practice in call centres as they enable the most common call patterns to be met quite well. These are also easy for staff to understand. What is important at this stage, rather than the exact shifts being offered, is to build-in flexibility. The easiest way of achieving this is to have flexible start times. For example, a normal full-time day shift might start anywhere between 8.00 a.m. and 9 a.m. Similarly, a flexible late shift might start anywhere between 1 p.m. and 2.30 p.m.

Flexibility of shift patterns
There is only a certain degree of flexibility that can be achieved using regular full-time shifts. There are two common ways of adding variability to the mix of shifts. The first is to operate long shifts on a three-on three-off, or four-on four-off basis. For example, an agent works an 11-hour shift for four days, then has four days off. This inherently leads to Sunday staffing levels at 50 per cent, which is usually acceptable. A number of staff on this kind of pattern provides a good core level of staffing through the busy period of the day, which is usually 9 a.m. to 9 p.m. Flexible starts can be used with this type of shift to maintain a high level of flexibility. It is best to limit this type of shift to a maximum of 20 to 25 per cent of the workforce or there will be too many staff at the beginning and end of the day, creating excessive staff availability.

To ensure flexibility within the day to be able to accommodate the minor fluctuations of the call patterns, specify shifts with flexible slots for breaks and lunches. For example, the first break might start between one and two hours into the shift, lunch between three and four and a half hours, and so on. Remember to make sure that the slots are spaced fairly evenly through the day, so that agents do not find themselves coming back from a break 15 minutes before lunch. Manual scheduling makes this easy to avoid, because the resource planner will always ensure the scheduling works. Scheduling software usually follows the rules it is given blindly, and if the windows for breaks and lunch are wide enough it will put them next to each other. As a final point, make sure that the lunch window, when counted into the shift from the start time, fits in with any canteen opening hours. With flexible starts, this can sometimes require care to get right.

PART-TIME WORKERS

The second way of adding flexibility is to use part-time workers. These can be quite successful, but attention does need to be paid to the hourly rate for such workers. If an agent does not work enough hours in a week they can struggle to maintain their call handling and sales skills at a satisfactory level. For this reason, operations where this is an issue usually have a rule that part-timers must work enough shifts to achieve a minimum amount of hours, typically about 20. The length and start times for part-time shifts will be tailored to each operation, but again there are some common practices that work well. Centres with a strong evening call traffic often use shifts between four and six hours long, starting between 4 p.m. and 6 p.m., working on five days a week for shorter shifts or four days a week for longer shifts. Flexible start times are uncommon on part-time shifts, but there is no reason why this cannot be done.

UNSOCIABLE HOURS

In areas of low unemployment it can be hard to find full-time evening-shift staff and full-time night-shift staff. Most call centres are purposefully located in areas where this is not the case. Multi-site operations may want to consider the option of only opening certain call centres when volumes are low, rather than deal with the cost of recruiting and retaining a level of staff in an area where more popular daytime work is readily available. However, in some cases, the company has one location and a recognized difficulty in staffing less sociable hours. In such cases, having a shift-pattern option where staff work late two days out of five each week can be a way of making evening work more palatable.

HOW TO DESIGN SHIFT PATTERNS AND WORK ROTATIONS

A shift pattern determines what shifts a member of staff could work each day to make a working week. Shifts made up of normal-length working days are usually offered on an 'any five days out of seven' basis, although most companies add a rule to this to assure the agent of a guaranteed level of Sunday and Bank Holiday working. Over a period of several weeks, the company may wish to add other rules to this to give agents other assurances, for example guarantees of full weekends off or midweek breaks of two consecutive days. This is called a work rotation, where every fourth week, for example, an agent is guaranteed the weekend off, or has to work the whole weekend.

To design a work rotation you need to ensure that, on each day of the week, enough staff are guaranteed to be working, or be available for working within their shift pattern, so that enough people are available for the contacts. Table 26.1 gives an example of a simple four-week rotation. This rotation ensures staff work one Sunday in two, have equal weekend working, and in a four-week period have one weekend and one other block of two days off together guaranteed. It provides a good basic match of staff distribution through the week to the contact distribution. There is enough flexibility in the non-fixed weeks to adjust the spread of staff through the week to meet movement in the call distribution up to a certain point. If the call distribution changes significantly, other shift patterns, part-time staff or a new work rotation will be needed.

Table 26.1   Simple four-week rotation

	Monday	Tuesday	Wednesday	Thursday	Friday	Saturday	Sunday
Week 1	X	X	X	O	O	X	X
Week 2	X	X	X	X	X	O	O
Week 3	X	X	?	?	?	?	X
Week 4	?	?	?	X	X	?	O
Percentage of staff at work on each day	15–20	10–20	10–20	10–15	10–15	5–15	10
Percentage of contacts by day of week	18	16	16	15	13	12	10

Key: X = must work, O = must be off, ? = may be at work

HOW TO TURN OVERALL STAFF REQUIREMENTS INTO NUMBERS OF STAFF BY SHIFT

With a workforce management system, turning overall staff requirements into numbers of staff by shift can sometimes be done using computer software. Some simpler systems can only provide workforce numbers according to shift for single-skill environments. Manual planning can be quite time-consuming, although it can be done easily enough.

Design the table

Set up a table for each day of the week, for each time interval and each skill. For each slot, add in the contact forecasts produced earlier. Using the agent productivity rates (for example, contacts handled per logged hour), calculate for eachslot how many agents need to be logged on. Then start to add in the agents according to shift, and build up a picture of how many agents will be present for each interval. Add in a number of agents for each shift and start time to try to get the 'agents present' pattern as close in shape to the 'agents required' pattern as you can. For example, each time you add a day-shift person starting at 8.30 a.m., this will give you one agent present during every slot from 8.30 a.m. to 5 p.m. Don't worry about breaks and lunches at this point!

Each day of the week will give a different picture, so remember to be consistent through the days – you need to find a mix of shifts that is similar each day, even if the volumes change. The actual schedule production can take care of the variations, but if a third of your staff are employed as full-time day-shift agents then every day you should plan to have around a third of your staffing provided by day-shift people. You cannot vary between 10 per cent one day and 50 per cent the next unless your other staff are on exceptionally flexible contracts.

Allow for 'down-time'

During the day each full-time person may be present for eight and a half hours, but they will usually take one hour for lunch and two breaks of ten minutes (total 1.33 hours). So, at best, the agent will be logged on for 7.2 hours out of 8.5, that is, 85 per cent of the time. So you need to 'overshoot' the requirements curve to allow for this. Over and above this, you then need to allow for off-phone activities – such as training and meetings – in the same way that these were allowed for in the long-term planning. Then, add on the same provisions you used earlier for sickness and holiday. You will probably end up needing to add about 40 per cent on to the requirements to arrive at the actual number of staff you need during each interval of the day. So, if it took 100 day-shift people to meet the 'agents required' curve, you would need to plan for 140.

Table 26.2   Example staff plan

Business stream	P/t day shift	F/t day shift	P/t late shift	F/t late shift	4 on 4 off	Total FYE	Total heads
Skill or media #1	0.5	5	5	3	10	23.5	28
Skill or media #2	3	7	7.5	0	10	28.5	34
Skill or media #3	0	20	9	10	23	62	65
Skill or media #4	1	5	10.5	10	12	38.5	46
Skill or media #5	0.5	7	2.5	4	16	30	31
Skill or media #6	0	0	4	1	20	25	29
Skill or media #7	6	2	2.5	3	15	28.5	34
Totals	11	46	41	31	116	236	267

Table 26.2 provides an example of a staff plan, having broken down the number of agents by skill and basic shift to give the required coverage for each skill. Multi-skill agents have been allocated proportionally in line with the skills they cover.

Creating a staff 'database'

If the company uses a workforce management system then this will provide a staff database. Otherwise, the operation needs to build and maintain a record in the resource management area of a number of things, depending on the exact remit of the resource team but usually including items such as:

- what hours the agents are contracted to work
- the call types they take (and can take if needed)
- a record of annual leave taken
- sickness
- overtime taken.

This list provides the reference for managing the detail in the scheduling. Remember the Data Protection Act: whichever way you decide to keep track of this information, it needs to be secure.

How to produce and manage a schedule

This is one area that is becoming more and more the domain of software applications. There are simple scheduling applications that are affordable for many smaller operations. At the other end of the market, there are sophisticated packages which can deal with pretty much any degree of complexity, skilling and multimedia. However for those without the luxury of this kind of system this step is not too difficult, although for the inexperienced it can be very time-consuming.

Adding names to numbers and patterns

Having decided on the shifts and the number of people in each shift and work pattern, the next step is to match the staff names to the patterns that are needed. A number of the days for each employee will be fixed each week, due to Sunday and weekend-working rules and other fixed days in the work patterns and rotations. The variables in each work pattern can be used to fill in the other gaps in the schedule.

Scheduling with multiple skills or media types

Next is to create a schedule for each skill, with agents assigned to each skill. In this context, multiple media and multiple skills can be treated the same. If some agents are multi-skilled then a simple but effective approach with manual scheduling is to split these agents *pro rata* between the two skills in question, for example, if one skill requirement is twice the other, assign one third of multi-skill agents to the smaller skill and two thirds to the larger. When the detail of the schedules is being worked out, it just needs to be remembered that if one skill is understaffed and one overstaffed at a particular point in the day, providing the contact routing has been set up correctly the multi-skill agents should even this out.

Understanding the multi-skill debate

A debate that seems to cause considerable controversy in some operations is how many agents to multi-skill. Articles have been written and talks have been given along the lines of 'is a multi-skilled agent an impossible goal?' The reality is, of course, that it depends on how many skills, how different the skills are and the individual agents concerned. Typically new joiners have one skill and then acquire others. Ultimately, is important to remember why multi-skilling is necessary. The reason for it was outlined in the previous paragraph: to smooth out the forecasting deviations in each skill to try make a large operation with multiple skills as cost-effective as a large operation with one skill. To achieve this you do not need all agents to have all skills, or anything remotely close to it. If one-third of agents assigned to a skill were given a second skill then this should give more than enough flexibility. As management of multiple skills improves, agent productivity will rise. This improved productivity can be reflected in the long-term forecast modelling, and result in less agents being used in the future to handle a given volume of calls.

Planning breaks, lunches and off-phone time

Using manual scheduling, planning breaks, lunches and off-phone time is another step that is simple in practice but time consuming to get right. If all the previous steps in the planning have been worked out properly then when the staff are scheduled, the numbers of staff present will be more than the numbers of staff required. Into each shift can now be slotted the breaks and lunches. These should be allocated to slots according to any rules agreed on when breaks will happen (for example, between one and two hours into the shift). Providing the rules are met, off-phone time should be spread across the day to try to even out the impact on the resourcing and always keep the numbers of staff present above the numbers of staff required. After breaks and lunches, any windows in the schedule where staffing exceeds requirements can be used for team meetings, training, and any other planned off-phone activity.

Managing annual leave

The best way to manage annual leave is to plan the amount of annual leave in advance outside the schedules. Annual leave has to be given and, while the amount of leave available on a given week can be varied through the year, this is a very sensitive topic and needs to be treated accordingly.

Holidays

In the high-level planning, a provision for annual leave each week is included in the resource equation. Remember, when adding in this provision, that staff will have times of the year when they prefer to take leave – school holidays, summer months, bank holiday weeks – and providing the seasonality in the call centre permits, a higher provision for leave should be given during those weeks. For most industries, bank holiday weeks are quieter thus allowing more time for leave, for example. However, there is unlikely to be enough flexibility in the operation to allow huge variations in leave week on week, and by announcing how much leave is available each week well in advance, staff can plan their leave to fit in with the operation. Providing there is a reasonable amount of leave available during popular times, most people will accept taking at least some of their leave at less popular times.

The percentage of staff that can be allowed leave on a given week will usually be between 10 per cent and 20 per cent. This can be turned into a number of hours of activity. For example if the payroll is 100 staff then 10 per cent leave means 10 FTEs can be on leave that week, which, on a 37.5-hour week, equates to 375 hours. This can then be spread across the days of the week in proportion to the staffing, for example, 18 per cent on Monday, 16 per cent on Tuesday and so on. The hours for a day can then be spread over the day. So if 75 hours leave was available on a given day, in a contact centre where the main traffic is spread over 15 hours from around 8 a.m. to 11 p.m., that equates to five people off at any point in the day. This could be presented to the staff as five early/day shift slots available and five late shift slots available. If the operation uses long shifts, for example, the four-on four-off approach, then this may need presenting as, say, four early, four late and two four-on four-off slots.

DELIVERING THE PLAN

This section will help you to ensure that the schedules are used and service is delivered.

THE CONCEPT OF A 'COMMAND AND CONTROL' TEAM

On the day, managing the activities in the operation to deliver the target service depends upon understanding how the schedule was put together, and also depends upon using whatever tracking tools exist to monitor agents in real time (ACD screens, real-time adherence). This can be time-consuming and does not naturally sit with the team that produced the schedules. In many centres, the on-the-day management sits with the team managers, but there is a growing trend towards the use of 'command and control' teams in contact centres. This ensures consistent monitoring throughout the day and a central point of coordination for arranging off-phone activity.

This command and control team is used for daily control of agents, as well as centralizing various support tasks that would otherwise fall upon team leaders and reduce the amount of time they spend coaching and supporting their agents. The control team can also act as the business focus for telephony changes and ensure that agents are correctly configured on the ACDs to match the schedules.

MAXIMIZING CALL HANDLING REAL TIME

On-the-day management relies upon two key tools. The first is the ACD or routing system viewer, which enables the observance of what the agents are doing when they are logged on – talk, after-call work, idle, outbound, email, and so on. The second, which becomes available with workforce management systems, is real-time adherence. This allows controllers to see who is logged on and who is logged off, and by comparing the schedule can provide an easy view of who is where they should be and who is not.

The goal of maximizing call handling can be aided by careful consideration of incentives. It is common to improve some productivity measures into incentives and balanced scorecards. Some of these do not actually add much to productivity without appropriate tracking. Here are a couple of common pitfalls:

- **Targeting calls per hour.** When a centre does not have real-time adherence, agents can influence this productivity measure by keeping their logged hours down by logging off. Also, the easy way to increase calls per hour is to cut calls short. If this productivity measure is to be used, make sure that reports are run to look for five-second calls to control short calls.
- **Targeting idle and wrap.** Agent time is a little like a toothpaste tube with the cap on – if you apply pressure in one place, the contents squeeze around but you don't get anything out. Targeting idle time usually pushes agents to use wrap more. Targeting both usually pushes agents into talk, which can be done by dragging out the call with the customer and keeping them on the phone when ideally the agent should be in wrap. Then, wrap is used to get some idle time. You should monitor average talk time – agents who increase call length to reduce idle and wrap percentages should be noticeable this way.

Where a centre uses call recording, if there are any suspicions about agents who are manipulating their productivity figures then retrieve their calls to check.

HOW TO ACHIEVE MAXIMUM FLEXIBILITY AND MANAGE DOWNTIME

A key to flexibility is the routing of contacts. Flexible staff cannot be leveraged without the routing of contacts overflowing between agents of different skills. Responding to changes in demand by moving agents between groups or skills is being reactive. The proactive approach is flexibility of routing, so that the calls move automatically. Waiting for calls to abandon before moving agents is inherently less effective.

Keeping good control of on-the-day activities is also essential. It may seem bureaucratic, but not allowing any significant off-phone time without the permission of resourcing or command and control is effective. Allowing team leaders to take staff off the phones when calls are quiet has two weaknesses. First, if too many team leaders have the same idea (especially in multi-site operations) the operation suddenly becomes understaffed, and, second, team leaders may not be aware of other planned off-phone activity about to start, which will take agents off the phone anyway.

WORKFORCE MANAGEMENT SOFTWARE

This section will describe the key issues concerning workforce management software.

INVESTING IN CHANGE

The main reason why large centres find themselves still using simple approaches to staff management is the cost of investing in change. A large operation can get by using spreadsheets to produce schedules, if experienced users are producing them. The operation grows used to a level of call performance that is not ideal – either mediocre abandon rates, or, if the centre increases staff numbers to drive abandon rates down, higher staff availability. On the face of it, investing in workforce management software can appear an expensive luxury, even though most people would agree that software should be able to produce a more accurate match of staff to calls. It is more difficult to see how the costs justify the change.

REPORTING

In the 'spreadsheet' scenario, other workforce information is managed on disparate systems. Often, absence and overtime are reported using HR department formwork and managed on HR-owned systems. This means that the centres have to create duplicate processes for tracking these areas internally because on the day they need to know who is ill and who is working overtime. As HR systems are really designed for payroll purposes, and not on-the-day management of staff, they will not give the operation this kind of real-time information.

Producing next-day reports is also harder when using separate systems. The main source of activity information in a centre is usually the ACD, but this only gives information about what happens when agents are signed on to the ACD. In most cases this only accounts for about two-thirds of what staff are doing. When the call performance is poor, the ACD is a limited source of information to analyse the problems and develop recovery plans. The rest of the time, staff are taking leave, off sick, in training, coaching, being coached or trained, in meetings and briefings, and sometimes just finding a reason for not taking calls when they should.

THE SCHEDULE PRODUCTION MODULE

Most workforce management solutions are component based, but as the components are all part of the same package, integration is inherent. The core of all systems is a schedule production module, which takes data from the ACD and possibly other media-routing systems such as email management systems, and uses this as the basis for planning agent requirements. It also holds information on all the staff – their hours of work, shift patterns, work rules – and combines this with history-based call forecasts to help produce the best possible schedules. The less expensive systems usually do this in a simple fashion, and some of them require a degree of user intervention to arrive at the best possible schedules. Others are more sophisticated in the rules they can hold and thus can produce a complete schedule with negligible intervention. Furthermore, the more sophisticated solutions usually provide a range of add-ons, such as facilities for absence and leave management, reporting, and real-time adherence. Some of these facilities, while sold as extras, can have a significant impact on the overall return on investment.

BUILDING THE BUSINESS CASE FOR WORKFORCE MANAGEMENT SOFTWARE

The basis of the business case will be defined by the components being purchased. There are two areas where workforce management software delivers quantifiable cost savings that can be used for a business case:

- **Customer service.** By using the latest call data, an accurate pattern of calls is held which will match staff to calls more closely than a manual estimate. No degree of sophistication in using manual spreadsheets can match the bespoke packages in this area. So, for a given number of staff, a workforce management solution will produce schedules that provide a better service. In a sales environment this translates to more sales. In a service environment, attrition to reduce the workforce size, and therefore less resources to deliver the same service, would usually be used.
- **Cost savings.** The second area of definable cost saving is in the use of real-time adherence. At the time of writing this is an 'optional extra' with all the main suppliers and not part of the core system. However, it often delivers a comparable level of savings to the core system itself, but at a cost increment of about 25 per cent. So, for most centres, taking the real-time adherence option should be a very easy extra to justify. Obviously though, if budgets are tight then even a good business case may not be enough.

A common pitfall to avoid, when the workforce management system is in place, is assuming that fewer staff will be needed in the support areas. Many of the tasks that support staff perform will remain. All the administration is still there – instead of updating a spreadsheet, now all the staff changes are updated on to the workforce management system. The main task that is removed is the schedule production itself. Some workforce management products have 'self-service' functions for agents to request leave and shift changes, but in practice, for most call centres these requests will require manual approval. However, in place of the tasks they performed previously, the support team will have much greater opportunity to assess the accuracy of the schedule and to look for ways to improve it. This can include accurate offers of overtime, offering of shift swaps, closer management of annual leave requests, all working towards handling more calls for less cost.

POSSIBLE LIMITATIONS OF PRODUCTS

It is worth making clear at the outset that a workforce management solution is not the contact centre's panacea. Most solutions are built around schedule systems and some of the peripheral functions are not core to the product and often not as well-developed. The common examples of this are call forecasting and report production. Expert users of workforce management systems are probably producing their own weekly call forecasts and adding these to the system, and combining these with the captured call profiles to produce schedules. Similarly, some are also taking data from the system and using it in a reporting package to improve analysis of the standard reports provided. Therefore, the analytical experience in the support teams will probably still be required.

PRODUCT SELECTION

When selecting a work management product it is worth looking at the contact centre environment and assessing its complexity. Complexity is the main factor when deciding on the best choice of solution. Think of it as like renting a lorry. You have to get a lorry big enough for the load you want to move, but if you get one way too big there is no real benefit (other than maybe some improved resilience) and the cost is a fair bit more. Working out what are the key factors that influence the choice of solution seems, in my experience, to be the area that users find hardest. It is also essential to visit an existing user, but try to make sure that you are comparing a similar type of contact centre operation. If you are multi-site, insist on visiting an existing multi-site customer.

Other important factors when selecting a work management product are:

- the number of different **skills** in use (possibly called call types or agent groups depending on the ACD in use) and levels of multi-skilling
- the number of **locations** and how many time zones they are in
- the number of call routes and the **volume** of calls received, on each and in total
- the total number of **staff** being scheduled at the same time due to multi-skill dependencies (not necessarily the total staff in the operation).

Let us now look at how each of these affects the product choice.

THE NUMBER OF SKILLS IN USE

There are two ways in which the number of skills in use influences the product selection. The first is fairly obvious: you need to be sure that the product you are reviewing is capable of modelling skills in the way that you use them in your organization. Some products have a fairly simple approach to skills, which in some cases is adequate. For instance, you may have a small number of skills and no multi-skilling, in which case only simple modelling is needed to simulate the schedules and produce quite accurate results. If you have a large number of skills, a high level of multi-skilling, and the same skill used at more than one site, then you will need a more sophisticated product to accurately model these scenarios. In particular, if multi-skill agents handle one type of call in priority to another (for example, sales agents who only handle service calls when there are no sales calls), then you should examine in detail how the product under review assigns priorities to the types of call received by agents. There are products that model these scenarios well, and you need to select one of these.

If you are a multi-skill environment then there is a second question that needs to be asked, which may need the help of IT support to provide the answer. Enquire as to the underlying structure in the database and the logical process followed by the software in calculating schedules. The reason for this question is that some products on the market are fundamentally single-skill products that have been modified to produce multi-skill schedules; the underlying database is, however, single skill and while the set-up would appear to capture the multi-skill information, the modelling probably uses this only in a limited fashion. Be particularly critical if 'multi-skilling' is an add-on to a core product. This would tend to indicate the core product is not multi-skill. Most products charge extra if you wish to produce multi-skill schedules, but there is usually a functional difference between products where it is an add-on, and one where multi-skilling is a feature that is disabled unless you pay the extra amount.

NUMBER OF LOCATIONS AND TIME ZONES

Essentially, the issues with regard to locations and time zones are the same as for skills. Make sure the set-up allows for the same structure as your organization, and also, if you are multi-site, that the underlying product structure is using this information correctly in its calculations. Site information is less important than skills in creating schedules that work but when you are using the product to produce management information or for real-time adherence it becomes important.

NUMBER OF CALL ROUTES

In an operation with a large number of call routes then almost certainly some calls will be more important than others. The ability to model the priorities of the call routes will be important in the choice of solution. If a large number of access numbers are used, the ability to treat these in clusters will also be required, in other words, the ability to define a queue or business area as a group of access numbers of call routes.

Once this is defined, it should be possible to assign agents to a business area, either directly, or by assigning a skill to the business area and then having agents linked to the skill. Either way, it should be possible to link agents to more than one skill and more than one business area.

SITE VISITS

Your prospective workforce management product will need to interface with other systems – ACDs or multimedia routing products – and, where possible, you should talk to other system users who have implemented the same combination of products. Ask about any technical issues they had during implementation, especially the ease of making any interfaces work and the stability of the links to ACDs and other systems. Another key issue to assess is the ease of use of the software. In particular, try to find out how long it takes a user to become proficient with the software – some packages are notably easier to learn than others. This learning curve will need to be built into the project planning and the speed at which a return on investment can be achieved.

IMPLEMENTING WORKFORCE MANAGEMENT: THE PROJECT

There are several key parts to the project that need to be considered. There is much more to a successful implementation than installing the software and training the resource team. The software supplier should be able to give detailed advice on this part of the project, but confirm what they say at the site visit.

DOCUMENTATION

The project needs to identify all the call routes, how they are routed and any time-of-day routing, if this applies. In an ISO or BS-approved organization there is some chance of there being a contact centre manual where this is documented. It is also quite likely to exist in operations that use a network call-routing product, because they will have had to introduce a process to ensure the network and the ACDs remain aligned. However, in many centres, maintaining the ACD is not under any serious change control process. In these cases there is no change request form, nor any manual of how the calls are routed which is updated each time a change is made. In such an informal environment there is a piece of work to be done to document this. Also, moving ahead, it should become fairly obvious that the project will need to include the implementation of a change control process for the ACDs (and any other call routing system used) to ensure the workforce management system is updated at the same time. Without parity between the two systems, the effectiveness of the workforce management system will drift.

AGENT DATABASE

A similar situation applies to information about the staff. In a well-structured operation, an agent database should exist with information on their skills, date of joining, skill/seniority levels, and so on. However, again, most contact centres are simply not that formalized. The data sources will probably be the HR database for basic details and then operational files for agent skills and productivity statistics.

TERMS OF EMPLOYMENT

The agent information that is usually particularly elusive is contracted shift terms. Organizations where all agents are on one contract are very lucky here. Most call centres use part-time employees to some degree with a range of contracted hours. Quite possibly there are different versions of full-time shift patterns and contracts too, depending on when the employee joined the organization. And finally, part-time staff in particular often change their hours with the agreement of local management, which is then never updated in their contract, in which case examining the HR files will provide the wrong information. In organizations where there is informal changing of hours there may be no alternative other than to have the resource team(s) document all the current work arrangements, which could take some time.

LICENCES AND TECHNOLOGY NEEDS

Early on, you should ensure that you do not need any additional licences or hardware from other suppliers, and ideally talk to the suppliers directly. Your workforce management supplier will also advise you of the technical requirements in order for your other systems to successfully interface with the workforce management product. As quickly as possible you should identify if any existing hardware needs to be upgraded, as the lead-time on some ACD components may be a few weeks and could be critical to the project.

IMPLEMENTATION TIPS

- Ensure there are sufficient resources to implement the system.
- Parallel run. The best way of implementing any new workforce management system is to run it in parallel to the existing system for a short period of time.
- Take time to explain the system to centre management and team leaders.
- Phasing – a gradual deployment.

REALIZING THE BENEFITS

CREATING AND LEVERAGING FLEXIBILITY

There are several ways to build flexibility into a contact centre operation, some of which are easier to operate than others, and some of which can have more impact on staff working conditions. I would tend to recommend the ones that give maximum flexibility with minimal impact on working conditions. Without a good workforce management package this can be difficult, but with one in place, staff contracts can be managed and scheduled easily. The options are:

- Flexibility on start times (for example, 7.5 hour shift starting between 8 a.m. and 10 a.m.)
- Flexibility on shifts worked (for example, five days per week, three days and two evenings)
- Flexibility on notice (schedules can be changed/issued at very short notice to suit operation)
- Multi-skilling where multiple skills exist.

Flexible start times

Flexibility of start times is becoming increasingly common as a contractual arrangement. It is usually fairly popular with staff, but on spreadsheet-level scheduling it is hard to use it effectively. Being able to model call volumes down to the level of detail where staff start times can be confidently planned at 30 or 15-minute intervals is beyond all but the most expert of users. However, this type of flexibility is easily optimized by workforce management products. In such cases, the system produces schedules with staff being progressively brought on at each interval, providing a build-up of staff as close to the build-up of calls as possible. In such cases it would be unusual to mix the flexibility of shifts as this may leave staff with too much uncertainty. If call volumes are very flat across the day and the organization has adopted on/off shift rotations (for example, working 4 four days of 12-hour shifts then four days off) then this is the only way to create flexibility.

Flexible shifts

Flexibility of shifts does not really add much to the flexibility of a workforce despite first appearances. It is one of two ways of achieving staffing in the evening. The alternative is the simpler approach of having staff either on permanent days or permanent late shifts. (Night-shift working is ignored here because very few organizations operate a significant night shift and they are usually managed with staff on permanent nights.) In my experience, both approaches to evening working are equally valid. Employing staff on permanent evening work is perceived as bad for retention by some, while others say that staff like the stability of working the same core hours and do not like their start times to vary by several hours between one day and the next.

In reality everyone is different, and some people will prefer one and some the other. Running both methods of staffing the evening shift will introduce a high degree of complexity, but this could be managed with a workforce management system, provided there are not too many work patterns overall. Either way, flexibility will come from having flexibility of start time for a given shift. Typically, 60–90 minutes of variability is optimum – this gives the operation scope to vary staff levels without creating to much uncertainty for the employees.

Flexible notice

Flexibility of notice of schedules is really a way of compensating for limitations or weaknesses in the planning process. In some cases, particularly outsourcing, this is unavoidable because call volumes are, of course, volatile. For most in-house contact centres it should be possible to confidently plan several weeks in advance, and this is certainly made easier by the use of accurate call profiling that a workforce management system provides. The more notice that can be given, the easier it is to manage staff expectations.

Multi-skilling

Multi-skilling speaks for itself – the more staff that can be given more than one skill the better. A good workforce management system can cope with almost any degree of multi-skilling. In fact, the limitation is more likely to lie in the ability of the call and other routing systems to physically manage call volume load balance to the same extent that the workforce manager can model, particularly when trying to load balance across multiple locations.

OVERALL RESOURCING KEY FACTORS

The key factors for successful workforce management are:

1   A good forecasting process – not just to achieve accuracy but to understand the degree of uncertainty.
2   Accurate analysis of contact patterns and demands.
3   Flexible shift working – flexible start times or flexibility between day and evening working.
4   Making adequate provision in the staff planning for holiday, sickness and off-phone time, and understanding the gap between staff required to handle contacts and the staff needed on the payroll.
5   Incorporating breaks, lunches and off-phone time in the planning to match the staff productive time as closely as possible to the contact patterns.
6   Effective on-the-day control processes to deliver the plan.
7   Effective use of software, where it exists.
8   Intelligent use of management information to improve future schedules and to manage productivity of less efficient agents.

27 *Resource Management*

Carol Borghesi, Director of Customer Contact Centre, British Telecom

This chapter discusses aspects of resource management which includes financial and business planning, workforce management, and recruitment and training.

WHAT IS RESOURCE MANAGEMENT?

Resource management is the practice and procedures that provide the correctly skilled people at the right time and place to deliver a customer experience within budgets and on time. End-to-end resource management comprises:

- Financial and business planning
- Workforce management
- Recruitment and training.

There is a requirement for these functions to work in one coordinated and integrated manner to deliver proper results. Without a solid foundation on which to plan and execute resourcing this vital function can be the source of sub-optimal performance, unnecessary cost and poor customer service.

BACKGROUND

The battle for customers (or clients or citizens or donors) is familiar to all contact centre operators, and battles are intensifying in relation to their frequency, duration and what's at stake.

The battle is won by giving your customers access to your business or operations where and when they need it and for your business to be able to respond to change faster and more efficiently than your competitors. This is well understood in contact centres, but strikes fear in the hearts of practitioners. How do we crack the code of effective, efficient customer access? The answer is through effective and efficient end-to-end resource management. The key to delivering customer satisfaction at an affordable cost is in the delivery of the right person in the right place, at the right time. Easy to say, difficult to do.

There are issues of unpredictable call volumes; uneven or volatile call duration, driven by unexpected customer reactions, or lack of adequate advisor training; inaccurate or downright wrong forecasted response to a campaign and, of course, pressure to manage within a tight or even unrealistic budget. On top of all that, contact centres are not exempt from demands to do more with less: productivity improvement targets, cost-reduction edicts and speeded-up product and service introductions and innovations are more and more typical. Research shows customers are increasingly more demanding and sophisticated, which makes it tougher to earn their approval and therefore their custom.

Getting the basics right may sound an overly simplistic strategy for delivering business results, but that is exactly what more organizations need to do but fail to do. There is no more critical element of basic contact centre operation than end-to-end performance management and it is often the most abused and defective component of the contact centre operation. Getting resource management right, whether it's the initial start-up of operations or the need to overhaul existing performance, is the single greatest source of cost reduction and customer satisfaction.

CUSTOMER NEEDS ARE BALANCED

Contact centres are overwhelmingly people-dependent and, despite predictions to the contrary, will remain so in the foreseeable future. Resource management done properly encapsulates the functions of acquiring the right people, ensuring they have the requisite training and then experience (for example, on-the-job training) and, most importantly, that they are there when customers need to talk to them. That should be in accordance with the customers' preferred time to talk, but is dependent on employees preferences in terms of hours of work, shifts and flexibility. That's when it starts to get complicated.

The challenge of balancing people-centric practices, policies and procedures, for example, creating a workplace that is responsive to individual needs and allows people enough autonomy and freedom with the obligation to serve customers when and how they want and need service, is very difficult to get right. If an operation takes the approach of enabling maximum autonomy and individually tailored shift patterns, resource efficiency levels out. It costs more to manage a blizzard of shift patterns and creates complexity in ensuring management, team leaders and coaches are available to support team members. However, the opposite end of the spectrum is equally ineffective. Rigid, overly strict rules and procedures that restrict people from taking time to do their job properly or, even worse, that they lead entirely by statistics and actively prohibit freedoms, create an unhealthy and unhappy work environment which ultimately costs in unexpected absenteeism and poor schedule adherence.

Resource management is but one element of a successful contact centre operation, but it is the most important. Its relationship to related and dependent functions is essential for optimizing resource utilization, which really shows how well the skills, knowledge and abilities of advisors are bought to bear on the questions, problems and opportunities customers bring, when they bring them. That is why end-to-end resource management and the positioning of it in the contact centre organization structure is so important. Equally critical is to get the processes that link into business planning, campaign management, capacity management, training and systems support aligned and orientated around best delivery of job-ready advisors.

BEYOND FORECASTING AND SCHEDULING

In the past, we have often treated resourcing as though it comprised just two or three components: usually forecasting, scheduling or rostering, and recruitment. Today there is a strong trend towards integration of these functions together with a more sophisticated business planning process, induction procedures and call management systems. The benefits of this more integrated approach are:

- Stronger linkage to other functions that generate calls or act as internal clients, for example, marketing campaigns, leading to tightened alignment between planned and actual results
- Greater control over costs, including the ability to plan contingency should call volumes not materialize or are well above forecast

- More responsiveness should contingency management necessitate alternative routing
- Better assurance that agents are 'job ready'
- Greater cost-effectiveness.

The components of resource management demonstrated in Figure 27.1 will be examined in turn, under the broad categories of planning, workforce management, and recruitment, including references to the kind of tools you'll want to consider as the scope and scale of resource management grows and changes. Some space will also be devoted to special kinds of work that require particular consideration, namely non-call activity such as correspondence, email and web support.

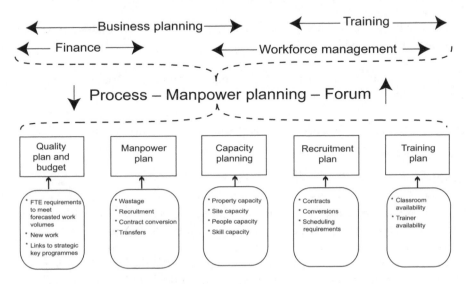

Figure 27.1   Resource management model © BT

FINANCE/BUSINESS PLANNING

As the call centre operates as part of the overall business plan, financial and business planning must provide the overall quality plan and budget for the year, covering the budget available in terms of headcount and money. There will necessarily be negotiation about the budget, probably on a quarterly basis, and the debate needs to be based upon historic call volumes, productivity requirements and plans for the coming year, expressed as call volumes, by function. For example, if your call centre handles sales and service enquiries for multiple product lines, you will require a detailed picture of the requirements, complete with assumption underpinning the numbers, that is response rates, percentage of market penetration expected and so on. In the case of inbound operations, if there are few and/or simple initiatives planned for the upcoming period, the process will be relatively straightforward. If there is a lot of new work planned or significant strategic programmes that will have ramifications on the call centre, the exercise becomes more involved. In the case of outbound operations, the process is more straightforward as there is more control over the volume of calls made. Both processes combine budget and actuals with other factors such as new campaigns, operational initiatives (for example, changes to call steering) and productivity improvement targets to establish the base line of work volume. It is essential that volume forecasts accurately reflect reality and that all 'knowable' campaigns and events are built in to this manpower plan.

The plan must also factor in the following:

- Wastage – the term used to describe the number and percentage of agents who leave the call centre resource pool
- Transfers – referring to people who will be promoted or will move to another part of the organization and are no longer available to handle calls
- Other considerations such as the use of agency or contract staff in combination with permanent staff. Are there differences between the two groups, in terms of wastage? Are you planning to convert any agency people to permanent status?
- Call and contact volume
- Shrinkage and ineffective time – ensures that indirect impacts on available headcount are deducted from the top-line calculation.

These two major components of manpower planning base data and shrinkage factors provide the actual full-time equivalent requirements.

- Erlang modelling to accommodate the unpredictable and uneven arrival pattern of calls.
- Seasonality is also key to ensuring the resource plan is calendarized correctly.

Once the basic components are in place, it is essential that FTE numbers are maintained and that the assumptions used in the model are accurate. Without these two critical success factors, it will be difficult or impossible to maintain efficient and effective delivery of service. This means that full recruitment, training and job proficiency lead times must be adhered to and factored into the plan, along with expected attrition. Failure to do so will result in a mismatch of 'effective' FTE – those able to perform to the standard of service and required FTE – the number of advisors needed to meet the service parameters of AHT (average handling time) and abandoned rates. It is as critical to have the right skills set and experience level as it is to have the right number of advisors, thereby dispelling the myth that this business is only about 'bums on seats'.

RIGHT PEOPLE, RIGHT PLACE, RIGHT TIME

Workforce management (WFM) is the industry-standard term that applies to forecasting, scheduling and monitoring of advisors and has evolved over time in parallel with the increasing size and sophistication of call and contact centres. It is covered extensively in the next section; however, it is worthwhile highlighting the key components. The overall goal of WFM is to ensure the 'right' people – those with the correct skills and knowledge – are at the right place – their workstations are enabled to deliver the service – at the right time – in accordance with call volume arrival. There are a number of considerations when delivering the promise of right people, right place, right time, but the most critical are:

- Organizational ability to attract and retain good quality advisors. This ability refers to the reputation or brand of the organization as well as its competency in recruitment and ability to pay a competitive salary.
- Call centre location, number of sites and equipped workstation availability. Much depends on where the call centres operate, if the sites are networked together and the flexibility of the desktop capacity. Local labour market conditions are important, for example, how competitive is the area, how much unemployment exists, and so on.

- Capability of the line management team to operate efficiently and effectively. Strong, results-focused and people-oriented managers who understand resourcing and have good relationships with those responsible for end-to-end resourcing are key. Equally, the resourcing team must be respectful of the views and needs of line management.
- Real-time monitoring of service to identify where quality of service is failing or at risk.

There are many workforce management tools on the market with varying capabilities. However, these days a workforce management tool should be able to provide the means to integrate skills-based routing and skills-set scheduling in an increasingly complex call delivery environment.

- Skills-based routing refers to the intelligent routing of calls/contacts from diverse sources, for example, different product or services that require different service to the rightly skilled advisor.
- Skills-set scheduling is the process of optimizing the scheduling of agents with different skills to meet the demands from skills-based routing.
- Call delivery platform capability including CTI, soft ACD (automatic call distribution), automated speech application platforms, call blending and call delivery prioritization, increase the complexity of calls and in turn the ability to route to the right advisor, ensuring seamless integration of workflows.

Skills-based scheduling is a means by which the effectivity of the call centre operation can be optimized without compromising effectiveness. However, it should be based on the needs of the business such as:

- ACD functionality
- Size of operation
- Need for permanently available advisors
- Cost of over-staffing.

and consideration of:

- Quality of service
- Customer perception
- Mix of advisor skills required
- Types of service.

WORKFORCE MANAGEMENT MADE SIMPLE

Workforce management comprises three processes – forecasting, scheduling and real-time monitoring – which transform the manpower plan into reality. Forecasting has already been covered in detail in this book, however, it is critical to ensure that input data captures sufficient data to create meaningful and accurate forecasts.

SCHEDULING

Using the contact forecast, the WFM tool produces individual schedules for each advisor, usually two to four weeks in advance. The schedules need to take into account individual contract agreements and governing rules, if applicable. All advisors should be scheduled for on-line duty, to enable the scheduling of exceptions. Exceptions include all factors discussed earlier, such as unusual call volumes, sick absence as well as non-call activity. This is key to effective WFM and the test of the proficiency of the resourcing team.

There are three elements of non-call activity that need to be scheduled:

1   Investment time
2   Regular training
3   Non-call activity.

This, of course, is only possible as a result of a very good manpower plan and disciplined commitment to ensure people are properly trained, communicated to and coached in their roles. These are often the areas that suffer most when forecasting has been inaccurate and/or unexpected volumes hit the organization.

'INVESTMENT' SCHEDULING

Each advisor requires individuals and personal investment and indeed should be entitled to such development time. Investment time should include 1:1 meetings at least once per quarter but more appropriately once a month; monthly team meetings, daily or weekly pre-shift briefings with other team members and coaching time. Coaching feedback should be provided weekly or monthly, depending on the nature of the role.

Regular training

Training needs to be planned at least one month in advance and delivered to all advisors in as narrow a window of time as possible. Training for marketing campaigns, system upgrades, policies, practices and procedures should be prioritized and distinction made between what needs to be trained and what can just be briefed.

WMF, training and operations management should be responsible for development and delivering the training plan for the following months or quarter. However, it is wise to establish a baseline of days needed to ensure advisors maintain proficiency in their roles, in terms of company products and system knowledge as well as customer skills.

Many organizations sacrifice quality (including quality of training) in order to meet service level agreements, at their peril. It is highly unlikely that customer satisfaction will result from under-trained or poorly informed staff, and it is essential to bear in mind that the overall goal of resource management is to ensure customer needs are met.

Non-call

Non-call work is often referred to as offline or support work but, regardless of name, it refers to the work that cannot or was not done on-line. Non-call work is as important as on-line work and should be scheduled using the same principles. Non-call work is often scheduled in the troughs of on-line demand in a blended environment; however, many organizations manage it as a separate operation, often using the same resource pool.

Non-call work also includes correspondence, email, order fulfilment and, in some instances, outbound follow-up calls. It is vital that non-call work is scheduled in direct association with on-line activity to make the best use of resources.

REAL-TIME MONITORING

The whole planning and scheduling process needs to be monitored in real time to enable the sensitivity and responsiveness to changes that threaten service performance and to compare actuals and to forecast the identification of inaccurate assumptions. Typically, this responsibility comprises:

- Monitoring queues across multiple physical and virtual call centres
- Manipulating the ACD network dynamically for optimum results
- Managing all non-forecast incidents
- Increasing/decreasing offline quantities to maximize performance
- Protecting service by queue/centre isolation or restriction
- System health checks
- Monitoring adherence
- Managing all contingency processes.

Real-time monitoring must be done in collaboration with resource and line management teams. WFM is a team effort; however, the skills, knowledge and experience of those directly responsible need to be highly specialized. In particular, the relationship to the line managers is key, as in effect, real-time monitoring measures compliance in adherence to schedule and sign-on time – both line management responsibilities – as well as systems up time and quality of forecasting.

Where there are attendance patterns commensurate with volumes and great discipline on adherence as well as reliable systems and stability of inbound volumes, real-time monitoring manages exceptions only and is reasonably light of touch.

QUALITY OF SERVICE KEY PERFORMANCE INDICATORS

The key to a cost-effective, high-quality customer experience is understanding the relationship between customer satisfaction with perceived performance and the internal measures to deliver that level of satisfaction. Customer expectation varies between transaction type and even between industry. However, research shows that customers have higher expectations of service providers than ever before, and of course, organizations must manage the cost of delivering to those expectations. Hence the importance of carefully balancing the break-even point of service level performance and perceived speed of answer. For example, 80 per cent service level in 15 seconds can result in 90 per cent of customers reporting that their call was answered promptly. Thus it is not necessarily true that higher quality of service results in higher costs, if the drivers of satisfaction are clearly understood.

Other relevant factors of quality of service:

- High volume, short duration calls in stable environments can be tweaked to deliver better service levels without increasing costs.
- IVR (interactive voice recognition) or call steering processing time should be part of the speed-of-answer calculation as it can have significant impact on customer perception.
- Other dimensions of service performance such as abandoned calls, hit rate and time to answer are important to understand real performance.

A myopic view of internal key performance indicators (KPIs) without the 'voice of the customer' input can also create the belief that performance is better than it is.

RECRUITMENT AND RETENTION OF THE BEST PEOPLE

The ability to accurately predict calls and deliver the right skills at the right time and place is of little consequence if the processes by which advisors are recruited and inducted into the business are not in place. It is often the case that organizations pay little attention to developing a recruitment strategy, creating a model and managing the process end to end. It is particularly worrying that few organizations engage partners in the exercise, for example, agency employee suppliers, to ensure consistency across the organization.

Difficulty in attracting, recruiting and retaining people with the appropriate skills, behaviours and experience is not uncommon. In fact, this is probably the number one challenge for most contact centre organizations. It is critical that recruitment and induction is part of the end-to-end resourcing model as this has such an impact on overall performance in terms of quality, cost and results.

Some of the pitfalls to avoid are:

- Uncompetitive pay and benefits. It is possible to pay above market rate and be uncompetitive in terms of cost structure, but it is more common to pay below market rate for the skills, knowledge and experience needed to meet the needs of your customers. Be sure you really understand the profile and prerequisites of the roles you recruit.
- Little or no pay or career progression. People don't respond well to an environment that holds no improving fortune nor the opportunity to develop and move onward and upward.
- No overall owner for recruitment results in inconsistencies and lack of structure and good practice.

There are other challenges that are industry related, such as staffing evening and weekend hours; increased contact centre competition; and alternative employment that offers more traditional hours of work. It is necessary to think through the approach that most closely balances the demands of the call centre and the needs and desires of advisors. One of the strategies to consider is the quid pro quo approach, which provides additional benefit for working less popular hours, for example, four rather than five-day attendance in exchange for evening hours. Part-timers who want permanent additional hours can be scheduled in the difficult-to-cover periods and new attendance patterns that tap into niche employment markets can be created. Examples of this are daily shifts of short duration, which are popular among students, and split shifts that cover peak morning and evening hours which are attractive to those with school-age childcare responsibilities.

Some organizations are increasingly using annualized hours, which equates to a part-time contract but is deployed tactically at seasonal peaks, for example term-time working which gives parents the advantage of being available for their children during school breaks.

Homeworking has been introduced in some businesses with good results in terms of people satisfaction and peak/unpopular hour coverage.

RECRUITMENT MODEL OF SUCCESS

A successfully executed recruitment strategy will require a recruitment model. The basic components of the model must include:

- job purpose clearly defined, responsibilities and behaviours required, for example the job purpose of a service rep is to deliver customer satisfaction and engender customer loyalty

- competency requirements agreed, including those essential to the role and those that are not essential but are desirable
- selection process documented, which includes relevant interview techniques and tests to provide a basis for consistent, equitable assessment of candidate quality
- induction training should be relevant, timely, topical and fully support the new recruit into the organization
- compensation review capability, which ensures pay and benefits keep pace with market conditions.

Consistent execution of a well-considered recruitment strategy and model will result in a higher level of quality recruits overall, who require less time to reach job proficiency and stay in the job longer. This, in turn, means resourcing needs are more consistently met on time and budget and that, of course, means customers have optimal access to more consistently satisfying interactions with the business.

SUMMARY

End-to-end recruitment management is about more than forecasting, scheduling and monitoring. In best-practice organizations, business planning, including finance together with workforce management and HR/recruitment, comprise an integrated approach to resourcing. Many organizations now combine contact delivery and resourcing responsibilities to ensure alignment and optimal performance of resources against contact volumes. While contact media is changing and expanding to include multiple methods of interaction such as email, text or web chat and call-me buttons and other eCRM technologies, the requirement for human interaction has not dissipated. To that end, the basic principles of excellent resource management apply, regardless of how contacts are processed, or what media delivers the contact to an agent.

Becoming proficient in the basics of resource management in terms of planning, forecasting, scheduling, monitoring, and recruitment and training may seem unglamorous and old-school in the environment of the Internet, mobility and CRM; however, it is the most important competency that a contact centre organization must possess in order to provide credible customer experience at an affordable cost. Without efficient, effective resource management, costs increase unnecessarily, people cannot be treated properly and developed to higher levels of performance, and customers won't be able to enjoy ease of access and highly satisfactory interaction.

28 Quality Monitoring and Service Improvement

Costas Johnson, Managing Director and Founder, Qualtrak Ltd

This chapter outlines quality monitoring and service improvement advice covering people performance, quality, systems and internal processes

USING QUALITY MONITORING AND COACHING TO CREATE A CONSISTENT CUSTOMER EXPERIENCE

It is well recognized that customer loyalty is created only when the experience matches the expectation. That makes service experience the only lasting loyalty differentiator and selling through service the only intelligent strategy to adopt for effective selling. The need for a consistent customer experience is therefore imperative.

The vision adopted by many companies is to grow revenue and profitability by delivering an excellent service, thus creating loyalty to the brand. It makes more sense to retain existing customers and increase their value. However, this will only happen when the company has earned a close and trusting relationship with the customer. Once again, this calls for an ability to deliver a consistent customer experience.

Companies launching a new product and creating a new market initially go through a frenzied period of acquiring customers with possibly little regard for the need for retention. But eventually such companies have to acquire a new set of competencies based around the need to retain their customers, particularly the high-value ones.

PEOPLE PERFORMANCE

Retaining customers requires contact centres to put in place an effective 'people' performance management programme, which carries the same level of priority and focus by senior management as that given to technology. Perhaps the most important contributor to delivering a consistent customer experience is quality monitoring and coaching. Yet there are some fundamental principles that need to be considered when implementing the programme in order to gain the desired outcomes.

With any culture change programme, there is the temptation to jump in and initiate lots of activities without setting the necessary foundations. Customer experience consistency will not be achieved through exhortation, slogans or 'sheep-dip' customer care training courses. The starting point is for senior management to realistically count the 'cost' required to achieve consistent performance (both financial and personal).

QUALITY AT A PRICE

Creating and sustaining a culture based on continuous feedback and learning doesn't come cheap. Therefore the potential benefits and need for action must be clearly articulated. For example, what will the benefits be to each of the stakeholders, including the employees? How will such a strategy differentiate the brand and gain competitive advantage? How does such a commitment fit into the bigger picture?

Quality doesn't come cheap; an initial investment is required. For example, to delight the customer and create loyalty may mean the productivity levels deteriorate. This is an incremental cost that will eventually deliver a return through increased customer value, word-of-mouth advertising, lower cost of sales and so on.

The cost of doing nothing should also be considered. Effective coaching is not cheap either. It requires quality time, typically 45 minutes per session, to be spent preferably in a private environment. Employees will not be won over if there is a half-hearted commitment to excellence by senior management. The worst thing that can happen is to launch a programme of 'service excellence' with full fanfare, raise expectations and, after the initial 'honeymoon' period, resort to the way it was before.

THE ADVISOR AND THE TEAM LEADER

The single most significant influencer to achieving a consistent customer experience is the role and relationship between the advisor and team leader. Team leaders should be role models and in a position to inspire the advisor to reach ever-increasing heights in their performance. Their most important task is to work with their team to help them grow in competence, confidence and strive for excellence.

Coaching is a core competency for all managers, especially team leaders. But how well do we equip them? This is not about training courses but individual support, especially from managers. If you ask a team leader what help they most need, second only to 'less administration' is regular coaching from their manager.

If we choose to ignore the needs of team leaders, we are risking the entire programme. Not only should there be some kind of contract to coach advisors regularly, but it should permeate all the way up the line and make coaching one of the cultural norms.

GOOD EVALUATION

Evaluation is an important component of continuous learning and improvement. However, if the measurement is suspect, this minimizes the usefulness and the potential good it can deliver. Ask any advisor how they feel about their evaluation, though, and they will refer to inconsistencies, unfairness, lack of objectivity and favouritism, among others. Ask the same of team leaders and they will refer to differences in team leader scoring. The opportunity to internally benchmark is then forfeited.

It is important to have realistic expectations about the rate of change. After all, the objective of an effective quality monitoring and coaching programme is to align the behaviours, and therefore the customer experience, to the brand values. This requires time and patience.

GET THE SUPPORT SYSTEMS YOU NEED

When choosing your quality monitoring IT system, don't let the salesman blind you with science. What really matters is the effectiveness of the system to support two key objectives: being able to analyse and present data in a helpful way to support the coaching event and the ability to customize the system. The ultimate requirement of a performance management system is to provide the advisor with online and real-time performance data across all the key performance dimensions, including quality, productivity, attendance, sales, customer satisfaction and so on.

What is it that enables Michael Schumacher to achieve peak performance from his Ferrari? The steering wheel contains instrumentation that provides the information he needs to take proactive actions, which – together with his competency and motivation – achieves peak performance.

Advisors need to be equipped with a real-time, online total performance management system that empowers them to proactively manage their own performance. The team leader, meanwhile, should act as a highly professional coach.

TAKING DATA MONITORING BEYOND PHONE INTERACTIONS

It would seem that, with true voice and data monitoring, for call centres at least, customer loyalty is a reality. But how do you extend the benefits of this monitoring beyond telephone-based interactions? After all, many companies are increasingly implementing web-based technologies to offer customers a wider range of contact points, and therefore promote greater customer loyalty. A diversity of communication channels, from phone to fax, email to web self-service and collaborative web chat are now commonly supported across a host of customer service businesses.

Web-based interactions clearly function differently from telephone calls, demanding different skill sets from agents and evaluation criteria. A collaborative chat system, for instance, enables an agent to interact instantly with customers by sending them messages and documents. Even more advanced applications enable them to take remote control of the customer's browser, such as web self-service, for a more direct resolution of queries. But, despite their cross-training, how can you be sure that agents with first-class telephone skills are consistently able to interact with customers on an electronic level, while still providing the highest standard of service? Furthermore, how can you measure their skills, calibrate the results across a range of diverse media while highlighting specific individual training needs, safeguarding quality assurance and driving your business forward?

BENEFITS FOR THE ADVISOR

Performance analysis software has other immediate and obvious benefits for the agent. By viewing the entire agent/customer interaction in real time and watching how agents manipulate data, managers can see clearly how effectively agents are operating. Where there are any discrepancies, tailored training can be arranged instantly through electronic learning software.

E-learning represents an automated way to bring training and development courses directly to the agent's desktop. In this environment, the e-learning enables companies to augment existing one-on-one coaching and training sessions – which will continue to have an important role in the development process – with newer methods that allow agents to drive training and learn at their own pace. Research has indicated that e-learning is retained at a rate of more than three times that of classroom training, largely because agents are becoming active participants in their own development. The benefits are clear. Agents needn't leave their desks to attend training courses, and, better still, receive individually targeted coaching. And thanks to the monitoring nature implicit in the software, managers can effortlessly perform continuous assessment to gauge the effectiveness of the training.

THE CLOSED LOOP PHILOSOPHY

To truly improve business performance, new processes need to be added to today's call centre operations. Internet interactions and calls need to be recorded, but more importantly evaluated. In turn, feedback and corresponding training options, such as e-learning, must be provided to individual agents to help them become more effective. Ultimately, this has the desired impact on the business in the form of customer service.

29 *Outsourcing*

Mike Harvard, Managing Director and Founder, CM Insight

This chapter addresses how the chances of success can be improved through the way the outsourcing process is conducted, and how to resolve problems if, and when, they do arise. It should be read as a guide to best practice in managing the outsourcing evaluation, contracting and management of a contact centre, and a primer on the key issues and pitfalls to be aware of.

BACKGROUND

The choice of contact centre delivery options available to organizations always used to be summed up in the phrase 'Make or buy?' or 'in-house or outsource?'. How irrelevant this question seems now, considering the vast array of choices available to the business manager – joint ventures, hosted solutions, co-sourcing, insourcing, hybrid options, alliancing – and on it goes. But the principles remain the same and that is what we will start with, moving on to the practicalities of evaluating, justifying, planning, implementing and managing the 'external' resource. Please consider the generic term 'outsourcing' in its broadest sense.

Outsourcing is a mature, yet still growing, practice in business and government for an increasing range of activities – from catering and security to IT and customer management. Deciding whether it is the appropriate solution depends on a variety of factors specific to each organization. In considering outsourcing, I have been neither pro- nor anti-outsourcing; I am on the side of improving the performance of outsourced resources in the customer management sector. There are good examples to be found of well-run outsourced contact-based activities and, unfortunately, plenty of bad ones.

Call centres and outsourcing have long been bedfellows. The requirement for an external resource to handle elements of an organization's telephone-based activity has been recognized as an integral part of the successful management of those activities. The capacity, skills and cost base of third-party suppliers have been leveraged in a number of ways – for short-term relief, mid-term knowledge transfer, or long-term competitive advantage.

A TIME OF CHANGE

However, there is a significant change taking place in the nature of both contact centres and outsourcing. This requires managers to be aware of the new possibilities and issues relating to a third party provision of contact centre services. In both cases, increasing maturity and complexity changes the character of the outsourced service providers, the processes required to appoint and manage them and the nature of the activities that can be outsourced.

REAPING CUSTOMER BENEFITS

Organizations need to catch up with technology, customer expectations and their competitors. Depending on the company's attitude towards risk, and its capital resources, outsourcing may be the quickest and easiest way to reap the benefits of effective customer management. If there is a lack of management experience and knowledge of remotely-based customer interaction, then using an external supplier is also an appropriate way forward.

Customer management initiatives are also providing a significant drive forward for contact centres, since these provide the evidence that the customer experience is being re-engineered to be simpler, quicker and more efficient. Increasingly, outsourced service providers have become (or are attempting to become) more strategic partners, delivering a full range of services, which embrace IT, project management, and process re-engineering, as well as contact handling. New approaches to pricing and managing outsourced contracts are allowing for IT business models to be applied, with both positive and negative implications for resources. There are now many businesses that outsource both customer contact and technology support to one partner.

BECOMING COMMERCIAL

A further development is the way in which an outsourcing project is managed. It has been relatively common for some telephone services to be outsourced on an ad-hoc basis, often with no contract in place. Especially for short-term marketing projects, an incumbent supplier may be repeatedly called upon – often at short notice – to provide call-handling facilities.

This type of management process is no longer acceptable. Purchasing disciplines are being brought to bear which require a more considered approach and an objective validation of decisions. The scale of longer-term outsourcing of call centres will logically require a clear business case, together with sophisticated measurement of the service delivery and the risk-reward ratios.

Senior directors and managers are therefore being asked to consider outsourcing call centres against a background of considerable change. Previous knowledge and experience are still vital, but these need to be augmented by an awareness of the bigger picture of both activities.

In summary, the principles for managing effective external partnerships are to:

- Be clear on why you need to outsource and ensure you understand the benefits and the risks, the available options open to you as well as the financial models and implications for your organization.
- Apply a disciplined methodology to finding and assessing potential outsourcing partners. Taking shortcuts without expert guidance carries a high risk.
- Be robust and balanced in your contracting.
- Be diligent in your implementation.
- Be fair in your engagement and management of the outsourcing relationship.

THE BASICS: DRIVERS AND PRINCIPLES OF OUTSOURCING

It is a combination of changing social attitudes to the use of the telephone as well as the focus for business to attain maximum value at least cost that is fuelling the growth in outsourcing. Rates of growth and adoption of outsourced contact centres vary according to market sector and countries within Europe. However, almost universally this growth is predicted to continue.

THE CUSTOMER SERVICE PERSPECTIVE

In both business and consumer markets, important changes are taking place in the delivery and demand for services. A remarkable convergence of interest is occurring between companies' desire to improve service levels, increase added value and broaden access to the market; and the customer's desire for optimal service performance, lower-cost channels, and faster response. Outsourcing is seen as one of the opportunities to be grasped by organizations to help meet the commercial and customer pressures that they face. It is not without its critics – and in many cases fairly so – but any disregard for the underlying principles and opportunities would be an unfortunate position for the modern manager to adopt.

THE GROWTH OF OUTSOURCING

There is a high level of consensus on the current size and potential of the outsourced contact centre market overall, valued at around $5.1 bn for contact centre outsourcing in Europe in 2001, rising to $10.5 bn in 2005 (Datamonitor Report 2002). Both Giga and Datamonitor estimate that approximately 10 per cent of contact centre seats are outsourced in the UK (slightly higher in Europe at *c.* 12 per cent and higher again in the US at approaching 20 per cent). Currently the growth curve for the adoption of outsourcing varies depending on market observers from 3.5 per cent to 18 per cent.

Economic recession has been shown in the UK and the US to stimulate interest and demand – organizations seek out alternative business and financial models by which to survive, or to weather downturns in the economy. This has the potential for further evolution of an already highly dynamic market, in terms of the supplier base.

TYPES OF SUPPLIERS

There are three broad categories of supplier to be considered:

1 **Traditional:** Organizations that have a heritage in teleservices and customer management activity. The UK position is dominated by US-parented organizations, counterbalanced by a disparate, fragmented array of niche or mid-sized national entities. There is often little, genuine competitive differentiation, the main marketing platforms being proposition (quality, sector, 'style', and so on), technology, brand, and extended service offerings (back-office, billing, data management, customer relationship management (CRM), among others). These organizations tend to have a strong understanding of customer management and competency in contact management systems development. They are less strong in the areas of bid management and contracting, being generally weak at sharing core business risk and reward elements.

2 **Diversifying:** Typically, these are organizations that see the continued growth curve and opportunities in customer management outsourcing, bringing in competencies, finance or relationships from other fields of activity. These could be large IT and systems integrators, moving into other areas of outsourcing, or recognized corporations seeking to exploit a particular in-house competency in order to gain a contribution to overhead, by making a competitive offering in the marketplace. This could be for either short-term margin gain or longer-term value realization.

3 **Emergent:** This is a highly interesting and dynamic part of the market, with new types of entrant appearing regularly. They are often sector biased; based on an accepted market

leadership for customer management in their area, they believe there is opportunity in 'selling' this competency more widely, either to create a revenue stream or to act as a cost contributor. This is a broad category that also includes offshore developments, hosting, alliancing and new venture-backed entities, which all have distinctly different propositions, strengths, weaknesses and risks.

The market has therefore experienced the entry of 'grown-up' suppliers – organizations with mature delivery capability and contracting experience, which distinctly contrast with the telemarketing and small-scale enterprises that originally dominated the sector.

HOW SUCCESSFUL IS OUTSOURCING?

There continue to be high-profile successes and failures, but there is *inconsistent sizing* of the issue, with COPC Inc. in the US suggesting that 73 per cent of outsourcing service provider (OSP) contact centre contracts are 'unlikely' to be renewed at the next contract renewal date.

TOP TEN REASONS TO OUTSOURCE

According to the Outsourcing Index, the top ten reasons for outsourcing are to:

1 Reduce and control operating costs
2 Improve company focus
3 Gain access to world-class capabilities
4 Free up internal resources for other purposes
5 Provide resources that are not available internally
6 Accelerate re-engineering benefits
7 Improve functions that are difficult to manage/out of control
8 Make capital funds available
9 Share risks
10 Provide a cash infusion.

As can be seen from this list, a combination of tactical and strategic issues support the decision to outsource. There is a very strong emphasis on cost management, which is most frequently identified as the key benefit of using an external facility. Releasing capital and benefiting from a cash injection can be important dimensions of the business case.

However, other major process benefits also emerge strongly in the survey, especially around improving the focus of the company and changing its approach more rapidly. There is a recognition that the company may not be performing an activity well, may lack the ability to do it better, or would get to world-class performance more quickly if it outsourced. These reasons are very true for the contact centre, which is only rarely a core competency in most organizations.

A survey conducted by Morgan Chambers revealed that around 20 per cent of outsourcing relationships were deemed unsatisfactory to either or both parties and a further 20 per cent were neither satisfied nor dissatisfied – leaving around 60 per cent of relationships that could be said to be entirely satisfactory.

WHY ARE THERE PROBLEMS WITH OUTSOURCING?

The main reasons for dissatisfaction were stated as:

- outsourcing for the wrong reason – often to get rid of a headache rather than to move the business forward
- poorly specified outsourcing requirements, with assumptions made by both parties, leading to inappropriate implementation
- pricing that prevented the service provider from making a suitable margin, removing the incentive to perform well and reducing the ability of the service provider to invest in development
- inadequate investment in management on the part of the outsourcing organization and poor communications between the two parties
- the inability of the service provider to innovate within a rigid contract specification
- inexperience of supplier management on the part of the outsourcing organization
- lack of diligence in selecting the right outsourcing partner.

Additionally, in our experience, many outsourcers expect too much too soon. The cost-savings from any outsourcing contract are likely to be maximized over many years, as processes and operations are refined and improved. A good working relationship, essential to optimize such savings, needs time to develop.

INVEST IN PLANNING TIME BEFORE YOU OUTSOURCE

It is vital, therefore, that before you begin your search for an outsourcing partner you are able to:

- identify the parts of your business that are non-core and therefore appropriate to be outsourced
- establish robust reasons for outsourcing and demonstrate the business case for outsourcing, in order to understand the fully loaded cost implications and return on investment
- evaluate outsourcing against other options for achieving your objectives, such as business process improvement, joint venturing, hosting or insourcing
- ensure you have buy-in and support from the top down within your organization
- define meaningful measures of success and set realistic expectations of the outsourcing contract
- commit an appropriate level of experienced resource to managing the outsource relationship.

Existing in-house call centres are increasingly being examined for their potential to be transfered to a third party. The Outsourcing Index examined functions that were currently outsourced and that were being planned. Traditional call centre activities that have been shared by both in-house and external call centres are being replaced by more strategic requirements. Elements of customer service and marketing that would previously have been considered as essential company activities are now recognized as being ripe for transferral.

CAPACITY AND CULTURE

The balance between functions that companies have been determined to carry out in-house and those that they have preferred to outsource is often driven by both capacity and culture. Although many organizations perceive customer relationship management as central to their business, the operational delivery of it may require too great a resource for the shape of the organization to sustain. For this reason, inbound customer service continues to represent the single largest task that is outsourced.

Business-to-business calling will also grow strongly, particularly around high value-added sales lead-generation campaigns. Many technical help-desk calls are also business-to-business functions, and this area is set to grow as well. In general, outsourcing in this sector yields higher margins, although contact volumes are lower than in the business-to-consumer scenario.

STRATEGIC SOURCING OPTIONS

Reviewing the elements that can and should be outsourced is a critical evaluation. Determining which options best suit and support the business and its objectives must be discussed, accounting for current demands as well as foreseeable future demands that may be placed upon the contact centre, such as Internet or e-commerce support. The options extend beyond the binary 'make' or 'buy' decision, with a complex and often sophisticated range of hybrid and emerging opportunities, including rapidly developing potential for offshore partnering. The various out-sourcing options are detailed below, with a balanced evaluation of the benefits each could deliver.

ACTIVITY

For the majority of companies, contact centre activity will have developed at differing rates within different functions. There may be short-term, tactical outsourcing of marketing response handling, with insourced long-term technical help-desk operations. Examining each of these in turn for the appropriateness of the supplier, the quality of the service provided, and the fairness of the contract will present opportunities for improved outsourcing arrangements.

OUTSOURCE OR IN-HOUSE OR BOTH

Theoretically, any customer management activity can be outsourced or operated in-house with no variation in performance. In reality, this is seldom the case. What will usually have driven the decision in the past are cultural issues, cost issues and company policy. To be effective, a review of outsourcing should be undertaken to consider the options freely for every activity, with 'fresh eyes', unconstrained or inhibited by previous arrangements.

A spectrum of outsourced activities exists in most companies. At one extreme, the front end of marketing activity will have been handed to a third party, for example lead generation, sales, response handling, outbound contacts. At the other extreme, the company itself will remain responsible for customer service activities. These two arrangements can coexist, but there is a risk of losing revenue, efficiency and customer benefit by not having a more structured, integrated approach.

CORE COMPETENCY

Few organizations have customer relationships as a core competency. Instead, their skills are in manufacturing, product design and innovation, or distribution. For example, a telecommunications company's core competencies are operating the network, devising and delivering services, not in managing customers.

Understanding where an organization's core competencies are is therefore critical as a first step. To begin the review of what to outsource, it is therefore important to consider two dimensions:

- Activities that are currently handled by phone and are capable of being outsourced
- Processes that might be outsourced in order to improve or create better service.

There does not need to be a presumption that every activity should be outsourced – or, conversely, be retained. The goal must be to understand which arrangement would best support the business objectives.

AGENT PROFILE

When considering outsourcing a multimedia contact stream, the agent profile will become more significant. Written communication with a customer has a different legal status to a conversation. This creates the potential for greater exposure if standards and safeguards are not high enough. Agents will also need to be able to write clearly and concisely, and to represent the client company in an appropriate way.

Just as many call centres have blended inbound and outbound calls for their agents, a similar blending of voice and data is occurring. A 'super-agent' group may well be established to handle both streams, with the majority of agents remaining purely telephone based. Consideration needs to be given to the way in which an outsourced service provider will handle each stream and especially to the service level agreements that will apply. These blended groups may initially operate across multiple clients, rather than as a dedicated resource, which might have implications for the contractual arrangement.

OUTSOURCING AND THE NATURE OF THE ENTERPRISE

Two important trends are helping to drive outsourcing, especially of contact centres. These are the concepts of core competency and the unbundled corporation. Tom Peters, the management guru and author of *Thriving On Chaos*, foresees the days of the three-person organization in which just about every function is outsourced. Either as part of an ongoing drive for efficiency, or within the context of business process re-engineering, many companies are questioning what it is essential for them to do, and what activities can be handed over to third parties.

John Hagel and Marc Singer (*Net Worth*, Harvard Business School, 1999) have identified three core competencies around which any company can be said to operate:

- Customer relationships
- Product innovation
- Infrastructure.

They have argued that competitive advantage can best be leveraged by a focus on the second two competencies, allowing the first to be handled elsewhere.

As has been noted, many companies struggle with this concept, as they view the customer as the most important asset of their business. However, the management of relationships does not require the customer to be 'decentred' from the organization. In any outsourced relationship management arrangement, the customer will usually remain unaware that the contact is with a third party. This allows the company to pursue a partnership with the most effective supplier in this area.

What then results is an 'unbundled' organization, where the operational processes do not stop at the formal boundaries of the company, but cross over into third-party partner companies. This type of arrangement is already being pursued in other areas. For example, retailers and their manufacturing suppliers are cooperating to improve the supply chain by sharing information and systems.

Control and confidence are the emotional issues at play. Just because the contact centre is located two floors down in the organization's own building does not necessarily mean that management has any greater level of confidence in its reliability, performance or quality than if it was based in Alaska, for example. The issue is one of effective management information and well-structured service level agreements that give rise to confidence and control. These are independent of geography and supplier.

OUTSOURCING OPTIONS

Where outsourcing has been identified as an option for some, or all, of the customer-facing activities in an organization, consideration needs to be given to the type of outsourcing structure that is to be pursued. There are five potential options (other than DIY – the 'make it yourself' option):

- **Insourcing**: Component parts (staff, training, systems support, and so on) are sourced individually against supplier competencies but the infrastructure is retained by the client.
- **Selective outsourcing**: Component parts are outsourced to one or more suppliers while certain elements are retained, based upon the respective competencies and ambitions of the various parties.
- **Alliancing**: Two organizations work together to service or support each other in a mutually beneficial arrangement; for example, non-competing companies may have alternating peaks and troughs, or cycles of activity, so that each can cover the other's peaks. The UK utilities and travel industries have led the way in this area. A risk with this type of venture is that the organization's own customers would always take priority over the partner's, which has created tension in these relationships.
- **Co-sourcing**: This involves greater degrees of partnership or venturing and has included, for example, locating the entire management structure of the outsourcing company on the outsourced service provider's premises, through to more formal joint venturing.
- **Total outsourcing**: All processes, infrastructure and service responsibility can be handed over, for example the entire front-office structure, but increasingly also the entire customer experience structure, such as back-office billing systems, and so on.

These five options are usually based upon three scenarios:

1 Migration or expansion of the business.
2 A new business requirement.
3 Incubation, hosting or 'hotelling' of a new business concept in its early stages, whereby the client manages the operation and own the service responsibility but the physical infrastructure (premises, workstations, IT and telephony hardware) is rented from the host organization. Usually the client would be responsible for the systems integration and application software as well. Potentially, any or all of the other component parts (staff, training, and so on) can be provided by the client, contracted via the host company or sourced separately.

All of these options should be available to the company, although not all suppliers offer each one. The outsourcing market for contact centres is still immature, especially compared to the maturity of IT outsourcing, but many of the models developed for outsourcing technology are beginning to be applied to contact centres. The majority of interest is currently around selective outsourcing.

INSOURCING

Insourcing the contact centre can be approached in two ways – set-up outsourcing and in-house resource. Set-up outsourcing involves a company hiring a contact centre outsourcer to help set up its own in-house operations. This often takes place as part of a process re-engineering project to refocus the company on the customer. The aim is to leverage the expertise of external specialists during the initiation of an in-house call centre, but with the clear goal of fully taking over the facility within six months to a year.

Insourcing can also be useful during later stages of contact centre operation, and can be especially valuable during periods of transition, development or organizational stress. The company leases human or technical resource for a given period of time. The success of this approach relies on effective knowledge transfer. Insourced teams can provide a vital source of process and culture knowledge, where this is lacking internally. Leased technical resources can also be used to gain best-in-class technology, to ensure that capacity is available, or that capital expenditure is reduced.

SELECTIVE OUTSOURCING

The majority of outsourced service uptake is provided on a selective basis. It offers some benefits, such as immediate access to best-in-class systems, cost reduction, improved capacity and phased learning.

Transitional outsourcing relates to the use of a service bureau while internal infrastructures are being revamped, rebuilt or upgraded, which forces a company to temporarily scale back its in-house call centre operations. In this case, an outsourcing bureau will provide services on a short-term basis while the client upgrades its own facilities. In many cases, this can involve simply handling overflow calls for a client. Caution needs to be taken with this approach, however. If too few calls are overflowed, the OSP does not build up enough knowledge about the client's business. Without sufficient volume, it will not gain a feel for the customer or the issues that are emerging. A better way of partially outsourcing capacity is to assign a fixed percentage of calls to the third party, which then handles a defined volume during peak times. While this does require letting go of some of the business, it will produce a better quality of call handling and customer views.

It is likely that, as in-house call centres age, more and more companies will be turning to outsourcers to help them through the transitional period between phasing out an old call centre and installing and integrating updated equipment in their in-house operation. There is also a growth in the use of 'incubator' facilities. These are call centre operations that have fully-configured telecommunications and workstations, but no permanent staff.

Co-sourcing as a model has the potential for greater prevalence in the future; operating almost as a joint venture agreement where the various requirements for service infrastructure, for example, people and IT are dealt with by a supplier. An alternative approach might mean that the business management of the client company is co-housed within the operational infrastructure of the supplier, to improve its visibility, communications and relationships with the third party.

The advantage of this type of outsourcing environment is its potential cost advantage, because the outsourcing company is pulling apart the various components and getting the best-of-breed suppliers for each. However, there is an increased management overhead for the client. Despite the cost advantage, flexibility is likely to be the key factor in choosing this approach. The incubator facility can be grown rapidly, or downsized if the Internet and self-help technologies replace calls, for example. Forecasts for volumes three years out do not need to be made to justify capital investment, as the only overhead is likely to be people costs.

TOTAL OUTSOURCING

Handing an entire business line or area of activity to a third party is still relatively rare. One of the drivers of this type of outsourcing is customer relationship management (CRM). For many companies, CRM is beyond their existing capabilities and outside of their culture, but could potentially be effectively handled by a third party with the experience and technical capability. That said, there is often confusion around CRM and what can realistically be achieved in partnership with an outsourcer. It is usually rather a euphemism for 'multi-channel contact centre capabilities' – a more realistic objective, though somewhat different from a business objective of realizing full CRM potential across the organization.

A totally outsourced call centre contract may involve one complete area of customer interaction, such as a help desk, enquiry line, or customer service centre. By assigning a clearly defined activity in this way to a supplier in its entirety, the contracting and measurement become easier to handle and the focus easier to maintain, although the perceived risk of 'letting go' often overrides this benefit. A company may choose to outsource all of its telephone-based customer contact. By having a third party at the front-line of interaction with the market, many of the difficulties of dealing with the customer alongside everyday business processes are removed.

A BALANCED EVALUATION OF OUTSOURCING

Outsourcing needs to be considered and understood as an option that meets certain business requirements at certain times. It is not a panacea for business problems, nor is it purely a short-term fix for capacity or capital issues – outsource a headache and you will still have to deal with the pain. In modern business, an outsourced resource is as much a part of the main business process as any internal function. The key differences relate to flexibility, capital expenditure, and risk.

Retaining everything in-house is not always the best choice, as internal functions can cost more, be harder to manage and may not relate well to the rest of the organization. In the case of contact centres, this is often reinforced by their position within the organizational structure, with most centres operated separately from the business, frequently with a different culture and system of rewards.

Conversely, fully outsourced operations may deliver better standards for an activity that is a necessary cost. The risk is that the outsourced service provider could take advantage of the situation and, therefore, the company. To understand how the business will react to each approach to outsourcing, some form of internal assessment needs to be carried out. This will help to predict internal reactions to the resource once it has been set up.

A matrix of factors has been used at a basic level to determine whether or not to outsource. The four options are determined by the degree of internal competency and advantage to be gained. Self-evaluation of the activities under consideration can be carried out using the matrix in Figure 29.1, with each activity mapped against the two axes. If a clear grouping emerges, then following one approach for all activities might be appropriate. If they fall into a variety of quadrants, then selective outsourcing may be the way forward.

In summary, the choice is no longer between an outsourced and an in-house solution; there are many hybrid models offering viable alternatives. In some cases, the solution may seem obvious and clear-cut; in others there may be more than one option that could fit the bill.

In either case, it is essential to carefully evaluate each option in terms of the proposed benefits, all the costs (including overheads, redeployment or redundancy of existing staff and so on) and the risks you will incur, whether in changing your customer management model or in maintaining the status quo.

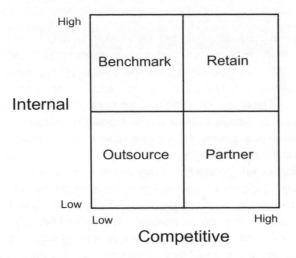

Figure 29.1   Mapping outsourcing against advantage gained © CM Insight

OVERSEAS OUTSOURCING: FACT OR FICTION?

The debate surrounding call centre outsourcing – always strong – is hotting up again as the economic arguments in favour of moving operations offshore become increasingly evident and, given today's tough economic climate, ever more compelling. To date, India has been the favoured location. English-speaking business culture, world-class operations, strong technology, facilities and an educated, motivated, IT-literate labour pool, are powerful lures for companies seeking more cost-competitive ways to keep pace with increasingly sophisticated customer service expectations. After all, operating costs in India can be as much as 40 per cent lower than the UK in an outsourced environment, and up to 70 per cent lower for self-build options.

Around five UK companies a week were taking some call centre or back-office work to India in early 2002. For most, this amounts to little more than 'testing the water' with projects that are relatively small and experimental in nature. The tide, however, is inexorable and the current hardening of the economic climate in Europe will turn the trickle of work moving to India into a flood, swelling the ranks of larger programmes and companies that have already proved the advantages of outsourcing to the region: British Airways, American Express, GE Capital, Willis Faber and others.

But just how real are the financial incentives and are they sufficient?

Salaries for entry-level call centre staff are around 85 to 90 per cent lower than their European counterparts and the quality of personnel is extremely high. Even at these levels salaries are above the service-sector average, making call centres an attractive and even aspirational option for the two million graduates that enter the Indian job market every year (over 70 per cent of whom will remain unemployed). Given that around 60 per cent of call centre costs are in people, these figures are enticing. On the flip side, however, the cost of installing high-quality international telecoms links, IT and power systems is higher when developing offshore locations. Combined with travelling expenses and management time spent overseas it's likely to cost around twice as much to move a project to India as to keep it in the UK. However, the wage savings, combined with the concessions offered by state and national governments to attract inward investment, can bring the overall costs down dramatically. Savings of between 30 and 40 per cent – enough to make any finance officer's eyes light up – are realistic, and are being achieved when in partnership with an outsourced service provider. To place that in context, a 50-seat project is likely to recoup the cost of the move to India, for example, within only three months.

FAR-REACHING BENEFIT

The benefits are not just financial. So far the call centre industry in India is avoiding many of the negative characteristics that have beleaguered it in the UK. Most significantly, Indian call centres are outdistancing their UK counterparts in their commitment to rigorous and internationally recognized business process standards. Many have already gained ISO 9001 accreditation and others are working towards the stringent COPC (Customer Operations Performance Centre) US standard or the GE-perfected Six-Sigma quality standard. All of this makes for highly robust operations with good working environments and strong personnel management.

In the area of technology, too, India is strong. Its IT software and services industry, long its pride and joy, has grown at a rate of 50 per cent per annum since 1991 and is expected to top $67 billion by 2008 (approximately 12 per cent of the world's software development). As a result, India's contact centre operators are up to speed with the latest and best developments and have had the sagacity to invest in them, recognizing that nervous clients need the reassurance of systems and platforms they know and trust.

Similarly, in anticipation of client concerns about the robustness of their telecoms and power back-up systems, Indian contact centres have covered all eventualities. Experience shows that disaster recovery infrastructure in India is comparable, if not better, than anything in the West. Frankly, it needs to be so. Power cuts around 10 to 15 per cent of the time are an accepted way of life in India, and the situation isn't getting better quickly. As one Indian organization's CEO quoted: 'If we don't have power we know we don't have a business – our business continuity preparations should therefore be unrivalled.'

In the final analysis, the fact that leading western businesses, such as BA, GE and American Express, now have well-established in-house operations that have been successfully operating out of India for many years, should be sufficient to allay any outstanding concerns about infrastructure, people or technology. But the picture can't all be rosy. There are challenges that any company considering a move to India, or elsewhere, must confront and overcome.

CHALLENGES FOR OFFSHORE

One of the most significant challenges is the threat of adverse publicity or customer reaction, in two key areas: companies fear accusations of worker exploitation in developing markets and of contributing to UK unemployment figures. This still means that, for many organizations, the subject of outsourcing offshore remains taboo. But this challenge must be faced head on. After all, overseas outsourcing in other industries, including manufacturing, is now an accepted commonplace. Actual examples of bad practice, though shocking, are relatively few.

Simply, the attractions of offshore outsourcing are based upon low-cost labour. With this advantage will then come the myriad of risks associated with the countries or regions able to provide this resource: those being language, infrastructure, accessibility, telecoms, political, and business climate and investment challenges. It is therefore essential to fully explore each of these elements before investing in any given offshore location. This suggests that the interesting markets for the UK will be South Africa, Malaysia, the Philippines and possibly some north and eastern European locations – for example Turkey and Lithuania.

CHOOSING A COUNTRY

Like any outsourcing project, choosing the country where it will operate should be approached with a clear set of objectives and measurements in mind. Every element of the solution should be considered and its pros and cons weighed up. Ultimately, an outsourcing decision is a balance and understanding of three factors: the risk, the financials and the quality. There are, however, a number of issues specific to offshore outsourcing, which should be given extra consideration. Among these are:

- **Telecommunications**: In many cases, there are some significant challenges and hurdles. For example, calls to India across a standard PSTN (Public Switched Telephone Network) are subject to echoing and voice delay. To counter this, however, many of the major Indian suppliers have set up their own high-bandwidth IPLC (international private leased circuit), usually involving satellite links, which provides the same high level voice quality as we can get at home. In addition, all the 'last mile' and resilience risks should be well considered.
- **Language and accent**: It's very important that the agents be understood, and are capable of working not just to the word that is being spoken by the customer, but also to the context within which it is said and the social norms for interaction and behaviour. There are now a number of call centre colleges that train agents in the language and colloquialisms of the customer countries. Accent is not as relevant – many calls managed today within the UK are handled by staff with distinctive regional accents and this does not generally create a problem with the wider public. Do beware of claims that accents in India, for example, can be 'negated' or 'neutralized' – this is not necessarily realistic and best treated with caution.
- **Culture**: Obviously, this varies greatly from country to country, so an outsourcer should make sure that the culture and business practices of their service provider complements their own and is aligned with their requirements and their consumers' expectations.
- **Risk**: To what degree are you risking your important customer communications by offshore outsourcing? What if it all goes wrong so far away from home? One way of reducing this risk is to start by outsourcing non-critical functions (for example back office, basic enquiry activity, low-value interactions). If this proves successful, and any wrinkles are ironed out as confidence and understanding increase, then you can then begin to outsource the more business-critical elements of your service.
- **Attitude towards offshore outsourcing**: It is certainly a different business relationship from that which most companies are used to, so it is important to have the support of all interested parties within your own organization for your offshore strategy, and to enlist expert support in managing the relationship.
- **Exchange rate fluctuations**: Even with additional travel and accommodation costs included, it can still be significantly cheaper for you to outsource to another country. However, exchange-rate fluctuations may take some of the edge off your savings. This can be managed in three ways; first, by paying in your own currency. If paying in local currency, 'hedge' your exposure by agreeing a fixed rate of exchange with your bank for a period, such as 12 months, ahead. This latter option might be desirable at times when sterling is strong. Third, and certainly the most preferable, contract with a UK entity or arm of the Indian service provider. This way you will be covered under English (or Scottish) law and have a local billing relationship.

However you choose to outsource offshore, you can be sure that there is an increasing number of businesses doing the same as you.

ASSESSING THE BUSINESS CASE FOR OUTSOURCING

Developing the business case for outsourcing needs to be a thorough and well-considered process. Ensuring the correct accounting approach and inclusion of all appropriate cost elements is essential. This can often encompass not just first-line support costs, but also associated administrative and back-office functions, overhead allocation and partner margin expectations. The range of charging options is discussed in this section, along with how to strike the right balance between the risk and reward structure of the contract for both parties.

CORE ELEMENTS OF THE BUSINESS CASE

Writing a clear, detailed business case is one of the most important steps in outsourcing. And one of the key elements of the case is an assessment of the risks involved, balancing the opportunities and benefits in retaining a call centre in-house with those to be secured from outsourcing. Understanding and quantifying the risks is critical.

One thing that can be predicted with confidence is that objections to contact centre outsourcing will be raised internally. Unless the objectives have been established and costed, and the benefits outlined for the project, it will be difficult to respond to challenges that arise from within the business. The source of these protests will vary, depending on the nature of the activity being outsourced, but will almost certainly include the finance department, staff associations, the in-house contact centre, which might be subject to or feel threatened by outsourcing, and the sales, customer services and marketing departments, which might be affected. There is also a significant degree of sensitivity surrounding the people who are directly affected by a decision to outsource, such as front-line agents and team leaders.

Within the business case there should be precise quantification of what an outsourced contact centre will deliver for each of the stakeholders in the project. By having this documented upfront, many of the objections in the early stages can be reduced to symbolic protests. The logic of the business case should counter any complaints about loss of control, loss of territory, or increased cost.

According to KPMG Consulting, developing the business case should involve consideration of four key aspects:

- Determining whether the activity is non-core, and therefore whether it should be outsourced.
- Documenting clearly the reasons for outsourcing the activity.
- Benchmarking the activity; first understanding the real internal costs to then allow for comparisons in improved performance through outsourcing.
- Understanding the strategic, political and managerial implications of outsourcing.

Experience suggests that communication (from effectively 'socializing' your ideas to executing persuasive strategies with good, clear documentation and financials) is a vital addition to the above list.

Benchmarking is one of the most overlooked aspects of any outsourcing project. Unless current metrics exist for the activity (excluding where the outsourcing is for a start-up function), it will be difficult to prove why there will be improvements in performance through outsourcing, or even if this is the case.

Table 29.1   Business benefits from outsourcing © KPMG Consulting

	% of companies mentioning benefit
Enables the company to concentrate on core business expertise	76
Flexibility for future workload planning	67
Reduction in operating costs	65
Reduction in staff costs	63
Improved customer service	57
Streamlining of the company/downsizing	51
Reduction in management effort	50
Increase in profitability	41
Motivated staff	37
Flexibility in contract	36
Reduction in bureaucracy	34
Unambiguous contract	33
Competitive edge	29
Decentralization	14
Don't know	4

One critical requirement is to define the commitment on the part of the company to manage the relationship with the outsourced service provider. It is easy to assume that outsourcing is a one-off management decision that results in handing the processes over to a third party with no need for further supervision.

TUPE

If the project is to replace an in-house resource, redundancy and tax implications need to be considered. Exposure and liabilities may arise from replacing an internal resource under the Transfer of Undertakings (Protection of Employment) Regulations 1981 (TUPE). This is a critical area to understand if you are in any way potentially exposed or liable – or indeed if your preferred partner assumes any liability.

The potential liabilities likely to arise from the outsourcing of a function or call centre process (or the liabilities that it is likely to take with it) need diligent and specific legal clarification. The complex European legal framework surrounding TUPE can have a dramatic effect on the viability of the business, specifically the inheriting supplier, and requires special care and consideration prior to commitment and contracting. Where TUPE is a major issue, for example with many Government outsourcing contracts, OSPs exist with specialist knowledge or expertise.

There are three key areas within the business case that may generate opportunities to justify outsourcing the contact centre:

1   Reducing costs by freeing up overhead, both through redeploying the space in which a call centre was housed and allocating staff to other roles.
2   Adding value through the greater expertise of the OSP – this is their core competency, after all – whereas for the client managing the resource can be a major headache. The experience of the outsourced service provider gained from other sectors and clients can help to introduce new ideas and innovations in processes and learning.
3   Shared technologies and infrastructure can bring considerable efficiencies within a third-party operation, together with dedicated staff, ongoing recruitment and incentive schemes, and operational and management practices that are focused purely on the contact centre.

In assessing the cost savings and added value that will be introduced by outsourcing, the benchmark for comparison is whether it will be equal to or less than the margin that the supplier is seeking to make. Where the benefits and savings exceed the margin, the case is positive, but if they are less, then it will be harder to justify.

More complex financial models may also demonstrate the case for outsourcing. With new business ventures especially, removing the capital base of an in-house call centre may be the only way to enter a new market. It may also reflect the recognition that the company's core competency relates to product innovation or distribution, rather than customer contact.

PAYMENT MODELS FOR OUTSOURCING

Table 29.2 outlines outsourcing pricing options and their respective advantages and disadvantages. The most appropriate method of contract pricing will vary according to individual circumstances and drivers for outsourcing. It is important, though, to enter these discussions from a position of strength, to understand that there are options and to be aware of the various pros and cons of each. Experience shows that a combination of the above, where there is a shared risk between the parties, is most beneficial. Where performance-related payment is incorporated, this has to be related to measures within the supplier's control. Where trying to reduce absolute costs, it is good to eradicate irrelevant costs, but you must ensure that investment in critical areas remains, for example ensuring the appropriate level of account management. At the start of the

Table 29.2 Advantages and disadvantages of outsourcing pricing options

Payment structure	Advantages of this approach	Disadvantages of this approach
Cost per unit (that is, per minute or per call)	• Simple to budget • Simple to measure and validate • Simple to allocate to departments/cost centres • Inter-supplier comparisons simple • Low calls, low fee	• No risk taken by supplier • Minimum guarantees on volumes/capacity • Inappropriate focus may be placed upon maximizing revenue-earning units
Cost per call outcome that is, per sale, or per appointment)	• Shared risk • Results based • Direct ROI calculations • Clear focus for supplier	• Can be complex calculation and be spread over time • Spin-off impact if over-emphasis on results (at any cost) • Factors outside supplier's control can cause angst (and complex caveats)
Fixed fee (that is, agreed fee per year)	• Known absolute cost • Zero financial risk • Reduced management time in validating and checking fees • Financial security of supplier can fund required investment in the contract	• Unknown value – may be overpaying • Limited visibility of supplier's performance • Quality often focuses only on volume management capabilities • Supplier's margin is a key driver
Open book (that is, true cost plus X% – linked to performance)	• Balanced risk • Avoids overpaying • Comparable model to conducting activity in-house • Excessive supplier margin only paid on excessive ROI	• Little incentive to reduce cost base • Difficulty in understanding the 'true costs' • Understanding of fixed costs and overheads • Complex to manage, especially auditing

contract, ensure that the supplier is entering into the delivery stage, happy to undertake the contract and not feeling as if they have been beaten up! The use of independent experts to strike this balance and achieve a fair contract is proving to be very successful.

EVALUATING POTENTIAL PARTNERS

Evaluating which organizations to pursue and invite to reply to tender is difficult. Initially a desk-based approach is sufficient, but this needs to be backed up by a more formal qualification process to identify appropriate OSPs that will receive your proposal request. This pre-proposal evaluation needs a careful and fair selection process. It should take account of the emotional element of assessing the potential relationship and 'fit', as well as the rational consideration of infrastructure, competencies, capabilities and experience.

Maximize your chances of finding the optimum partner by adopting a proven methodology. There is no 'right way' to buy. However, summarized below is CM Insight's proven methodology for outsourcing both large and small operations. Applying a procurement methodology doesn't necessarily involve undue delay; the key point is to have a process and framework for reference and comparison.

1. Define the requirement

Whether you are setting up from scratch or transferring (and improving) existing business areas, it is absolutely essential that you invest in the time to develop a full requirement specification. Depending on the area of the business to be outsourced, this will include key information, for example:

- the background to and reasons for the outsourcing decision
- your business objectives
- how the contract will be supported and managed within your organization
- descriptions of the services and processes to be outsourced – with documented business processes and flows, demonstrating the work requirements and links between the different areas of your organization
- current activity sources, volumes, durations and patterns
- forecast activity levels and reasons – marketing plans, organization growth forecasts, and so on
- current service level and key performance indicator achievements, plus objectives for the new contract
- systems requirements – existing platforms, new developments required, and so on
- management information and reporting requirements
- quality management requirements
- level of resource required to successfully deliver the work and definition of the skill-sets and training required
- definition of your organization's vision for the relationship between your organization and the outsourced service provider, including any 'ownership', branding and cultural issues and preferences
- timetable for the project with milestone dates to be achieved
- key personnel and responsibilities
- costs, budgets and projected return on investment
- restrictions such as location or potential conflicts of interest that may be encountered.

Once the requirement has been specified in detail, you will be in a position to identify the type of organization that is most likely to meet your objectives, in terms of experience, size, capabilities, location and management style.

2. Identifying and qualifying potential outsource service providers

With your primary qualification criteria in mind – type of outsource service partner, size of organisation, relevant experience (of handling the type of work you're placing and possibly also of your sector, although this may be less important), location and so on – you will need to draw up a list of organizations as your starting point.

Draw up a checklist of the basic information you require and make contact. Ask for:

- **Experience**:
  - Work types and vertical sectors
  - Number, size and duration of contracts
  - Client list
  - What your business would offer them
- **Company information:**
  - Size (for example, number of workstations, current contact volumes)
  - When founded, ownership, revenue, growth projections
  - Marketing literature and relevant case studies
  - Check the contact details
- **Business organization:**
  - Current workstation utilization (how much of their capacity is being used?), available capacity, growth plans
  - Management structure
  - Stability of the management team
  - Stability of the operations team – agents and team leaders
- **Company ethos:**
  - Quality accreditation, such as ISO, IIP, COPC or compliance with the Call Centre Association Standards Framework
  - Membership of industry bodies, such as the Call Centre Association
  - What sort of work are they looking for?

When asking for this information, did you feel comfortable with the way your enquiry was handled?

You may also wish to narrow the field by gathering additional information that will give you a better feel for the likely 'fit' between your company and the potential service provider. This can be done in a number of ways, for example:

- Visiting the company to experience the atmosphere of the operation(s) and meet some of the management team.
- Inviting service providers to demonstrate their position, intention and vision in relation to a specific area of your business, by means of a written response to a brief or set question(s). This might, for example, seek to uncover their understanding of your marketplace and the way in which they would need to approach the delivery of your brand values to your customers via the outsourced customer contact experience.

Put all your collected information and views into a spreadsheet to facilitate comparisons and, ideally, develop a scoring system to help you draw up the list of six or so companies that are to be invited to tender. Before issuing the invitation to tender, it is always prudent to ask the organizations to sign a confidentiality agreement.

3. The Invitation to Tender

Prepare the Invitation to Tender document, drawing from the Requirement Specification document. If you intend to have a high level of involvement in the ongoing management of the outsourced activity, you may wish to be very prescriptive in your requirements. Alternatively, you may be looking for a high degree of proactivity from your OSP and seek to be challenged with creative solutions. Whatever your preferred approach, the invitation to tender should enable participants to:

- understand the requirement in sufficient detail to identify how they will be able to meet your requirement
- propose their solution, or demonstrate how they intend to meet your requirements
- cost their solution.

The invitation to tender should include directions on:

- How to respond – what should be included and what to avoid (for example, how you wish costs to be presented, to facilitate comparison)
- Deadline for the response and format of the response (soft copy, hard copy, to whom)
- How to obtain answers to questions about the tender or the requirement and a deadline for so doing. You may choose to circulate answers to all the questions to all the tenderers, irrespective of the originator.

While there is often pressure to appoint a service provider and outsource the activity as quickly as possible, it is essential to allow the tenderers time for questions and enable all relevant staff within the organization to contribute to a worthwhile response. Between two and three weeks is usually sufficient, unless the requirement is extremely complex or key staff might not be available due to national holidays or some other reason.

4. Making the decision

Although price is important, it is not the only measure by which you should choose an outsourcing partner, if you are to avoid entering into a contract that is more likely to fail. When compiling your requirement specification and Invitation to Tender, you will become aware of the relative importance to your organization of a number of criteria that will need to be met by the service provider and will have a fundamental impact on the ability of a service provider to deliver your requirement successfully.

These will include, for example:

- Experience of managing contracts similar to your own requirement
- Availability of a stable, qualified workforce
- Calibre of management and organizational leadership
- Systems capabilities and support structure.

The criteria can be listed and weighted to create an objective, consistent benchmark against which each tender can be scored.

The CM Insight scoring model, PEACH©, includes a large number of variables, grouped in the following categories:

Physical capabilities
Experience
Attitude
Costs and contract proposition
Human factors

The weighting of each grouping and of each factor within the group ultimately depends on its relative value to the outsourcing client organization. The scoring method should be developed in line with the invitation to tender document, to ensure that all the factors are included that are of importance in making the decision. This will also help to make scoring the tenders more straightforward.

A note of caution – look beyond the sales presentation for evidence of real experience. Meet the team who will be delivering your requirement – can you work with them, do you trust them?

CONTRACTING, SERVICE LEVEL AGREEMENTS AND THE PITFALLS OF FORMAL ENGAGEMENT

Contracting is a critical process in outsourcing as it defines how the operation will be run, paid-for and managed. It should specify pricing, service levels, reporting and management processes, each of which can be set out in a separate schedule. The contract is a working document, the common point of reference for both parties. As such, it should be mutually agreeable, beneficial, and kept up-to-date throughout its lifetime by the ongoing incorporation of negotiated amendments.

Successful contract negotiations should address the following issues:

- the contract period
- definition and scope of services to be provided
- service levels required
- client obligations
- management structure
- confidentiality and data issues
- benchmarking criteria
- disaster recovery
- reporting and management
- exit management
- change management
- problem resolution
- price, performance and charging structure.

OPTIMIZING THE PARTNER RELATIONSHIP

With the supplier in place, the relationship requires ongoing management input and support. A positive relationship requires mutual respect, chemistry and appropriate inputs. These include the right kind of reporting at the right time, accurate benchmarking and monitoring, and validation of measures through third parties. Without correct usage of these, friction, misunderstanding and disputes will occur.

STARTING ON THE RIGHT FOOT

Throughout the specification of the outsourcing project, the evaluation of suppliers, the tendering process and the contract negotiations, it is important to keep in sight the fact that the activity being outsourced is an ongoing process. Having signed the deal, things are only just beginning, rather than coming to an end. It is at the inception of the contract that the effectiveness of the preceding stages will be realized. A well-managed process should produce a good relationship. Poorly managed outsourcing projects are likely to experience difficulties early on.

A number of factors will influence how well the outsourcing relationship progresses. These include:

- the supplier's style of management
- proximity of the outsourced call centre
- visibility of the supplier
- degree of openness, transparency and trust in the contract
- personal chemistry.

Depending on the level of performance being achieved, it is possible for these factors to become friction points, especially the interaction between personalities on both sides.

Managing the politics of outsourcing, through internal marketing, achieving early buy-in, and having high-level support and sponsorship for the objectives, should help to overcome resistance. In research conducted by Ventura, 60 per cent of directors expressed a fear of loss of control and 48 per cent feared a loss of contact. Another study by IBM amongst *The Times* Top 1000 found that 84 per cent of business directors feared a loss of control through outsourcing, yet 84 per cent (we would suspect a slightly different set) agreed that outsourcing reduces cost and improves efficiency. This shows the turmoil and conflict in the minds of senior management about the risk–versus–benefit argument. It also indicates that the relationship needs to be conceived and managed on an emotional level, as well as a rational one.

There are inherent differences between the various outsourcing relationships. For example, a utility that needs to adapt and improve its flexibility, weighed down by historic processes and encumbrances, being forced to work with a nimble, young, dynamic OSP. This may be the very competitive advantage that the utility needs, but it has to be recognized that in the working relationship there is likely to be some tension and frustration in the coexistence of two culturally opposed bodies.

CREATING SUCCESS

There are four hallmarks of successful outsourced relationship management:

- creating a shared vision;
- using effective performance measures;
- establishing clear communications mechanisms;
- developing a clear contingency plan and exit strategy.

Ongoing reviews of performance against targets are key to the operational management of the call centre. This can be made easier through exception reporting, whereby variances, rather than adherence, are reported to the client. However, hard data on its own does not tell the whole story. The quality of calls, the quality of service, and the impact on end customers will not be reflected in ACD and other technology statistics.

It can be difficult to persuade senior managers to look beyond hard data, not least because, while performance indicators provide a clear baseline, softer measures are often relative – even subjective. A high abandoned call rate can be understood as having an impact on the bottom line, because of the loss of potential business. But many directors and senior managers may not acknowledge the same impact from poor call handling quality.

DEALING WITH RELATIONSHIP 'CHALLENGES'

The scale of the resources employed within a call centre, the degree of contact with the customer base, and the dynamics of the operation mean that problems are commonplace. Rather than responding negatively, problems should be confronted and worked through. Information, negotiation, and, if appropriate, mediation are key to moving things on. Increasingly, outsourcing companies do not have the option of walking away, so resolving disputes is a skill that has to be learned.

Problems do occur, your situation may not be unique

There is a US military phrase that seems apt: *SNAMU – Situation Normal – All Messed Up*. All types of business activity suffer from problems at some time. The degree of complexity of the problem will vary, as will the ease with which it can be resolved. Call centres are not necessarily more prone to difficulties than any other activity. However, there are aspects of customer contact-based activity that mean that problems can rapidly escalate or expose the business to risk. And, by their very nature, they are often far more visible or detectable (being only a phone call away) than, say, production-line issues in a manufacturing environment, or system downtime issues in an outsourced IT environment.

There are five typical reasons that problems arise:

1   **Cost/pricing issues**. This is one of the most frequent areas of dispute and often arises because one party feels hard done by in a deal.
2   **Lack of management skills**. Experience of call centres on the client side is relatively shallow. This can create difficulties for the outsourcing client company in understanding the dynamics of how an operation works and what its limitations may be, and therefore how performance improvements should be pursued.
3   **Poor integration of the contact centre into the organization**. As an outsourced resource, the contact centre may suffer from a lack of ownership within the client's management structure. This can create differences between the objectives of the client company and those of the contact centre. It may also mean that the contact centre poorly represents the client's brand and positioning.
4   **Poor long-term strategic planning**. Often call centres have been outsourced for tactical reasons that are then superseded by other strategic objectives, without the necessary process change; or no consideration has been given to how to develop the contact centre service to align with the new objectives. Alternatively, call centres may be seen just 'at the end of the chain' when they are actually an integral and central part of the business.
5   **Service quality competing against supplier margins**. Neither side wants to feel exploited in the relationship, but there is frequently a heavy imbalance in favour of either the client or the supplier as a result of the way that the contract has been negotiated. This will rapidly escalate any service issues into a confrontation.

Getting the balance right between price and quality is difficult for both parties, especially if cost-reduction has been a driver in the outsourcing project, or where success is only being measured on hard performance data. Some organizations are beginning to address quality in balance with cost-efficiency, where they have a mature relationship with their outsourced service provider. The top level is to address value, but very few companies make it to that stage.

Aside from specific gripes about contracts, performance and payment, there are three other key reasons why problems tend to occur. These are:

1   **A significant skills gap at middle management level**. However high up the decision has been taken to run a call centre operation, the practical management is usually delegated to relatively junior or middle management. Executives at this level may not have the right skills and experience to deal with critical tasks such as effective forecasting, scheduling, quality and margin management, skills and people management.
2   **Over-selling and over-claiming by suppliers**. With the growth of outsourcing, suppliers have exaggerated their abilities and capacity in order to win an ever-greater share of the contracts being assigned. This means that they are pushing the boundaries of their competency on bigger projects, with the result that service levels and service quality suffer.
3   **Over-expectation among clients**. Poor procurement and poor benchmarking by client companies have created false expectations about what performance and delivery levels are possible at each level of investment. This ultimately leads to dissatisfaction with suppliers.

Resolving problems and using mediation

The response of clients or OSPs to problems often reflects a prevailing culture. Just as outsourcing projects are moving away from being tactical and directed towards achieving the lowest possible price for the contract, so too a new way of addressing problems is emerging. Across industry, there is a greater sense of the need to work with all partners in a business in order to maintain focus, innovation and advantage. This is exemplified by the perception that a company is responsible to its stakeholders, rather than just to its investors.

In the macro-socio-economic world, negotiation and mediation are beginning to replace conflict. Political settlements and the prospect of negotiated peace deals are remarkable indicators of how even the most intractable issues can be dealt with through persistent negotiation and a commitment to seeing a process through. A mediator can act as the honest broker, interrogating both parties from an independent and objective perspective.

There will be situations where the relationship has deteriorated to the extent where it is beyond salvage (or where the effort in salvaging the relationship is not considered a prudent investment by either or both parties). In these situations, three principles should be considered:

1   Call upon qualified legal support to ensure that the situation is commercially under control and that your risks are covered against claims of breach of contract and such like.
2   Maintain openness and dialogue with the supplier and their staff to ensure that there is good and clear communication in the winding-down and migration process to optimize the support and commitment for as long as possible. Even introducing a termination bonus for compliance and support in the exit, though contrary to generally held principles of failed commercial relationships, can help you through a difficult period where you may be dependent on the supplier for support.
3   Make sure that the reasons for failure are understood and that you do not, in the new relationship, go on to commit the same errors that led to the termination of the failed contract. This may be about the way you procure in the first place, the nature of the contract and charging structure, the team that managed the relationship or the measures used to control the supplier.

SUMMARY

In summary, the four key principles that I believe will be of most use to you in the future, and will make the biggest difference to your outsourcing success are:

1 There is no single 'right way' to outsource; don't feel constrained by previous or other approaches to the issue. New outsourcing models are emerging and these may indeed have more relevance to your business than the standard models that are commonplace. Creative solutions are possible and have shown to be highly successful.
2 Try not to generate a 'blame' culture when things go wrong nor assume that any issues are directly the responsibility of the other party. Successful outsourcing is a two-way street and the relationship (like any other) needs to be worked at.
3 Following on from point 2, the more you put into the outsourcing project and ongoing relationship, the more you are likely to get out. You should not consider outsourcing as your chance to get rid of a persistent headache and abdicate your responsibilities. As a strategy, this is destined to failure. Your customers will still be experiencing your brand, processes, product and service. Abdicate that responsibility at your peril.
4 Contract carefully and with good commercial diligence. Remember that outsourcing contracts, like most things (apart from car parking spaces), are easier to get into than to get out of.

RECOMMENDED READING

Peters, P. (1991), *Thriving on Chaos: Handbook for a Management Revolution*. SOS Free Stock.

V Building Profitable Customer Relationships

Understanding how to create sales and build loyalty via a contact centre is crucial to enhancing the customer experience. Furthermore, as margins become tighter and costs increase, seeking new and innovative ways to cross-, up- and even down-sell are essential. This section of the handbook shares ideas and proven methodologies to promote, market, serve and sell to customers (and prospects too!)

- Creating Profitable Customer Interactions
- The Inside Sales-Force
- High-Impact Telemarketing
- Managing Campaigns

30 *Creating Profitable Customer Interactions*

David Seccombe, Contact Centre Marketing Specialist

In the relatively short history of the contact centre industry, the telephone has evolved from being a tactical tool to being core to the proposition of many brands. Any company with 'direct' in their title will be a testament to this. What has catalyzed this evolution on customer relationships is making the most of each interaction with the customer, and delivering against customer needs. This chapter examines how an open two-way dialogue, enabled by the telephone, remains a powerful relationship-building tool, continuing to prove its effectiveness alongside traditional channels such as mail and in partnership with channels like the web.

THE RELATIONSHIP CYCLE

The 'relationship cycle' was developed by OgilvyOne to provide a framework for:

* Understanding the stages of development of a customer's relationship with an organization
* Identifying opportunities to maximize the customer's value at each stage.

There are six stages of the life cycle:

* **Market**: The set of all possible customers who potentially could become aware and build a lasting relationship with the organization.
* **Suspect**: A potential customer who is aware of a company (for example, recognizes it, may see unique value, and so on) but has not yet made a move towards commitment. This is generally called a 'lead'.
* **Prospect**: A potential customer who is on the brink of making an initial commitment to a company. In classic terms, this is called a 'qualified lead'.
* **Customer**: Once a purchase is made of the product or service, the purchaser becomes a customer.
* **Bonded customer**: A customer who is demonstrably committed to the organization, product or service. At this optimal stage of the life cycle, a bond has been established between the brand and the customer who is now known as a 'bonded customer'.
* **Lapsed customer**: A customer who has attrited from the brand. Once customers stop purchasing, they return to the 'Market' stage.

Each of these stages is separated by a gap as shown in Figure 30.1:

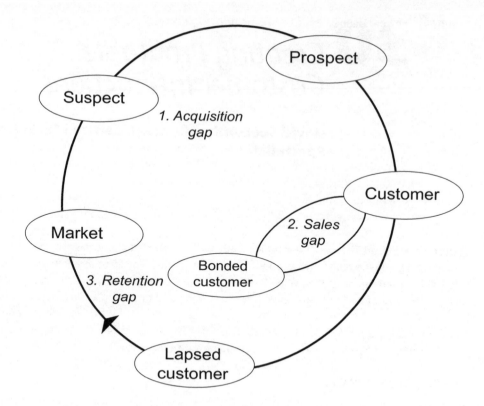

Figure 30.1   Where are the customers in the relationship cycle? © OgilvyOne

- **Acquisition gap**: the opportunity to acquire more profitable customers
- **Sales gap**: the opportunity to sell more to existing customers, to increase loyalty and profitability
- **Retention gap**: the opportunity to keep profitable customers.

Building individual customer relationships and realizing the potential value of a customer relationship requires closing these gaps. This is achieved by meeting customer needs and expectations through effective interactions with the brand or moments of truth.

MOMENTS OF TRUTH

A moment of truth (MOT) occurs when there is an interaction between the company and a consumer. As a result of this, the consumer has an opportunity to evaluate or re-evaluate their relationship with the company. The outcome of this evaluation can be positive, negative or even neutral.

A simple example is where a consumer rings in to complain. If the company acknowledges the complaint and resolves it then the consumer is likely to feel positive. If the company does nothing the consumer is likely to feel negative.

Another example is where a company recognizes an anniversary/change in lifestyle of a consumer and communicates with the customer. If the offer or communication is relevant then the consumer will feel positive towards the company.

OgilvyOne have defined three key moments of truth:

- Business driven
- Customer driven
- Environmental.

BUSINESS

A business-driven moment of truth is 'artificially' created by the business and generates a timed communication to the customer, for example, billing, product upgrade. Business-driven moments of truth by nature are easier to plan and manage because the business knows when it is likely to make contact with the customer and the type of customer (based on profile, behaviour and spend). Acknowledgement of a valued customer's anniversary is a good example.

CUSTOMER

A customer-driven moment of truth is initiated by any type of customer, an enquiry or complaint for example. It is therefore more difficult to predict and react to. These moments of truth tend to be customer life-stage dominant. Buying a new house or car, having a baby, moving jobs – all times when the consumer tends to make relatively rapid and important decisions that will affect their lives.

Customer-driven moments of truth are potentially more emotionally charged than business driven MOTs as the customer has had time to mentally 'prepare' for the contact.

ENVIRONMENT

Environmental drivers are factors such as a product withdrawal or a price change, which are likely to involve a level of 'planned' contact between customer and company.

Moments of truth can be mapped onto the relationship cycle to effectively develop a continuing series of contacts with customer groups. Sometimes these are referred to as 'relationship management strategies'.

TYPICAL EXAMPLES: BUSINESS-DRIVEN APPLICATIONS

For simplicity, consider the relationship cycle and map out a typical year in the life of a customer. At month one the customer is actually a prospect, and by month 12 the customer is either bonded or potentially lapsing.

FROM SUSPECT TO CUSTOMER

The time between being a suspect and a customer is an important moment of truth because it begins to set a precedent for the whole relationship. Think about the importance of a well-handled product enquiry call if the customer has made six or seven similar calls to other competitors. A simple and effective way is to mention your brand name several times to differentiate yourself from the competition.

Setting a precedent means taking an active interest in an enquiry, by asking the right questions, delivering what you promise or even actively following up an enquiry with an outbound call. It is in this area that many companies lose valuable business leads because process and technology are not geared around the potential customer.

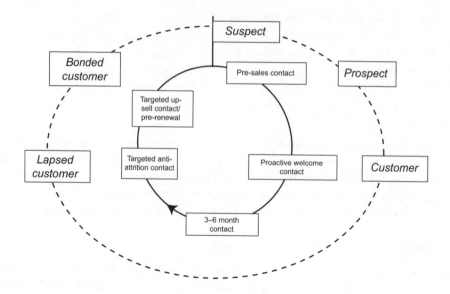

Figure 30.2   Business-driven applications © OgilvyOne

A typical solution is to understand why customers respond but do not convert. Often there is great potential in this data, which can be exploited based on an understanding of the customer needs, and overcoming those issues raised. If systems can be set up to gather this information, then subsequent programmes can be developed to re-contact customers at an appropriate time through an appropriate channel (typically telephone and/or mail). There are good examples within the higher-value end of the automotive industry of using the phone effectively at this stage with 'test drive' programmes, for example, a potential customer rings in to book an appointment and the manufacturer will not only arrange this but will also ask a lot of relevant questions about the potential purchase (age and type of current car, budget, finance options, and so on). The test drive will be preceded by an attendance confirmation call and followed up by a 'satisfaction call' which will cover both the customer experience/satisfaction of the process but also likelihood of purchase and next steps. These experiences can have a significant positive impact on the final buying decision.

NEW CUSTOMERS

The most lucrative time to make contact is within three months of acquiring a customer. Typically, customers are three to five times more likely to purchase products or services during this phase. This is because they have made a commitment to the brand and want to feel they have made the right choice. They will be interested in additional products and services. They therefore have a bond to the brand, which can be a combination of emotional, functional and rational reasons. It is a real moment of truth.

Active communication can only enhance these bonds. This has led to the practice of generating 'welcome calls' to customers. Typically, the objectives of welcome calls are to:

- establish the relationship (how, when and why will we contact you)
- understand customer satisfaction
- gather more information about the customer
- and cross- and up-sell where appropriate.

Welcome calls can be achieved by asking customers to ring the company (inbound) or can be achieved by an outbound call. Welcome calls are generated as a result of a company-driven reason to communicate with the customer or more specifically positioned as a process-driven reason – to activate an account or mobile phone, for example. Therefore, for process-driven customer contact, a compelling reason is needed to inspire the customer to make contact. A year's free insurance on a product is a compelling reason to complete a warranty; a warranty card on its own is not.

ONGOING DIALOGUE

Within a three to six-month period, a company should have begun to understand its customers better. Hopefully, this will be as a result of basic transactional data (spend, usage, payment methods) as well as other data sources (contact history with the company, satisfaction surveys) and even external sources such as lifestyle data. This information will 'segment' customers into groups to develop tailored communication plans for certain groups of customers. Based on the profile of the customer it is common to re-contact customers with an outbound call, or generate an inbound call, at this stage. There are normally specific objectives, to cross- and up-sell relevant products or services, but these can be underpinned by the additional welcome-call objectives listed above. This type of contact is designed to reinforce and build the customer relationship.

CONTACT WITH LAPSING AND BONDED CUSTOMERS

Towards the end of the first year, and again based on customer data, it is important to recognize and react to differing types of customer behaviour. This is typically done between months 10–12. Clearly, where there is a process-driven reason, such as a renewal of contract, then this will need to be carried out nearer the month 12 stage because the communication will be more relevant to the customer. In a positive circumstance this may be to reward a 'bonded' customer for being a good customer. In a negative circumstance it may be to understand why a customer has not used, or has a low usage of, the product or service. The worst case may be to 'save a customer' from defecting to a competitor, particularly if this customer has historically been a valuable customer, or has the potential to be one. Again this will be a key moment of truth, particularly if it coincides with the customer's decision-making process of whether to renew a contract. Both inbound and outbound calls can be utilized in these circumstances.

Outbound calls are used to target known customers who:

- look like they will attrite based on spend and behaviour
- would benefit from a recognition and reward call.

Inbound calls are used when the company has adopted a 'please contact us' policy typically generated by mail.

PRACTICAL EXAMPLES: BUSINESS-DRIVEN APPLICATIONS

The practical examples, described below, are depicted on the business-driven MoTs diagram (Figure 30.3) to help put the customer relationship cycle in context.

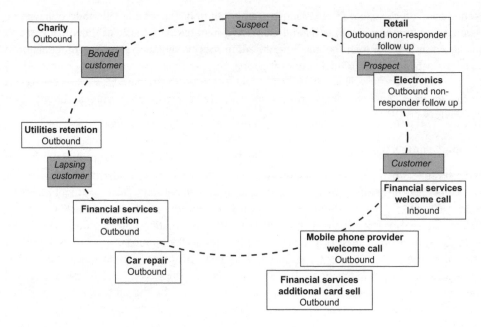

Figure 30.3 Business-driven moments of truth © OgilvyOne

SUSPECTS AND PROSPECTS

Retailer

A major retailer ran a card-based loyalty points scheme. One particular target group of customers and potential customers were new mothers. This is because families tend to have higher shopping budgets and generally stay loyal to one particular store. A mailing was sent to potential and existing customers offering a £100 worth of free spend for every £1000 spent, achieved only through the loyalty card scheme. The potential benefit to the company was that they would attract new high-value customers and maintain the loyalty of existing customers.

Although the mailing was generally successful, outbound follow-up was initiated to convert more customers and potential customers to the scheme. A secondary objective was to ascertain why the offer had not been taken up. The calls increased the overall response by 10 per cent. In addition, it was determined that some elements of the offer needed clarification in the letter, something that had put off recipients from responding.

Electronics

An electronics manufacturer is so confident in the quality of its product it offers a free home trial of its product, although the consumer has to leave a deposit. Towards the end of the two-week trial at a key moment of truth, an outbound call is made to encourage the consumer to purchase the product in order to reduce product 'returns'.

NEW CUSTOMERS

Financial

A leading financial services company have used 'welcome calls' successfully for many years. It sends its card product in the post to new customers. On the back (where consumers sign the card) is an invitation to phone in and 'activate' the card. At this stage, and following security questions, card members are cross-sold a loyalty scheme and offered direct debit as a method of payment. Additional supplementary cards can also be offered where relevant. Statistics show that not only does this process reduce fraud but has a significant impact on retention (60 per cent reduction in attrition) and spend (typically up 45 per cent).

Mobile

A mobile phone provider adopts a similar practice. It tested an outbound call on its new customers. The purpose of the call was to establish the relationship, signpost relevant support contact numbers and briefly introduce some of the functionality that the mobile phone could deliver. Ironically, many people only use a small percentage of the features that mobile phones are capable of providing.

This programme contributed to a 28 per cent reduction in churn from first-year customers.

THREE TO SIX MONTHS/ONGOING CONTACT

Financial

A leading financial service provider segments its customers and where relevant (typically based on usage and spend) offers supplementary cards with an outbound call. This achieved a conversion rate of up to 20 per cent.

Car repairer

A nationwide car repairer undertakes post-repair customer satisfaction calls – a key moment of truth. A high proportion of calls are simply satisfaction measurement, any that need escalating are dealt with immediately. This has enabled the company to gauge customer-facing service levels and has significantly contributed to the service reputation and brand of the company.

ANTI-ATTRITION CALLING

Financial

A leading financial service provider segments its customers and is able to determine which customers are likely to lapse. It then makes outbound calls to these customers and can achieve conversion of up to 50 per cent in attracting these customers to its loyalty scheme. This then forms a structural and emotional bond that contributes to keeping the customer loyal.

Utility

A utility company can identify which customers typically delay renewing a yearly agreement, which costs the company money. These customers receive an outbound payment reminder call. At the same time as chasing the debt, they are also offered a direct debit facility for payment. Conversion of up to 40 per cent is achieved. An additional longer-term benefit is that once direct debit is adopted, customers are more cost-efficient to serve.

BONDED CUSTOMERS

Charity

A charity typically sold its products (and therefore donations) to customers via a catalogue. It was able to determine which customers had ever made a financial donation in addition to buying products. Outbound calls were made to these customers to thank them for their support and to ask for a one-off donation. A conversion of 15 per cent was achieved at a return on investment of 3.6:1.

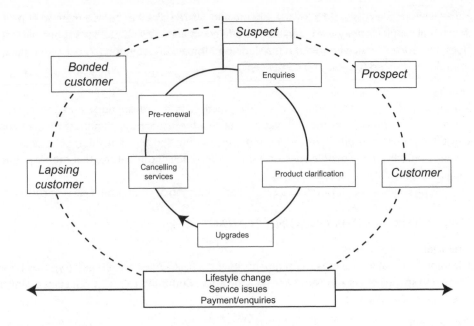

Figure 30.4   Customer-driven moments of truth © OgilvyOne

TYPICAL EXAMPLES: CUSTOMER-DRIVEN MOMENTS OF TRUTH

The principles behind the timing of business-driven moments of truth also apply to customer-driven moments of truth (shown in Figure 30.4). The key difference is that, as discussed earlier, they are more difficult to predict and plan because the customer drives the timing and content of the call. This is particularly true of lifestyle changes, service issues and generic enquiries.

What is key, therefore, is putting in place processes and procedures to react effectively to these types of call. Across the relationship cycle these can be applied to more distinct moments of truth:

- at enquiry level
- in the first three months when a customer requires product or service clarification
- three to six months when upgrades may be required
- when a customer rings to cancel a product or service
- at renewal stage.

Because these are 'situation dependent' it is easier to demonstrate these at a practical level.

PRACTICAL EXAMPLES: CUSTOMER-DRIVEN APPLICATIONS

ONGOING/THREE TO NINE MONTHS

Utility
One area that is not generally exploited is in maximizing inbound enquiries. A utility company, which took a large number of general enquiries, set up a screening matrix which would enable them to define whether the customer, after their general enquiry had been handled, would

benefit from transferring their account onto direct debit. Under strict screening criteria the percentage of conversion across the general enquiry line increased from 7 per cent to 14 per cent.

Mobile

A mobile phone provider offered a product upgrade to customers making inbound general enquiries. Despite the incremental cost to the customer, a conversion rate of 35 per cent was achieved.

Airline

An airline set up a loyalty scheme. It then profiled its customers and built a matrix of offers which it considered would appeal to distinct customer groups. When customers rang up on inbound enquiries they were offered one of the following:

- a new product with a discount
- a double points promotion
- a seasonal discount.

This is a good example of surprising and delighting a customer.

Catalogue

A high-street catalogue company realized that many customers rang the local store prior to visit in order to check that the product they were going to buy was in stock – a real customer-driven moment of truth. This was, however, not something that the local stores were set up to handle effectively. Consequently, an automated line was set up. Customers could key in the product number and were informed if the product was in stock. If it wasn't, then a live agent offered a home delivery service to the customer.

ANTI-ATTRITION/NINE TO TWELVE MONTHS

The highest levels of service are achieved where companies have geared themselves around being able to react to defecting customers. This approach has been applied across the mobile phone sector and general utilities, as well as financial, but basically any sector with an interest in retaining high-value customers.

Specialist inbound teams are created over and above generalist inbound enquiry handling. These teams are highly trained, motivated, rewarded and empowered. They are trained specifically in being able to offer customers solutions to their issues, for example tariffs, rates or monthly fees. If a customer rings in to make a cancellation, calls are forwarded to these teams and typically in the contact centre industry, specialist teams are able to retain or 'save' between 20–35 per cent of defecting customers. These are generally called 'customer saves teams'.

THREE GOLDEN RULES

By following the three golden rules outlined below, organizations will be able to consistently achieve positive call outcomes.

CALL OBJECTIVES

Always have an objective! Calling a customer for no particular reason undermines credibility. It is important to establish the *primary* objective of the call. Having too many objectives and/or having conflicting objectives will compromise the activity. It is possible to have primary and secondary objectives as long as they are balanced, which should reflect in the call structure. A typical example of conflicting objectives are sales *and* research based. You cannot achieve either effectively on a call if you attempt both in equal measure. A sales call structurally means creating an opportunity and closing it down, while a research call requires a lot of open questions conflicting with closing an opportunity down.

HONESTY

Be clear why you are calling the customer. A sales call disguised as a customer service call will fail because you will not manage the expectation of the customer and leave a bad impression. It is also a requirement of the DMA (Direct Marketing Association) telebusiness guidelines for best practice.

TEST

Allow enough time to test a programme effectively. Try to measure both the *claimed* customer behaviour (derived from calling reports) against the *actual* customer behaviour (derived from company databases). Experience suggests some apparently negative call outcomes actually convert, thus increasing the overall real conversion.

FINDING MOMENTS OF TRUTH AND BUILDING ON THE RELATIONSHIP CYCLE

EXISTING CUSTOMER PLANS

The most robust source of moments of truth is the existing marketing, sales and service plans. These will translate to a proposition and time-based customer contact plan, which may already be implemented or planned. You may find that channels such as mail/web are already being adopted alongside call contact.

CUSTOMER CONTACT PROCESSES

The second area is to review existing contact process documentation. You may find existing customer contact processes that would benefit from the testing of different channels to the customer. Typically, process activity such as invoicing, payment reminders and subscriptions is mail- (and increasingly web-) driven.

CUSTOMER BEHAVIOURS

The third level of sourcing should involve a series of observations and actions based on analysis of customer behaviour across :

- websites
- databases
- satisfaction surveys
- focus groups
- competitive activity.

Within all these information sources are indications of what your customers need, when they need it and why they need it. But you can't beat the most interactive of channels to understand customer behaviour: listening into calls and subsequent debriefing with your customer-facing staff. All of these sources should allow you to identify opportunities based on existing customer behaviour, many of them moments of truth.

31 *The Inside Sales-Force*

Richard Stollery, Global Consumer Service Director, LEGO

This chapter shares insights into how substitution of the telephone-based salesperson with a field sales force can successfully take place.

BACKGROUND

By its very nature any contact centre should be integrated with the organization's sales activities, either directly or indirectly. It is very likely that the contact centre is 'making' (outbound) or 'taking' (inbound) contacts, whether they are calls, emails, faxes or post, from more customers than other perhaps more traditional or well-established parts of the organization The contact mix is changing, with field sales operations, for example, being reduced as organizations discover faster and less expensive ways of reaching more customers and making sales. It can be estimated that contact centres are responsible for around 70 per cent of an organization's customer contact.

A typical breakdown of customer contacts in a business-to-business organization is represented in Figure 31.1. Additional segments that are more significant in certain industries, markets or individual organizations, could include website 'hits', advertising, sponsorship, public relations, events, hospitality, direct mail and email marketing.

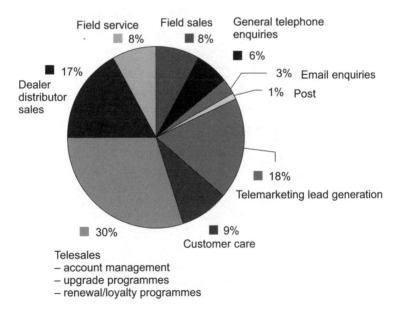

Figure 31.1 Total number of customer contacts

STRATEGIC ROLE

Realization of the potential strategic role of an integrated contact centre is driving the reconsideration of them as more than just a cost centre that is mentally, and more often than not, physically located on the periphery of the organization. More customer-centric, enlightened organizations see their contact centre in a central role, with an opportunity to capture customer data, turning it into knowledge and competitive advantage.

However, it is not just about the number of contacts. In the same way a contact centre can help traffic more buying decisions, it also has the potential to damage sales by inappropriate, ill-timed and low-quality contact. To expand this further and achieve a basis for making better investment decisions, it is necessary to assess the quality or the 'depth' of the contact. For example, at The LEGO Company, someone seeing an advertisement for a LEGO® product on the television is not probably as 'deep' a brand experience as visiting www.LEGO.com to place an order, or visiting a LEGOLAND® park.

The 'depth' factor applied to each method of contact should therefore depend on the duration and intensity of the contact and will result in a very different-looking pie chart from that in Figure 31.1.

Field sales, directly or via dealers, becomes more important in Figure 31.2 in comparison with Figure 31.1. Its focus is on face-to-face contact and building strong longer-term relationships. However, contact centre activity remains over 50 per cent and will continue to grow as more and more organizations learn to integrate their web presence and develop contact centre-backed activities such as email marketing. This is not to say that traditional sales efforts are dead; only that the contact mix is changing. More successful organizations in the future will be those that achieve the synergies from integrating web, phone and face-to-face methods of customer contact.

The economic advantages of selling through a contact centre are clear, as is demonstrated in Table 31.1.

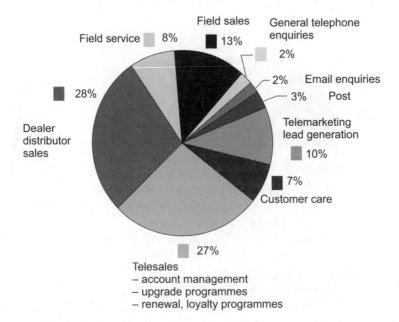

Figure 31.2   Depth of customer contact

Table 31.1   Annual cost per sales contact figures

	Field sales representative	Contact centre advisor
Salary and related costs	£60 000	£25 000
Effective customer contacts (based on 200 days)	1200 visits/calls	4000 calls
Infrastructure/overhead costs	£40 000	£30 000
Fully loaded cost	£100 000	£55 000
Cost per sales contact	£83.33	£13.75

These figures act only as an illustration of two different contact methods, and ignore the *quality* of the two different contacts. The point is to deploy these resources in an integrated way that achieves the maximum coverage of buying decisions, consideration by the customer and, ultimately, profitable business. Web contact, in sufficient volume, can bring the cost per sales contact below £1, and is also part of the contact mix.

It is useful to plot the contact centre's selling activities in a diagram and to focus on how to drive more and more contacts towards winning profitable sales (see Figure 31.3).

Of course, all of the above potential won't be realized if the contact centre staff aren't well trained and motivated. A lot will depend on the culture and the importance the organization places on its contact centre operation.

Essentially the contact centre is the 'inside sales-force'. Its potential is to cover many more buying decisions in a week than a field sales-force can do in a month and at less than half the cost. But rather than pointing out the differences and putting up the fences between 'outside' and 'inside' sales-forces, the real gains come from an integrated selling approach.

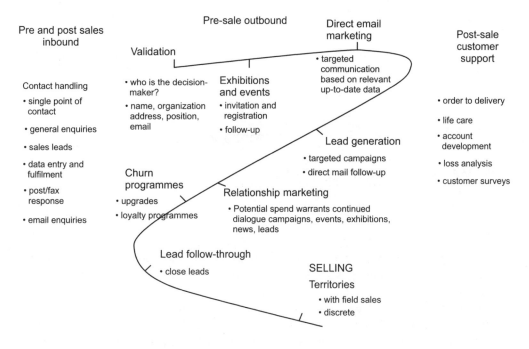

Figure 31.3   Contact selling cycle activities © LEGO

DELL'S MODEL

Dell and similar organizations realized a long time ago that integrated selling was the way forward and continue to outperform their competitors in a fiercely competitive market. Of course, Dell in the beginning had an advantage over its competitors of low overheads, a good product and speed to market, but it is now over 20 years since Dell was founded and it continues to stay one step ahead. Michael Dell continues to challenge his organization to improve the business model still further by making it more and more convenient to buy Dell products, while lowering the cost of sale, selling through the web in preference to the contact centre, and selling through the contact centre in preference to field sales staff. Along the way, Dell have learnt how to deploy their field sales, contact centre and web resources and to push products down into the lowest-cost channel feasible.

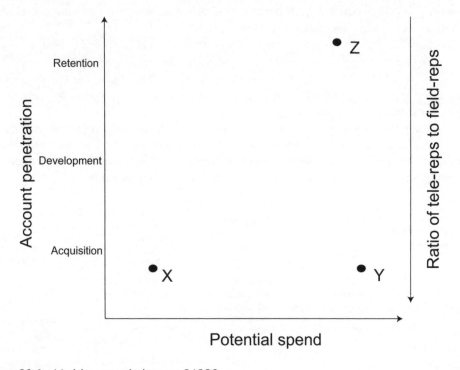

Figure 31.4   Model resource deployment © LEGO

In Figure 31.4, customer X is not yet a customer and a potentially low spender so it is uneconomic to chase this business. However, if customer X contacts Dell then the order is taken in the contact centre or on the web.

Customer Y is also not yet a customer, but has a high potential spend which warrants concentrated effort by dedicated new business field sales staff (supported by targeted direct marketing for lead generation). These staff are rewarded for acquiring these significant new customers. At this point, telephone account advisors (typically one-third of the cost of a field salesperson) increasingly nurture and develop the account at the expense of Dell's competitors. The approach aims to turn customer Y into customer Z.

Customer Z chooses to place the vast majority of all their transactional orders with Dell, either through their dedicated telephone account manager, or via the web, where they enjoy a tailored web page provided by Dell for their use. More specialized or strategic consultancy-type sales may still be concluded through a field-based account manager, but even here, as relationships develop, some of these sales are concluded over the phone and on the web.

Other companies, such as IBM and Xerox, following Dell's approach, have experienced a similar trend that once customers have enjoyed the benefits, particularly the convenience, of dedicated telephone account management, they become increasingly comfortable placing higher and higher value orders though this channel, in particular, repeat purchases. Furthermore, these companies have experienced another phenomenon that contradicts the conventional thinking that customers demand a lower price on the web or over the phone than they do through other channels. The facts may actually be to the contrary, depending on how the service has been marketed. The customer value of providing key customers with dedicated telephone support, tailored web pages or face-to-face contact if preferred, should be made clear. Selling the way the customer wants to buy should be a new added-value service. It enhances the relationship and reduces the cost of doing business for both parties but primarily through convenience and saving time, making it easier for the customer to do business with the selling organization.

PEOPLE: THE INSIDE SALES FORCE

Realizing the benefits of an inside sales force depends greatly on having well-trained and motivated staff in your contact centre. Below are the five key points to remember:

1   Recruit the right staff. Assess the skills needed for the role and match accordingly.
2   Don't mislead applicants that the role is something that it is not. Be very clear on what is expected, the challenges, and the support they will receive.
3   Demonstrate the personal development plan opportunities for those wishing to progress within the role. Individuals should see how they could acquire new skills, improve their performance and be rewarded against objective criteria.
4   Discuss the right things! Focus should be less on call length, wrap-up time and logged-on time, and more on customer satisfaction, contact quality, sales performance, team goals and behaviours.
5   The physical environment must encourage staff to do their job. Think about the desk area in the contact centre as equivalent to the salesperson's car. It 'belongs' to them. If anything, furniture, lighting, space, break rooms, refreshment, and so on, should be better than that enjoyed by general office-based staff who maybe do not spend as much time at their desk, can move around more freely, attend meetings and visit other companies.

RECOMMENDED READING

Furey, Tim and L. Friedman (1999), *'The Channel Advantage': Going to Market with Multiple Sales Channels to Reach More Customers, Sell More Products, Make More Profit*, Butterworth-Heinemann.
Peppers, Don and Martha Rogers PhD (1997), 'Enterprise One to One: Tools for Competing in the Interactive Age', Bantam Doubleday Dell.

32 *High-Impact Telemarketing*

Fabienne Tyler, Head of Marketing, Thomas Sanderson

The trend towards greater integration of all the marketing functions has heightened the need for contact centre managers to appreciate how different marketing tools interact when they are combined with the telephone. This chapter looks at how the telephone can be used as a valuable marketing tool.

BACKGROUND

There is significant impact when the telephone is integrated with other direct marketing activities, and it is important to understand how to harness different elements for the best possible results. The high costs associated with the telephone means that a fundamental shift in focus is often required, away from the single dimension of resource and cost measures and towards a more holistic focus on value, in terms of the overall return on the marketing investment.

Call centre managers are increasingly expected to understand the dynamics of the telephone within the marketing mix, so that they are better equipped to add value to their organizations' marketing activities and in turn maximize customer potential.

INTEGRATION WITH THE MARKETING MIX

The telephone is one of the most versatile tools available to today's marketers, and when applied with skill it is also one of the most powerful and profitable. Used appropriately, the telephone can deliver a high return on investment – but the high costs also represent a risk that must be managed by understanding how to use the telephone effectively.

Here are some 'typical applications' to consider – all of these have the potential to be highly profitable or just highly expensive, depending on the skill with which the telephone is integrated within the marketing activity or campaign:

- Direct generation of sales, leads and appointments
- Handling of incoming enquiries and customer calls
- Database building
- Gathering and/or exchange of information
- Sales and other customer transactions
- Customer acquisition and retention
- Handling complaints
- Warm-up to direct-mail activity

- Follow-up to direct-mail activity
- Research
- Testing.

THE COMBINATION EFFECT

In particular, the telephone is most effective when properly combined with other 'direct' tools, especially direct mail and, increasingly, email. Figure 32.1 highlights the typical impact of combining the phone and mail approaches.

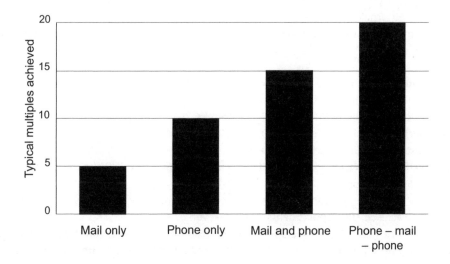

Figure 32.1   The combination effect © Thomas Sanderson

The multiples that can be achieved will vary with every application, and it is important to test carefully to determine the true potential for improvement in the overall results. The actual cost-effectiveness will be determined by the value of the improvements, and these must obviously exceed the additional cost of the high-impact approach.

BE BOLD

A bold increase in investment can result in dramatic improvements in the overall return on investment. It is important to apply these principles to the kind of activity that has the potential to deliver high value for the business. Some specific case studies are detailed later in this chapter. To illustrate the shift in focus required, the two examples below demonstrate ways in which investment and value might be increased for typical call centre activities, in order to cost-justify a high-impact approach.

LEAD AND APPOINTMENT GENERATION

The phone – mail – phone approach is particularly effective for lead and appointment generation, especially where the customer value is high. Spending up to ten or even 100 times more on the approach may seem excessive, but the investment can pay handsome dividends. By investing in an initial phone call to verify the correct contact details, wastage is minimized and effective contacts are maximized. In some cases, the verification call can also prepare the ground so that the prospect is more receptive to the mail communication. Knowing that only qualified prospects are now on the mailing list, it is easier to justify an increased investment in written communications.

Consider the real value of a customer, then imagine that you have 10 per cent of this available to create a really high-impact campaign to attract them. Think about how you could invest this amount in order to deliver higher-value conversions and outputs from the activity. This could take the form of a highly creative mailing, or a high-value response incentive, or the investment could finance the phone – mail – phone approach. Finally, calculate what improvement in conversions to appointment and to sale would be required to fund this investment. The sum may look something like this:

Target £75 000 worth of revenue to generate

- Average customer value = £3000 = 25 new customers
- High-impact marketing investment @ 10% = £300 each to invest
- 25 new customers @ £300 each = £7500 investment
- Based on a 25% conversion to sale, it would be necessary to create 100 appointments in total to create 25 new customers
- Based on a conversion of lead/appointment of 20%, it would be necessary to contact 500 prospects to achieve 100 appointments and breakeven
- **Total cost to target 500 propsects and deliver 25 new customers would be £7500. This provides a marketing investment of £15 per contact, more than enough to invest in verification, a highly creative mailing, and a follow-up call.**

HANDLING COMPLAINTS

Handling complaints may not seem an obvious opportunity for high-impact marketing, but applying the same principles can deliver surprising results. For example, a typical process for complaint handling would be to receive an incoming call, take details, resolve the issue either immediately or as soon as possible, and confirm the outcome to the customer. Total cost would probably be approximately £3, with no apparent value other than eliminating the problem.

The high-impact approach starts by looking at the value. Let's imagine that one in 100 customers typically complain. The customers have an average value of £100 each per year, and an average lifetime value of £500. So the value of 100 customers is £10 000 per year, and £50 000 is the average lifetime value. Taking 10 per cent of the annual value as a starting point, consider the value of an investment of £1000 per 100 customers, or £10 each. If an investment of £10 each could deliver an improvement in loyalty and lifetime value, as well as flushing out any customer problems along the way, then there may be a justification for investing in outbound customer contacts once or twice a year. This kind of customer contact programme can deliver improved retention, higher loyalty, and the company could also benefit from referrals, up-selling and cross-selling!

By shifting the focus from marketing cost to marketing investment, the role of the telephone in this example is transformed from being a reactive low cost, low-value (but necessary) function, to a high-impact lever for additional profits.

PRINCIPLES FOR HIGH-IMPACT MARKETING

Adopting a bolder approach to the entire marketing process can significantly increase the effectiveness of the telephone marketing activity. The three high-impact principles most likely to deliver a higher return on investment are as follows:

1 When determining how much to invest, focus on value, not cost.
2 Invest boldly in processes that combine the telephone and direct mail.
3 Test and evaluate the full impact through to sale and measure the overall return on investment.

CRITICAL INGREDIENTS FOR SUCCESS: PLANNING, PEOPLE AND PROFIT

PLANNING TO WIN

For the call centre to deliver an effective performance, the use of the telephone must be carefully defined and managed through the application of some basic marketing disciplines:

1   Define the overall business objectives
2   Identify the potential telephone marketing application
3   Create an outline budget and cost-benefit evaluation
4   Eliminate or accept any risks involved
5   Test the proposed approach
6   Evaluate initial results and feedback
7   Calculate actual cost-effectiveness of the activity
8   Identify improvements and implement them
9   Repeat steps 5–9 until the process is complete
10   Document the final results and learning for future reference.

All too often, this basic planning process is sacrificed. A wise call centre manager will recognize that it provides the key to effective performance management and improvement, and the time dedicated to planning and monitoring will ultimately determine the extent to which the activity fulfils its potential.

BEYOND BRIEFING: THE HUMAN ELEMENT – PEOPLE

In addition to the basic planning disciplines, it is vital to remember the human element that distinguishes live operator telephone calls from every other direct marketing activity. Training operators on how to give objective feedback when evaluating activities can help to ensure that opportunities for improvement are highlighted – after all, they are on the front line and directly experiencing the interface with the customer or prospect on the telephone. It is often worth going beyond the basic briefing processes and involving operators more actively in the feedback loop, providing them with updates and information on individual wins as well as the overall performance, and seeking their input on improvements. Some companies will go so far as to provide incentives and rewards for operators who correctly identify opportunities for improvement – this helps to build a culture where the return on investment is focused on at every level for maximum impact.

As well as standard briefing and training practices, some additional forms of operator involvement can have a positive impact on results:

- Meeting real customers/prospects/clients
- Introducing incentives/competitions to reward successful improvement suggestions
- Providing information on individual wins to personalize the process more
- Experiencing the product (where appropriate!)
- Providing samples of all relevant literature and letters
- Setting up campaign-specific recognition boards/certificates
- Inviting someone important to attend the briefing and debriefs.

Above all, it is the power of personal connections that provides the best results, and anything that enhances the operators' ability to relate personally to the process will contribute positively to the outcomes. Help them to appreciate the importance of their role. Be creative! It doesn't cost a great deal to provide a relevant personal and meaningful experience for the operators, and like any effective motivational tool it can pay great dividends.

PROFITABLE INTERVENTIONS

The cost of the high-impact approach is balanced by the creation of incremental revenue, and there are a number of opportunities to consider when looking for ways in which telephone marketing can deliver added value:

- Can you gather extra pieces of information that could help to improve conversions at the next stage of the process? If so, what is the potential value of an increase?
- Can the connection being made help to increase customer loyalty? If so, what is the potential value of the additional retained customers?
- Can you generate opportunities to sell additional products and services? If so, what is the potential value of the incremental sales?
- What is the value of higher productivity? Are there savings in staff costs, or lower production costs? What is the value of these savings?

Most companies are harbouring many untapped opportunities for increasing the profitable use of the telephone and adding significant value to the business. It is worth investigating every opportunity along the sales and marketing chain in order to identify key areas in which to test an investment. The call centre should be run as a centre for generating profit, rather than just being considered a cost to the business. Involvement in the full marketing process will help to ensure that profitable interventions are maximized.

DEMONSTRATING THE RETURN ON INVESTMENT

Having identified opportunities for improvement, it is then necessary to provide a persuasive rationale for increased investment. Most telemarketing activities are measured primarily on response rates, but of course this only forms part of the equation for a profitable return on investment.

Taking the example of a young business providing computer services to a small but distinct business sector, Table 32.1 is typical of the initial calculation made when evaluating the use of telephone marketing to attract new customers. Arriving at this calculation, the company was hesitant about investing as much as £6000. This represented a great deal of risk to a fledgling business. The instinct was to seek ways to reduce the costs and minimize the risk, but this would only reduce the contribution to the business and was unlikely to deliver enough new business to

Table 32.1   Basic cost and breakeven calculation

Cost per decision-maker reached by telephone: (*Based on five decision-maker contacts per hour*)	£6
Number of contacts planned: 1000 @ £6	£6000
Estimated response rate of appointments made	4%
Cost per appointment	£150
Conversion to a sale within six months	10% of appointments
4 sales at an average value of £10 000	£40 000 revenue
Sale value on average £1500 profit each	£6000 profit
4 sales delivers breakeven @ £6000 investment	
Cost-to-profit ratio	*1:1*

justify the time and energy involved. The company had actually been hoping to add £500 000 worth of new business in the next 18 months, and with this calculation they found themselves hesitating to invest in just £50 000 worth of business. The numbers were realistic based on their experience of making telephone calls, and it was not easy for them to see how the telephone marketing activity could be justified. In addition, the market was so highly defined that only 3500 companies fell within their selection criteria, so even on rollout this approach could not deliver the business growth they were seeking.

After adopting some of the levers for improvement and changing the focus from a short-term cost focus to a long-term value focus, later that day the company happily signed off a test budget of £12 500 based on the calculation shown in Table 32.2.

Table 32.2   Advanced cost and breakeven calculation

Phone – mail – phone cost per contact	£25
Data verification call *£1*	
High-impactr mailing *£19*	
Decision-maker contact call *£5 (6 per hour)*	
Number of contacts planned 500 × £25	£12 500
Data verification *£500*	
High-impact mailing *£9500*	
Decision-maker contacts *£2500*	
Estimated response rate for appointments	15%
Number of appointments	75
Cost per appointment	£167
Conversion to sale	10%
7 new customers with an average value of £40 000 over 18 months	£280 000 revenue
Customer value over 18 months is £6000 profit each	£42 000 profit
Cost-to-profit ratio	*1:3.3*

Now the company had a basis for investing in the test. The proposed approach also had the following safeguards built in:

- The campaign could be stopped at any time if the results did not support the investment.
- The fixed costs amounted to just £2000, by negotiating for the high-impact mailing to be hand-created in batches of 50.
- 95 per cent of the wastage was eliminated by the data verification call.
- The decision-maker contact rate was confidently planned at a higher rate due to the verification having taken place, and due to the high-impact mailer that was designed to be unforgettable.
- The data cleansing and warm-up mailing would make it possible to achieve at least the same number of appointments from half the size of the mailing list in question.
- Given the small size of their market sector, this approach also made it much more likely that they would achieve their overall objective of £500 000 on rollout to a universe of just 6000 companies.

The company was rewarded for its courage by exceeding all the volume, response and conversion estimates after just 100 verifications, despatches and follow-up calls. The return on investment was 1:6, almost double the hoped-for improvement that the test was designed to deliver.

A similar approach for a London printing company delivered all its new business targets with just two out of seven campaigns designed to attract new customers over an 18-month period.

A CONSUMER EXAMPLE

It is sometimes easier to justify the high costs of investment in business-to-business activities, due to the high potential customer values. With the high volumes and often more limited lifetime values associated with consumer marketing, it takes even more courage to adopt a bolder approach. Yet it can pay great dividends, and the cost of testing can be kept low to minimize the financial risk.

Table 32.3 is an example taken from a company manufacturing and selling high-value home improvement products to individuals. The company has high acquisition costs and few opportunities to extend the customer lifetime value, and it was seeking ways to attract new customers more cost-effectively. The table shows the company's typical approach to the conversion of prospect data.

Table 32.3   Typical return on investment calculation

Per 10 000 prospects:	
Mail low-cost flyer to warm up @ £0.25 each	£2500
Cost of follow-up calls to convert to appointment @ £2 each	£20 000
Conversion to qualified appointment @ 1%	100
Cost per appointment	£225
Conversion to sale @ 40%	40 sales
Average order value @ £2500 revenue	£100 000
Average profit per customer @ £1000	£40 000 profit
Return on investment – cost-to-profit ratio	*1:1.8*

The company was seeking to improve the cost-effectiveness of its activity by lowering the costs of mailing and improving conversions. This focus on cost provided little hope of significant improvement, and instead the company decided to test a bolder approach to delivering a better return on investment.

The calculation is shown in Table 32.4.

Table 32.4   Maximizing return on investment

Per 10 000 prospects:	
Mail high-impact full brochure to warm up @ £0.75 each	£7500
Cost of follow-up calls to convert to appointment @ £2 each	£20 000
Conversion to qualified appointment @ 1.5%	150
Cost per appointment	£183
Conversion to sale @ 40%	60 sales
Average order value @ £2500 revenue	£150 000
Average profit per customer @ £1000 profit	£60 000
Anticipated return on investment – cost-to-profit ratio	*1: 2.18*

The calculation allowed for the higher cost of a full-colour brochure to go to each prospect. While no savings could be made in the cost per contact on the follow-up calls, it was anticipated that there would be a significant uplift in the conversion to appointments. With the return per £1 spent increased to £2.18, this would represent an uplift of over 20 per cent in the return on the marketing investment.

The test was successfully implemented, with some surprising results (see Table 32.5).

Table 32.5   Return on investment – final results

Per 10 000 prospects:	
Mail high-impact full brochure to warm up @ £0.75 each	£7500
Cost of follow-up calls to convert to appointment @ £2 each	£20 000
Conversion to qualified appointment @ 1.3%	130 appointments
Cost per appointment	£212
Conversion to sale @ 45%	58 sales
Average order value @ £2650 revenue	£153 700
Average profit per customer @ £1150	£66 700 profit
Actual return on investment – cost-to-profit ratio	*1: 2.93*

The uplift to appointments was lower than expected at just 1.3 per cent. This generated an additional 30 appointments per 10 000 mailed, but the appointment cost rose to £212. While this conversion to appointment was not as high as was hoped, it still delivered an improvement on the current cost per appointment. Less expectedly, there was an upturn in the conversion to sales, plus an increase in the average order value. While the desired uplift in appointments had only been partially met, the new approach helped to ensure that more of the right kind of customers were appointed, and the provision of more product information at the front end also increased the likelihood of a higher spend. The final result was an uplift of over 60 per cent in the return on marketing investment, from £1.80 per £1 spent to £2.93 per £1 spent.

THE KEY TO IMPROVED RETURN ON INVESTMENT

There are a number of important principles that are prerequisite to achieving the maximum return on the marketing investment:

- **Focus on improvements in value and profits, rather than just on reducing costs:** A purely cost-based method of evaluation is unlikely to show enough benefits to justify investment in a new approach. Calculate the real value of a customer, and think about how you might invest to deliver significant improvements in conversions.
- **Don't underestimate the value of high-impact marketing:** In addition to the obvious benefits of improved conversions, a bolder approach to marketing can help to significantly reduce costs and increase profits. Costs are reduced because growth can be achieved with a lower marketing investment, and also because of the resulting reduction in the overall resources required to support the marketing process. Profits are often increased by the extended effect of high-impact marketing, and this is not always limited to the initial activity. Always measure through to final sales and profits, because improvements can be experienced at any of the lever points along the selling chain.
- **Recognize the importance of extracting greater market share:** Improved conversions deliver more than new opportunities for revenue and profit. They also provide the basis for increasing overall market share, by extracting more customers from an often-limited universe of prospects. Generally, the smaller the universe, the greater the justification for increased investment in improved conversions. This provides the organization with the option to reduce the overall investment required to deliver the desired results, or, if equipped to do so, the company can opt for maintaining the current level of investment in order to achieve higher growth.
- **Planning, testing and measurement skills are vital:** Testing new approaches provides the only means for significant performance improvement. This means that call centre managers need to understand the implications of a bolder, high-impact approach to marketing, so that lever points can be measured and incentives for improvement attached to the most appropriate outcomes.
- **Go for the big picture:** Small-scale changes can deliver modest improvements, but a significant improvement in the return on marketing investment can only be achieved through a bolder approach to the overall marketing process. The telephone is the most powerful lever point in the process, and even minor increases in effectiveness can deliver a high uplift in the return on investment.

33 *Managing Campaigns*

Laurin McDonald, Managing Consultant, SITEL

With contributions from:
Antonietta Caprano-Wint, Telephone Marketing Manager,
Customer Service, NatWest
Juan Sotolongo, Business Consultant
Alyson Jordan, Contact Centre Consultant
Mary Cooke, Consultant

Managing campaigns successfully takes time planning, involving careful execution and comprehensive reporting. Often the bridge between marketing plans and operational delivery lies in how the campaign is managed. This chapter provides a format for ensuring the results are achieved with maximum positive impact.

BACKGROUND

The first thing to remember about marketing campaigns is that they rarely do what you expect them to do. The vagaries of media, weather, environmental, political and sporting events and life in general mean that nothing will happen quite as you expect. If the mechanism driving the response is television or radio, then the programmes will run over. If it is direct mail then it won't leave or arrive as you expect and if it's press or magazines then respondents will call months after the campaign is terminated. If it is outbound, in other words customer retention, then it is also reliant on customer availability. Within this chapter we focused predominantly on the principles of developing, implementing and evaluating inbound campaigns.

PLANNING

AGREEING THE OBJECTIVES

Clarity on objectives is the starting point. This will set the campaign in context and support your decision-making throughout.

First, the campaign manager or agency must provide a brief overview explaining how the project fits into the overall strategy. Following on from this there are the specific questions relating to the campaign itself. For example:

- Is the target audience existing customers or new prospects?
- Is the campaign designed to maximize the overall number of responses, or generate a small number of quality leads?

- What are the specific requirements of the campaign: is it about generating direct sales or qualifying the leads and passing them on to a dealer network or salesforce; the establishment of a qualified mailing list for future activity; building the database information; increasing awareness of products?
- When is it to start?
- What media will be used?
- Is there any other marketing activity at that time that might affect response rates?
- Are there budgetary constraints?
- What response mechanisms will be used, for instance email, web, telephone, interactive voice recognition (IVR) and mail?

If this is the first time you have completed this process in your current role and if no template exists for the briefing, then developing a briefing process for future campaigns will be worthwhile. A template that acts as a checklist to cover all the initial information needed will be useful in the future, not just for you and your team, but as a guide for those briefing you.

Additionally you will need to calculate your overall capacity to handle campaigns as demonstrated in Figure 33.1.

HARD MEASURES

With these fundamental questions answered it is possible to move forward, discussing your proposed solutions to optimize service and agreeing the objectives for your team, together with the success criteria they will be measured against. These objectives should take the form of hard and soft issues. The hard issues will be those 'nuts and bolt' items that are generally easy to measure, such as:

- target answer times
- average call length
- number of calls per hour per agent
- average answer time
- abandoned rates
- metrics in the use of IVR equipment, for instance target number of calls to use this route (if this is appropriate)
- web support targets
- mandatory information collection requirements
- target number of sales/quality leads (or other measurable objective as appropriate)
- back-office requirements and turnaround times such as mailing/quotation/contract turnaround, email response targets, outbound follow-up timescales and so on.

SOFT MEASURES

The soft measures will normally be those that cover qualitative issues which will directly affect the respondents' experience, such as:

- attitude
- call control
- helpfulness
- enthusiasm.

Capacity planning for unit

Campaign name	Tel. number	Volume	Start date	TOTAL	January – week commencing				
					31st (Dec)	7th	14th	21st	28th
Mastercard – direct mail	0800 XX XX XX	n/a	01-Jan	1075	100	100	75	75	75
Call me – Internet	0800 XX XX XX	n/a	01-Jan	850	50	50	50	50	50
General calls – non campaign	0800 XX XX XX	n/a	01-Jan	38750	2500	2500	2250	2250	2250
Current accounts (switchers) – In-branch	0800 XX XX XX	n/a	01-Jan	0					
Chequecard renewals – direct mail	0800 XX XX XX	4,000 pm	28-Jan	650					50
Youth accounts – various	0800 YY YY YY	n/a	02-Apr	0					
Customer review – in-branch	0800 YY YY YY	n/a	01-Nov	170	10	10	10	10	10
Savings and investments – Non campaign	0845 AAA AAA	n/a	01-Jan	1325	100	100	75	75	75
Savings and investments – In-branch	0845 AAA AAA	n/a	01-Jan	275	50	50	25	25	25
Savings – statement Insert	0800 YY YY YY	5,200,000	08-Jan	2050			150	200	300
Customer review – in-branch	0800 YY YY YY	n/a	01-Feb	200					50
Bonds – direct mail	0800 YY YY YY	300,000	22-Apr	1000					
Business/company card – leaflet	0800 XX XX XX	1,000	05-Feb	10					
Business card – direct mail	0800 XX XX XX	70,000	11-Mar	600					
Credit cards – leaflet	0845 AAA AAA	n/a	01-Jan	1700	100	100	100	100	100
Small business – leaflet	0800 YY YY YY	n/a	01-Jan	4150	200	200	250	250	250
ISAs – non campaign	0800 ZZ ZZ ZZ	n/a	01-Jan	4750	250	250	200	250	250
ISAs – Magazines	0800 XX XX XX	1,200,000	29-Jan	3700					3000
ATM limits (current account) – direct mail*	0845 AAA AAA	300,000	07-Feb	2875					
Students – non campaign	0800 YY YY YY	n/a	01-Jan	5400	300	300	400	350	350
Cash machines – non campaign	0800 YY YY YY	n/a	01-Jan	360	30	30	20	20	20
Generic – welcome brochure	0800 YY YY YY	n/a	20-Nov	850	50	50	50	50	50
Sharedealing – non campaign	0800 YY YY YY	n/a	01-Jan	4100	200	200	200	250	250
Miscellaneous (old campaigns)	n/a	n/a	01-Jan	1275	75	75	75	75	75
TOTAL				76115	4015	4015	3930	4030	7230

January total   23220

	31st (Dec)	7th	14th	21st	28th
Actual calls received	4094	4679	4148	4356	7367
Actual calls handled	3939	4515	4084	4232	7203
	730.00	730.00	714.55	732.73	1314.55
Prediction difference :	-79	-664	-218	-326	-137

Figure 33.1   Capacity planning for unit © Natwest

There is much evidence to suggest that a company's reputation is built on these direct interactions with consumers and all the investment in the campaign can be won or lost by a poor experience when communicating through the contact centre.

These quality issues are just as critical as the other more measurable elements, so assign them equal importance.

DEFINING THE KEY ELEMENTS OF THE CAMPAIGN

It is likely that there will be a number of work streams critical throughout the campaign which impact on contact centre performance. These will include:

- information technology
- telephony
- human resources and training
- operations
- management information and reporting
- quality
- facilities
- other nominated departments that are directly involved, such as fulfilment and sales.

Defining the key events within each of these areas will lay the foundation for your project planning and delivery. Depending on the scale of the project you may choose to use a formal planning tool such as Microsoft Project, or for those smaller tactical campaigns a manual process will do. What really matters is making sure you account for all key elements of the project that will need to be considered for successful implementation.

These will cover:

- activity schedules for media and mailing
- software and database definition
- website programming
- email response definition
- call guidelines and scripting if appropriate
- data interchange
- staffing and training
- forecasting and scheduling
- telephony including IVR
- quality plan
- hours of operation
- risk assessment and contingency planning
- change control process
- testing
- reporting and communication
- target definition and monitoring
- budgetary issues.

Figure 33.2 shows many of the key events and items you will start with but there will always be items specific to your business that you will need to consider. All events will need to have assigned deadlines, with time allowed for slippage. These deadlines will be prioritized and worked back from the 'live' date when the response commences. It is advisable to make your deadline for implementation at least one working week before that live date to give you that time to test and refine when everything is in place.

ID	Task name	Duration	Start date	Finish date
1	**Campaign implementation project**	55 days	Mon 11/02 08:00	Fri 26/04 17:00
2	**Initiate**	13.7 days	Mon 11/02 08:00	Thu 28/02 14:36
3	Decision to use partners	5 days	Mon 11/02 08:00	Fri 15/02 17:00
4	Identify Steering Group members	3 days	Mon 18/02 08:00	Wed 20/02 17:00
5	**Project kick off with Steering Group and project manager**	1 day	Thu 21/02 08:00	Thu 21/02 17:00
6	Define project goal	0.2 days	Thu 21/02 08:00	Thu 21/02 09:36
7	Define project objectives	0.5 days	Thu 21/02 09:36	Thu 21/02 14:36
8	Define project team structure	0.2 days	Thu 21/02 14:36	Thu 21/02 16:12
9	Define project workstream leaders	0.1 days	Thu 21/02 16:12	Thu 21/02 17:00
10	Steering Group sign off of goals and objectives	1 day	Wed 27/02 14:36	Thu 28/02 14:36
11	**Define**	20.7 days	Thu 21/02 08:00	Thu 21/03 14:36
12	Confirm project managers	1 day	Thu 21/02 08:00	Thu 21/02 17:00
13	Prepare scope document	1 day	Thu 28/02 14:36	Fri 01/03 14:36
14	Steering Group sign off of scope document	1 day	Thu 07/03 14:36	Fri 08/03 14:36
15	Define initial plan based on objectives and scope	1 day	Fri 08/03 14:36	Mon 11/03 14:36
16	**Project kick off with workstream leaders**	1 day	Mon 11/03 14:36	Tue 12/03 14:36
17	Review project objectives from Steering Group meeting	0.2 days	Mon 11/03 14:36	Mon 11/03 16:12
18	Define project tasks	0.2 days	Mon 11/03 16:12	Tue 12/03 08:48
19	Assign tasks to workstream leaders	0.2 days	Tue 12/03 08:48	Tue 12/03 10:24
20	Agree task deadlines	0.2 days	Tue 12/03 10:24	Tue 12/03 12:00
21	Agree task interdependencies	0.2 days	Tue 12/03 13:00	Tue 12/03 14:36
22	Prepare work breakdown structure	2 days	Tue 12/03 14:36	Thu 14/03 14:36
23	Steering Group sign off of work breakdown structure	1 day	Wed 20/03 14:36	Thu 21/03 14:36
24	**Plan**	53.7 days	Mon 11/02 08:00	Thu 25/04 14:36
25	Identify project streams members (HR/Finance/ Operations/IT)	2 days	Tue 12/03 10:24	Thu 14/03 10:24
26	Project team agree task responsibilities, timings and resource requirement	3 days	Tue 12/03 14:36	Fri 15/03 14:36
27	Prepare detailed project plan	2 days	Fri 15/03 14:36	Tue 19/03 14:36

Figure 33.2   Sample project plan. Project start: Mon 11/02 08:00; Project finish: Fri 26/04 17:00

Whether you have two months, two weeks or only two days' lead-time, this phase underpins your success. Short cuts will undermine the outcome. It is worth noting that it's usually the simple or obvious things that get forgotten, such as making sure the telephone number is live for instance! That is why the testing period is so crucial but that will be covered in more detail later on.

THE RESPONDER PROFILE

The target audience for the campaign will drive the style of your delivery. For instance, a financial services product targeted at people with high savings may require a very different style from that for a free mobile-phone subscription. The former respondent might be more mature and prefer to be addressed more formally by their titles such as 'Mr' and 'Mrs' than the latter, which might be a younger audience less sensitive to this type of detail. An existing customer may expect you to recognize them when they call, whereas a prospect will normally expect you to ask the obvious questions about their name, address and telephone number.

The specific call to action will set a level of expectation with the respondent about what will happen when they make contact. If they expect to receive a quotation you will need to give them one; if they want to find out their nearest outlet or register for a free sample of an item, make sure your systems are effective, speedy and up to date.

CALL-TYPE DEFINITION

As well as the known and expected response types as a direct result of the campaign call to action, there will always be those who contact you for reasons other than that defined as the objective of the campaign. It is not uncommon during marketing campaigns for 50 per cent of contacts to be unrelated to the core subject, but to relate to peripheral areas. In DRTV (direct response television) this can be higher, particularly if media is scheduled during school holiday periods when children are at home and tempted to call.

It is wise to anticipate what these calls might be and build a process to handle them. You will probably get a good idea of what to expect by investigating similar campaigns that have been handled in the past as well as day-to-day contact types. Team leaders usually have a good idea of these and examples might include:

- Children – many companies have special information and gifts for children that you can use as a positive outcome in dealing with contacts. Handling contacts of this type are seen as investment in future prospects and brand image.
- Subscribers with queries that relate to their accounts, such as billing queries – you will need to decide whether your agents will have access and are able to deal with these or should pass them on.
- Those interested in other products – can your agents give satisfactory answers on these or would you rather they were dealt with in some other way?
- Complaints about the company – a clear complaints handling procedure will be essential to allow agents either to deal with these themselves or escalate accordingly.
- Technical queries directly relating to the product being promoted but often about other products too – careful routing can again allow agents to deal with these themselves or pass them on to the correct person.

Ideally you will anticipate and plan for these types of call, but otherwise have the flexibility to build in processes rapidly to deal with any situations which arise that you didn't consider during the planning. In addition, you will need to account for these in your management information as there may be cost implications for the budget and impact on other metrics, such as the average call length if you do receive many more calls than you expect.

FORECASTING CONTACT VOLUMES AND SCHEDULING OF STAFF

There are some specific considerations which should be made when dealing with direct response campaigns.

The campaign manager will provide an overall forecast and has probably planned the budget based on generating an anticipated number of responses. This is a good start, but a more detailed breakdown will be needed to support the staff roster. It is desirable to break down the overall response according to each media type and then map this into a forecast to give volumes week by week, and hour by hour if it is TV or radio that is being utilized. Overlying this will be any other key events that will drive up volume or conversely depress it. Finally, this data will be fed into the forecast for other activities that will coincide and impact on traffic through the contact centre during the campaign.

While some organizations may have the benefit of a sophisticated software package and team of people trained to carry out the forecasting, others will not or find that they are limited in some way when it comes to the specific campaign in question. It is therefore relatively simple to develop the forecast through a spreadsheet or proprietary database using historic data.

Figure 33.3 takes a broad-brush view at the likely impact on volumes throughout a campaign and predicts the level of full time equivalent agents required to staff the campaign for the duration.

MODELLING

In order to maximize flexibility of the model employed, the information that feeds it must be as detailed and accurate as possible to ensure usable output. It should include:

- hours of cover required
- effective utilization per agent
- volumes expected according to day segments, for instance half hourly or hourly
- call length
- wrap and administrative time
- contact type
- contact method
- agent costs
- other fixed and variable costs.

Output you will need will be:

- contact activity volumes
- work times for all activities including administrative and back-office tasks
- number of staff according to day, hour and week
- budget.

The model must be flexible enough to recalculate on a dynamic basis so that if volumes or other metrics predicted change (and they probably will – several times) then it can recalculate, preferably showing the new actuals against your original forecasts. The model should be built robustly for it will continue to serve as a foundation for your staff planning and budgetary control throughout the project.

PREDICTIVE DIALLING

To fully utilize your staff accurately to run an efficient campaign, some form of dialler must be in place. Depending on your budget, the type of campaign depends on which dialler to use. Predictive dialling is discussed in Chapter 18 of this book.

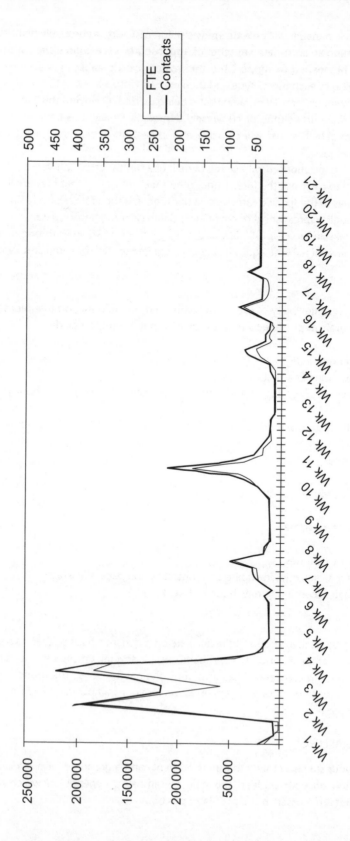

Figure 33.3 Extrapolated volumes and FTE requirement

Technology is so advanced in contact centres these days that various types of dialler are on the market. Larger companies run various types of campaign from one main dialler. Some key aspects of predictive diallers are:

- ability to connect to your host systems to access your call-list database
- ability to switch from different campaigns and lists
- can schedule callbacks
- able to perform call blending between outbound and inbound calls.

The dialler is loaded with tasks, which, depending on the type of campaign, can be loaded daily, weekly or monthly. The dialler is a sensitive piece of kit; it dials the customers on the task list, taking out all the busy tones, corrupt telephone numbers, and so on. Most diallers have call line identification (CLI) embedded in the software application, which means that when a ring tone is received, it puts the call through to the next available agent and the customers' details pop up on screen, simultaneously.

There is also on the market a more sophisticated type of dialler, which controls a variety of campaigns and links to relevant software applications. Multi-skilled agents can work on different campaigns and the technology does the hard work – the agent hears a whisper announcement of which type of call is coming through and with the screen pop-up can deal with that customer. This maximizes productivity and associates utilization. The downside of this type of dialler is, that if it is not functional due to a technology fault, your staff cannot make telephone calls. Experienced IT support desks have to be available during all hours of operation.

DATA MANAGEMENT

In an ideal world, the agent has one view of the customer and can see a full contact history for that customer. However, many contacts come from prospects rather than existing customers, or indeed the respondents are customers but the company does not have the benefit of integrated software. In this latter case it is likely that data will be moved around during the campaign and careful controls are needed to protect data integrity.

Figure 33.4 gives an example of possible data flows. It assumes data will be coming from the marketing database where it is then used for a mailing; it is then forwarded to the contact centre to ensure that agents identify respondents when they make contact. Once the data has been updated, it is fed back to the central marketing database. At each point of transit, a strict quality process is undertaken where the data are checked and any exceptions are rejected. Any rejected data are dealt with through a further process to find out where the data does not comply and the necessary steps are taken to correct and reformat it.

In the case of campaigns targeting new prospects, there may be no original data and this data will be created at the first stage when the respondent engages with the contact centre. In addition, there may be external movement of data through partners (see below). It is critical that the same controls exist for moving data externally as well as internally, and partners must be briefed thoroughly.

DATA TESTING

Once the process has been mapped and implemented to control data flows, it is vital that dummy data interchanges take place that replicate the live situation as closely as possible. Flaws can then be rectified prior to live transfers. This testing should be rigorous, not just checking that a file moves between point A and B, but ensuring that every field can be checked thoroughly.

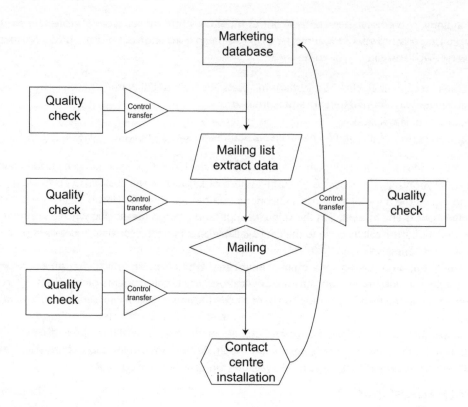

Figure 33.4   Data flows

As with all these matters, it is often the simplest item that gets missed, and with data transfer it is frequently entire records that are not transferred correctly because they are not picked up at the data selection stage. To avoid this, the checking process must follow a full audit which includes reconciliation on the number of records sent. Quite simply, if 1000 records are sent then 1000 must be received and accounted for. It is all too common to find, three or four weeks into a campaign, that some respondents have not been followed up in the designated way because the selection criteria checks have not been rigorous enough.

Remember to close the loop throughout the data interchange process.

WORKING WITH PARTNERS

EXTERNAL CONTACT CENTRE PROVIDERS

It is common for companies to partner an external contact centre provider who is trained to deal with tactical campaigns. If tactical activity seems likely to impact on day-to-day customer service requirements this can be an important way of ensuring service standards are met at all points. For instance:

- where peaks of activity are generated from DRTV or radio advertising
- major company events, such as restructuring announcements, may increase volumes periodically
- unexpected activity can be a result of faults in merchandise and product recalls.

These types of event can be managed through partner programmes thereby protecting the in-house resource from saturation. In addition, there may be mailing houses dealing with fulfilment as well as the initial direct-mail campaigns.

Many years and many campaigns have led to one conclusion about the success of such partnerships: communication and early engagement is the key. Treat these partners like another department and communicate consistently and clearly with them. If you engage them at the planning stage they will be able to assist you in forecasting and contingency planning. They will have infrastructure and facilities that may complement your own and they will certainly form a key part of your contingency plans through offering scalability and flexibility.

WORKING WITH THE MARKETING TEAMS

Probably one of the most important elements of good campaign management is the relationship you hold with the marketing team. It forms the foundation of mutual respect and understanding. It is worthwhile putting yourself in your marketing colleague's position and trying to understand their needs, pressures and goals from both a personal and business perspective. Ensuring that you both have common ground for critical success factors is important.

Here are some things to consider when dealing with your marketing colleagues:

- Have a named contact for each campaign; keep a list of contact details handy.
- Make sure your name is on the sign-off list; try to get included in 'nice to know' information as well – often this can have an impact on how a campaign will be executed.
- Invite marketing colleagues to visit the contact centre; having an understanding of each other's working environments can often increase the effectiveness of working together.
- Be honest; don't commit to elements of a campaign that you know you cannot deliver. Don't commit to something just to get the business, otherwise you will lose credibility as well as future business. Profitability is also likely to take a hit.
- Don't be frightened about offering your opinion and advice; you have probably managed more campaigns than they are ever likely to and your previous experiences will be worth sharing.
- Always ensure marketing have involved the legal and compliance teams where appropriate. This can be especially prominent in the financial services sector.
- Make sure your marketing colleagues know what your team is capable of, in terms of inbound, outbound, Internet fulfilment services, what volumes you can cater for and, of course, what a typical lead-in time for a campaign would be.
- Involve the marketing team with the product training; invite them to present and brief the telephone operators.

Set up regular communication meetings with the campaign manager. By having regular two-way dialogue you will ensure that the campaign runs smoothly and that there are no major last-minute surprises. If there are any changes to the campaign you will be kept informed throughout.

QUALITY MEASURES

As outlined earlier, your success will be evaluated not just against quantitatively accountable performance indicators, but on the quality of the contact handling and data collection.

Quality can be measured via three methods:

- Dedicated quality management team
- Team manager monitoring
- External mystery shopping or post-contact research.

The ideal world would give you a rounded perspective of all three views, but not every contact centre has this. Whichever solution you have available to you (the very minimum will be team manager monitoring), integral to success is a documented quality management assessment process that identifies the key quality thresholds to be achieved and indicates remedial action.

The basic quality process involves:

- specifying the goal
- creating a plan to achieve the goal
- articulating the expectation and making assignments to the team and agents
- conducting follow-up at all levels
- managing variance and taking action.

The sort of action you might take can include:

- side-by-side monitoring
- 'buddying'
- re-training
- improved help-screens or knowledge base.

The quality process should also encompass agent data-capture accuracy and relevance of call outcome logging. During training, the quality process should be outlined to the agents so that they are clear on the quality success measures and how they can impact on them.

GETTING THE SOFT SKILLS RIGHT

Consider the soft skills needed to be a good agent. These are often specific and relate to the way in which the call is handled. The usual measures include greeting, establishing callers' needs, tone of voice, pacing the call, handling conflict and closing the call.

For each campaign, be specific in terms of your requirements at each stage of the call (see Figure 33.5). Additionally, pacing the call is important. The advisor needs to make a judgement about the customer. A business person, used to making many telephone calls, and orderly in approach, will require a fast, accurate, short reply. Someone less confident may have to be led more slowly and would appreciate some time invested. In all cases the call must be paced in a way to ensure that the caller 'hears' the reply. Not to do so, to be too fast, is a false economy as the customer will undoubtedly make another call.

Figure 33.6 shows an example of the quality measures used on a specific tactical campaign, both from a technical and soft skills perspective, and gives insight into the different quality of delivery achievable. Figure 33.7 is an example of a follow-up quality script where customers' perceptions are sought within a couple of days of their original response call.

TEAM STRUCTURE AND STAFF PROFILES

A key ingredient to the successful execution of your campaign will be the structure, experience and skill-set of the management team and agents.

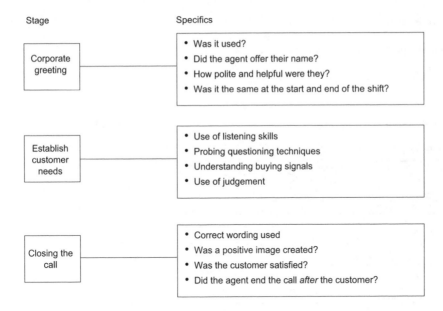

Stage

Specifics

Corporate greeting
- Was it used?
- Did the agent offer their name?
- How polite and helpful were they?
- Was it the same at the start and end of the shift?

Establish customer needs
- Use of listening skills
- Probing questioning techniques
- Understanding buying signals
- Use of judgement

Closing the call
- Correct wording used
- Was a positive image created?
- Was the customer satisfied?
- Did the agent end the call *after* the customer?

Figure 33.5   Soft skill requirements

TEAM MANAGER

First and foremost there must be one manager with overall accountability for the project within the contact centre. Their function will be to lead and direct the team and to manage communication between the original owner of the overall campaign and the contact centre. They will have ultimate responsibility for the design and implementation of the project and delivery of the service and quality measures. They will manage the communication on a daily basis and prepare an end-of-programme evaluation and review.

TEAM MEMBERS

Within the team working with this manager should be a nominated person to lead each work stream, including recruitment and training, technology and telephony, operational management, management information and quality monitoring. The overall manager will ensure that each team member is clear about what is expected from them during implementation and the daily running of the live campaign and will organize and chair the project review meetings which will be run on a regular basis. Once the project is live it is likely this team will communicate very frequently throughout the first few days. There is likely to be fine-tuning of the operation to reflect what has actually occurred. For instance, if calls are more or less than planned, rescheduling of staff may be necessary or if an unexpected issue is being raised frequently by responders, the call guidelines and knowledge base may need updating.

AGENTS

At operational level it is likely that there will be an agreed ratio of team managers to agents – this is usually between 1:5 to 1:15. During the first few days it may be necessary to supplement this with other members of the management team until a 'steady state' is achieved. It is critical that the live feedback on what is taking place during calls is carefully monitored through dialogue with agents

Name of agent:

Team Manager:

Date:

Technical skills	Score	Comments

Technical skills	Score
Opening/Introduction	
Correct introduction and name given	1 2 3 4 5
Total	
Front Screen	
Name, initial and title asked for	1 2 3 4 5
Asked for spelling of surname	1 2 3 4 5
Customer asked to read back address	1 2 3 4 5
Are home, work and mobile phone numbers asked for?	1 2 3 4 5
Are all details entered correctly?	1 2 3 4 5
Total	
Media	
Correct media flagged	1 2 3 4 5
Total	
Script	
Correct script route followed	1 2 3 4 5
Any appliances in the property?	1 2 3 4 5
Owner or tenant	1 2 3 4 5
Does customer have service cover?	1 2 3 4 5
Age of current appliance confirmed	1 2 3 4 5
Explanation of visit	1 2 3 4 5
Decision-maker question discussed	1 2 3 4 5
Has the appliance broken down?	1 2 3 4 5
Total	
Appointment Booking	
Was satisfactory appointment negotiated?	1 2 3 4 5
Was necessary information entered in notes?	1 2 3 4 5
Reference number given	1 2 3 4 5
Representative name given	1 2 3 4 5
Inbound phone number given	1 2 3 4 5
Close of call conducted appropriately	1 2 3 4 5
Total	
Sub total	
Technical Skills Percentage	%

Figure 33.6 General advertising response monitoring form (*continues*) © SITEL

Soft skills	Score	Comments
Customer Impression		
Tone	1 2 3 4 5	
Clarity/Clear diction	1 2 3 4 5	
Pace	1 2 3 4 5	
Demonstrated empathy	1 2 3 4 5	
Rapport-building skills	1 2 3 4 5	
Demonstrated excellent customer care	1 2 3 4 5	
Customer expectations met	1 2 3 4 5	
Total		
Client Impression		
Agent demonstrated positive attitude to brand	1 2 3 4 5	
Showed good campaign knowledge	1 2 3 4 5	
Explanation of outcome	1 2 3 4 5	
Business expectations met	1 2 3 4 5	
Total		
Call Control		
Questioning skills – good variety, effective	1 2 3 4 5	
Assertiveness	1 2 3 4 5	
Listening skills	1 2 3 4 5	
Recognized behaviour type and adapted accordingly	1 2 3 4 5	
Negotiating skills	1 2 3 4 5	
Total		
Problem Solving		
Objection handling	1 2 3 4 5	
Dealing with difficult people	1 2 3 4 5	
Correct complaint procedure followed	1 2 3 4 5	
Total		
Cross-selling		
If relevant was cross selling attempted?	1 2 3 4 5	
Total		
Grand Total		
No. of criteria measured against		
Average score		
Soft Skills Percentage	%	

Other		
Subtotal		

Overall Total	%

Signed..   60–69% – Poor (refer to Team Manager)

70–84% – Development Area

Signed..   85–89% – Good

90–94% – Very good

95% +   – Outstanding

ACTION POINTS:

Figure 33.6   General advertising response monitoring form (*concluded*) © SITEL

Customer Service Professional: ....

Auditor: ....

Date: ....

Good morning/afternoon/evening, my name is ...., a Quality Assurance Representative calling on behalf of (insert Company name) I understand you recently spoke to ...., one of our Customer Service Professionals and wondered if you would answer a few questions about the service we offered you?

Using a score of between 1 and 5 (1 being bad and 5 being excellent), how would you rate the following:

1 Very Poor   2 Poor   3 Average   4 Good   5 Excellent

	1	2	3	4	5
Overall manner of CSP?	1	2	3	4	5
Willingness to help of CSP?	1	2	3	4	5
Knowledge of CSP and ability to help?	1	2	3	4	5
Customer needs understood and met?	1	2	3	4	5
How well did our service meet your expectations?	1	2	3	4	5

Are there any other comments you would like to make?

....

....

Thank you for your time.

Figure 33.7   Customer perception follow-up © SITEL

to ensure they have all they need to fulfil the brief and ensure the customer interaction is first rate. Where they haven't got what they need to achieve this, action must be taken swiftly to give them what they need to enhance the customer experience.

At agent level it is advisable to analyse programme objectives and devise an agent profile and then screen agents against the skill-set required. For instance, if the campaign is aimed at taking simple name and address details for despatching a brochure the skill-set is basic and the pool of agents available probably wide within the existing resource. However, at the other end of the scale, if the campaign is focused on selling a highly technical product suite or developing individualized quotes it is likely you will need a much higher level of competency from the agent. This may give rise to some limitations and necessitate contingency planning.

TESTING CYCLE

Earlier in this chapter we recommended that a testing period be built into the project plan before going live. At this stage all infrastructure should be in place and the agents trained. It is then possible to implement a full testing phase which will take the programme through data load (if applicable) and various contact-handling scenarios, evaluate call outcomes and reports and data interchange. These initial test results have a habit of throwing up surprises and highlighting any weaknesses or errors that will allow you to act and refine the programme.

The scale of the testing will depend on the scale of the programme and the budget available. I have known literally hundreds of test calls to take place if the profile of the project demands this. In others, just a few scenarios exist for calls and the testing is scaled accordingly. Whatever the scale, try to involve as many different perspectives in the testing as possible. If you ask colleagues to make test contact then give them guidelines:

- **Customer perspective:** First, they must make the contact from the point of view of the customer or prospect. It is very easy for a colleague who has an intimate knowledge of the product and campaign to ask questions from that perspective, putting the agent into difficulties by asking questions that wouldn't normally arise. This can throw the system into disarray. For example, it is not unknown for directors to call in without even having seen the call-to-response mechanism (be it advertisement, letter or whatever). They have no insight into what customers' expectations might be, ask questions that would not arise, then complain to the team, putting unnecessary pressure on the operation, which is probably already feeling considerable pre-live tension in any case. This sort of scenario ultimately helps no one, so issue guidelines and control the test process.
- **Feedback:** Second, feedback should never be directed straight to the agent, but through the nominated team member to ensure that feedback is administered to the whole team in a consistent and effective manner. Feedback given inappropriately to an agent can often undermine the confidence of the whole team.

ESCALATION PROCESS

When you detail your communication process, make sure all involved are aware of the escalation procedures and points of contact for all matters arising in the live environment. A fully defined and open discipline for communication of all matters, especially complaints, will underpin their swift and consistent resolution.

Again, this may change as the campaign matures. In the early stages of the project campaign managers may want very direct involvement and ownership themselves, but as the project settles down, this is probably not necessary.

Ensure that all the team knows that if they are directly approached about any matters, they must communicate them in the defined manner straightaway.

BUDGETARY CONTROL

Your briefing process and forecasting will have given you the budgetary outlines. Reporting and monitoring on the key measurements for this must be adhered to throughout and it is recommended that this be broken down into the smallest component. If it is feasible to break down the budgetary components into their smallest elements, that is to team manager and agent measurement factors, then do it. For a team manager and agent this might be based on the number of calls you need them to take per hour and shift. Giving them these targets will control budgets at the point of impact. This can then be incorporated into team performance and overall contact performance measurement against the budget. The more frequently performance is reported, the sooner adjustments can be made if things are not working according to plan.

RISK ANALYSIS AND CONTINGENCY

It will have become clear by now that inbound response campaigns can generate many unexpected events. Where much activity has gone before, your forecasting of responses can be very close, but it is not uncommon that some unexpected event will impact on the campaign. It is therefore advisable to conduct a risk analysis of the overall project in order to define likely impacts on the contact centre and develop contingency plans.

It may be that you have already defined contingency and crisis plans within the contact centre and you can plug your campaign into this process. More often these do not exist, so take a common-sense look at the stages and key events and ask yourself what you will do if certain events occur:

- What are the thresholds on volume that will affect your staffing and what will you do if you need more or less people at very short notice?
- What will happen if there are technology or telephony failures?
- If you are incorporating IVR and web or email responses, what will you do if the ratio of these is not what you have planned for?
- How will you handle unexpected media coverage?
- What will happen if your mailing doesn't land in the pattern you expect?
- What will you do if there are unexpected agent shortages through illness or other events?
- How will you manage communication internally and externally in the event of such occurrences?

It is not possible to provide a definitive list of unexpected events. However, a discussion with your contact centre team managers will probably give you a good idea of what they've come across and what resources can be brought to bear in these circumstances. It is, however, vital that whatever you are able to define and plan for, you have scope to develop plans dynamically as events happen. Be flexible and open to ideas.

IMPLEMENTATION AND MANAGEMENT OF THE LIVE CAMPAIGN

The emphasis in campaign handling is without question on thorough and detailed planning. However, there are a few additional considerations to be taken into account during the implementation of your plans.

PROGRAMME INITIATION AND DEFINITION

All functional areas should by now clearly understand their responsibilities and points of delivery as defined in the project plan. However, sometimes during this phase of the project the team can become fragmented, falling back into their functional silos and losing identity with the cross-functional team whom they have worked with during the planning stage.

Good project leadership can overcome this. If there is strong identity with the project team then loyalty and focus will remain on making the project a success, so continue to engage all areas and communicate with them as one team. Importantly, remember that communication is a two-way process so if you ensure that they are reporting back on their areas during the implementation they will be forced to remain focused and accountable.

Gain their cooperation by recognizing their positive contribution. For instance, if the software is successfully implemented, make sure thanks are communicated to the team and all key management. Where the implementation fails, work alongside the programming team to support the extra efforts needed. Also, don't leave HR and recruitment to appoint the staff. Work with them by attending assessment centres or interviews and contributing to the training. Get to know the agents who are to work on the project and ensure they know other members of the team. Close attention to the team interaction at this stage will galvanize the energy of the team and underpin your success. One way or another, contact centres are about people and your leadership and people interaction skills will gain loyalty and commitment to the campaign.

MANAGING COMMUNICATION

The importance of setting expectations for the campaign has been touched on already. It is all too easy for a project to be undermined by false expectations of what it is to deliver, and all too often the pressure that this creates flows into the contact centre as implementation gets underway and tensions mount. It is not unheard of for directors who have not been briefed thoroughly to expect sales from an awareness campaign, for instance, or to test the system and expect to receive some follow-up when none is planned.

Much of this can be avoided if clear and simple communication continues during implementation. People may not have much time to assimilate information, so the process for telling them what is happening as the planning evolves should be simple but thorough. For instance:

- Concise bulletins can be sent by email or posted on notice boards
- Mechanisms can be put in place for senior teams to feedback to the management team where they have concerns (this ensures problems are dealt with prior to going live)
- Key people, whose perspective you consider to be particularly important, may be contacted.

Whatever it takes, don't neglect this area; stay in control to support the team in the contact centre, who will feel the effects if negative perceptions arise.

TEST CALLS

Encouraging people at all levels to engage in the testing process, by carrying out test calls for instance, can also uncover any hidden concerns or inaccurate expectations. Getting these issues in the open before the live date will again ensure your contact centre team can focus on successful interaction with customers and not be diverted in the live scenario by new issues emerging.

Be proactive in this area, communicating not just your successes, but those negatives that also need to be raised. By managing the communication of any less than successful elements of the project you will have the opportunity to set them in context and not allow negative internal messages to emanate from rumour and speculation.

GOING 'LIVE'

Finally, when you are fully tested and the systems are in place and you are ready to go live, move calmly into this state. The bigger the profile of the event, the more pressure the contact centre will feel under. A positive atmosphere coupled with a calm and steady hand on the project tiller will help them do their best for you. It's okay to panic, but not in the middle of the contact centre floor – go behind closed doors, work issues through, and present solutions to the team in a considered and professional way.

The pressure on budget owners can be enormous, particularly if responses are low, and it is not uncommon for them to pass that pressure on to agents if they are not managed firmly.

MANAGING THE LIVE CAMPAIGN

So your planning has paid off, the campaign has begun, systems are fully operational and your contact centre is confidently handling the response. Now you just need to keep your hands on the steering wheel to make sure the vehicle stays on course.

Monitoring results

Table 33.1 is a typical report of the key measurements of a response campaign. It evaluates some key dimensions of the project including quality measures; in this case the need to keep the percentage of calls to IVR below an average of 10 per cent. You will probably want to supplement this data with anecdotal feedback from agents to give you a full perspective on how the campaign is working. Use these reports to keep control and to communicate to the rest of the team and management.

DYNAMIC GOAL SETTING AND REFINING YOUR PERFORMANCE

As the campaign evolves, you will need to evaluate your original goals for each criteria and assess if they are still appropriate. It is most important that you regard these goals as changeable and react swiftly to what actually happens when the response starts. For instance, your call length may be shorter or longer than anticipated – though it will perhaps be longer in the first few days as agents get used to the campaign. However, ultimately, you may need to readjust your call guidelines to keep to the expected goals or readjust them to accommodate the actual call length because there is no scope to change the call content. If you do adjust this goal then you will need to adjust every point of contact for this metric and ultimately re-evaluate your staffing plans. Another example might be that call peaks or troughs are occurring in a way that was not anticipated. Again, if you cannot alter the fact – for instance, DRTV (Direct Response Television) causes such peaks and troughs that you may be able to adjust the advertising schedule – it may be necessary to look at shift patterns to ensure you get the right people in the contact centre when you need them. Similarly, if the mix of response methods is not as expected you may need to adjust the mix of skills available in the agent team.

Constantly challenging your expectations and the goals set and acting to refine delivery will optimize the ultimate success of the project. Even when a campaign is several weeks old it pays to take 'new eyes' to the goals to see if anything can still be done to improve your performance. Finally, document and communicate to all concerned those changes you make and the reasons why you have made them. Again, it's a question of setting expectations of project delivery at the correct point and putting the reasons for this in context.

COMPLAINTS HANDLING AND PROBLEM RESOLUTION

A successful process for managing complaints or problems will have been mapped out and implemented. Monitoring the types of complaint, and success in resolving them will enhance the positive impact created by the project. Particularly where products or services are highly regulated, such as in insurance and financial services, this aspect of the project will be heavily

Table 33.1 Sample inbound campaign monitoring report. © SITEL

Date	Total calls forecast	Calls arrived	% diff to forecast	Calls answered	Calls abandoned	% Abandoned	Calls to IVR	% IVR	Calls aban. during/ after IVR	% Aban. during/ after IVR	Call duration (MIN)
1-Sep	2970	3858	130	3666	80	2.07	493	12.78	107	2.77	3.95
2-Sep	2760	3000	109	2891	41	1.37	406	13.53	66	2.20	4.01
3-Sep	2528	2913	115	2839	48	1.65	187	6.42	24	0.82	3.98
4-Sep	2451	2771	113	2717	33	1.19	144	5.20	19	0.69	3.96
5-Sep	858	1420	166	1298	50	3.52	274	19.30	72	5.07	4.32
6-Sep	234	320	137	295	16	5.00	34	10.63	9	2.81	3.22
7-Sep	4428	3780	85	3649	80	2.12	343	9.07	50	1.32	3.78
8-Sep	4107	3087	75	3037	27	0.87	131	4.24	23	0.75	4.18
9-Sep	3796	2870	76	2824	24	0.84	149	5.19	21	0.73	4.11
10-Sep	3480	2812	81	2775	25	0.89	82	2.92	10	0.36	4.08
11-Sep	3374	2999	89	2904	51	1.70	230	7.67	44	1.47	4.24
12-Sep	1158	1623	140	1470	50	3.08	425	26.19	102	6.28	3.96
13-Sep	313	482	154	458	11	2.28	57	11.83	13	2.70	2.95
14-Sep	3843	5630	147	5038	205	3.64	1387	24.64	381	6.77	3.52
15-Sep	3560	4224	119	4149	43	1.02	255	6.04	31	0.73	3.67
16-Sep	3286	3814	116	3722	66	1.73	195	5.11	25	0.66	3.87
17-Sep	3011	3241	108	3141	46	1.42	230	7.10	52	1.60	3.94
18-Sep	2920	3050	104	2982	40	1.31	233	7.64	26	0.85	4.19
19-Sep	1007	1421	141	1338	35	2.46	216	15.20	47	3.31	3.73
20-Sep	275	299	109	283	9	3.01	15	5.02	7	2.34	3.74
21-Sep	5314	3685	69	3513	79	2.14	359	9.74	91	2.47	4.01
22-Sep	3991	3035	76	2953	49	1.61	270	8.90	70	2.31	4.09
23-Sep	3399	3037	89	2951	42	1.38	216	7.11	42	1.38	3.9
24-Sep	3319	2855	86	2753	47	1.65	219	7.67	49	1.72	3.8
25-Sep	3319	2837	85	2745	63	2.22	238	8.39	29	1.02	4.09
26-Sep	1468	1248	85	1226	13	1.04	58	4.65	11	0.88	4.19
27-Sep	402	298	74	292	4	1.34	7	2.35	2	0.67	3.4
28-Sep	4972	4036	81	3798	108	2.68	504	12.49	123	3.05	3.7
29-Sep	3734	3316	89	3197	61	1.84	253	7.63	57	1.72	3.87
30-Sep	3606		0								
TOTALS	83883	77961	93	74904	1446	1.85	7610	9.76	1603	2.06	3.88

The report is produced here to show the full extent of the figures but can be presented graphically if desirable.

scrutinized. Sometimes problems arise out of aspects of the product itself; at other times the problem requires internal investigation and follow-through and may highlight shortcomings in your internal administration process.

When a complaint occurs:

- Communicate it speedily through the designated process.
- Manage the complainant's expectations and make sure that you then act when and how promised.
- Investigate as quickly as possible.
- Decide on action required to deal with the complainant and make recompense if appropriate.
- Decide if this complaint is symptomatic of a deeper issue and, if it is, take necessary action.
- Communicate the nature of the complaint to all of the team as appropriate and ensure they know what action was taken and why.
- If it is a problem that is likely to have occurred with other respondents, update your call guidelines and knowledge base to equip agents in dealing with it.
- Document the occurrence and the action time and keep a record for audit purposes.

CLOSING THE CAMPAIGN

The campaign has run its course and the peak of activity has passed. Calls are still coming in, but volumes are lower and the close date is in sight.

It will be helpful to you and the entire team if you conduct a full review of the project to ensure that any key learning is documented and passed on. This review will consider all actual outcomes against the original plan and cover all functional areas. In particular, media effectiveness should be assessed in detail.

- Did the media reach the targeted audience and did the audience respond to specific incidents of the media in the numbers expected?
- Was the target cost per response and cost per outcome achieved?
- If the target costs were achieved, would it be feasible to continue with other waves of similar activity? If the target costs were not achieved, what can be recommended to improve the media buying in future?
- Did the technology work and did the knowledge base develop any insight into customer behaviour that would assist other areas of the business?
- Was the agent training effective or could refinements be made to enhance agent confidence at the point of customer interaction?
- Was the data management effective?
- What perceptions do management within the company have of the campaign? Is it what you want or could you improve communication in future campaigns?
- Did the management information provide you with what you wanted or could you add new dimensions for future activity?
- Have you conducted external customer research which will give you direct feedback on their experience of this specific campaign?

Seek feedback wherever it is appropriate and available, then prepare a comprehensive post-campaign evaluation.

Finally, don't forget to close those lines and release numbers and other contact medium, and take steps to redirect any trickle of response that might continue.

VI *The Future*

This section of the handbook looks into the future and how consumers and technologies will adapt over the coming years.

- The Information Revolution
- Preparing for Tomorrow's Customer

34 *The Information Revolution*

Graham Whitehead, Principal Consultant, BTexact Technologies

In the last few years, small changes have produced massive, unpredictable effects, changing the way we live, work and socialize – in fact everything. We have always managed (eventually) to accommodate the changes, embrace them and use them to our advantage. This chapter looks at the next change that is about to happen, and that is the Information Revolution.

BEFORE THE INFORMATION REVOLUTION

If you think that we have already been through the Information Revolution, think again – it has not yet even started. We simply throw around concepts such as the Internet and World Wide Web so that we completely overlook the implications for our life and our work. It is so easy to think that these new technologies are simply an extension of the old telephone network.

The telephone liberated our ability to communicate over vast and increasing distances. The device was not universally welcomed initially. The Minister for Posts in her Britannic Majesty's House of Commons is quoted as saying, 'Whilst this new-fangled telephonic apparatus might be all well and good for our colonial cousins, it will serve no use in the United Kingdom because we have a surfeit of messenger boys'. Not to be outdone, the Chief Engineer of the Post Office wrote, 'My office is in full knowledge of this device, and we can see no merit in it at all.'

Indeed, by the early 1990s, browsers were developed and allowed point-and-play graphical interfaces which allowed general users a simple, easy and fun method of using the system. At this point commercial interests started to show interest in the new system and soon the World Wide Web (as it became known) became the dominant means of passing information. November 12 1998 was the first day in the BT network where there were more data calls (machines talking to machines) than voice calls (people talking to people)!

Very soon the data calls started to swamp the telephone network, so by the end of the year 2000 the whole of the BT phone network had been overlaid by a new data network called the colossus network, using routers rather than telephone exchanges.

The foundation is now in place to start the Information Revolution …

THE HOME OF THE FUTURE

These changes will become most apparent in the home, where we are seeing for the first time the first skirmishes in the information battle. For years the only information connections we had in the home were letters, a telephone and a TV antenna. Then there were satellite TV and cable connections. Suddenly there is the 'Could I interest you in a bundle of services, TV phone and Internet access?' offer. In the future people will not care, let alone worry about, how the information arrives in their homes any more than they strive to understand how their car engine works. Plugging into information will be as easy as plugging in a power cord, and when was the last time you questioned whether electricity would flow out of the socket?

In the near future, information will arrive across the whole spectrum of services and be combined at the point of human interest. That point is likely to be the television, which in practice is likely to be a very powerful digital computer, but will display a movie if that is what is wanted. The television will become an information portal, with probably the ability to display different things on different screens in different room. The advent of the wireless local area network (LAN) (such as IEEE802.11) will remove the constraints and cumbersome expense of cables.

THE CUSTOMER'S PERSPECTIVE

The delivery of the information will be easy; the real challenge will be how we are going to be able to accommodate and assimilate all the information that is so readily available. To this end, we will require some assistance, and this will be in the form of artificial intelligent agents. Now at this point most people become fearful, which I feel is unnecessary as these agents will not be artificial nor intelligent, just small packages of software to assist the user. They will learn the user's interests and preferences and actively seek out information that might be of specific interest. At a convenient time this information will be offered for one's perusal. Just imagine that the first agent that will be used will be a TV-watching agent. In only a few years' time, when there are thousands of digital TV channels available, how is the viewer going to know what is available? Will they really read a programme guide that is over a metre thick every day? Rather, the TV agent will be sitting aside the viewer on the sofa watching viewing patterns and suggesting suitable viewing. The TiVo system is probably the first such intelligent system to be demonstrated.

These agents will also have voices and speak in a natural human-like voice. They will listen to and understand what you say without having to train your voice to the machine nor the machine to your voice. They will even have faces. These agents will not expect to be programmed; they will engage in conversations and ultimately it will be like talking to a friend.

PURCHASING WILL BE DIFFERENT

General information will be simply collected at the appropriate times; take household insurance as an example. The insurance agent will know the date of renewal and in the last 30 days of the cover period will be seeking suitable terms and conditions from commercial agents in the insurance business, using data stored from last year's exchange and any new changes that have been acquired during the year, such as new furniture from the shopping agent. This data will then be offered to the consumer for a decision, as I do not see these agents making executive decisions. The customer will then make a decision based on their priorities (cheapest is not always best), and at that point will probably seek personal contact with the organization of choice. If this contact is a simple telephone call to a call centre, then we are back in the Dark Ages: Name? First name? Address? Post code? All tediously done by voice and keyboard at the far end.

This is where we step into the future of communications. In the old days we could just talk over the phone, which made the transfer of data tedious. Once we step into the Internet-working Protocol (IP) world things get much simpler, quicker and easier. When we start using systems where voice, data and vision are one simple connection over one network, not three separate connections on three networks, the exchange of information becomes effortless. The voice channel is established to a call centre. My intelligent agent passes all the data that has been used and collected over the simultaneous data connection (no more re-entering of data) and I can browse. At that point I might be comfortable to complete the transaction without further recourse to a human operator. I frequently these days make purchases by entering personal details and a credit card number, and complete without talking to anybody. If, however, I need further details, explanations and confidence, I will be passed to a human call centre agent who instantly can see all the previously entered data and is only involved at a level in the transaction that requires the human intellect.

On the Internet today you will often see 'call me' buttons. By clicking one of these you will be asked 'at which phone number?' and 'at what time?' The latter most people find strange, but today most people surf down the phone line, which makes talking to them on the phone impossible. They have to close down their browser – hopefully they have printed-off all the pages they had been looking at – and wait by the phone for the call to be made. In the data-world of tomorrow, one will click the button and instantly a voice will arrive through the screen. A conversation will go something like: 'I see that you are looking at Caller Display 20; could I interest you in Caller Display 50?' might well ensue.

Once voice, data and vision are one simple connection over one network, not three separate connections on three networks, the button will become a 'discuss with me' button – face-to-face communications over a device that you will still call a TV. This, of course, raises the issue that if contact centre staff are to be seen as well as heard, will they have to be dressed in corporate clothing with a bustling office behind them?

THE IMPACT OF MOBILITY

It would appear that everything is going mobile, a further example of the disruptive technologies. Just look back to the early 1980s, when there was a man walking down the street talking to a house brick apparently clamped to the side of his head. Did anyone really believe that it was anything but a fad? But it happened. There are now more mobile phones in the UK than people.

In the near future people will insist that they have access to everything via a mobile appliance. The advent of 3G mobile systems means that there is an equivalent connection in the mobile world as we have become used to in the wired world over the last few years. Bandwidths and data transmission rates have become large enough to ensure that there will be no waiting in wanting. Unlike the WAP phones of the late 1990s there will be 'permanent connection always on' data, so the retrieval of data will be a background activity. No delay means that humans will use the system without frustration.

The new 3G phones have a landscape, rather than portrait, orientation. They have larger, colour screens with higher definition, and no buttons to press so voice dialling will become the norm. With such equipment, people will start demanding information from their mobile devices. 'What's the balance in my current account?' 'What's on at the cinema?' 'I would like one of those. Where can I buy it?' There is also a great likelihood that by carrying a mobile device the user will be tracked and information that is pertinent to the user in that location will automatically be fed to them. There will be a great demand for information and the contact centre, be it an artificial agent or a human agent, will be the centre of this demand.

E-FRIENDLY

Above all, in this new instant interactive information world, systems must be e-friendly. The human-fronted call centre was the ultimate interface for most people. Almost everyone can talk and listen and the customer could leave all the difficult details to the call centre operator. As more and more of the process is handled in the automatic machine world, we must take great care to ensure that it works well, to the point where it becomes transparent.

In the days before the complete transfer of all personal data from my 'secure card' or 'secure memory' location there is a need to remove the complexity of the system front end. Most people these days are familiar with the data entry boxes on Internet pages. At best they are simple; at worst they are tedious. New systems are being designed to make use of the ability to combine phone calls and data calls.

While addressing a web page on the Internet one has the option to phone the page as well, using a standard phone or a mobile device. As one looks at the page a realistic voice asks for the data, such as 'What is your family name?', and one can enter the data by typing or speaking. Furthermore, while the system is entering the user's name, by voice, the user can add the data for their date of birth in another part of the screen, by keyboard; the system acknowledges that input and this data is not requested by the voice system.

Recently I used such a system to request house and contents insurance. Having conveniently filled in the data, I was transferred to a human agent who undertook the higher-level requirements capture. But the best part of the system was that both the agent and I could see exactly the same web page, different options being detailed in a manner similar to being sat at the same table looking at the same piece of paper. Gone are the days of having to listen at apparently supersonic speeds to an agent who has done this procedure a hundred times already today and then being expected to make choices. Similar procedures will be undertaken in call centres to address customer complaints and queries. For example, an enquiry about a phone bill is so much easier to handle if the conversation starts 'Here is the bill, and can you see this number?' and on the screen is not only the bill but a highlighted area that is being discussed.

The whole aim of customer relationships in the future is to give the impression that that customer is the only person who is being addressed, and more than that, the most important person in that group of one. Stroke the customer, make them feel wanted and they will return.

Unfortunately, a bad customer experience is more and more likely to result in that customer going elsewhere. After all, the new information systems will make the ability to set up customer centres relatively easy, and moderately cheap. All a dissatisfied customer needs to do is click and they have found one of your competitors. And the total lack of effort required to produce that single click will mean customers will be very quick to change allegiances. I was surprised recently to be told that many people are changing their house mortgages every few months to get the best interest deals. Only a few years ago most people would have only changed a mortgage once they had gone past the level of being totally dissatisfied with their old supplier, as the process was perceived to be too complex and difficult.

Ease, simplicity, good visual appearance and accuracy are the main stays of good customer engagement.

WORKING IN A CONTACT CENTRE

As we move into the technology age, however, I do not see the bad call centre surviving. The ease of connection will enable more and more people to connect to the contact centre facility, and the ease of being able to register one's dissatisfaction by a mere click will ensure that the poor ones do not survive.

I see a lot of effort being put into the call centre environment in the near future. The customer expectation is speed, accuracy and a good experience. In order to provide this, the environment of the call centre must be maximized. The environment must be productive, protective and enabling, and people are most productive when they feel safe.

THE CONTACT CENTRE ENVIRONMENT

Historically, call centres by their very size have required large open spaces. Dividing the floor into functional areas or team units has to some extent reduced the expansiveness, and the inclusion of low dividers to create the open-plan pigpens has had a unifying effect. But little else has been done to address the working environment.

There has been a lot of research undertaken recently, both in the USA and in the UK, looking at the call centre experience from the agent's point of view. Most call centre agents these days work from a computer screen, but that screen is still used in the same way as paper;, it is vertical rather than horizontal when the paper used to be flat on the desk surface. As humans we are able to assimilate information that surrounds us, not just information delivered directly to the eyes and ears. As an example, in the USA one researcher injected noise into a call centre. The more calls being handled the greater the sound of rain falling. Most people would think that the noise would be distracting and irritating, but humans have the ability to filter sounds – next time you are in a crowded room just imagine how confusing it would be if you tried to listen to all the conversations all the time. We filter and concentrate on the one immediate conversation. However, this does not blunt our ability to home in on the remote comment, which contained our name. We are listening to everything and filtering that which is not appropriate at the time. Similarly, the noise of the rain gave people a feeling of being involved in the greater environment without being distracted from the task in hand.

We can also change the visual environment. At the moment we have a telephone, a screen and a keyboard. Text is read from the screen and typed into the keyboard, which is simple but very limiting. Computers these days are very powerful and we can use this power to make them deliver information in an analogue manner rather than in the digital computer way. As a human I am wonderfully powerful in the analogue world. My eyes can accept gigabits of information every second and I have an analogue computer in my head working at the same data rates. I have spent all my life living with coloured moving pictures. So why when we go to work does everything become so boringly digital?

New technologies will enable an environment that is a point and play area. The view from the patio doors is of a seascape and sky – infinitely adjustable to personal requirements – and messages, in this case towed in by a hot-air balloon, can be of a general nature. The working environment will be laid out pictorially as a desk, with the phone keypad and the customer data areas clearly visible. A hand in the centre of the picture will be a pointing device that activates the environment. Pointing to the customer data causes, for example, a phone bill to fold out and the image can be shared with the customer, highlighting areas of interest or discussion as mentioned above. At the end of the customer exchange the customer can be 'dragged' into the filing cabinet – very satisfying at the end of a tedious interaction.

THE HOME WORKER

'Do not talk to me about home workers!' said the managing director of a well-known high street company, 'all they do is skive all the time. I would never get anything out of them.' This is far from the truth. Granted, some home workers will be cyber-skivers, but these would have been the very same ones that skived in an office!

The addition of modern networking allowing email and file transfers has meant that the home worker can have access to communications and information from the home just as easily, conveniently and simply as being actually in the office. Eventually full-fibre optic connections will increase the desirability of remote working, while road and public transport congestion over the next decade will further enhance its desirability. The technology is not the problem in this area; the problems we need to address are people issues. We will have to start measuring performance by output and not by input and attendance.

The ability to split shift becomes a pleasure if clocking-off entails only getting up from a desk and closing a door. Being on-call in an evening is not arduous if it can be done from your home. Work is becoming an activity, not a place we travel to.

A DELIGHTED CUSTOMER

What we must strive for in the near future is a delighted customer. The creation of a good and sound working environment is just part of that greater goal. The customer experience must be one of an easy and convenient conversation – a totally one-on-one experience.

In the electronic information age of the future, not only will we be able to collect more and more information about our customers, but we must also ensure that this information is correlated and used in a proper manner. To find a customer takes months, to lose one can take seconds. Let's use the new technologies to ensure that our customers are delighted customers. We need to embrace the new technologies and marshal them as we engage our customers. And if you thought that technology has attained all that it can, think again. The scientists at Cerner Corporation have just built the Haldon Collider – a machine that can produce Pita bits of information every second. (Pita = 10^{15} bits every second). They are already creating networks (called the grid) that can handle these amounts of information. Just like the scientists in the 1960s and 1970s, they are creating the next Information Revolution. At the moment the systems are confined to a few academic institutions but they are heading our way. Do you think that you will be ready for them? Just like the web, the grid is coming.

35 *Preparing for Tomorrow's Customer*

Melanie Howard, Co-Founder, Future Foundation

This chapter is designed to provide an overview of the key consumer trends that are evident today, which give a pointer to the way in which businesses, and in particular those responsible for the primary customer interface in the contact centre, should be thinking and responding in anticipation of the customer of the future.

BACKGROUND

While the past may not necessarily be a good guide to the future, its seeds can always be found in the present, at least from a social and consumer perspective. Rather grandly called 'the principle' by sociologists Willmott and Young in their 1970s book *The Symmetrical Family*, this idea proposes that it is always possible to find, within the present, people who are the early adopters of social, consumer and technological change. Properly analysed in the context of wider trends, their behaviour will point to how people are likely to act in the future. This chapter looks at this principle, which underlies much of our work at the Future Foundation and provides an excellent guide to future changes and demands from customers.

In attempting to describe the emerging consumer needs that will increasingly make themselves felt in the contact centre of the future, it is likely that these will be demands that are already beginning to make themselves felt today and will be recognized by many readers. One of the main benefits of futurology and future-focused research from a business perspective is that it forces the organization to look outside of itself and at least catch up with the present – often surprisingly difficult given the complexities of everyday operational management and pressures on performance and margins. Additionally, as highlighted by Stewart Brand in his excellent discussion of the nature of change in *The Clock of the Long Now*, because change happens at different speeds in different areas of human activity, it is always more difficult to change the corporate culture and infrastructure within an organization to match the speed of change in the outside world amongst consumers. This is one of the reasons that businesses should be led by consumers. Successful companies, as Tom Peters identified as long ago as 1983, are those that are 'close to their customers'. This is as true today as it was then, and good examples are as hard to come by despite the fact that this has become a virtual mantra of business strategy in the meantime.

THE NETWORK SOCIETY

The technological revolution is just one of four interlocking revolutions that create what we call the 'network society' (see Figure 35.1). The role of technological change is explained by reference to the way in which it intersects with the contemporaneous social and consumer revolutions happening simultaneously. These are driving the trend to greater individuality and self-expression in all aspects of our lives. Definitions of families, communities, and businesses are becoming more fluid and flexible as is the experience of 'self'. Thus the network society is created by the actions and choices of individuals participating in key emotional, social and economic networks, rather than consisting of fixed social structures and groupings.

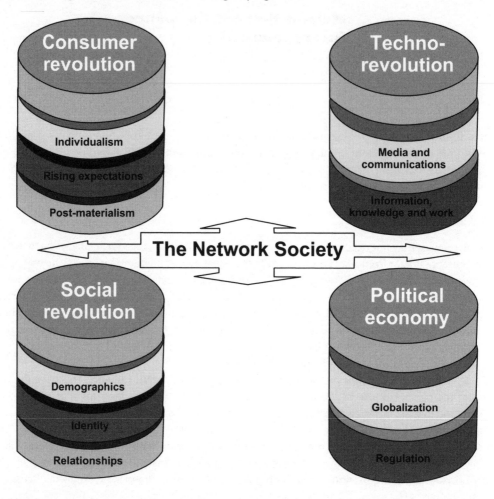

Figure 35.1   Four interlocking revolutions © The Future Foundation

Communications technology is an essential component in this increasingly networked world, offering as it does an intertwined and invisible additional 'space' for creating connections and meaningful interactions between network members, which reinforces and shapes the reality of our daily face-to-face meetings and experiences. It is also an increasingly fertile and extensive environment for 'real time' interactions with companies and brands through an expanding array of interfaces.

The extent of this infrastructure is evident in much of the research that exists on the access and usage levels of the technologies that provide the communications tools. Not only is the telephone in 97 per cent of homes and mobiles used by nearly 70 per cent of the population; the Internet is now accessible to about half of us either at work or at home. And as Future Foundation forecasts suggest, this growth will continue. Over 90 per cent of the UK population will have Internet-type access via one channel or another by 2010 (see Figure 35.2).

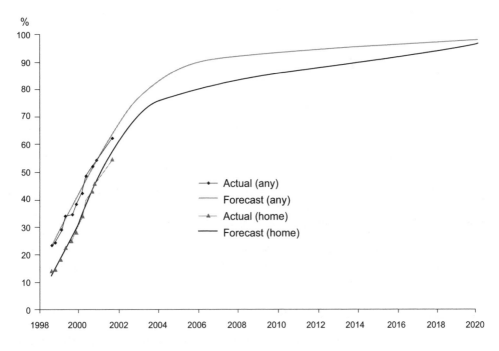

Source: 'Changing Lives', 'Charity Awareness Monitor', The Future Foundation nVision
Base: 1000 adults 16+

Figure 35.2   Growing access to interactivity. Proportion of adults 16+ with access to interactivity at home and anywhere – nVision forecast © The Future Foundation

More tellingly, as a result of our need to interact, the volume of calls, emails and text messages continue to grow substantially as they become integral to the creation and functionality of the many networks of which we are a part. Nor do these new communications channels result in significant substitution of existing forms of contact. Our own recent research (see Figure 35.3) shows that bank customers who use the Internet are the most frequently in touch with their service providers – new technologies encourage more communication.

Implications for the contact centre of the future:

- The network society is creating a virtual communications infrastructure that is mediating every aspect of our daily lives.
- Commercial interactions and 'relationships' are part of this, but not necessarily seen as important or emotionally significant by customers.
- The challenge for companies is to engage and service customers in ways that will earn 'stand out' appeal in this growing sea of constant communication with which the individual is going to be assailed.

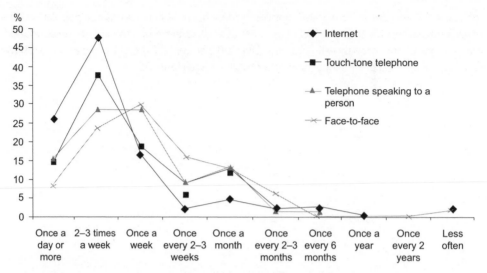

Source: Self-service Society Consortium/The Future Foundation. Base: 446 respondents

Figure 35.3   Customer contact with banks. © The Future Foundation

- The new channels will create more communications for contact centres to deal with, as proliferation rather than substitution seems to be the rule and there seems to be no physical limit at present.

THE INDIVIDUALIZATION OF SOCIETY

In this networked world, there are many factors contributing to the profound shift that we are already experiencing in many aspects of life today – the individual is becoming the basic unit of society. Thus the shape and function of social structures and activities are increasingly determined by individual activity and participation facilitated by interactive communications technologies. The old rules are gone and fewer people feel the need to the conform, as the long-term trend from Future Foundation research going back to 1980 shows quite clearly (see Figure 35.4).

This individualization is the result of the interaction of many different trends, demonstrating perfectly the interconnected nature of change:

- More liberal social attitudes towards difference with less pressure on people to 'fit in' to proscribed social roles.
- In turn, this makes it more acceptable for people to live outside traditional family units for longer periods of their lives – later marriage, more cohabitation, high levels of divorce, lone parenthood, same-sex relationships and declining birth rates. Already fewer than a quarter of households are occupied by anything resembling a 'nuclear family' which was for so long held to be the norm.
- Ageing society further compounds the tendency towards individualization as older women (who continue to outlive their male partners) will make up over a third of single households, themselves already comprising a third of UK households.
- With this there is a growing interest in self-expression and self-fulfilment, promoting the idea that individual experience and meaning is critical to achieving a good quality of life (a concept that is generating growing interest in social analysis today).

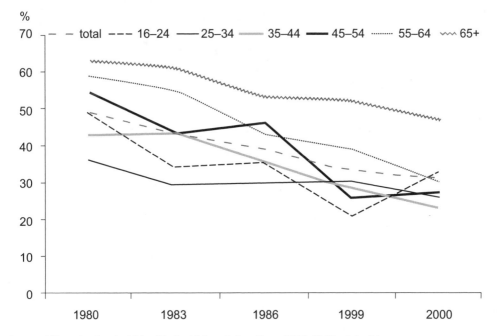

Source: 'Changing lives', nVision/Taylor Nelson Sofres. Base: 1000–2000 adults 16+

Figure 35.4   Percentage who agree that it is important to fit in rather than be different from other people.
© The Future Foundation

Taken together, all these factors add up to an individualizing, ageing and feminizing population overall, and despite relatively flat population growth we will see an increase in the actual number of households in the UK (see Figure 35.5).

Implications for the contact centre of the future:

- Understanding the varied and shifting nature of household composition and the increasingly individual nature of life today.
- Identifying and recognizing customers as individuals without making assumptions about their circumstances or situation.
- Dealing gracefully and seamlessly with change such as divorce and re-marriage.
- Recognizing the effect of changing circumstances on customer's needs, interests and information requirements.
- Showing sensitivity to titles, different and varied surnames, as well as the effects of different ethnic and religious affiliations on timing of communications.

CHANGING PATTERNS OF BEHAVIOUR

Education is enjoying a whole new emphasis in the twenty-first century, with creativity, knowledge and enterprise highly prized as components of a competitive service economy. Call centres themselves have been the biggest engine of employment growth in many parts of the UK. This is intimately intertwined with changes in the workplace – both driving and being driven by the many elements making work more subject to fluctuations in a variety of ways:

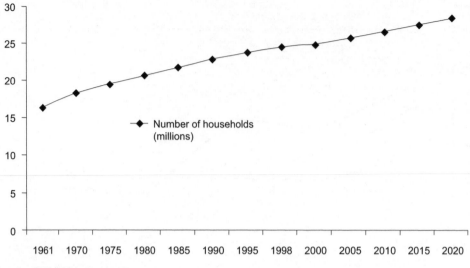

Source: ONS/nVision

Figure 35.5   Absolute numbers of households. © The Future Foundation

- We spend more time in further education, with women now outperforming men in many areas of tertiary education (making them more attractive in the knowledge economy arena).
- Despite 30 years of equal pay legislations, it is estimated that women who give up work or reduce their hours due to childbirth and childrearing can lose up to a quarter of a million pounds in income over the course of their working lives, encouraging mothers to continue to work, particularly given the high rates of divorce which disproportionately damages women's financial position.
- More people are working part time and flexible hours as women begin to outnumber men in the workplace, and mothers continue to work outside the home in ever greater numbers.
- Growing numbers of jobs are held by each individual throughout their adult working lives.
- As more young people stay in education longer, and compounded by the effects of a reduced birth rate over time, the workforce, like the society around it, will continue to age.
- Attitudes generally for both men and women are moving towards a stronger desire for better work–life balance, as demands and pressures on the individual from their family, social and community commitments require time and energy outside the workplace.
- While self-employment and genuine teleworking has not increased as much as some forecasters suggested it would, there is evidence that a growing proportion of workers are now working from home on a regular basis.

Implications for the contact centre of the future:

- Customers are more likely to be working, whether male or female, with consequent pressures on their time and greater demand for accessible services at times that suit them.
- The service economy has to respond to the growing 24-hour society and therefore as more people provide extended-hour service to others, so they in turn will be consumers of 24-hour services at the margins of their working days. This snowball effect will continue.

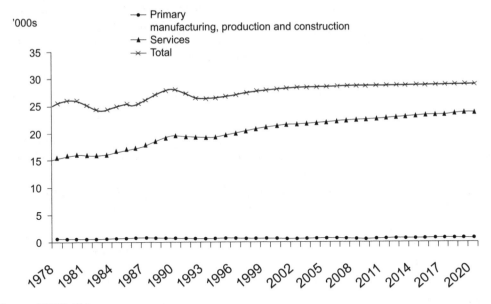

Source: DETR/n Vision

Figure 35.6   Workers in the service industries compared to other sectors. © The Future Foundation

- The more highly educated workforce will need greater challenges and opportunities to flex their intellectual muscles if they are to remain loyal over time.
- Women will continue to be prime employees in contact centres that offer flexible work conditions that suit family and other commitments.
- Service-economy workers are more likely to have access to computers and telephones at work as well as at home, with awareness of the basic principles of service provision accelerating their learning curve as consumers and professionalizing them as users of new technology interfaces.
- Older workers will be an invaluable and growing resource in this market.

DEMOCRATIZATION OF DECISION-MAKING AND TIME CONSTRAINT

Profound shifts in gender roles have also contributed to what has been the biggest consumer change since the 1960s and 70s: effectively the disappearance of the role of housewife as professional consumer on behalf of the family unit. Again there are many contributing factors that have transformed the face of the typical consumer over the last 15 years and will continue to create further diversity and change in the future:

- High levels of time pressure are experienced by both men and women – while women continue to do a disproportionate amount of the domestic tasks and shopping, men do work longer hours out of the home than their female counterparts.
- Men are increasingly becoming targeted as shoppers in a range of markets and over time are becoming more educated and experienced as consumers.
- Women may not be earning as much as their partner, but they are taking an equal involvement in financial decisions and increasingly developing their own financial portfolios.

- Only 12.5 per cent of households now conform to the nuclear family model of the 1950s with a female partner remaining at home to care for dependent children, while a breadwinner husband goes out to work. There is some role reversal but this is still negligible statistically.
- Choice in most markets has proliferated almost exponentially over the past 20 years, further requiring greater knowledge, energy and time in making consumer decisions.
- Family life is becoming more democratic in every sense and children are increasingly becoming involved in big decisions about family purchases, as well as influencing expenditure on themselves.

The degree of time pressure and the extent of experience as consumers are both critical factors in determining consumer behaviour. The disappearance of the 'housewife' means that most women responsible for children are time pressured (often part-time working women as much as full-time working women, as the latter tend to get more professional help) and indeed, men who tend to work longer hours out of the home also experience as time pressure (see Figure 35.7).

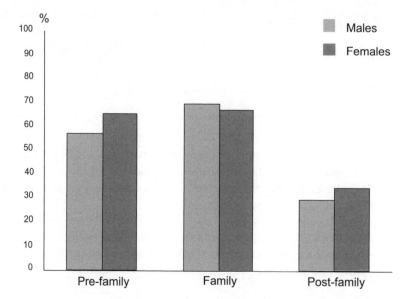

Source: Labour Force Survey/The Future Foundation

Figure 35.7   Time pressure in everyday life. © The Future Foundation

Also due to growing affluence and the proliferation of products and services both men and women are obliged, as participants in the advanced consumer society, to spend more time and energy and, of course, money on buying goods and services – feeding into the steady growth of the retail and service sectors in the UK. The effects of time pressures are also evident from the widespread use of the telephone and the Internet in the evenings – 50 per cent of the population have used the telephone after 10 p.m. to contact companies and nearly a third have used the Internet for this purpose (see Figure 35.8).

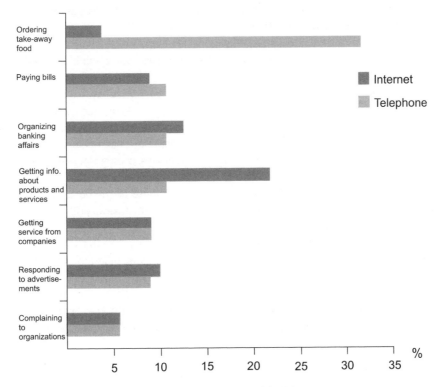

Source: 'Changing lives'/The Future Foundation. Base: 1000 adults 16+

Figure 35.8   Internet and telephone comparisons by contact type. © The Future Foundation

Implications for the contact centre of the future:

- All but the companies targeting the most or the least affluent will continue to need to find ways of reducing time and simplifying the means by which customers can get access to the service they need.
- The value-for-time equation is already an acid test of new services and channels of delivery and will continue to be paramount in the way that contact centre services are judged.
- The way in which trusted brands can develop a role as 'choice' manager in markets other than retail, where this principle is already well established, is an opportunity that both service providers and customers, who would prefer a limited array of choices, could benefit from.
- This position of trust has to be earned through the provision of consistently excellent service now and into the future.

THE EXPERIENCE ECONOMY

Another significant component of the changing consumer marketplace that will increasingly impact on service provision in the future is the phenomenon of the 'experience economy'. This summarizes a number of converging trends that result in a growing proportion of time being spent literally 'out and about' involved in leisure activities and eating out. It chimes entirely with the concept of the more active, involved individual who expresses themselves as much as through participation as more abstract notions. These include:

- Time spent out and about has practically doubled since 1965, although it still makes up less than 15 per cent of our time awake.
- While in some respects this contributes to the reality of greater mobility, distances travelled to most consumer and leisure destinations tend to be within a 14-mile radius, with differences according to gender, age, class, urban/rural and region of the country lived in.
- Therefore the greater distances being travelled by people are not necessarily taking them further away from home; they are undertaking more journeys, mostly by car at different times of the day.
- Growth in eating out has been significant, partly in response to the decline in housewives discussed above and consequent reduction of time to spend cooking, and partly due to the proliferation of high-quality, reasonably priced options.
- The appetite for new experiences is growing steadily, as is the desire to try out new products and services, fuelling an enthusiasm and interest in new and different ways of satisfying consumer needs and desires.

Forecasts for growth in-out-of home leisure spending confirm the importance of the experience economy as an impetus to spending and consumer engagement in the coming years (see Figure 35.9).

At current and constant prices – nVision UK forecast

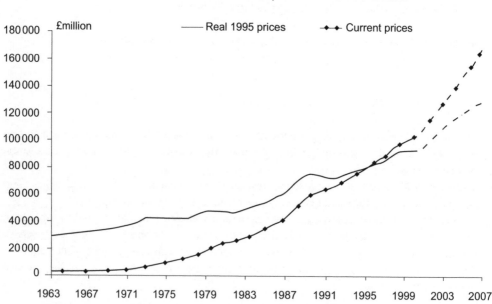

Source: Self-Service Society Consortium/The Future Foundation. Base: 1008 respondents.

Figure 35.9   Out-of-home leisure spending. © The Future Foundation

The popularity of mobiles and email and their patterns of use offer a powerful demonstration of how these highly individualized tools enable whole new ways of interacting and communicating with key networks from different geographic locations, facilitating the blurring of the lines between different environments and locations. Once such tools are in place, patterns of communication can change quickly, capitalizing on the opportunities they create for useful networking activity. In a recent Future Foundation survey 15 per cent of respondents use their home Internet connection for work purposes and similarly around 17 per cent of workers are accessing personal content via work connections (see Figure 35.10).

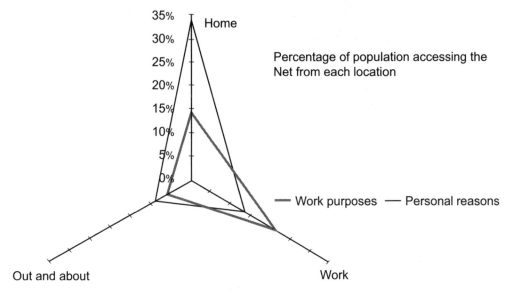

Source: M-Commerce/The Future Foundation

Figure 35.10   Prevalence of Internet use by location and purpose of access. © The Future Foundation

Not only are old barriers to communication disappearing, increased mobility is creating more reasons for interaction. We now make more calls on the move in relation to the time spent proportionately than we do at home, as our latest analysis shows (see Figure 35.11). This is fascinating in itself – not only do modern communications *not* turn us into couch potatoes as anticipated by many commentators, but we also appear to become more gregarious while on the move. This provides yet another example of the proliferation of communications that is integral to the network society.

Implications for the contact centre of the future:

- Consumers will spend more time out of the home, with a growing proportion of potentially 'dead' time travelling to leisure destinations either in cars or in public transport.
- Customers will also welcome ways in which companies can deliver relevant services to them on the move, and drive extended hours of access so that they can choose when to interact and how.
- All leisure destinations need to provide readily accessible information and service to customers planning outings and trips.

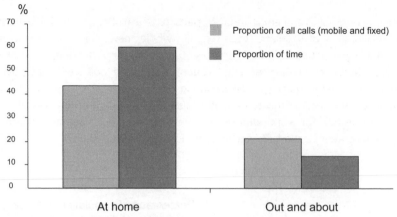

Source: M-Commerce, The Future Foundation/OPCS Time-use survey

Figure 35.11   More communication on the move. Time spent in certain location and percentage of calls per week from those – fixed and mobile–combined. © The Future Foundation

- The whole emphasis on experience will further heighten the demand for something different and involving in the way service is delivered – the pressure will be on to add 'experience' into service itself.
- It will be increasingly difficult to identify the appropriate mode to approach the customer, based on the access used and the time of day – customers can be literally anywhere, requiring a growing array of services and information to suit their more mobile lifestyles.

NEW TECHNOLOGY INTERMESHED

Cynicism about the Internet in the wake of the dot.com fiascos is proving to be entirely misplaced. Evidence suggests that this is becoming an ever more popular channel of accessing information and transacting as part of a portfolio of service delivery in a range of sectors, to which it is particularly suited. The market was simply not ready to take advantage of the new channels at the time the majority of the Internet-only services were being launched. Most people need to go through a learning curve once they encounter and begin to use a new technology and gain valuable and necessary experience and confidence over time. The longer people have spent online, the more activities they are able to perform as data from a year-long research programme into online consumers for First Direct shows (see Figure 35.12). However, it is worth noting that it takes nearly three years for more than a third of the online population to feel comfortable with the full range of applications.

Experience is critical, and it seems that as people gain confidence they create their own implicit rules on how to use the telephone (mobile or fixed) or the Internet to maximum advantage. Based on actual levels of purchasing and interaction, Future Foundation forecasts for the levels of consumers that will be able and willing to transact online in various markets are currently fairly positive (see Figure 35.13). Contact centres need to find ways of encouraging and integrating this growing stream of potential orders. The question of integration has always been key for call centres and will become more so, due to the plethora of different contact methods that will be available and used by customers. Individual variation and personal preferences also play a significant part in how people use the tools at their disposal. This is a logical outcome of the fact that the individual is in charge, and can decide what works best for them. Clearly, as research

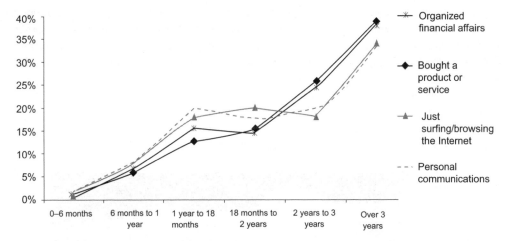

Source: E-service Monitor/First Direct – The Future Foundation. Base: All respondents, Wave 3, approximately 500.

Figure 35.12   Emerging relationship between experience and activities. Percentage doing the activity according to the time they have been online. © The Future Foundation

has confirmed over the years, some people prefer the intimacy and personal touch of voice communication over the telephone, others like the control and efficiency of email, while some love the constant contactability conferred by mobiles and text messaging. Currently, as the self-service society research shows, the expressed preference is for human contact amongst the majority, despite the popularity of self-service alternatives.

As other media come online and mature from a consumer perspective over the coming years, it would be a mistake for companies to decide how customers should contact them. Cynicism about the future impact of broadband access and the advent of 3G mobile services, while currently understandable due to the considerable delays in the availability of both to the wider

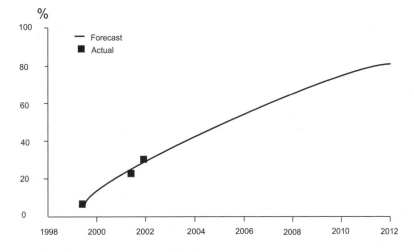

Source: 'Changing lives'/nVision. Base: 1000 adults 16+

Figure 35.13   Percentage of adults who do at least some online purchases. © The Future Foundation

public, is certainly misplaced for the longer term. It is vital that contact centres are in a position to extend their interface with customers in time and space as these become available. It is this, in the mobile network society we are envisaging, that will go a long way to ensuring that you become an indispensable service to your customers rather than an inconvenient bottleneck on their day's activities.

The Future Foundation's approach is to describe continuing technological change as the continuing evolution and hybridization of existing media and channels – the coming together of voice and Internet services, vision and interactivity, email and voice, as the broadband platforms become more widely available and competitively priced (see Figure 35.14).

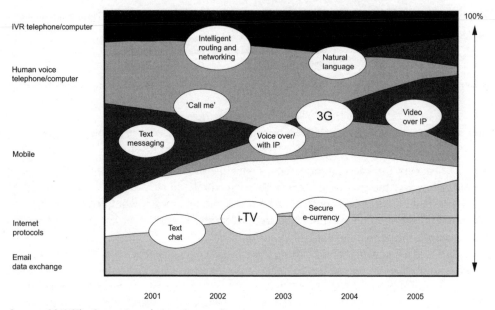

Source: C&W/The Future Foundation: Contact Zone

Figure 35.14   Planning in the context of evolving platforms. © The Future Foundation

Implications for the contact centre of the future:

- Beware the hype, but assess the real potential of new media by looking at the unmet needs of your customers and how these can be fulfilled in new ways.
- Interactive digital TV has failed to develop attractive consumer applications as yet, and though this might be some time coming, it should not be written off as the majority of homes will have access via this route within the next few years.
- Anticipate slow startup and commercial payback with new technologies as consumers acquire the necessary skills to use them as commercial interaction tools – this will always be behind their social and networking activities.
- More technology will generate more communication overall – this should be planned for and accommodated into the plans for the contact centre.
- Key to success will be the effective integration of different tools and platforms, with the ideal scenario being the smooth transfer of data so that the customer can be recognized and identified at every interface if this will improve the service offer.

THE EFFECTS OF THE AGEING POPULATION

Having highlighted the fact of the ageing population earlier, it is worth considering what this is going to mean in customer service terms in the future.

While the spread of technology and the potential for merging of interfaces in the broadband environment could fire considerable enthusiasm for the technological potential for service improvements, a note of caution should be sounded. While the ageing of the population will see millions of baby boomers moving into the 55+ age bracket over the coming years, and this group is established as being more adventurous and technologically adept than previous generations, it is going to be vital to ensure that the service delivery mix is right for these increasingly lucrative older segments who, as Figure 35.15 shows, are already responsible for a significant proportion of expenditure in many markets and this will grow to over 50 per cent in the coming decades.

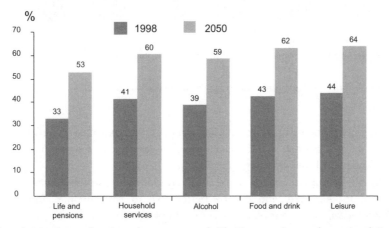

Note: based on changes in numbers in each age group only (that is, assuming no change in relative amounts spent).
Source: Family Expenditure Survey/ONS/The Future Foundation

Figure 35.15   Spending for the 50+ age group. © The Future Foundation

Recent research conducted by the Future Foundation for a consortium into the self-service society has identified that older segments are more likely to express a preference for human service (see Figure 35.16). Interestingly, this human contact is now as acceptable over the telephone as it is face-to-face in the service sectors researched. This points to an inevitable fact about the evolving media environment: with experience over time, consumers' perception and experience in use of media will develop. Thus, ten years ago, telephone service in its relative infancy was seen as somewhat remote and less personal; with the spread in use of the Internet the telephone has shifted towards becoming a more 'personal' medium than other options.

Only 8 per cent of the consumers interviewed by the self-service society consortium expressed a preference for self-service at every stage of the buying cycle. This research showed some variation between younger and older consumers in terms of what they are prepared to undertake for themselves, which highlights the danger of assuming that younger consumers, because they are more adept with new technologies, are going to be more able to 'serve themselves'. In fact, because they are less experienced in many markets, their need for advice and reassurance in many circumstances is actually greater than their older counterparts. Older respondents were more

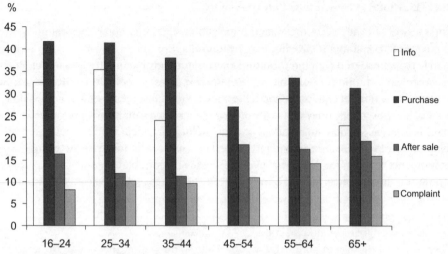

Source: Self-service Society Consortium/The Future Foundation. Base: 1008 respondents

Figure 35.16   Proportion of age group using self-service at each stage of sale. © The Future Foundation

confident and more prepared to complain using remote methods and to obtain after-sales service. So, from both ends of the age spectrum, the need for continued access to human contact and reassurance remains and will remain strong (see Figure 35.16).

Obviously the young are already more adept and familiar with the new interfaces, such as text messaging for example, and will be better able to navigate new interfaces as these emerge. One shortfall of many mobile devices could be screen size, which would preclude easy use by long-sighted older consumers (just as most packaging is difficult to read for older consumers). However, in the more fluid and flexible world of the network society, these tendencies are not hard-and-fast rules and the general principle of individual variation and preference remains.

Implications for the contact centre of the future:

- Older consumers are going to be a major customer group in most markets and their needs must be properly researched, identified and catered for in order to capture a slice of this lucrative market.
- Baby boomers are maturing into the most experienced consumer generation ever, with high standards in every area of purchasing and service – they will be relatively open to new platforms and means of service delivery but will have neither the time or inclination to give service providers the benefit of the doubt: these will have to add value-for-time from the first test.
- While young people may be more experienced and enthusiastic about using new technologies, it is important to remember that they need more help in other areas due to relative inexperience as consumers.
- Service components will be the same for both younger and older groups, but will need to be mixed in different ways to meet the needs of the segment but also recognizing individual variation within these.

WORD OF MOUTH

Whether young or older, it is a fact that customers in every age group are becoming increasingly discerning and demanding. An important by-product of the network society, and again, intimately interconnected with the social and consumer trends pointing to lower levels of respect and authority in institutions and declining trust in companies generally, is the rise in influence of word of mouth and other communications between customers, unmediated by companies. Thus, in financial services, family members are more trusted for advice than bank managers and friends are seen as being as good as independent financial advisors!

Not only is personal recommendation and advice seen as being more valuable, Future Foundation research shows that the effect of network communications is to increase and accelerate the speed at which word of mouth spreads through a population. This is the basis of the widely hyped concept of viral marketing. However, for most organizations, the priority must be to provide service of a standard that generates positive word of mouth – recognized as an ever more vital component of brand building.

Mathematical modelling conducted by the Future Foundation shows that the effect of the Internet on the speed of news travel, as depicted in Figure 35.17.

As consumers become more experienced in using the new channels available to them, their critical faculties will be sharpened. While the standards of service for telephone contact are well known and widely applied by consumers, they are still learning what good Internet service might actually be like. First Direct research shows that in the last quarter of its year-long online programme, the proportion of respondents who experienced bad service and told someone else about it almost doubled, in comparison to earlier results that indicated that Internet users have been more likely to spread good news about sites they like than bad. This can now be seen as an 'early adopter' effect which is beginning to wear off. As the online population matures and extends its use of interactive media, so the standards applied to the service delivered will increase and word-of-mouth effects will become more potent.

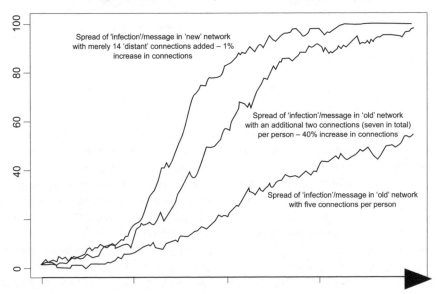

Figure 35.17   Networked world – speed of news travel. © The Future Foundation

Implications for the contact centre of the future:

- Encourage positive word of mouth from satisfied customers – either through 'more formal member get member'-type schemes, but also through facilitation of emailed hyperlinks to friends and colleagues.
- Recognize and encourage the significance of the personal consultation and either emulate this in marketing communications, or acknowledge its importance in the decision-making process.

CITIZEN BRANDS AND THE DEMAND FOR RESPONSIBLE ORGANIZATIONS

The sad fact of the matter is that consumer trust in companies of all kinds has been declining consistently over recent decades. An equal proportion of consumers disagree as agree with the statement that companies are fair to consumers, with a growing number falling in the middle (see Figure 35.18). This is a savage indictment of business by its customers, and explains why a growing proportion now feel that more regulation should be imposed on businesses.

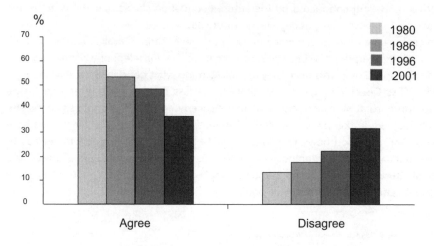

Source: 'Changing lives', The Future Foundation/Taylor Nelson Sofres

Figure 35.18   The level of trust in companies in recent times. © The Future Foundation

In terms of building trust and brands, research conducted with the Consumer's Association and the Industrial Society has shown that nothing is more influential on a consumer's view of an organization than the service experience. This will continue to be the case, however far in the future we might care to look, and is the ultimate acid test of the advanced consumer society – no matter by what medium the service is delivered. Thus, providing a 'good and consistent service' continues to be the top factor influencing trust as Figure 35.19 shows, although other more nebulous factors such as 'fairness' and 'honesty' are on the increase.

The treatment of employees has become more important in the three years since these questions were first asked, pointing to another vital arena of corporate responsibility which is increasingly becoming a means by which consumers judge companies, with a growing amount of discussion in the media and through word of mouth. More importantly, our research shows that over 30 per cent of consumers now fit into the post-material category, whereby they are both cynical of businesses and prepared to apply ethical or environmental criteria to purchasing (see

To what extent do you trust (company X) to .... 'a great deal' or 'mostly'

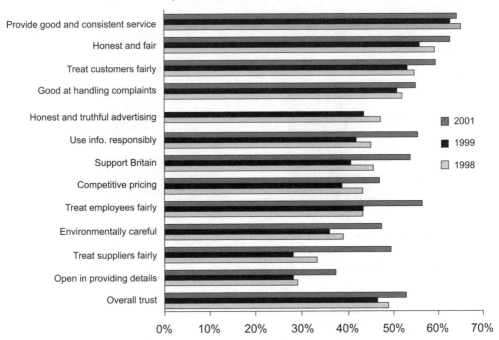

Source: Consumers' Association/Marketing Forum/Industrial Society/The Future Foundation

Figure 35.19   Contributors to trust in companies in the UK. © The Future Foundation

Figure 35.20). With increased affluence, which we anticipate despite recent scares, this will continue to grow as a proportion of the population.

Implications for the contact centre of the future:

- The contact centre, as the point of contact with customers, should be seen as strategically highly significant in the battle to rebuild consumer trust.
- The contact centre must be at the heart of the organization, providing genuinely responsive customer-focused service and response to needs.
- The treatment of employees working in the contact centre, and in turn their approach and interaction with customers, will contribute to the overall brand building and reputation of the company.
- Companies must become 'citizen brands' reflecting the wider values and concerns of their customers. For the more educated, ethical consumer the contact centre will be a vital means by which they acquire information on the provenance of the products and services they buy. No longer can 'ethical' and 'environmental' concerns be seen as being specialist or unimportant.
- Standard consumer standards of value for money and service need to be satisfied as a basic competitive requirement, but beyond that, softer factors will play a growing role and the contact centre has to be able to embody and communicate the wider corporate mission and values.

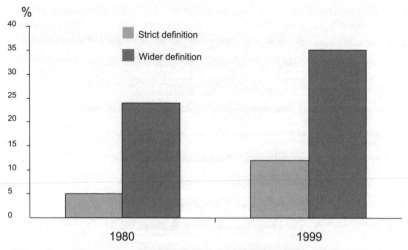

Source: Citizens Brands, Michael Wilmott/The Futures Foundation, 2001

Figure 35.20   Evidence for growing proportion of post-material consumers. © The Future Foundation

CRM, e-CRM AND THE REST

The consequence of the converging and integrating trends described in this chapter for the contact centre of the future are clear. Nor are they any different to those that emerged from earlier analysis of consumer trends when I wrote *Teleculture 2000* in 1997. This highlighted the opportunity and challenges facing call centres from an extensive programme of consumer research and analysis. At that time, the Internet was a distant rumour and interactive digital TV a mere dream, mobile phones were the size of bricks and the telephone was only accessible to some 30 per cent of the workplace.

In the early 1990s the already time-pressured consumer was crying out for the modern, accessible, open-all-hours telephone call centre. And, to some extent, they have got it. Call centres have become an integral part of the growth in the service economy in the 1990s, as a provider of jobs and a provider of service. However, despite the high hopes for many professionals involved in the industry at the beginning of the 1990s, it has failed to fulfil its potential. Then, as now, it was clear that call centres needed to be fully integrated into the company service mix, not seen as an add-on or operationally separate. It was also clear that the call centres, while offering savings over other forms of contact, should not be judged or set up on this basis. Investment in improving service standards would pay off in terms of customer 'longevity' and positive word of mouth.

Instead, with a few notable exceptions, call centres became synonymous with the 'sweat shops' of the twentieth century; automated call services were widely and badly deployed, reducing the perception of good service; and many organizations thought they could drive customers onto the Internet to save the cost of human contact altogether. This is the heritage that the contact centre industry of the future needs to dispose of, if the new array of technologies and solutions are going to be deployed in ways that will genuinely bring satisfaction to the customers. However, it is not going to be easy. While customers and fashions change, technologies evolve and reduce in price, corporate culture is often the most resistant to transformation. And nothing less than transformation is required if business is to remedy the shortcomings of the current service offerings and genuinely adapt and add value to the customer.

Interestingly, the advent of customer relationship management (CRM) as the new marketing mantra is both a help and hindrance in achieving the necessary focus on the customer. On the one hand, it has become a fashionable umbrella or bandwagon on which many software vendors have attempted to sell technology solutions that have failed to deliver because of the lack of corporate commitment. On the other hand, in its more advanced expression, it is being used to encourage a management philosophy that requires the integration and cohesion of the organization around the focus of the customer.

Recent research by BT amongst members of Insight Interactive – its online community for people interested in CRM – highlights the degree to which the same old problems dog the application of these CRM principles: lack of integration, lack of board-level champions, the intransigence of the culture (see Figure 35.21).

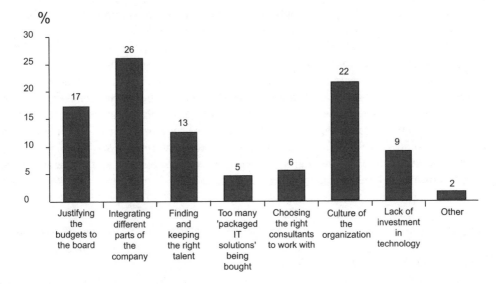

Source: BT Insight Interactive. 107 respondents

Figure 35.21   Issues facing the implementation of a CRM strategy. © The Future Foundation

These responses are little different to those that would have arisen from a discussion of call centres some ten years ago. However, this is not to say that the concept of the integrated, modern, flexible and customer-responsive call centre is not valid nor that it cannot be achieved in the future; simply that the barriers to success and to delivering the all-important outcome of customer satisfaction en route to increasing customer value are significant.

e-CRM, despite the allure of the new and technological, has no magic wand to offer in this respect, except for the possibility of further cost-cutting due to the non-human nature of the interactions on offer. But where nearly all CRM theorizing falls down, in my view, is in the assumption, now wildly out of date, that it is any way possible for the company to manage and control communications with the customer. Everything we have looked at in this chapter would suggest otherwise:

• More individuality and difference
• More technologies and access channels

- Varying patterns of time use and location through the day
- Growing needs for information due to post-material selection criteria
- More customer-to-customer interaction in the buying decision
- Consumer participation in growing numbers of markets
- Continuing appetite for new products and services
- Greater experience and higher standards for judging service
- Less respect and trust for organizations.

This is not an environment in which the words 'relationship' or 'management' are likely to have resonance with customers or hold much sway with consumers. The big problem for most organizations is the difficulty they have with really getting up to date with their customers' lives and then changing the inside of the organization fast enough to keep up with the outside. This is largely due to continuing corporate self-obsession (resulting from internal hierarchies, operational silos, power struggles and history) – easy to recognize, difficult to overcome.

Our research for the Self-service Society shows clearly that while human contact is valued, the ability to reach in to an organization through 'self-serve' is considered important by many (see Figure 35.22). Given the empowered, facilitated and experienced consumers of all ages that are emerging as a result of the many factors described above, this trend will doubtless grow. Self-service is not about the customer being in control of the 'relationship' with companies; again, the research shows that 'relationship' is too strong a term for consumers to use when talking about brands and companies. Essentially, what they want is service, information and products when and where they want it, in a manner that is convenient to them, saves time and adds value to their lives. No small order –welcome to the customer of tomorrow!

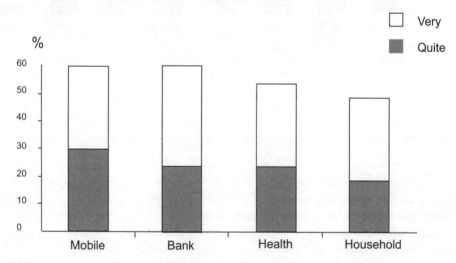

Source: Self-Service Society Consortium?The Future Foundation. Base: 1008 respondents

Figure 35.22   Importance of self-service in current choice of supplier. © The Future Foundation

SUMMARY

CRM should be replaced as a mantra for the future with the three 'F's of the customer interface for the twenty-first century:

- Flexible
- Facilitated
- Freedom.

Discussions of the contact centre of the future need to increasingly focus the attention not on the internal structure and investment needs, but on the nature and quality of the changing interface with the customer. This is the real challenge facing the industry – to reinvent itself away from the damaged roots of the call centre heritage and the overblown promise of the dot.com boom and become the focal point by which the organization is able to anticipate customer needs, provide effective and flexible interfaces, and adapt and evolve to meet the ever-changing needs of customers in the future.

RECOMMENDED READING

Brand, S. (2000), *The Clock of the Long Now: Time and Responsibility*. Phoenix.

Howard, M. (1997), *Teleculture 2000*. Henley Centre.

Young, M. and P. Willmott (1975), *The Symmetrical Family: Study of Work and Leisure in the London Region*. Penguin Books.

Glossary

Abandoned call:	where a caller hangs up before the call is answered by an agent. If there is an ACD and the call has been accepted, it will be registered as an abandoned call.
ACD:	see Automatic Call Distributor.
ADSL:	see Asymmetric Digital Subscriber Line.
Agent:	a term for a contact centre employee interacting with customers and end-users of ACD equipment.
Analogue:	a type of voice transmission where the telephone system transmits an electrical current, which is analogous to the human voice. The louder the voice – the stronger the current. Still used in many telephone systems and most homes, although the trend is now moving towards digital systems.
Answer Detect:	where the telephone system makes outbound calls and on answer identifies network tones such as ringing, engaged, unobtainable, fax phones and answer phones and filters these out, only sending live calls through to an agent.
API:	see Application Programme Interface.
Application:	software that carries out a specific task, such as word processing or spreadsheets.
Application Programme Interface (API):	this is a piece of software that connects the telephone system to the host computer system and allows them to communicate with each other.
Architecture:	the overall design of hardware or software. If the description is 'open architecture' this means it is generally compatible with major (as opposed to proprietary) applications.
Asymmetric Digital Subscriber Line:	low-cost, high-speed Internet access technology.
Audiotex:	an automatic voice-responsive service where a caller dials a number and receives a recorded message. This can be anything from weather reports and horoscopes to adult entertainment.
Auto Attendant:	where an inbound call is answered by a recording which asks the customer to either choose from a menu of options or select the extension they want. The system then automatically routes their call.

Automatic Call Distributor/
Distribution (ACD): a system for handling call volumes that automatically offers the next call to the agent waiting for the longest period. These systems can be configured with a variety of parameters in order to give priorities to different callers and route certain types of call to specific groups or individuals. ACDs also provide a range of reports.

Automatic Dialler: also called Outbound Dialler. These automate outgoing calls and have various levels of sophistication. See also Screen Dialling, Power Dialling, Predictive Dialling and Progressive Dialling.

Available time: the total time an agent was in the available state, but not handling calls, during a given period of time.

Average speed of
answer: the total amount of time all callers have had to wait for an answer, divided by the total number of calls.

Back office: those business activities that do not involve customer contact.

Bandwidth: the speed of transmission. When a system lacks bandwidth, it is a way of saying the transmission is not fast enough for it to accomplish its tasks speedily.

Bit: in the digital universe, numbers are represented as a series of zeros and ones, and these are referred to as bits.

Blending: where the same agents work on both inbound and outbound calling during any day or working shift.

Blocked calls: calls that cannot be connected. This may be because all lines are busy or the ACD has reached the threshold of its queue(s).

Browser: a software program, with a graphical user interface, for navigating the Internet and viewing World Wide Web pages. Examples include Microsoft's Internet Explorer and Netscape's Navigator.

Bulletin board: a place on a network where electronic messages are left for others to read. It is also used in Internet newsgroups, where information on various topics is left for the world to read.

Call handling statistics: numerical data and information on calls being handled and waiting to be handled. These statistics, real-time and historic are available from PTOs, ACDs and associated systems such as diallers. The information can include, for example, the number of calls arriving at the ACD, the number passed to agents, numbers holding and for how long, the duration of calls and their outcome. This information is used to help monitor and manage operational efficiency and maintain optimum performance.

Calling Line Identity (CLI): a feature which enables the caller's own telephone number to be forwarded at the same time as their call, enabling identification.

Call recording:	the recording of conversations with contacts, used for quality control, training needs identification and in compliance procedures. Some systems can be managed from a standard PC. Options include total recording, recording-on-demand, selective recording, and call monitoring for quality assurance.
CBT:	see Computer-based Training.
Centrex:	generic term for a service offered by network providers (PTOs) which in the context of call centres, enables organizations to use the provider's ACD facilities at the exchange.
CLI:	see Calling Line Identity.
Client:	a personal computer in a client/server environment. When called a thin client, this refers to a network computer.
Client/Server:	a computer network. Each agent has an intelligent PC (called the client), which is loaded with the appropriate software applications and is connected by a LAN to the server which houses all the major software programs such as the database. Files can be sent and shared. The client accesses the server each time it requests information or changes data.
Compliance:	complying with legal requirements, such as those deriving from the Consumer Credit Act or the Financial Services Act.
Computer-based Training (CBT):	where the learning process takes place at the desktop through exchanges between the learner and a pre-written program. It is particularly useful where there is just one right answer and one right way of doing something. It allows training to proceed at the learner's chosen pace.
Computer Supported Telephony Applications (CSTA):	the language, set to a specific standard, used between computers and telephone systems.
Computer-Telephone Integration (CTI):	where the computer and telephone interact with each other, enabling you to give commands to the telephone through your PC.
Contact management:	organizing and managing customer and prospect information, for example, contact dates, information sent and personal data.
CRM:	see Customer Relationship Management.
CSTA:	see Computer Supported Telephony Aplications.
CTI:	see Computer Telephone Integration.
Customer Relationship Management (CRM):	where companies use a variety of methods, customer

databases, product directories and contact strategies to build lasting and profitable relationships with customers, retaining their custom and generating more revenue.

DASS or DASS II: Digital Access Signalling System – the method used in the UK for communicating in ISDN.

Database: a named and ordered collection of data, usually stored on a computer.

DCL: see Distributed Collaborative Learning.

DDI: see Direct Dial Inwards.

Desktop: a term used to include the agent's PC, telephone equipment and any specialist peripheral equipment, such as video/Web camera.

Dialled Number Identification System/ Service (DNIS): where more than one telephone number terminates on one queue, this facility enables the system to recognize the different numbers dialled and therefore identifies the call volume made to each number.

Digital: data represented by binary code (a series of zeros and ones) used in telecommunications, computing and recording. Once data is digitally encoded it can be easily manipulated, stored and transmitted.

Digital Private Network Signalling System (DPNSS): the main type of digital private networking, it is similar to ISDN in that it comes in two megabit blocks, each capable of carrying up to 30 simultaneous telephone calls.

Direct Dial Inwards (DDI): where you can dial directly into a company and reach an extension without going through a switchboard operator.

Disaster recovery: a term for the planning (and implementation of plans) in order to restore a company's computing or telecommunications after they have failed for some reason.

Distributed Collaborative Learning (DCL): the concept of people learning together through the Internet without necessarily physically being together.

DNIS: see Dialled Number Identification System/Service.

DPNSS: see Digital Private Network Signalling System.

DTMF: see Dual Tone Multi Frequency.

Dual Tone Multi Frequency (DTMF): a method of telephone signalling via tones; the audible tones when you dial a number and that all digital exchanges can recognize. Touch Tone is a BT trademark using the technology.

E-commerce: trading where the transaction including payment takes place over the Internet.

Email: text communication transmitted over the internet and handled by client software, such as Outlook.

Extranet: a network using the Internet, which can be viewed as part of

	a company's intranet that is private but extended to specified users outside the company such as special customers or suppliers.
Fax:	a method of transmitting text and images over the telephone line. The image to be sent is scanned by a fax machine and transmitted electronically to a receiving fax where a facsimile (exact copy) is printed out or reproduced electronically.
Forecasting:	the ability to take current trends and past history and extrapolate them into views about the future.
Frequently Asked Questions (FAQ):	a set of questions that new users of the website or contact centre are likely to ask and for which answers are already prepared and available.
Front-end:	the part of a computer system with which the user interacts.
Front office:	that part of a business, and the systems used by it, that comes into contact with customers, for example sales, marketing, service.
Full time equivalents (FTES):	the total number of hours worked equated to a full-time rather than part-time head count.
Gbps:	Gigabits – 1 000 000 000 bits per second.
Graphical User Interface (GUI):	pronounced 'gooey'. This is a generic term for presentation on screen of computer information in a graphical format (simply put, using 'easy-to-identify' pictures such as icons).
GUI:	see Graphical user Interface.
Handled call:	a call that has been answered, as opposed to blocked or abandoned calls.
Hot-desking:	the ability to log-on to any computer and have all other systems on the network know, through the identification code used, who is using which computer. In a call centre it means that agents can sit at any workstation and still be logged on as part of their normal agent group.
HTML:	see Hypertext Mark Up Language.
Hypertext Mark Up Language (HTML):	the language protocol of the Internet, enabling all computers, PC or Mac, anywhere in the world to share information. All documents need to be 'translated' into HTML in order to be viewed on the Internet. There are now many packages that can do this automatically from word-processed documents.
Imaging:	the scanning of images for storage in electronic format.
Inbound calls:	incoming calls made by customers and prospects, or other groups, in response to an advertised telephone number that may or may not form part of a specific short-term or ongoing campaign.

Integrated Services Digital Network (ISDN):	an all-digital network, which may carry both voice and data and is usually leased in bundles of 30 trunks.
Intelligent Routing:	this will route callers based on a number of parameters including information on the caller, on the call itself, queue status, agent skills and the present situation.
Interactive Voice Response/ Recognition (IVR):	where an inbound call is answered by a recording that requests the customer to press buttons on the keypad, or speak, in response to a menu of options. The choices selected may instruct the system to search host systems for specific information that is then converted into the spoken word, for example, a bank balance.
Interactive Web Response:	enables customers to transact business on the Internet, interacting with the company's database, with the ability to connect to an agent in the call centre, continuing the enquiry over the phone, or by using Web chat.
Internet:	a global system of computer networks where information available on a computer can be viewed by other computers throughout the world, messages can be sent and received, programs can be downloaded and transactions can take place electronically.
Intranet:	a network of PCs that uses the Internet but is contained within a controlled environment, for example internal company information that is viewed only by its employees.
ISDN:	see Integrated Services Digital Network.
IVR:	see Interactive Voice Response/Recognition.
Kbps:	Kilobits – 1000 bits per second.
Knowledge-based system:	a system that stored the knowledge and experience of experts in their field in a structured form. Less skilled people can interrogate the system to obtain 'expert' responses to the situations described by the user.
LAN:	see Local Area Network.
Landline:	a telephone circuit that uses terrestrial (land-based) cables or microwaves to transmit the signal. It can interconnect with communications generated by radio signal, for example calls from mobile phones.
Local Area Network (LAN):	used to link computers and other devices, such as printers and faxes, a LAN enables computers to share files and resources.
Management Information Services (MIS):	reports from the ACD showing data on agents and agent groups, inbound and outbound calls, and exchange lines.
Mbps:	Megabits – 1 000 000 bits per second.
Megastream:	the commercially available leased circuit operating at 2.048 Mbps.
Middleware:	is an extra layer of software that sits between the switch (or

	front-end application) and organizational databases (or existing application programmes). For example, this could enable bolt-on software programme modules giving dumb switches the intelligence to automatically distribute calls. Additional modules could offer all levels of functionality including computer telephony integration, interactive voice response and workforce scheduling.
MIS:	see Management Information Services.
Multimedia:	the combination of different media in communications, for example voice and video, which is being greatly facilitated by advances in telecommunications technology.
Multiplexor:	a device that enables several different signals to be sent down the same line. Sometimes referred to as a 'mux'.
Natural language:	in speech recognition, recognizing natural language – words spoken as in normal conversation – is the ultimate goal.
NC:	see Network Computer.
Network Computer (NC):	where you put most of the intelligence back into the server (similar to a mainframe system and dumb terminals where you use the desktop PC merely for input, output and presentation with all the applications running only on the server). However, the NC does have its own intelligence.
Network provider:	see PTO.
Network services (NS):	the infrastructure over which voice and data travels.
Noise cancelling:	a feature of telephone headsets that reduces background noise and amplifies the user's voice.
NS:	see Network services.
Number portability:	the facility to transfer existing telephone numbers to a new service provider (PTO), a new service (for example to ISDN) and/or a new geographic area.
Occupancy:	the time agents spend handling calls compared to waiting for calls.
Offered calls:	all calls arriving at the ACD (whether they are accepted or not). Telephone companies (PTO/network provider) are the only way to get a true picture of all calls offered, since the ACD will not usually register calls arriving beyond its queuing threshold.
Outbound Dialler:	also called Automatic Dialler. This automates outgoing calls and has various levels of sophistication. Also see Screen Dialling, Power Dialling, Predictive Dialling and Progressive Dialling.
Overflow:	the movement of calls from one place to another, for example from one queue, when it reaches its threshold, to another; or from one answering facility, when all agents are busy, to another (perhaps automated).
PABX:	see PBX.
PBX:	originally PBX was Private Branch Exchange and PABX was Private Automated Branch Exchange, but only the latter now

applies. This is a generic term for a telephone system that is found inside a company's premises (as opposed to one serving the general public). Automation has meant that employees can dial out themselves (by pressing a number, say nine) rather than having to request a line from the switchboard operator.

PDA: see Personal Digital Assistant.

Personal Digital Assistant (PDA): a device, similar in size to a calculator, that offers a range of functions including electronic diary, memo taker, calculator, alarm clock and personal communicator. May be used as an alternative to a laptop PC for simple mobile tasks.

Ports: in a telephone switch, a port can be used for either an agent/employee extension or a trunk. The number of ports available in any switch including ACDs is finite, unless extra cards/cabinets are purchased.

POTS: Plain Old Telephone Services – a single-line telephone service with no frills. You can simply make or receive one call at a time.

Power Dialling: is often used as a generic term for all diallers but specifically is where the telephone system dials as many calls as it has lines available and, using Answer Detect, puts through live calls to agents. If no agent is available when a call is answered, it will simply drop the call and cause a 'nuisance' call.

Predictive Dialling: similar to power dialling but more sophisticated. This uses a pacing algorithm, which regulates the number of outbound calls made, based on the probability of an agent being available. Minimizes the number of 'nuisance' calls.

Preview Dialling: uses screens of data downloaded from a central database. The agent then initiates the call, usually by using a pre-programmed button on the keyboard, or screen.

Progressive Dialling: the most sophisticated of all the diallers, this goes one stage further than predictive dialling and actually monitors the status of operators before calls are made. It keeps agents supplied with live calls and virtually eliminates 'nuisance calls'.

Proprietary: a system or software design which means that the system or software may only be compatible with other products from the same vendor.

Protocol: the language used by a software program.

PSTN: Public Switched Telephone Network – the public telephone network.

PTO: Public Telephone Operator – also called Network Provider. Originally this was BT in the UK. Now a range of operators provide public services and supply exchange lines (or trunks).

Quality Management: a term used to describe quality evaluation ranging from supervisor monitoring through to sophisticated systems for recording customer contacts, analysis and remedial training.

RAN: Recorded announcement – an intercept message controlled by the ACD using parameters such as the ring time, or the time of day (for night messaging).

Rostering: a shift system that rotates the employees through each of the available shifts, for example night shifts, early morning, late start.

Routing: the planning and assigning of a communications path for a telephone call to reach its destination.

Scanner: a device similar to a photocopier that, rather than producing a paper copy, creates a file on the computer that is a digital copy of the input. It enables text, photographs and transparencies to be filed and edited on the computer.

Scheduling (and forecasting): predicting work volumes and staffing requirements based on historical data, usually using software that automatically creates staff schedules.

Screen Dialling: where you select a number on the screen using a mouse to point and click so the system dials the number for you.

Screen Popping: where integration between the computer and the telephone (CTI) enables the system to attempt identification of each call and look into the database for a match. If that match exists, the data attached to it will then be displayed on the agent's screen just prior to the call arriving at the agent's ear.

Script: a document containing the agent's side of a dialogue for use when handling calls. When computerized it can contain huge amounts of embedded information and multiple links to different host systems and databases for direct access and data entry.

Server: architecture for systems called client/server. Each agent has an intelligent PC (called the client) that is connected by a LAN to the server which houses all the major software programs such as the database. Files can be sent and shared.

Service level: the percentage of calls answered within a specified number of seconds over a particular period of time. It is a widely used measure of call-handling efficiency.

Short Message Service (SMS): a feature on most digital mobile telephone networks enabling users to send short alphanumeric messages to other mobile phones.

Silent monitoring: in call centres, silent monitoring is generally used for quality control. A supervisor may listen in to a call to check if an agent is responding correctly, though they cannot break in to the call. For silent monitoring to be legal, both the agent and the customer must be aware that the call may be monitored.

Skills-based routing: where calls are identified and then routed through to the most appropriate agent, for example calls from France would be routed through to a French-speaking agent.

SMS:	see Short message Service.
Speech recognition:	the ability of a voice processing system to recognize spoken words and numbers.
Switch:	the simplest explanation in the context of a call centre is the generic word for all telephone systems.
TAPI:	see Telephone Applications Programming Interface.
Talk time:	the total time an agent spends talking to a contact, as opposed to time between calls spent on administration.
Tbps:	Terabits – 1 000 000 000 000 bits per second.
Telephone Applications Programming Interface (TAPI):	a software protocol loaded onto the PC itself. It allows you to use the keyboard to dial instead of an actual telephone (screen-based telephony).
Telephone Server Applications Programming Interface (TSAPI):	a protocol that links the telephone and computer to the host system, rather than the PC.
Text chat:	see Web chat.
Thin client:	a network computer (NC).
Tie line:	a private line between the ACD and PBX enabling call transfers.
Top and tail recordings:	Where an agent's opening and closing greetings are pre-recorded and therefore sound fresh and enthusiastic all day.
Trunk:	each telephone or exchange line is called a trunk.
TSAPI:	see Telephone Server Applications programming interface.
Unified messaging:	The technology used to place all messages from whatever source into one message box, including all emails, voice mails, faxes and Web requests.
Voice mail:	enables callers to leave a message much like an answer phone but this message can then be reviewed, copied, sorted, annotated and forwarded to one or many people in one go. Sometimes called voice messaging.
Voice over Internet Protocol (VoIP):	the process by which a voice conversation with an agent is maintained over the same telephone line as the Internet connection.
Voice processing:	a generic term for a variety of applications such as IVR, voice mail and auto attendants.
Voice recognition:	technology that converts speech into data that can be understood by the computer system.
Voice Response Unit (VRU):	a system that enables IVR.
Voice synthesis:	where data from the computer system is converted into speech.
VoIP:	see Voice over Internet Protocol.
VRU:	see Voice Response Unit.
WAP:	see Wireless Application Protocol

Web call me button: a 'press to talk' icon on a web page, which customers can click. This will either initiate a call back at a time to suit the customer, or an immediate contact with the call centre using VoIP.

Web chat: where the customer using a website can initiate a 'text conversation' with an agent, each typing dialogue on screen. Also called text chat.

Web-enabled: a call centre environment where in addition to handling voice calls, the customer can use Web call me and/or VoIP and/or Web chat. Web-enablement also allows the agent to 'push' web pages onto the customer's screen, so directing the customer to any page in the World Wide Web.

Wireless Application Protocol (WAP): the language protocol used to allow mobile phones to accept and display large volumes of information (similar to Internet access via a mobile phone).

Workflow: the way work progresses through an organization. A customer order or instruction is progressed in logical steps by the supplying organization, for example the order is approved by sales control, sent to stock holding for fulfilment and then to dispatch for delivery; concurrently, stock control replenishes supplies, the customer's order history is updated and an invoice is issued to the customer by the finance department.

Workforce management: various programs that offer features such as calculation of staffing requirements, creation of schedules, call load forecasts and real-time performance monitoring.

Workstation: Workstation may also include desk, chair and associated furniture. See also Desktop.

Wrap-up: the time spent by an agent completing administrative/data input/follow-up work after finishing communicating with one customer and before accepting the next call.

Wrap-up codes: codes entered by agents on their computer terminal to indicate the type of call they have just handled. These form part of the reports of call-handling statistics.

Useful Addresses

Calcom Group Limited

Tuition House
27–37 St. Georges Road
Wimbledon
London
SW19 4EU
Tel: +44 (0)20 944 9669
Fax: +44 (0)20 944 9779
Email: contactcentre@calcomgroup.com
Web: www.calcomgroup.com

CCA

The Call Centre Association
Strathclyde House 6
Elmbank Street
Glasgow
G2 4PF
Tel: +44 (0)141 564 9010
Fax: +44 (0)141 564 9011
Email: cca@cca.org.uk
Web: www.cca.org.uk

CCMA

Call Centre Management Association
International House
174 Three Bridges Road
Crawley
West Sussex
RH10 1LE
Tel: +44 (0)1293 538 400
Fax: +44 (0)1293 521 313
Email: admin@ccma.org.uk
Web: www.ccma.org.uk

CIPD

Chartered Institute of Personnel and
Development
CIPD House
Camp Road
Wimbledon
SW19 4UX
Tel: +44 (0)20 8971 9000
Fax: +44 (0)20 8263 3333
Web: www.cipd.org.uk

CSM Group

Customer Service Management Group
21 High Street
Green Street Green
Orpington
Kent
BR6 6BG
Tel: +44 (0)1689 862 999
Fax: +44 (0)1689 862 455
Email: info@csm-europe.com
Web: www.csm-europe.com

CWU

Communication Workers Union
150 The Broadway
London
SW19 1RX
Tel: +44 (0)20
Fax: +44 (0)20
Web: www.cwu.org

DMA

Direct Marketing Association
1 Oxenden Street
London
SW1Y 4EE
Tel: +44 (0)20 7321 2525
Fax: +44 (0)20 7321 0191
Email: dma@dma.org.uk
Web: www.dma.org.uk

DTI

Department of Trade & Industry Enquiry Unit
1 Victoria Street
London
SW1H 0ET
Tel: +44 (0)20 7215 5000
Email: dti.enquiries@dti.gsi.gov.uk
Web: www.dti.gov.uk

eCustomerServiceWorld.com

eCustomerServiceWorld.com
Treadwell House
High Street
Bloxham
OX15 4PP
Tel: +44 (0)1295 722 500
Email: info@ecsw.com
Web: www.ecustomerserviceworld.com

e-skills

e-skills UK
1 Castle Lane
London
SW1E 6DR
Tel: +44 (0)20 7963 8920
Fax: +44 (0)20 7592 9138
Email: info@e-skills.com
Web: www.e-skills.com

FSA

Financial Services Authority
25 The North Colonnade
Canary Wharf
London
E14 5HS
Tel: +44 (0)20 7066 1000
Fax: +44 (0)20 7066 1099
Email: consumerhelp@fsa.gov.uk
Web: www.fsa.gov.uk

HDI

Help Desk Institute
21 High Street
Green Street Green
Orpington
Kent
BR6 6BG
Tel: +44 (0)1689 889 100
Fax: +44 (0)1689 889 227
Email: support@hdi-europe.com
Web: www.csm-europe.com

HSE

Health & Safety Executive Infoline
Caerphilly Business Park
Caerphilly
CF83 3GG
Tel: +44 (0)8701 545 500
Fax: +44 (0)2920 808 537
Web: www.hse.gov.uk

IC

Information Commissioner
Wycliffe House
Water Lane
Wilmslow
Cheshire
SK9 5AF
Tel: +44 (0)1625 545 745
Fax: +44 (0)1625 524 510
Email: data@dataprotection.gov.uk
Web: www.dataprotection.gov.uk

ICS

Institute of Customer Service
2 Castle Court
St Peter's Street
Colchester
Essex
CO1 1EW
Tel: +44 (0)1206 571 716
Fax: +44 (0)1206 546 688
Email: enquiries@icsmail.co.uk
Web: www.instituteofcustomerservice.com

IDM

Institute of Direct Marketing
1 Park Road
Teddington
Middlesex
TW11 0AR
Tel: +44 (0)20 8977 5705
Fax: +44 (0)20 8943 2535
Web: www.theidm.co.uk

LSC

Learning & Skills Council
Cheylesmore House
Quinton Road
Coventry
CV1 2WT
Tel: +44 (0)870 900 6800
Email: info@lsc.gov.uk
Web: www.lsc.gov.uk

MRS

Market Research Society
15 Northburgh Street
London
EC1V 0JR
Tel: +44 (0)20 7490 4911
Fax: +44 (0)20 7490 0608
Email: info@mrs.org.uk
Web: www.marketresearch.org.uk

Ofcom

Office of Communications
Riverside House
2A Southwark Bridge Road
London
SE1 9HA
Tel: +44 (0)20 7981 3000
Fax: +44 (0)20 7981 3333
Email: wwwenq@ofcom.org.uk
Web: www.ofcom.org.uk

Oftel

Office of Telecommunications
50 Ludgate Hill
London
EC4M 7JJ
Tel: +44 (0)20 7634 8700
Fax: +44 (0)20 7634 8845
Web: www.oftel.gov.uk

QCA

Qualifications and Curriculum Authority
83 Piccadilly
London
W1J 8QA
Tel: +44 (0)20 7509 5555
Fax: +44 (0)20 7509 6666
Web: www.qca.org.uk

TMA

Telecoms Managers Association
Ranmore House
The Crescent
Leatherhead
Surrey
KT22 8DY
Tel: +44 (0)1372 361 234
Fax: +44 (0)1372 810 810
Email: tma@tma.org.uk
Web: www.tma.org.uk

Index